Graphics Shaders

Second Edition

Graphics Shaders

Second Edition

Theory and Practice

Mike Bailey

Steve Cunningham

CRC Press
Taylor & Francis Group
Boca Raton   London   New York

CRC Press is an imprint of the
Taylor & Francis Group, an **informa** business

AN A K PETERS BOOK

CRC Press
Taylor & Francis Group
6000 Broken Sound Parkway NW, Suite 300
Boca Raton, FL 33487-2742

First issued in hardback 2019

ISBN: 978-1-56881-434-6 (hbk)

Library of Congress Cataloging-in-Publication Data

Bailey, Michael (Michael John), 1953-
    Graphics shaders : theory and practice / Mike Bailey, Steve Cunningham. -- 2nd ed.
       p. cm.
    Summary: "This book uses examples in OpenGL and the OpenGL Shading Language to present the theory and application of shader programming. It explains how to program graphics shaders effectively for use in art, animation, gaming, and visualization. Along with improved graphics and new examples and exercises, this edition includes a discussion on handling OpenGL's evolution beyond its original built-in functionality, including four new appendices that provide C++ class code to help in this transition. It includes a new chapter on tessellation shaders. It also discusses shaders in multipass rendering and presents new applications including terrain bump mapping, morphing 3D geometry, and wavy glass."-- Provided by publisher.
    Includes bibliographical references and index.
    ISBN 978-1-56881-434-6 (hardback)
     1. Computer graphics. 2. OpenGL. 3. Three-dimensional display systems. I. Cunningham, Steve. II. Title.

    T385.B3455 2011
    006.6'6--dc23

                                                                                        2011031720

Visit the Taylor & Francis Web site at
http://www.taylorandfrancis.com

and the CRC Press Web site at
http://www.crcpress.com

To my parents,
Ted and Anne Bailey,
whose respect for both curiosity and books
made a project like this inevitable sometime.
– MJB

To the other writers in my family:
Judy,
for her collaboration on so many projects
and her patience with my work on this one, and
Rob and Rick,
for their own past and future writing projects.
– SC

Contents

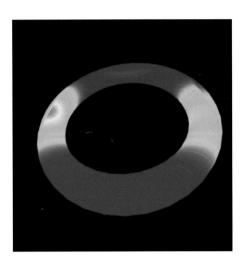

Foreword

Excellent! I am glad that you are reading this book. You might want to skip straight ahead to the good stuff, but as long as you are here…

Computer graphics is a fascinating and fast-changing field that didn't even exist when I was born. I was attracted to it because it is a field with a unique mix of engineering and artistry. In the computer graphics industry, people with engineering skills design graphics software and hardware products that offer ever-increasing levels of performance and image quality. These products inspire people with artistic skills to use the resulting products to create amazing visual experiences that entertain, teach, or help others create or design. This in turn inspires the engineers to create even better hardware and software in order to improve the visual experiences created by artists. This symbiotic relationship between engineers and artists has never let up and has resulted in photorealistic effects for movies and near-cinematic quality experiences for computer games.

You might be reading this book because of your interest in the computer graphics field. Perhaps you are an engineer looking to develop another tool for your toolbox of software development skills for computer graphics. Perhaps you are an artist who is interested in learning a little more about the bits and bytes of how computer graphics images are created. Perhaps you are that rare breed, an engineer/artist, and you have in your mind's eye a vision of what you want to create, and you need only to develop an understanding of this new medium in order to bring your vision to reality. If any of these are true, you have selected an excellent guide book to help you on your journey.

You are holding in your hands a book written by two people who share two passions. Mike Bailey and Steve Cunningham both love computer graphics, and they are absolutely passionate about teaching. This book allows them to combine both of these passions into a form that is sure to benefit you, the reader.

Actually, the word "passionate" understates the impact that Mike and Steve have had on computer graphics education. Mike is a "lifer" in the computer graphics industry. I met him some 15 years ago when we asked him to lead an effort to define industry-standard benchmarks for computer graphics systems (which he graciously agreed to do). He has been teaching or practicing computer graphics for almost 30 years now. He has won numerous awards as a professor of computer graphics. His dedication to educating people new to graphics is demonstrated by the fact that he annually prepares and delivers the "Introduction to Computer Graphics" tutorial at SIGGRAPH (ACM's Special Interest Group on Graphics).

Steve is a similarly dedicated, accomplished, and award-winning educator. He was a co-founder of the SIGGRAPH Education Committee and co-chaired this activity for many years. He served in countless leadership positions in the SIGGRAPH organization and for the SIGGRAPH conference itself (the largest, most prestigious, and longest-lived conference focusing on computer graphics). For his lifelong efforts, he was given the 2004 ACM SIGGRAPH Outstanding Service Award. His influence on the computer graphics industry is global, as witnessed by the fact that he was the first Eurographics Education Board chair and he has been named a Eurographics Fellow.

So it is certainly the case that these two authors can tell you a thing or two about computer graphics. But even more importantly, they can tell it to you in a way that you will understand and remember.

The topic of this book, writing shaders with the OpenGL Shading Language, is both important and timely. OpenGL and its companion shading language are industry standards. This means that they are supported by a variety of hardware companies on a variety of operating environments. OpenGL and GLSL are available on Macs, PCs, and Linux systems; on workstations, towers, desktops, laptops, and handhelds. The goal of a standard is simple: to make it easy for you, the programmer, to deploy your code on a diverse range of products without requiring any changes to the source code. The resulting portability amortizes the cost of the software development by creating a bigger market for software products based on industry standards.

But the most important part of this book is that while it is teaching you how to write programmable shaders, it is also teaching and reinforcing the fundamentals of computer graphics. As a result, you will be able to easily adapt the lessons learned here to other shading languages and graphics paradigms. This is becoming increasingly important since the trend for graphics hardware is to offer more general programmability and less fixed functionality built into hardware. In other words, we are returning to the days where computer graphics innovation occurs in software. The knowledge and skills that you learn while reading this book can be adapted to the even more general graphics programming environments of the future.

At the end of each chapter in this book, you will find some exercises that will help develop your knowledge of graphics and programmable shading. In that spirit, here are the exercises that I would prescribe for you:

1. Read this book.
2. Use computer graphics and programmable shading to create beauty.
3. Share your creation and your knowledge with others.

Most importantly,

4. Have fun!

Randi Rost
December 31, 2008

Preface

Does this remind you of yourself?

http://xkcd.com

You have lots of great, creative ideas in your head, but can't seem to get the right pixels to come out onto your graphics screen. Then, you are our type of person. And, this is your type of book.

Welcome to the second edition of *Graphics Shaders: Theory and Practice*. As the name implies, this book deals with both the theory and equations behind what shaders do, as well as lots and lots of code examples of putting the theory into practice. To help you, this book has been printed with color throughout. That means that the lots of examples have lots of images to go with them to help understand the concepts. So stop and stay for a while. Put your feet up and start reading. You are really going to enjoy this.

This book has over 100 more pages than the first edition did. Here are the major improvements:

1. This book is written against the most-recent specification releases: OpenGL 4.x and GLSL 4.x0.

2. All code examples have been brought up-to-date with the current standard of the GLSL language.

3. There is an entire chapter (with examples) on the new tessellation shaders.

4. All chapters have more examples and more exercises.

5. Many diagrams have been improved. The ones involving GLSL functionality levels have been brought up to 4.x0.

6. The OpenGL Architecture Review Board (ARB) has depecated some portions of OpenGL, but has not eliminated them. This edition discusses that, and presents a strategy to write your own code with that in mind. All code examples in this book now follow that strategy. Also, by following that strategy, you will be prepared for migration to OpenGL-ES 2.0.

7. Appendices have been added showing the use of C++ classes to make writing OpenGL shader applications easier, and help with the post-deprecation strategy.

Programmable computer graphics shaders have had an interesting history. In not-too-distant memory, at least for some of us, *all* aspects of computer graphics were programmable. In fact, "programmable" is probably not a good term, because that implies that there was a programmability option when creating an image. There wasn't. If you wanted *anything* to happen, you had no choice but to program it. Yourself. "Involuntary programmability" might be a better way to put it.

Computer graphics APIs changed that for most graphics practitioners. With a good API, you could write very good graphics programs much more easily because you could let the API's functionality take over large portions of the graphics process. However, you paid for this in giving up any functionality that the API didn't know how to handle. A good example is surface shading, where most of the 1990s APIs could not support anything beyond simple smooth lighted surfaces.

Fortunately, neither the computer graphics research community nor advanced graphics practitioners were satisfied with this. First in software and then in hardware, as graphics processors were developed, specific functionality was developed to support the programming of features that fixed-function graphics APIs had fenced off. This functionality has now developed its own standards, including the GLSL shader language that is part of the OpenGL standard. Programmable graphics shaders, programs that can be downloaded to a graphics processor to carry out operations outside the fixed-function pipe-line of earlier standards, have become a key feature of computer graphics.

This process is now being paralleled in the teaching and learning of computer graphics. Just as students usually first learned computer graph-ics through a graphics standard, most often OpenGL, students now need to understand the role of programmable shaders and to have experience in writ-ing and using them. One of the remarkable things about shader-level pro-gramming is that it brings us all back to the same kind of graphics questions that were being examined in the 1970s. We can now manipulate vertices and individual pixels while still having the full OpenGL API high-speed support whenever we want to use it. This gives students and practitioners a wonderful range of capabilities that can be used in games, in scientific visualization, and in general graphical communication.

This book is designed to open computer graphics shader programming to students, whether in a traditional class or on their own. It is intended to com-plement texts based on fixed-function graphics APIs, specifically OpenGL. It introduces shader programming in general, and specifically the GLSL shader language. It also introduces a flexible, easy-to-use tool, *glman*, which helps you develop and tune shaders outside an application that would use them.

This book is intended as a text for a second course in computer graphics at either the undergraduate or graduate level. It is not a textbook for a first course in computer graphics, because it assumes knowledge of not only OpenGL, but of general graphics concepts. Knowledge of another graphics API, such as Direct3D, will work, but we focus on GLSL and will use OpenGL terminology consistently. Because shader programming lets you work in areas that APIs might hide from you, sometimes you will need to work at fundamental levels of geometry, lighting, shading, and similar concepts. You will benefit from a prior understanding of these. You will also find that shader programming exposes some areas of API operation that you may not have fully understood, so you may need to review some of these details.

Our choice of GLSL as the vehicle for teaching shaders is based on its integration into the widely-used OpenGL multiplatform API and its solid per-formance. The concepts presented here will also help anyone who works with other shader APIs such as Cg or HLSL, because the basic ideas of shaders are all similar. The book is designed to take the student from a review of the fixed-function graphics pipeline through an understanding of the basic role and functions of shader programming to solid experience in writing vertex, fragment, and geometry shaders for both *glman* and actual applications.

While it might seem logical to treat shaders in the order in which they are applied in the expanded graphics pipeline, with vertex shaders first, followed by geometry shaders and then fragment shaders, we have chosen to lay out their order a little differently. Again, it might seem logical to treat shaders in the order of frequency of use, with fragment shaders first, followed by vertex shaders and then geometry shaders, but that also does not quite seem to work. Because many of the operations of a fragment shader depend on things that come out of a vertex shader, we treat vertex shaders first, followed by fragment shaders, and finally geometry and tessellation shaders.

The overall outline of the text is straightforward. In the first chapters, which make up the background for the rest of the book, we begin by covering the fixed-function graphics pipeline of OpenGL in **Chapter 1,** and OpenGL shader evolution in **Chapter 2**. We then present the basic principles of vertex, fragment, geometry, and tessellation shaders in **Chapter 3**, including several examples, using the GLSL shader language. **Chapter 4** introduces the *glman* tool with a kind of mini-manual on its use. Finally, **Chapter 5** presents the GLSL shader language and discusses its similarities and differences from the C programming language.

The next set of chapters sets up vertex and fragment shader concepts. **Chapter 6** covers lighting from the point of view of shaders and introduces the ADS (ambient, diffuse, specular) lighting function that we will use several times in later chapters. This is fundamental in both vertex and fragment shaders, since vertex shaders often need to compute lighting for each vertex, and fragment shaders may want to compute lighting for each pixel. In **Chapter 7** we cover vertex shaders, emphasizing their inputs and outputs as well as the ways they can be used to modify vertex geometry. Finally, in **Chapter 8** we cover fragment shaders, again emphasizing their inputs and outputs and showing how they can be used to replace the usual fixed-function fragment operations.

The next three chapters discuss particular capabilities of fragment shaders. In **Chapter 9** we describe the way fragment shaders handle texture mapping, including bump mapping, cube mapping, and rendering a scene to a texture. **Chapter 10** discusses noise functions and their role in writing textures and shaders, and introduces a tool, *noisegraph,* that lets you experiment with the properties of 1D and 2D noise functions. Finally, **Chapter 11** examines some ways you can manipulate 2D images, treated as textures, with the tools that fragment shaders make available.

Chapter 12 presents geometry shaders, including how they are related to vertex and fragment shaders as well as their own capabilities. Several examples highlight the way geometry shaders can expand the geometric capability of your models or show the capability of geometry shaders to handle simple level-of-detail operations. **Chapter 13** discusses tessellation shaders. We show how they are somewhat similar to geometry shaders but have important enhancements.

The final set of chapters focuses on computer graphics shaders in applications. **Chapter 14** describes the GLSL API that lets you compile, link, and use shaders in an application. It also discusses passing data and graphics state information to shader programs and introduces a simple C++ class that encapsulates the process of incorporating shader programs in an application. In **Chapter 15**, we focus on how shaders can be used in scientific visualization applications, and show examples of a number of specific visualization operations. And in **Chapter 16** we explore some fun things you can do with computer graphics shaders, under the guise of getting real work done. (Don't tell anyone.)

Four appendices have been added showing the use of C++ classes to help write OpenGL applications and handle some of the post-deprecation challenges.

While many of the topics in this text are straightforward, some are tricky or deserve special attention. We have followed the lead of the Nicholas Bourbaki mathematics texts of the early 20th century and have highlighted these with a "dangerous curves ahead" sign as shown to the right. We hope this will help you notice these points.

Because shader functions are changing, there are times when we want to highlight things that have evolved or things we introduce to deal with these changes. We have used a second sign, shown at right, to draw your attention to these points.

We are confident that the tools and capabilities we describe in this book will both make you a better graphics programmer and make graphics programming a much more interesting experience for you. As OpenGL evolves toward the future and shaders become the only way that geometry and rendering are handled, we believe that you will find this text to be an invaluable guide.

Thanks

The authors of this book owe thanks to a number of people, primarily on Mike Bailey's side.

To faculty colleagues at Oregon State University for their support and camaraderie: Ron Adams, Bella Bose, Terri Fiez, Karti Mayaram Ron Metoyer, Eric Mortensen, Cherri Pancake, Sinisa Todorovic, and Eugene Zhang.

To the superbly talented UCSD and OSU graphics students who have shared this shader expedition: Tim Bauer, William Brendel, Guoning Chen, Matt Clothier, John Datuin, Will Dillon, Jonathan Dodge, Chuck Evans, Nick Gebbie, Kyle Hatcher, Nick Hogle, Chris Janik, Ankit Khare, Vasu Lakshmanan, Adam Leibel, Jessica McGregor, Daniel Moffitt, Chris Moore, Patrick Neill, Jonathan Palacios, Nadia Payet, Randy Rauwendaal, Dwayne Robinson, Avneet Sandhu, Nick Schultz, Sudarshanram Shetty, Evon Silvia, Ian South-Dickinson, Madhu Srinivasan, Michael Tichenor, Christophe Torne, Ben Tribelhorn, Ben Weiss, and Alex Wiggins.

To professional colleagues: Ryan Bailey, Mike Gannis, Jenny Orr, Todd Shechter, and Justin Spencer.

To the folks at NVIDIA for their support, especially Gary Brown, Greg Gritton, Jen-Hsun Huang, David Kirk, Dave Luebke, and David Zier.

To the folks at AMD/ATI for their support, especially Bill Licea-Kane.

To Randi Rost, for his support from positions at both 3D Labs and Intel, and for writing his "Orange Book," from which so much of what went into this book was learned.

To Paramount Pictures for their permission to reprint the image in Figure 2.2. and to Pixar for providing the original image.

To xkcd.com for the comic used at the front of this Preface.

We also thank Alice Peters and Sarah Cutler for their advice and assistance in developing this project, and the reviewers for helping us refine some key points in the text.

Mike Bailey   Steve Cunningham
Corvallis, Oregon   Coralville, Iowa

1

The Fixed-Function Graphics Pipeline

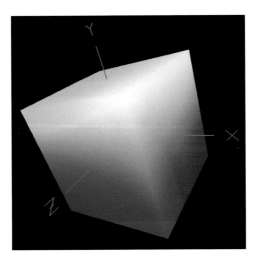

In your first course in computer graphics, you probably used a graphics API to help you create your projects. Because this book focuses on graphics using OpenGL, we assume that your API was OpenGL, and in this chapter we review the graphics pipeline as it is expressed in OpenGL versions 1.x. If you used a different API, especially in a first graphics course, your experience was probably very close to the OpenGL approach. These APIs used a *fixed-function pipeline*, or a pipeline with a fixed set of operations on vertices and fragments. In the rest of this book, we will look at the shader capabilities of OpenGL versions 2.x and how you can use them to create effects that are difficult or impossible with the fixed-function pipeline.

The Traditional View

When you develop a graphics application with the OpenGL API, you define geometry, viewing, projection, and a number of appearance properties. Objects' geometries are defined by their vertices, their normals, and their graphics primitives, specified by `glBegin–glEnd` pairs that encompass points, lines, geometry-compressed groups, or polygons. Viewing and projection are each defined with a specific function. Appearance is specified by defining color, shading, materials, and lighting, or texture mapping. This information is all processed in a very straightforward way by the fixed-function OpenGL system, acting either in software or in a graphics card.

The simplest way to view OpenGL's operations is to think of it as using two connected operations: a *vertex-processing operation* and a *pixel-processing operation*. Each operation in fixed-function OpenGL has a pre-determined set of capabilities. It is important to understand how the geometry and appearance directives you give are carried out in the pipelines. When you work with shaders, though, it is more than important to understand the pipelines; your shaders will actually take over part of these operations, so you absolutely *must* understand them.

The Vertex Operation

To create the geometry of a scene, you specify primitives and vertices, and operations that act on each vertex and create its pixel coordinates in screen space. The primitive you specified then determines the pixels that must be filled to represent it, and any appearance information you specified is used to determine how those pixels are to be colored in the pixel-processing operation. The geometry part of the vertex processing follows the flow in Figure 1.1. The geometry processing is carried out for each vertex independently of any information on grouping in your specified primitive; the grouping information is only used after the vertices finish the vertex processing.

The first stage of the vertex operation defines the fundamental geometry of your scene. The input to this stage is the set of vertex definitions (your `glVertex*`, `glNormal*`, and `glTexCoord*` function calls) and the grouping definition (your `glBegin(...)` and `glEnd( )` function calls) that you set for the scene. Each piece of geometry is created, or modeled, in its own model space. This coordinate space can be anything that makes it easy for you to define the vertices and relationships for your model. Modeling functions include any operations you may need to create these definitions and often use mathematical functions operating in the model space. As we noted, the geometry might include normal vectors and texture coordinates. It also includes primitive specifications that specify how pixels are to be assembled from your vertices. It may also include lights when you want the lights to have specific relationships with your geometry. You are probably used to including other definitions, such as colors and material properties, as you define your geometry. These are appearance factors for the scene and are used later in the vertex pipeline, as we will see. The output of this stage is a set of vertices in model coordinates, with other geometric information and with primitive information.

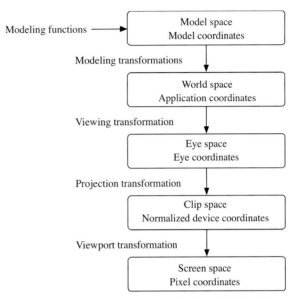

Figure 1.1. Vertex processing in the OpenGL pipeline.

The second stage of the vertex operation defines the world space that will hold the entire scene and puts all your individual models in that space. Each geometric primitive is placed into world space by modeling transformations such as scaling, rotation, or translation transformations, so the input to this stage is your set of modeling transformation specifications (your glRotatef(...), glTranslatef(...), and glScalef(...) function calls). These transformations convert the individual model space coordinates into a single set of world or application space coordinates. They do not affect color or material definitions, texture coordinates, or groupings, but they do modify vertices, normals, and the geometry of lighting. Often, lights are defined directly in world space when you think of lighting a whole scene instead of a single object. Light geometry, such as position or direction, is affected by whatever modeling is in effect when the light is defined. The output of this stage is a modified set of vertices and normals, representing the original geometry in a different space.

The third stage of the vertex operation defines the eye space that is created when you specify viewing information for your scene. The input to this stage is your definition of the viewing environment, often using the GLU function gluLookAt(...). This defines the viewing transformation that modifies your scene to create the standard eye view of a scene, a coordinate system with the eye at the origin, and the x-, y-, and z-axes in their familiar right-handed 3D orientations. This transformation modifies vertex, normal, and light information, so the output of this stage is the modified geometry with the original primitive information, with the geometry representing a standard viewing space. All depth information for later processing comes from the z-coordinates in this eye space. The *ModelView matrix* is defined at this point, and is used to transform the vertices for geometric computations, as well as to transform the values of the normals, light positions, and light directions for lighting computations.

Once you are in eye space, other information comes into play. As part of defining each vertex, you probably also provided some appearance information (e.g., glColor3f) or other information (e.g., lights or materials). This information can be used here to set the vertex color. The color of each vertex can be set as your color statements are implemented or any lighting operations you specified are carried out. If lighting is enabled, the light parameters, light position and direction, normal vectors, and material specification are used to determine a color for each vertex. Each vertex is assumed to have a color value from this point on in the process.

The fourth stage of the vertex operation defines the *clip space* that is created when you specify the projection of your scene to the viewplane. The input to this stage is your projection definition, either perspective or orthographic. This projection definition defines a projection transformation that is to be applied to the eye space. Your projection definition creates a *view volume*, and the projection transformation is applied to this view volume to create a rectangular 3D space that can easily be used for the next stage.

The final stage of the vertex operation uses your specified viewport information to create pixel-space representations for each vertex in screen space. There are two primary operations here. One is clipping the geometry you specified on the clip space boundaries in your projection definition; if any clipping is done, it may create new or modified primitives as vertex pixels are added or deleted. When there is clipping, the new vertex pixels will need to have their new colors or texture coordinates interpolated in the same way as edges are interpolated in the rendering process. The second is converting the 3D clip space coordinates into the 2D integer coordinates of the specified viewport. This is a simple proportion operation in the x- and y-coordinates plus homogeneous division, followed by a truncation of these real values to integers. At the same time, the z-coordinates are converted to depth values (usually integers) that can be used in rendering. The output of this stage, and thus the output of the entire vertex pipeline, is a set of vertices in integer pixel x- and y-coordinates with grouping, normals, depth, texture coordinates, and color.

While Figure 1.1 describes the actions of the vertex pipeline, it can also be useful to see the effects of these actions. In Figure 1.2 we describe this by showing how the overall graphics pipeline works on a simple triangle represented by the three (blue) vertices. These are sent to the vertex pipeline by

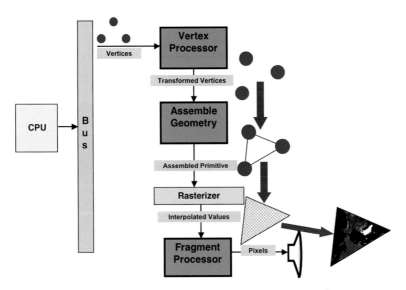

Figure 1.2. The actions of the overall graphics pipeline.

the CPU, are transformed into screen space by the vertex processor, are assembled to go into the rasterizer, and are turned into pixels by the fragment processor.

The graphics pipeline as described above includes a number of transformations noted in Figure 1.1: several modeling transformations, the viewing transformation, and the projection transformation. The actual OpenGL implementation of the pipeline uses a more unified version of these transformations, however; the modeling and viewing transformations are combined into the *ModelView transformation*, and new modeling transformations are multiplied into this as they are defined. A *transformation stack* is maintained for the ModelView and Projection transformations, with the current version at the top of the stack. The `glPushMatrix( )` and `glPopMatrix( )` operations let you save and restore modeling environments. The *ModelViewProjection transformation* is the product of the ModelView and Projection transformations, and is updated whenever the ModelView transformation or Projection Transformation is updated. The ModelViewProjection transformation is applied to individual vertices to place them into clip space. The system also maintains another transformation, the *Normal transformation*, calculated as the inverse of the transpose of the ModelView transformation, which handles the problem of ensuring that the normal can be correctly used for lighting and other operations. Later in the chapter we will describe how this is done.

The Fragment Processing Part of the Pipeline

OK, a moment ago we called it "pixel-processing," but the fact is that it is really called "fragment-processing." What is a *pixel*? A pixel, in GLSL terminology, is a set of appearance information (usually red, green, blue, alpha, z-depth, etc.) that is about to be written to the framebuffer. Then what is a *fragment*? A fragment is a pixel-to-be; that is, it is a pixel's worth of information necessary to compute that pixel's red, green, blue, alpha, z-depth, etc. The operation is called "fragment processing" because its job is to take all that information and produce the pixel appearance. We will now see how that operation fits in with the entire graphics pipeline.

The graphics pipeline takes the vertices in screen space and constructs the regions you defined in your grouping with the appearance you specified in the OpenGL rendering commands. This is described in the somewhat simplified diagram of the rendering pipeline shown in Figure 1.3. This takes as its input the output of the last step of the vertex pipeline in Figure 1.1.

Looking at this as we did at the vertex operation, we ask about the inputs and outputs for each stage. We start with the output of the vertex operation: vertices in screen coordinates with groupings, colors, depths, and texture coordinates. (Normals are not considered here; the fixed-function pipeline does not need them for fragment processing because lighting is computed per-vertex and only the resultant color intensities are interpolated per-fragment.) The first rendering stage takes the ordered vertices and creates the edges of the primitive. The colors, depths, and texture coordinates at the vertices are interpolated to define these same properties along the edges and are then interpolated left-edge-to-right-edge for each fragment.

The next rendering stage processes fragments. It takes that "pre-information" we just talked about and creates the appearance information that will be written into the framebuffer.

In the final stage of the graphics pipeline, the color of the pixel is integrated into the framebuffer by functions such as depth testing, blending, and masking that assemble the final framebuffer content. These processes might ignore the pixel (depth testing, masking) or might change the color of the pixel (blending). The final output of this stage is the actual color in the framebuffer.

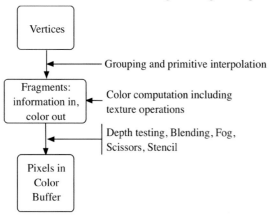

Figure 1.3. A simplified view of the OpenGL rendering pipeline.

There are, of course, many details in these operations, and we have only sketched the overall process here. Many of these should be familiar from your experience with graphics programming using OpenGL. Later in this chapter we will review some of these details and discuss some others that may not be quite as familiar. And in the later chapters that describe fragment shaders and show how you can use them, you will see how to control most of the details yourself.

State in the Graphics Pipeline

In order to manage the large number of OpenGL operations and all of the options they need, OpenGL sets and maintains a set of state information that is used in the vertex and rendering operations. A large number of OpenGL functions have as their only operation the setting of information in the graphics state. As these operations are carried out, they get their information from the state.

We need to be very aware of the OpenGL state in working with shaders, because we will have to replace some critical fixed-function operations. It will be useful to have a comfortable language and notation to talk about OpenGL state. We introduce the notion of a graphics context to describe the OpenGL state, and introduce a diagram of this context in Figure 1.4.

The initial graphics context has a number of default values (e.g., lines are white and one pixel wide, the background color is black, and there are no active textures.) When we set values with functions such as glColor3f(...), we will say that we "dock" the color value to the slot that holds the primary color value in the OpenGL state. If we change that color with another function call, then the slot holds the new value and the old value is lost. Thus, each "docking point" holds a unique state value that is used in the graphics process, and most values can be queried as well as set. We will see this from time to time as we discuss shader operations.

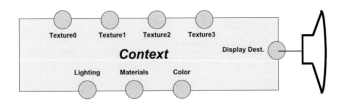

Figure 1.4. The OpenGL state as a graphics context object.

How the Traditional View Is Implemented

In the OpenGL system, the actual processes that implement the pipeline are grouped into different kinds of functionality. A block diagram of these functional groups in a generic graphics system is shown in Figure 1.5.

The first functional group handles the vertex processing that is shown in Figure 1.1. The input to this group includes vertices, normals, primitive definitions, colors, lights (and their parameters), materials, and texture coordinates. The output is a set of vertices as pixels with their color, depth, and texture coordinates, and perhaps as revised primitives.

The next step is rasterizing. This implements the Vertices-to-Fragments step in the rendering pipeline of Figure 1.3. The input to the rasterizer is the set of vertices in screen coordinates with their depth, color, and texture coordinates, along with how the vertices are to be connected. The rasterization process interpolates the vertices to create fragments, and the same interpolation is applied to determine the depth, color, and texture coordinates for each fragment.

The second functional group is fragment processing. The input to this group is a fragment rasterized from a graphics primitive. The fragment's color is determined by processing its color, depth, and texture coordinate information. The output of fragment processing is a set of completed pixels, the "RGBAZ Pixels" of Figure 1.5, with color (RGB), blending (A, for alpha), and depth (Z) values, ready to be integrated into the color buffer.

The final step is this integration of pixels into the color buffer. This corresponds to the Fragments-to-Pixels section of the rendering pipeline of Figure 1.3. The pixels from the fragment processor are integrated into the color buffer by raster operations that merge the fragment with the pixels in the framebuffer. This is the same for both fixed-function and shader-based graphics.

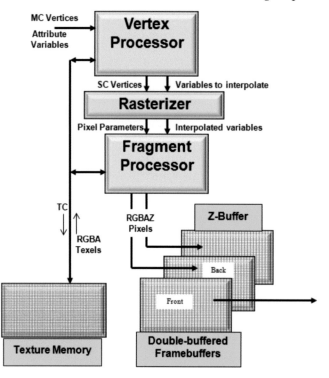

Figure 1.5. The OpenGL pipeline in graphics hardware.

Vertex Processing

There are many details of this fixed-function vertex pipeline process that must be understood in terms of the hardware pipeline in order to work with shaders. The first is probably the *ModelView matrix,* the matrix that implements the ModelView transformation.

Whenever any vertex V is sent to the vertex processor, it is multiplied by the ModelView matrix M as $V' = M * V$ to convert it to eye space and begin its processing.

The second detail of the vertex pipeline process is the role of the projection and viewport transformations. After vertices are transformed from model space to eye space by applying the ModelView transformation, they are further transformed by applying the projection transformation (set by the functions glOrtho( ), glFrustum( ), or gluPerspective( )) into *clip space,* and the clipping is done by a separate operation. In fact, the ModelView and Projection transformations are combined to create the ModelViewProjection transformation that takes your model into clip space in one operation. The name "clip space" is used because the projection transformation maps the vertices into a coordinate space in which clipping is easily done. Finally, homogeneous division and the viewport transformation convert vertices in clip space to their integer screen coordinates.

Why is the normal matrix the transpose of the inverse of the ModelView matrix? Let's consider a normal vector N to a surface at a point P, and let's choose a point Q so that the vector $T = Q - P$ is tangent to the surface at P. Then $N \times T = 0$ or, using matrix multiplication, $N^T * T = 0$ (recall that if vertices and normals are expressed as column vectors, a transpose is a row vector, so this is a product of a 1×3 and a 3×1 matrix, or a scalar). Then if we apply the transformation M so that $P' = M * P$ and $Q' = M * Q$, the new tangent vector is $T' = Q' - P' = M * Q - M * P = M * (Q - P) = M * T$. Now if we define N' to be the normal in the transformed space, $(N')^T * T'$ must be zero. So if R is the matrix that transforms the normal N to the new normal N', we have

$$0 = N'^T * T' = (R * N)^T * T' = (N^T * R^T) * (M * T) = N^T * (R^T * M) * T.$$

Since $N^T * T = 0$, the middle term $R^T * M$ must be the identity, so $R^T * M^{-1}$ and finally $R = (M^{-1})^T$.

In fact, this process is less mysterious than it might seem, because if only rotation is done, the matrix is orthonormal. One property of an orthonormal matrix is that its inverse is equal to its transpose. In that case, the normal is transformed by the same rotation that transforms the vertices.

With this processing for vertex coordinates, what is done for normals? In order to compute normals accurately, OpenGL uses a Normal transformation that maintains the normal property: if the normal vector is transformed by the normal transformation, the result is still normal to the transformed surface. This is implemented by the *normal matrix*, computed by taking the transpose of the inverse of the upper-left 3 × 3 submatrix of the ModelView matrix. The normal matrix is updated automatically whenever the ModelView matrix is changed, so it does not need to be re-created each time a normal is processed.

We want to remind you that vertex lighting color computation is handled in the vertex processor. This is not always obvious. If you generate colors for your scene by using lighting and materials specification instead of simply specifying colors for each vertex, you define a number of parameters for the lights and for the materials of each object. This information is available to the vertex processor, and the lighting model you specify is applied to compute a color for each vertex. In any case, whether you use a lighting model or not, the color of each vertex is passed into the rendering process, not calculated while rendering.

Rendering Processing

In the rendering process, the vertex data from the vertex pipeline (pixel position, depth, color, and texture coordinate) is used to define the set of pixels that make up a graphical object and to calculate the color for each of these pixels. This process associates the graphics primitive specification, the appearance information you specify for each vertex, such as the actual texture to be used, and directions on how appearance processing is to be done, to create the actual image.

Primitive specifications define the way a sequence of vertices is to be used to define a geometric object, and this quickly reduces to the question of defining a single polygon. Polygons are defined to be planar and non-self-intersecting (though OpenGL does not check this). Further, in OpenGL a polygon is always assumed to be convex, that is, to have the property that any line segment whose endpoints are inside the polygon must itself lie completely within the polygon. This is shown in Figure 1.6 (although to be strict with the definition, the rightmost figure isn't really a polygon, since it self-intersects). If you should define a non-convex polygon, it is usually processed in a way that is inconsistent with your intent.

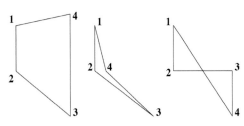

Figure 1.6. A convex (allowed) polygon (left) and two non-convex (not allowed) polygons (middle and right).

Any convex polygon can be triangulated, or broken up into triangles, by choosing any vertex and constructing a triangle fan by processing the vertices in order, starting with that vertex. (A non-convex polygon does not have that property, even though you might be able to find a way to make up the polygon from triangles, as is the case with the middle example of Figure 1.6.) This concept also extends to other geometry constructors, such as quad strips; an OpenGL quad strip is defined in such a way that it can as easily be viewed as a triangle strip. Since OpenGL only handles convex polygons, we can assume polygons are convex, and so we can simply use triangles as our model for polygon processing.

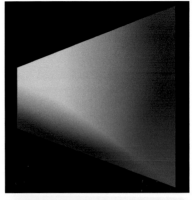

A key concept in rendering is *interpolation*. Given a set of vertices in screen coordinates and a polygon defined by their grouping, interpolation is needed to determine the edges that bound the polygon, and interpolation is again needed to fill the interior of the polygon. The interpolation not only creates locations to be filled, but also interpolates all the accompanying properties, such as depth, color, and texture coordinates. Interpolation is supported by graphics hardware; in the fixed-function rendering pipeline, this handles simple interpolation (needed for depth or smooth shading) and perspective interpolation (needed for accurate coordinates, especially texture coordinates).

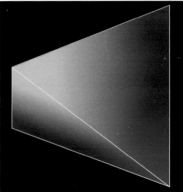

Figure 1.7. Linear color interpolation across a polygon.

The interpolation for smooth-shaded color or for depth is linear interpolation of these values at the vertices or the endpoints of an edge. This interpolation first interpolates the vertex colors along the edges of the object and then interpolates the edge colors across the interior of the object. This interpolation may not be exactly as you imagined it would be. Figure 1.7 (top) shows a simple quad having one blue, one green, and two red vertices, with fixed-function color interpolation across the interior. You see that the shading looks as though there were two triangles that were interpolated separately, one including the top right vertex and the other including the bottom left vertex, as shown in the bottom image in the figure.[1] This is obviously a weakness in simple interpolation shading that we would like to be able to deal with, as we will discuss in Chapter 15.

---

1. You can tell that something is not right in the way this quad is being rendered because the upper-left to lower-right diagonal has just green-blue colors on it. There is no evidence of red on the diagonal despite there being two vertices colored red.

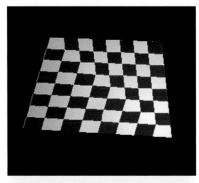

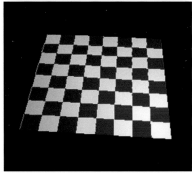

Figure 1.8. Texture mapping a checkerboard pattern on a quad without perspective correction (top) and with perspective correction (bottom).

There is also an interpolation for texture coordinates. The texture coordinates for each vertex are interpolated to get the texture coordinates for the boundary pixels, and the texture coordinates of the endpoints of a fragment are interpolated to get the texture coordinates for each pixel in the fragment. After the texture coordinates for each pixel are computed, the texture coordinates are sent to the texture space and texel values are returned to be combined with other pixel information as specified in your texture specifications.

The kind of interpolation done for texture coordinates depends on your texture quality hint. If you ask for "fastest" you might get a simple linear interpolation, but if you ask for "best" the texture coordinates are interpolated based on a perspective interpolation. Figure 1.8 shows the difference between linear and perspective interpolation for texture coordinates applied to a single quad seen as two triangles. Many graphics systems do not distinguish between "fastest" and "best," so you may not see this difference on your own system.

Simple linear interpolation is a familiar technique. Given a general data value f with values f_a and f_b at the two endpoints a and b of a line segment, linear interpolation with linear parameter t is typically given by the function

$$(1-t)f_a + t f_b.$$

If the data values f are in homogeneous coordinates (r, s, t, q) with $q \neq 1$, then you must convert the coordinates into standard form by dividing each f by the values of q and interpolate the f/q values:

$$(1-t)f_a/q_a + t f_b/q_b.$$

This last case clearly is the same as the first case if f_a and f_b are already in standard homogeneous form.

As usual in interpolations, we notice that if $t = 0$, the function has value f_a, while if $t = 1$, the function has value f_b. The value of the interpolating parameter t that would give a particular pixel in the interpolating line can be computed by

$$t = \frac{(p_r - p_a) \bullet (p_b - p_a)}{\|p_b - p_a\|^2} = \frac{(p_r - p_a) \bullet (p_b - p_a)}{(p_b - p_a) \bullet (p_b - p_a)}$$

where $p_r = (x_r, y_r)$ gives the coordinates of the pixel in pixel space and $p_a = (x_a, y_a)$ and $p_b = (x_b, y_b)$ give the screen coordinates of the endpoints in pixel space of the line segment containing the pixel.

Simple linear interpolation like this is readily supported by graphics hardware and is used to interpolate simple values such as depth and smooth-shading color. But it has some problems if we use simple linear interpolation in model space when the real graphical meaning of those values is determined in clip space. For interpolating these kinds of values, such as texture coordinates, we need to do the actual interpolation in clip space. That is more interesting. For these values, instead of linear interpolation, OpenGL uses a modified interpolation function (using the same parameter t as above) given by

$$\frac{(1-t)f_a/w_a + t f_b/w_b}{(1-t)\alpha_a/w_a + t\alpha_b/w_b},$$

where $\alpha = 1$ unless you are interpolating textures and the texture coordinates (s, t, r, q) have $q \neq 1$; in that case $\alpha_a = q_a$ and $\alpha_b = q_b$. Further, w_a and w_b are the fourth coordinate of the endpoints a and b in homogeneous clip space. Again, if $t = 0$, we simply get the value f_a and if $t = 1$, we get f_b (or their homogenized value if f is a texture coordinate). We may call this a *perspective interpolation*, because it is really only different from linear interpolation when clip space is different from eye space, which happens with a perspective projection. This interpolation can be quite non-linear if the original endpoints a and b have different z-values, because the values of w_a and w_b are generally the reciprocals of those z-values. Figure 1.9 shows how a value (in this case one of the coordinate values) is interpolated by this process between two endpoints; notice that this is not linear.

Although we think of depth in terms of the z-values in clip space, depth computations are not done with these values. That is, the depth buffer is not a traditional z-buffer. The depth value for a pixel in screen space is represented in fixed-point form (effectively as an integer) with at least as many bits as are in the depth buffer, and the depth buffer stores these values, truncated if necessary, for depth comparisons. Thus, the depth value is aliased, and to minimize aliasing problems, you want to define your near and far clipping planes so the distance between them is as small as possible. The near clipping

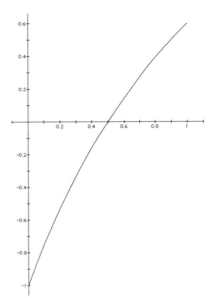

Figure 1.9. Interpolating the x-coordinates of two points in 2D eye space. The points are (-3, -1, 3, 1) and (3, -1, 5, 1) in 3D eye space.

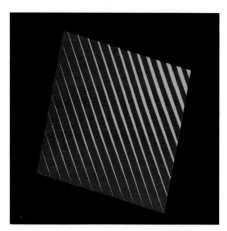

Figure 1.10. An illustration of *z*-fighting, with the area where two polygons intersect having depth aliasing problems.

plane has the smallest depth value, while the far clipping plane has the largest. The linear interpolation calculation based on the depth value of the endpoint of a line segment or fragment gives the depth for a given pixel.

In the final phase of pixel processing, these pixels are sent to the final stage of the rendering pipeline after they are computed, but before they are written to the framebuffer. These final stages handle several operations, including masking, depth testing, and alpha blending. The integer depth value is used in depth testing, and pixels are ignored if their depth exceeds the depth of that pixel already in the depth buffer. If the aliased depth values of two pixels are the same, only one of them can be used. This can lead to unusual surface behaviors such as uneven boundaries between objects that intersect at a very shallow angle; this is called *z-fighting*. This is illustrated in Figure 1.10, which shows two quads that differ in depth by only a very small amount; you can see that there is no consistent calculation of depth priority for the polygons. Blending uses the alpha value for each pixel, from the color setting, material definition, or alpha component of the texture, and should be familiar to you. Masking is handled by scissors testing, alpha testing, stencil comparison, or other logical operations.

So the overall geometry and rendering processing includes many steps, but OpenGL organizes them in a reasonable and manageable order and gives the programmer the tools to do sound basic computer graphics while working at a relatively high level. The success of OpenGL in making high-quality computer graphics accessible to the general computing environment is one of the true success stories in computing—but it has gone about as far as it can go, and this book is about the next step in making ever-better graphics widely accessible.

Homogeneous Coordinates in the Fixed-Function Pipeline

Homogeneous coordinates are often treated lightly, if at all, in a beginning graphics course, but it can be very important to understand them in more advanced work because they affect the way OpenGL works. *Homogeneous coordinates* refers to vectors in 4-dimensional real space whose fourth coordinate is often unitary. The components of a vertex have the name conventions (x, y, z, w), and a vertex in standard form has $w = 1$. You may have used 2D or 3D vertices in your graphics programs, but internally in OpenGL these are always treated as points in 4-space. If you specified a vertex with `glVertex2f(x,y)`, then the point $(x, y, 0, 1)$ was used. If you specified a vertex with `glVertex3f(x,y,z)` then the point $(x, y, z, 1)$ was used. And if you specified a vector with `glVertex4f(x,y,z,w)`, but the 3D point you specified was really $(x/w, y/w, z/w, 1)$. For example, the homogeneous points $(1, 2, 3, 1)$, $(2, 4, 6, 2)$, and $(-1, -2, -3, -1)$ all represent the same $(1, 2, 3)$ 3D point.

This apparent confusion between 3D and 4D space, and the apparently arbitrary decision to always want a unit value for w seem awkward; why do it this way? One reason is that it allows for perspective division within the matrix mechanism. The OpenGL call

```
glFrustum( left, right, bottom, top, near, far )
```

creates this matrix:

$$\begin{Bmatrix} x' \\ y' \\ z' \\ w' \end{Bmatrix} = \begin{bmatrix} \dfrac{2*near}{right-left} & 0 & \dfrac{right+left}{right-left} & 0 \\ 0 & \dfrac{2*near}{top-bottom} & \dfrac{top+bottom}{top-bottom} & 0 \\ 0 & 0 & \dfrac{-(far+near)}{far-near} & \dfrac{-2*far*near}{far-near} \\ 0 & 0 & -1 & 0 \end{bmatrix} \begin{Bmatrix} x \\ y \\ z \\ 1 \end{Bmatrix}.$$

This gives $w' = -z$, which is the necessary divisor for perspective.

This approach also gives us a way to work with a more general geometry than simple 3D space. As another way of thinking about homogeneous coordinates, consider the four homogeneous points $(1, 2, 3, 1)$, $(1, 2, 3, 0.1)$, $(1, 2, 3, 0.01)$, and $(1, 2, 3, 0.001)$. In standard form, these points are $(1, 2, 3, 1)$, $(10, 20, 30, 1)$, $(100, 200, 300, 1)$, and $(1000, 2000, 3000, 1)$. In mathematical terms, the homogeneous coordinates of a point in 4-space are the representation in three-dimensional projective space of the line through the point and the origin, and the point $(1, 2, 3, 0)$ is the "point at infinity" in the $(1, 2, 3)$ direction.

We will sometimes find it important to consider vectors defined by their two endpoints, and we often think of these as being defined by simply doing a vector subtraction of the coordinates of the endpoints. This is not exactly the case for vertices in 4-space, or more specifically, for vertices in homogeneous coordinates. In this case, as well as addition in homogeneous coordinates, we must think a little more carefully about the question.

To compute the difference between two points in 3-space when they are represented in 4-space, we start with the vectors in 4-space, convert them to

3-space, take the difference, and find an appropriate representation of that difference. We have

$$\left(x_b, y_b, z_b, w_b\right) - \left(x_a, y_a, z_a, w_a\right) = \frac{\left(x_b, y_b, z_b\right)}{w_b} - \frac{\left(x_a, y_a, z_a\right)}{w_a} =$$

$$\frac{\left(w_a x_b, w_a y_b, w_a z_b\right) - \left(w_b x_a, w_b y_a, w_b z_a\right)}{w_a w_b}.$$

Now the denominator in the right-hand side is a scalar, so if we only want a unit direction vector, we can simply normalize the numerator as

$$v = \text{normalize}\left(w_a x_b - w_b x_a, w_a y_b - w_b y_a, w_a z_b - w_b z_a\right).$$

If both of the original vectors were already in homogeneous form with w_a and w_b both equal to one, this reduces to the standard form for the difference of two vectors.

Light position is specified in homogeneous coordinates with four values that actually position the light in projective 4-space. If the w component is not zero, the light position is an ordinary point in 3D world space whose x-, y-, and z-values are given when the point is converted to standard homogeneous form. But if you use a light position whose homogeneous coordinate w is zero, the light is treated as a directional light, because the position is the "point at infinity" of projective space. Modeling and viewing transformations affect the direction of the light, but they do not affect light's position.

Texture coordinates are also stored as real 4-vectors, just like vertices, but they also include the possibility of a one-dimensional case. Texture coordinate components have name conventions, just as vertices do; for textures, these are (s, t, p, q). (The letter p is used for the third texture coordinate instead of r in order to avoid confusion with the letter for the color red.) If you specify a 1D texture with a value of s, the t and p values are set to 0 and the q value is set to 1. The 2D and 3D texture coordinates are set in the same way.

Color is also stored internally in four dimensions in RGBA form, and if you only specify a color in RGB form, its alpha component is set to 1. Normal vectors are always defined to be three-dimensional, as in `glNormal3f(x,y,z)`, so there are no homogeneous-coordinate issues with normals.

Graphics cards' reliance on 4-vectors lets them adopt a uniform data path that is four floats wide. This lets cards become, in effect, array processors, and is part of the reason that graphics cards can speed up the pipeline processes so effectively.

Vertex Arrays

Throughout this chapter, in order to keep the concepts clear, we have been talking about the graphics pipeline as it operates on simple vertices and primitives. In actual applications, however, there are techniques that greatly increase the speed of graphics processing. One such technique is called *vertex arrays*. You may have already met this in an earlier computer graphics course, but if you have not, we want to give you a quick look at it here.

Vertex arrays are created on the host CPU to store vertex coordinates and vertex attributes. These arrays are transmitted to the graphics card along with indices that tell what vertex numbers need to be connected in graphics primitives. This way, each vertex is only transformed once, and there are fewer overall function calls.

Vertex arrays are activated with the command

```
glEnableClientState( type )
```

where *type* includes

```
GL_VERTEX_ARRAY
GL_COLOR_ARRAY
GL_NORMAL_ARRAY
GL_SECONDARY_COLOR_ARRAY
GL_TEXTURE_COORD_ARRAY
```

This function lets you enable all the vertex arrays you need to describe vertex data.

To deactivate a vertex type, use

```
glDisableClientState( type )
```

Once you have activated the vertex state(s) you need, you can fill the arrays by simple array operations, such as these for vertex data:

```
static GLfloat Vertices[ ][3] = {
{
  { 1., 2., 3. },
  { 4., 5., 6. },
  . . .
};
```

Similar operations could fill arrays for colors, normals, and texture coordinates, as noted above. To specify that an array will be used as a vertex array, you use the functions

```
glVertexPointer( size, type, stride, array );
glColorPointer( size, type, stride, array );
glNormalPointer( type, stride, array );
glSecondaryColorPointer( size, type, stride, array );
glTexCoordPointer( size, type, stride, array );
```

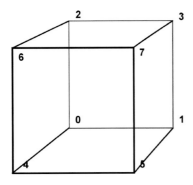

Figure 1.11. A cube with vertices numbered to match the RGB cube.

that let you specify that an array is to be used for vertex coordinates, colors, normals, etc. Here, *size* is the dimension of a vertex and can be 2, 3, or 4; *type* can be any of GL_SHORT, GL_INT, GL_FLOAT, or GL_DOUBLE; and *array* is the name of the corresponding data array. The variable *stride* is the byte offset between consecutive entries in the array (0 means tightly packed) and is most easily set with the sizeof( ) function.

As an example, let's draw the standard RGB cube whose vertices are indexed in Figure 1.11 by specifying its vertex coordinates and vertex colors. We set vertex 0 to be black, its adjacent vertices 1, 2, and 4 to be red, green, and blue respectively, vertices 3, 6, and 5 to be yellow, cyan, and magenta respectively, and vertex 7 to be black.

The following statements set up these arrays:

```
static GLfloat CubeVertices[ ][3] =
{
    { -1., -1., -1. },
    {  1., -1., -1. },
    { -1.,  1., -1. },
    {  1.,  1., -1. },
    { -1., -1.,  1. },
    {  1., -1.,  1. },
    { -1.,  1.,  1. },
    {  1.,  1.,  1. }
};

static GLfloat CubeColors[ ][3] =
{
    { 0., 0., 0. },
    { 1., 0., 0. },
    { 0., 1., 0. },
    { 1., 1., 0. },
    { 0., 0., 1. },
    { 1., 0., 1. },
    { 0., 1., 1. },
    { 1., 1., 1. },
};
```

Then we can draw the RGB cube using the glArrayElement( ) function and simply list all the vertices by their index. The geometry and color for each vertex is used as if the glVertex( ) and glColor( ) statements were given for each vertex.

```
glEnableClientState( GL_VERTEX_ARRAY );
glEnableClientState( GL_COLOR_ARRAY );
glVertexPointer( 3, GL_FLOAT, 0, CubeVertices );
glColorPointer( 3, GL_FLOAT, 0, CubeColors );
glBegin( GL_QUADS );
   glArrayElement( 0 );
   glArrayElement( 2 );
   glArrayElement( 3 );
   glArrayElement( 1 );
   glArrayElement( 4 );
   glArrayElement( 5 );
   glArrayElement( 7 );
   glArrayElement( 6 );
   glArrayElement( 1 );
   glArrayElement( 3 );
   glArrayElement( 7 );
   glArrayElement( 5 );
   glArrayElement( 0 );
   glArrayElement( 4 );
   glArrayElement( 6 );
   glArrayElement( 2 );
   glArrayElement( 2 );
   glArrayElement( 6 );
   glArrayElement( 7 );
   glArrayElement( 3 );
   glArrayElement( 0 );
   glArrayElement( 1 );
   glArrayElement( 5 );
   glArrayElement( 4 );
glEnd( );
```

This feels rather long and inelegant, and not very productive. But we can also define an array that holds the indices of the vertices on each of the six faces of the cube and use the glDrawElements( ) function.

```
static GLuint CubeIndices[ ][4] =
{
   { 0, 2, 3, 1 },
   { 4, 5, 7, 6 },
   { 1, 3, 7, 5 },
   { 0, 4, 6, 2 },
   { 2, 6, 7, 3 },
   { 0, 1, 5, 4 }
};
```

```
glEnableClientState( GL_VERTEX_ARRAY );
glEnableClientState( GL_COLOR_ARRAY );

glVertexPointer( 3, GL_FLOAT, 0, CubeVertices );
glColorPointer( 3, GL_FLOAT, 0, CubeColors );
glDrawElements( GL_QUADS, 24, GL_UNSIGNED_INT, CubeIndices );
```

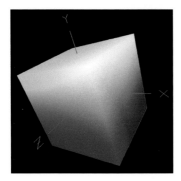

Figure 1.12. The RGB cube produced by the code above (with axes added).

which is certainly shorter and feels somewhat more elegant. Notice that the CubeIndices array is never named by a pointer-specifying function; it is simply an ordinary array of indices. The result is shown in Figure 1.12.

This is a very simple example, but in applications it is not uncommon to have these arrays contain hundreds, if not thousands, of vertices, and to have large portions of scenes captured in single arrays. This is sound data encapsulation and re-use, and it makes scenes much faster to render.

Vertex arrays are stored on the client, or host, side of the bus. That means that they are not as efficiently accessible to the graphics card as they could be. Vertex buffer objects (VBOs), which operate just like vertex arrays but live on the graphics card side, are a more efficient way to encapsulate graphics geometry. VBOs are created and used almost identically to vertex arrays, with a few small differences. See the OpenGL "Red Book" [41] for details.

Conclusions

The fixed-function graphics pipeline has shown itself to be very valuable in creating a model for computer graphics that has become widely used. It can be implemented in both software and hardware with predictable results across all computing platforms. Its fully determined processing lets most graphics operations be optimized and moved into silicon. These well-designed data paths let graphics use parallel processing to handle vertex data uniformly, and the parallel architecture of graphics cards lets the rendering processor handle many pixels simultaneously. The number of vertex and fragment processors on a card is continually growing, and as of this writing has reached as high as 128. This speeds fragment processing significantly.

As we go through the traditional fixed-function pipeline, however, we see that there are some kinds of graphics operations we would like to do that are simply hard to handle. All of these have been done in specially built computer graphics systems, often in research environments, and it is a goal of the evolving computer graphics APIs to provide more and more of these abilities. Among these are

- *Eye-space-dependent modeling*, in which objects are only defined relative to the eye. A good example of this is a rainbow, which depends critically on objects (water droplets) that define a particular angle between the eye and the light.
- *Ability to work in world space* as well as model space and eye space.
- *Phong shading*, in which the normal vector is interpolated across polygons, and the color of a pixel is determined by the standard lighting model applied pixel-by-pixel rather than by interpolating the colors of the vertex pixels.
- *Anisotropic shading*, in which light is reflected from objects differently than the assumptions on which the ambient-diffuse-specular lighting model is based.
- *Texture effects* that are completely scale-independent, for which you can zoom in on textured geometry and always get a texture that is exactly right for the scale being used.
- *Nonphotorealistic rendering*, in which the rendering creates effects that are not explicit in the geometry and appearance information.
- *Image processing techniques* that take advantage of the ability to access and work with individual values in a texture.
- *Creating geometry* as needed with the geometry shader to create effects such as level of detail that adapt themselves based on the nature of the screen space for the image.
- *Creating detailed tessellations* of an object based on relatively simple object definitions.

We will see all of these things as we move through the rest of the book.

Exercises

1. The perspective transformation into clip space is performed simply by dividing each of the x- and y-coordinates (as well as the w-coordinate, actually) by the z-coordinate for each point. Create a model that you will view with perspective, and hand-compute an alternate model by carrying out the perspective transformation yourself. That is, create a new model in which the old model's clip space is the new model's world space. Then draw both models and compare the results.

2. In this chapter, we claimed that it was easy to create the inverse of any transformation that is built with only rotation, scaling, and translation. Verify this symbolically and use the OpenGL matrix operations to verify it numerically.

3. When we use flat shading for a graphic object, we usually set the color before we define the first vertex. In principle, though, we could set a separate color for each vertex. Try this, creating a graphics object and calling glColor3f(...) with a different color before each vertex. What conclusions can you draw about when the color value is set for an object? For example, is it set the last time glColor3f is called? The first time? Compare your results with others to see if this is consistent across OpenGL systems.

4. The way the colors in Figure 1.7 are interpolated suggests that the quad is actually drawn as two triangles. First, verify this for your own OpenGL system, because your system may implement quads differently from ours. Second, extend this by adding more vertices in different colors to create polygons by extending the quad, and see if you can identify the way the polygon is implemented. (Our systems seem to implement polygons as triangle fans.)

5. Experiment with non-convex polygons by defining such a polygon with color or lighting information at each pixel and seeing what your OpenGL system actually draws. Carefully describe what you see, and develop an explanation for it.

6. While polygons are defined to be planar, you can readily give OpenGL a set of non-planar vertices within a GL_QUADS or GL_POLYGON primitive. Experiment with what happens when you give a set of non-planar vertices to a quad or a polygon, and discuss why your results are plausible.

7. Experiment with z-fighting by drawing two polygons that meet at a very shallow angle, as shown in Figure 1.10. When you get an example of this problem, look at the depth of your projection's viewing volume, and adjust its front and back planes to make the depth as small as possible. Does this reduce the z-fighting problem? Does it eliminate the problem?

8. Create a model with vertices, vertex colors, and normals and store it using vertex arrays. Display it without shading, using the vertex colors, with the glDrawElements( ) technique instead of the usual glBegin( )-glEnd( ) approach. Then change the model to use a single color and the normals and use smooth shading to display it.

9. Experiment with rendering efficiency benchmarks. Create a reasonably large amount of geometry and render it using

   glBegin-glEnd in immediate mode
   glBegin-glEnd in a display list
   Vertex Arrays
   Vertex Buffer Objects

   What do these results tell you about your graphics card and its driver?

2 OpenGL Shader Evolution

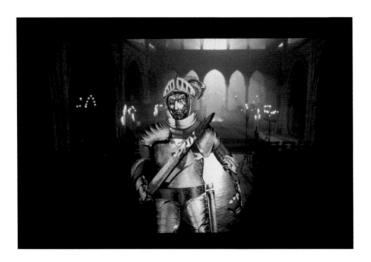

In its early days, computer graphics had no standard programming models. Vendors provided a low-level interface to their hardware, and each person or group then developed their own approach to taking geometry and appearance information and applying their particular algorithms to create a screen display. It was fun (in a geeky sort of way), but not very efficient or portable. While many of the images created in this period might seem very simple by today's standards, a lot of work went into them, and the basic ideas generated in those days still impact us today.

Early attempts to reduce the amount of development work needed for production focused on building graphics standards, but the standards generally provided only a least-common-denominator level of functions. However, as standards developed, they led to a growing understanding of the fundamental operations needed in the graphics process and provided a rising level

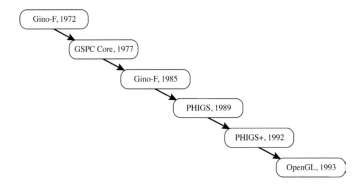

Figure 2.1. Some graphics standards that led to OpenGL.

of expectations for the quality of images they could produce. In turn, these led to the graphics engines developed by companies like Evans and Sutherland (E&S) and Silicon Graphics (SGI) and others that began to implement basic graphics processes in hardware. These again increased the expectations of performance and quality. A part of the "family tree" of public, non-proprietary graphics standards is shown in Figure 2.1.

Originally, graphics standards were meant to solve portability problems. That is, graphics standards enabled programmers to re-deploy existing applications on different hardware systems with a minimal amount of work. But as hardware acceleration became more common, graphics standards also became a blueprint for what operations needed to be accelerated.

For example, in order to take advantage of the SGI graphics engines, the engineers at SGI also developed a graphics API that mapped well to the engines' processes. This was Iris GL, and it made developing graphics applications so much more straightforward that an industry-wide version was created. The resulting OpenGL API can be said to have been one of the key factors that has made graphics so ubiquitous in the computing world. Of course, others have looked at OpenGL and have believed they could do better by matching the API more closely to their particular platforms or by extending the functionality of the API in different ways, so we continue to find ourselves in a world with many competing "standards."

OpenGL makes no assumptions of hardware support. The spec only says what should be done, not how it should happen, or how fast. It is possible to implement OpenGL entirely in software without affecting the applications in any way except speed. However, many—perhaps most—graphics applications need to create images at interactive speeds. This is particularly true for real-time applications such as games and simulation. So simple "graphics cards"—cards that contained a graphics memory and acted as a simple frame-buffer—were replaced by cards that included onboard graphics operations and eventually the full fixed-function graphics pipeline that we discussed in the previous chapter. These provided a great increase in graphics speed, but the graphics audience wanted more. It's a truism is that you can never be too thin or too rich—but in computer graphics you can never have too much speed or too much resolution or too many colors. As a community, we are very greedy—and proud of it!

While simple graphics cards were a great improvement over software rendering, they were restricted to what the fixed-function pipeline could do, and they did not support many effects and capabilities that a creative graphics programmer might want. The next step, where we are now, was to make the cards programmable so that extra functionality could be added as needed. With emerging systems such as OpenGL ES (for embedded systems such as PDAs and cell phones) having no fixed-function pipeline, and with core OpenGL 4.0 replacing the fixed-function approach with a shader-required approach, it seems clear that shaders are increasingly central to computer graphics applications and that anyone planning to do serious graphics work will need to become skilled in shader programming and development.

History of Shaders

Even though GPU-based shaders are a relatively recent phenomenon, the overall history of shaders goes back about 30 years. Looking back, it could be considered to have started in 1977, with the release of a low budget movie that was to grow into a cult phenomenon: *Star Wars Episode IV: A New Hope.*

Star Wars IV was revolutionary in using models and robotic-controlled cameras to create the illusion of actual moving space ships in a fierce battle. It did use computer graphics, but not much. What it did use was well below the capabilities of that time, but the astonishing box office success of the movie demonstrated that special effects sell tickets. But for future movies, it was realized that it would be difficult to greatly scale up the use of physical models. However, George Lucas was a man with a vision—and, more importantly, the movie had given him the funds to implement that vision.

Turning to computer graphics, Lucas hired Ed Catmull and others from the New York Institute of Technology around 1980 to become the Computer Division of Lucasfilm. Their efforts at Lucasfilm had three thrusts:

- Digital editing and compositing.
- Hardware for 2D image processing.
- Hardware for 3D graphics rendering.

In 1983, Lucasfilm spun off the 2D and 3D groups into their own company, called Pixar, and sold it to Steve Jobs in 1986. The 2D Image Processing group produced the *Pixar Image Computer* (PIC), a hardware device to perform image processing. The PIC used 4-way SIMD (single instruction multiple data) operations to perform image processing on all four RGBA components simultaneously. Thus, when we say in GLSL

```
vec4 rgba;
. . .
rgba *= 0.5;
```

we are using the modern-day evolution of the PIC SIMD paradigm. Despite its technical success, Pixar eventually discontinued work on the PIC to focus on 3D rendering.

The Pixar rendering group's intention was to create a hardware rendering device. But first, a software prototype of that device needed to be developed. This was known as the *REYES system*, a tribute to Point Reyes in northern California, and also an acronym for *Renders Everything You Ever Saw*.

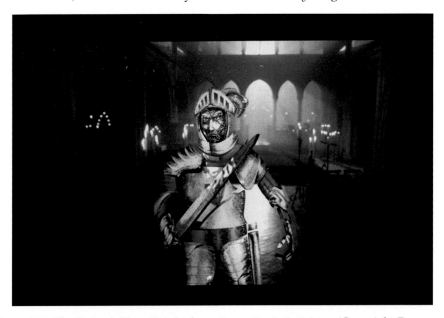

Figure 2.2. The Stained Glass Knight from *Young Sherlock Holmes*. (Copyright Paramount Pictures; used by permission. Image courtesy of Pixar Inc.)

In 1984, Rob Cook from Pixar published his landmark "Shade Trees" paper [10], in which he showed how the rendering process could be user-manipulated by writing "scripts" and inserting them in the proper places in the rendering pipeline. His paper's abstract says it all, and is still appropriate today:

> Shading is an important part of computer imagery, but shaders have been based on fixed models to which all surfaces must conform. As computer imagery becomes more sophisticated, surfaces have more complex shading characteristics and thus require a less rigid shading model. This paper presents a flexible tree-structured shading model that can represent a wide range of shading characteristics.

The *Shade Tree* concept allowed developers to create many different effects without having to constantly be adding new code permanently into the renderer. One of the first commercial uses of these shaders was in the movie *Young Sherlock Holmes* in 1985, which created the Stained Glass Knight shown in Figure 2.2. (If you've never seen this movie—egad!—you really need to go rent it! No computer graphics background is complete without having seen it.)

In the meantime, work on hardware rendering continued along with the REYES software prototype. Someone made the comment that someday every-one will carry a small rendering box around on their belt with them. It will be like a Sony Walkman, they said, but instead would be called a *RenderMan* [38] [43], and a name was born. Eventually, the hardware idea was dropped in favor of a general-purpose software solution, which became the package *Photorealistic RenderMan* (prman).

In the meantime, others took the idea of shaders and developed differ-ent software and hardware approaches to creating graphics scenes. In 1985, Perlin [34] published his landmark Image Synthesizer paper. His use of a pro-cedural noise function to make surfaces more interesting probably did more to promote the use of shaders than any other development. However, it is often overlooked that this work created surface shading functions with expressions and flow control, and thus also showed the graphics community how much could be done with procedural languages in the graphics pipeline.

In 1998, Olano and Lastra [31] developed a shading language for the *PixelFlow* graphics system. PixelFlow was a very innovative approach to fast graphics developed at the University of North Carolina. Some of its ideas on parallelism can be seen to have influenced today's graphics hardware. Their shading language achieved 30 frames/sec update rates—a first for a shading language. In 2001, Proudfoot et al. [39] at Stanford developed a higher-level shading language that could transparently spread its operations to a combina-tion of CPU and GPU, wherever it made most sense. It was important because it allowed a graphics programmer to ride the hardware acceleration capabilities curve without changing code. There were many others working in hardware shaders at that time, and we apologize to anyone whose work we omitted.

By the early 2000s, graphics hardware had become sophisticated and fast enough that people started thinking that it needed the same sort of flexible shading capability that Rob Cook had described nearly 20 years before. The first implementations of this were *Cg* [29] [16] and *HLSL* (High Level Shader Language) [33], which, while separate products, were developed in lockstep and thus look very similar. Cg was developed by NVIDIA Corporation, while HLSL was developed by Microsoft as part of its Direct3D graphics API. Close behind came *GLSL* (OpenGL Shading Language), created by the OpenGL Architecture Review Board (ARB).

These three hardware-oriented shader languages do things a little differently, but all have the same basic functionality: vertex, geometry, and fragment (or pixel) shaders, a C-like language, and access to key data values within the graphics pipeline. This book bases all its application examples on GLSL, but the same underlying concepts are common to all three languages, and the code can be readily translated between them. If you know one of the three, learning the other two isn't hard.

OpenGL Shader History

OpenGL Release	GLSL Release	When
1.0	---	1993
1.1	---	1997
1.2	---	1998
1.3	---	2001
1.4	---	2002
1.5	---	2003
2.0	1.10	2004
2.1	1.20	2006
3.0	1.30	July 2008
3.1, 3.2, 3.3	3.30	July 2009
4.0	4.00	March 2010
4.1	4.10	July 2010
4.2	4.20	August 2011

Table 2.1. Evolution of OpenGL and GLSL.

To understand the nature of OpenGL shaders, we need to look more deeply at OpenGL's evolution, and particularly to the evolution of shaders and shader technology in the last few years. Table 2.1 shows the timeline for OpenGL's versions.

OpenGL 2.0/GLSL 1.10

This version of OpenGL introduces shader-based graphics programming, including programmable vertex and fragment shaders and the GLSL language. Each of these is the subject of a later chapter in this book. These shaders restore an enormous amount of flexibility and creativity to OpenGL graphics programming, and in some sense all the later OpenGL developments are mainly evolutions of this approach. This version includes a few of these evolutionary steps, including

- Vertex buffer objects let you store vertex arrays in graphics memory to reduce the amount of communication needed between the CPU and card.
- Occlusion queries let you ask how many pixels a particular scene element would occupy if displayed.
- Texture-mapped point sprites let you create many small 2D objects for uses such as particle systems.
- Separate stencil operations for front and back faces give you better support for shadowing.

OpenGL 3.x/GLSL 3.30

OpenGL 3.0 and GLSL 3.00 is a major revision in the standard that reflected the growing processing power in graphics cards. It introduces geometry shaders, the next development in shader technology and the subject of Chapter 12. It also includes several new types of objects to store structured data on the graphics card.

- Frame buffer objects let you render into non-displayable buffers for such uses as render-to-texture.
- Texture buffer objects allow you to use much larger texture arrays.
- Uniform buffer objects let you define a collection of uniform variables so that you can quickly switch between different sets of uniform variables (typically different ways to present a set of primitives) in a single program object or share the same set of uniform variables between different program objects.

All OpenGL buffer objects share the capability to replace a range of data in the buffer instead of having to replace the data one item at a time.

The OpenGL 3.* and GLSL 3.30 standards also add several new capabilities not available in earlier versions:

- For textures, you can now define a texture array (sometimes called an *array texture*) that contains a sequence of 1D or 2D textures of the same size, so you can use different textures without having to do multiple texture bindings. You can use rectangular textures, which can be useful for video processing, though these do not have bias or level-of-detail capability. You can also query the size of a texture with the new `textureSize( )` function.

- When variables are interpolated in the fragment shader, you can choose different interpolation techniques with the interpolation qualifiers centroid, flat, invariant, or nonperspective. The differences are discussed in Chapter 8.
- There is now a layout qualifier that can be applied to either in or out variables for some shaders. This qualifier's effect varies considerably between shader types, but it includes specifying the position of a vertex shader input variable in an array, defining the input and output properties for a geometry shader, or the input coordinates of a pixel in a fragment shader.
- 16-bit floats and 16-bit floating point variables are added, which have less precision than 32-bit floats but are more compact and faster to compute.

This version also includes significant revisions of the GLSL standard, moving it away from fixed-function OpenGL by deprecating a number of capabilities that mirrored fixed-function operations. Because of the large number of applications that were built with earlier versions of OpenGL and GLSL, however, this version also supports compatibility mode operation that lets you use these earlier versions. This book uses GLSL 4.1, but we include several notes in the appropriate chapters that describe compatibility-mode alternatives. These notes are marked with flags like the one in the margin. Among the capabilities that have been deprecated are

- any use of the fixed-function vertex or fragment operations; you now need to use shaders for everything,
- the use of glBegin / glEnd to define primitives; you now need to use vertex arrays and vertex buffers for your geometry,
- use of quad or polygon primitives; you now only use triangles,
- use of display lists; you now use vertex arrays and vertex buffers,
- use of most of the built-in attribute and uniform variables in GLSL; you now need to define all these in your application and pass them all into your shaders.

While these features are deprecated, and are thus not guaranteed to be available in all future versions, you really need not be afraid to use them. They are said to be going away "at some future time," but there is some feeling that this might end up meaning, "when the sun burns itself out."

OpenGL 4.0/GLSL 4.00

OpenGL 4.0 introduces the final kind of shaders discussed in this book: tessellation shaders. These let you generate new geometry to provide greater detail in your geometry, and are covered in Chapter 13. One object of this version is to implement shader model 5 by applying more of an object model to the GLSL shader language. This includes such features as shader subroutines, giving you runtime selection of the particular function to be called so you can keep multiple ways of doing things in a single shader.

GLSL 4.00 includes significant developments for geometry shaders, which are discussed in more detail in Chapter 12. You can now have multiple iterations of a single geometry shader to create multiple instances of the shader, letting you recursively subdivide geometry primitives. You can also create multiple vertex streams from a geometry shader, with the first stream being the normal output to primitive assembly and the rasterizer, and with additional streams going to transform feedback objects.

Texture interpolation is enhanced in GLSL 4.00. It includes the texture gather operation, returning the four texel values that would be returned by standard texel interpolation so that you can apply your own interpolation to them.

The GLSL compiler is designed to optimize expressions for the sake of efficiency, but the optimization makes it impossible to know exactly how an expression is implemented. GLSL 4.00 introduces the `invariant` qualifier for a variable that requires the compiler to compute the same variable expression the same way in two different shaders. This lets you maintain computational consistency in multipass algorithms.

With GLSL 4.00, the shader language becomes even more C-like. You finally get the functionality of the `#include` statement, you get full 64-bit IEEE floating point variables with the keyword `double`, function overloading, and you get a wider set of implicit type conversions, including float → double, int → double, uint → double, and int → int. You also get a new operator, the fused multiply-add, written as `fma(a,b,c)`; this performs the operation `(a*b)+c` with a single operation and no loss of precision.

OpenGL 4.x/GLSL 4.x0

OpenGL 4.x and GLSL 4.x0 are probably best characterized by the way they increase the generality of shader operations. They support *shader binaries*, precompiled shaders that can be written to a file and loaded separately to save recompilation, as well as separable shader pipeline stages, linking shaders to a shader program at runtime so you can select different shader stages then. This standard level also supports viewport arrays, supporting drawing into multiple viewports by allowing the geometry shader to select which viewport to render into.

One of the newest features in OpenGL 4.x and GLSL 4.x0 is the ability to generate "side effects." GLSL programs can now read and write to image textures and can perform atomic arithmetic operations in uniform buffers. (This should keep algorithm developers busy for some time!)

The other key feature of this standard is its relation to OpenGL ES 2.0. The growing importance of OpenGL ES has made it important to support application development for both desktop and embedded systems, and this standard release makes desktop OpenGL a proper superset of OpenGL ES 2.0. That is, if you develop for OpenGL ES 2.0, your application will run correctly with OpenGL 4.x and GLSL 4.x0.

Finally, this standard extends the 64-bit floating point capability to vertex shader input variables (that is, to attribute and uniform variables), allowing you to do your application computation in double precision and maintain that precision when your data is sent to the shaders.

What's Behind These Developments?

This continuing evolution of the OpenGL and GLSL standards is driven by several factors. One is the continuing emphasis on speed by applications such as games, and several of the new OpenGL/GLSL features reduce the need for communication between the CPU and the graphics card or move computations from the CPU to the card. Another is the increasingly general architecture of graphics cards that corresponds to the increasing use of these cards for general-purpose computing with tools such as CUDA or OpenCL. These changes will continue to drive OpenGL and GLSL for the foreseeable future.

OpenGL ES

OpenGL ES 2.0 is designed to support high-quality graphics on embedded systems such as cell phones. It is based on OpenGL 2.0, but does not support any fixed-function operations—all the vertex and fragment processing must be done with shaders. It also does not support tessellation and geometry shaders, just vertex and fragment shaders.

The key issue with embedded systems is the need to operate with limited memory sizes and limited computing capabilities. Supporting the full set of fixed-function operations requires a significant memory overhead, but using shaders only requires memory for the data and operations you actually use. Only vertex and fragment shaders are supported, however, because geometry and tessellation shaders may expand the input geometry and require additional memory.

The OpenGL ES shading language is more restrictive than the GLSL 1.10 that is associated with OpenGL 2.0, however. It does not include the set of built-in attribute and uniform variables of GLSL 1.10, but requires you to create your own variables as needed. This is similar to GLSL 3.30, and in fact GLSL 4.10 is a proper superset of the OpenGL ES shader language 1.10—if you write a shader program in OpenGL ES, it will run with OpenGL 4.1.

How Can You Respond to These Changes?

There are two ways you can respond to the continuing evolution of the OpenGL shader standards.

1. Follow the standards and make continuing changes to your code to use the latest versions. Do everything the core profile requires. At the top of your shader sources, put the line

   ```
   #version 4.00 core
   ```

   The advantages of using the latest shader standards are performance and generality, and by using the right subset of the core profile you can be compatible with OpenGL ES 2.0. The disadvantage is that the latest graphics hardware is needed to use these standards and you must commit to continuing code maintenance to keep current as the standards evolve.

2. Adopt as much of the evolving standards as you want, to take advantage of ways the changes provide more performance without making your life too difficult, and use compatibility mode for the capabilities you want to keep from earlier standards. At the top of your shader sources, put the line

   ```
   #version 4.00 compatibility
   ```

   This will let you use whatever you like from any earlier version of the standard.

   For example, you may want to target an audience that could not be expected to have the latest graphics hardware. Or perhaps you may want to simplify your shaders by using built-in attribute or uniform variable names from OpenGL 2.1, but may want to use tessellation shaders, or perhaps vertex buffer objects because they are much more efficient than begin-end primitive definition and they can be disguised to look like begin-end.

   Your code will run at least as fast on the newer cards as it did on older ones, it may be easier to get people productive with the earlier versions, and you will not have to rework your existing code.

Our Approach in this Book

In this book we take something of a hybrid approach to the question of OpenGL standard levels. We generally use GLSL at the 1.50 level, but do use many of the more advanced constructions of OpenGL 3.* and 4.*. We do cover tessellation shaders and geometry shaders, and we use the most current syntax for passing data between shaders. For the most part, we don't use the deprecated built-in variable names in our sample code. However, to make life easier, later on we will show you a file we've created for our own use, *gstap.h*, which #defines the un-deprecated names to the deprecated names. In this way, you can get the best of both worlds—your code looks cleaner and more modern, but underneath you are still using the easy-to-get-at built-ins.

Variable Name Convention

As we will discuss in the next chapter, variables take on a number of different roles for shaders. Two kinds of variables are provided by your application (or by the OpenGL system, if you are using older OpenGL standards): *attribute* and *uniform* variables. Attribute variables are used to describe individual vertices, while uniform variables are used to define whole graphics primitives or larger-scale graphics concepts. Other variables are used to pass variables between shaders: *out* and *in* variables. Each shader passes data to other shaders or other OpenGL stages as out variables, and each shader takes data from other shaders or the application program as in variables.

In this text we will adopt a convention for variable names that are passed between the application and the various shaders that we will present. This convention is entirely arbitrary, but it helps us keep track of the source of variables that come into each of the shaders. We will use the convention in the

Prefix	Stage that wrote it	Example
a	Attribute (from application)	aColor
u	Uniform (from application)	uModelViewMatrix
v	Vertex Shader	vST
tc	Tessellation Control Shader	tcRadius
te	Tessellation Evaluation Shader	teNormal
g	Geometry Shader	gNormal
f	Fragment Shader	fFragColor

Table 2.2. Our initial letter naming convention.

shader sources throughout the book, and we hope you will not found it confusing. This convention is shown in Table 2.2.

Thus at the beginning of a vertex shader (for example) we might find data declarations such as

```
in vec4 aVertex;
in vec4 aTexCoord0;

uniform mat4 uModelViewProjectionMatrix;

out vec4 vST;
```

to pass the vertex coordinates (in model space), texture coordinates, and modelviewprojection matrix into the shader and the texture coordinates from the vertex shader to be used by the fragment shader. This kind of declaration set will become quite familiar as you read the examples throughout the book.

Exercises

1. Rent one of the movies mentioned in this chapter and look at the effects we discussed. You will only see them in TV resolution, but step through the stained glass knight or the Genesis effect (*Star Trek II: The Wrath of Khan*) sections frame by frame and note how each works. For the stained glass knight, notice the effect of a colored dirty surface that transmits light from behind it.

2. Take one of the simple vertex shader source files that we use to introduce the shader concepts. You will find some of the data coming from vertex attributes, some hard-coded, and some coming from uniform variables defined through *glman*. For each of these data, identify an original OpenGL function that would define the data, if possible (some of the uniform variables do not fit this), and identify the OpenGL 2.1 built-in variable that would contain the data.

3

Fundamental Shader Concepts

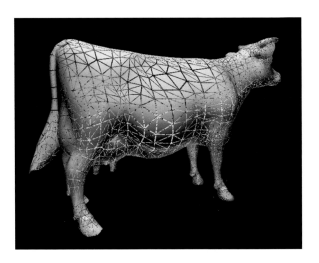

Shaders in the Graphics Pipeline

Let's have another look at the graphics pipeline, but let's break it out in a little different way than we did in the previous chapter. Let's add into the pipeline the five shaders we are considering in this book: vertex shaders, tessellation control shaders, tessellation evaluation shaders, geometry shaders, and fragment shaders. This expanded view of the pipeline is shown in Figure 3.1, where the positions of the shaders in the pipeline suggest the functions that each provides. While it is not obvious from the diagram, each shader block is in an alternate branch of the pipeline; they are optional capabilities that may or may not be used for any application. You may use any combination of vertex, tessellation, geometry, or fragment shaders in your program; you do not have to use any particular combinations, although, in general, if you use *any* shad-

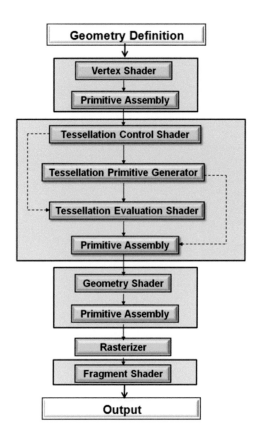

Figure 3.1. The expanded graphics pipeline, with programmable stages shown in green and fixed-function stages shown in orange.

ers, you usually are required to include a vertex shader, too.

When you're developing shaders, however, you don't necessarily need to think of the entire graphics pipeline like this. For each individual shader, it is helpful to understand what data comes into this shader, what this shader can do with it, and what new data gets transmitted to the next stage. For this, it's interesting to consider how the graphics pipeline looks to shaders; this is shown in Figure 3.2, with an emphasis on how data moves among the shader stages. Of course, if you choose not to include any shader stage, the in/out variables from the previous stage simply skip the omitted stage and go on to the subsequent stage.

Notice in Figure 3.2 that all attribute variables are input to the vertex shader, and all uniform variables are input to whatever shader needs them. Uniform variables are written by the application; none of them can be written by any shader. Any computation that needs to pass data on to the next shader must do so through an out variable, and that variable must be read (as an in variable) and passed along (as an out variable) by intermediate variables until it is used.

Let's consider how the separate functionalities of the graphics pipeline might be enhanced by using shaders. To begin, let's look at the modeling functions that begin the geometry pipeline. In the standard pipeline, you define the vertices of your model either by using specific statements, such as glVertex3f(2.0, -1.0, 3.0), or by using a computation to create the vertex coordinates. You can add other geometric information such as normals and texture coordinates as you need them and as they are available. You can also add appearance information. This may be done while the geometry is defined, as you might do with colors through the glColor*(...) function. Another approach to appearance defines and enables environments such as lighting, with its associated materials definition, or textures, with their associated texture parameters, texture environment, and texture image.

The geometry operations in the fixed-function pipeline can be replaced and possibly expanded by any (or all) of the GLSL vertex shaders, tessellation shaders, or geometry shaders. A vertex shader only operates on one vertex at a time and can take the initial vertex definition and alter it by changing the values of the position, normal, or texture coordinates. As we will see, the vertex shader must set the transformed position of each vertex. It may also set the color for the vertex, especially if per-vertex lighting is used.

The tessellation shaders take a set of points called a *patch*, which can represent anything, and interpolate the points to create a new geometry. You get to define what meaning these points have. The tessellation shaders will then assist you in creating new geometry from them.

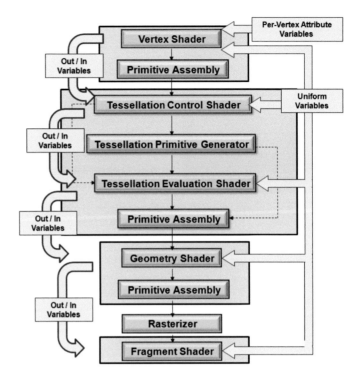

Figure 3.2. The shader's-eye view of the pipeline.

A geometry shader can take a graphics primitive from a vertex shader and create one or more new primitives. Geometry shaders can do the same computation as a vertex shader to compute the full geometry and color of each new vertex. They can also prepare variables for later use by a fragment shader.

The final shader capability is fragment processing, done by the fragment shader. This takes the information developed by vertex processing (vertex shader, tessellation shader, or geometry shader) and expands the traditional fragment operations by letting you operate on each fragment individually to generate the color of its pixel. This is a highly parallel operation that can apply traditional or procedural textures; special coloring, such as pseudocolor transfer functions; and advanced kinds of shading, such as Phong or anisotropic shading. The operation can also determine whether its pixel is to be retained or discarded for the final image. The fragment shader has the strongest impact on the visual effect of your images.

In the next few sections, we will look at the functionality of each shader by looking at simple examples. For reference, a sphere with only standard

Figure 3.3. A sphere with simple color, diffuse lighting, and smooth shading.

fixed-function processing is shown in Figure 3.3. In each section, we will outline the shaders' operations and give a short example of a vertex and a fragment shader that produce the figure; we will then give a brief description of the GLSL shader language, so you can see the language features that we use in the examples. A more complete discussion of GLSL will come in Chapter 5.

In the next chapter, we'll describe the *glman* tool that lets you create and experiment with shaders without having to write a complete application; here, it is useful if you see how you could define this image with *glman*. Here is the GLIB file that sets up the image and specifies the shaders to be used:

```
Vertex Sphere.vert
Fragment Sphere.frag
Program Sphere

Color  1 0.5 0
Sphere 2.0 100 100
```

We will provide the vertex and fragment shader files for this example later in this chapter.

Vertex Shaders

A GLSL vertex shader takes the vertex and environment information that is stored by the OpenGL system and makes it available to you through a set of uniform and attribute variables, so that you can do your own vertex computations. Later in this chapter, we will outline some of the highlights of the GLSL shader language, including these commonly used uniform and attribute variables. Vertex shaders act on geometry that is usually given in model space coordinates and produce geometry that is output in 3D clip space; all projection and clipping is done later in the graphics pipeline. Vertex shaders must do much more than that, however. A GLSL vertex shader replaces these operations in the fixed-function geometry pipeline:

- Vertex transformations.
- Normal transformations.
- Normal normalization (i.e., turn it into a unit vector).
- Handling of per-vertex lighting.
- Handling of texture coordinates.

These are very important operations. Fortunately, the necessary information is readily available, and the operations you need to perform are expressed well in the GLSL language, which handles vector and matrix operations with ease.

However, a GLSL vertex shader does not replace *all* of the operations in the geometry pipeline. In particular, it does not replace the operations that take the clip space to the final pixel space. The specific functions that are still done by the fixed-function pipeline are

- View volume clipping.
- Homogeneous division.
- Viewport mapping.
- Backface culling.
- Polygon mode.
- Polygon offset.

A key function of a vertex shader is to take all attribute variables and either use them or copy them into out variables for later shaders to use.

Vertex shaders have several kinds of output. The most important are the transformed vertices and the color associated with each vertex. Of course, the vertex shader can compute or re-compute normals and texture coordinates as well as vertex coordinates. If you use a fragment shader, the vertex processing can develop variables that let the fragment shader interpolate these properties as each fragment is developed. By setting up color, normals, or textures with variables from vertex processing, the fragment shader can carry out sophisticated operations on each fragment.

The vertex shader for the smooth shading on the simple sphere of Figure 3.3 is shown below. This shader code, and the other shader code examples in this chapter, will be better understood when we have discussed GLSL in more depth later in the book. For now, though, note that this shader calculates per-vertex light intensity by the standard diffuse lighting com-

The shader code in this chapter uses the name prefix conventions we introduced in Chapter 2. Variable names start with a character that indicates who created it:

a	attribute variable
f	variable from a fragment shader
g	variable from a geometry shader
tc	variable from a tessellation control shader
te	variable from a tessellation evaluation shader
v	variable from a vertex shader
u	uniform variable

As in C/C++, constants are generally written in all caps.

putation using the normal, vertex eye coordinates, and light position, and that it sets the required output gl_Position from the uModelViewProjection matrix and the vertex coordinates.

```
uniform mat4 uModelViewMatrix;
uniform mat4 uModelViewProjectionMatrix;
uniform mat3 uNormalMatrix;

in vec4 aVertex;
in vec4 aNormal;
in vec4 aColor;

out vec4  vColor;
out vec3  vMCposition;
out float vLightIntensity;

const vec3 LIGHTPOS = vec3( 3., 5., 10. );

void main( )
{
   vec3 transNorm   = normalize( uNormalMatrix * aNormal );
   vec3 ECposition  = vec3( uModelViewMatrix * aVertex );
   vLightIntensity  = dot(normalize(LIGHTPOS - ECposition),
                           transNorm);
   vLightIntensity  = abs( vLightIntensity );

   vColor           = aColor;
   vMCposition      = aVertex.xyz;
   gl_Position      = uModelViewProjectionMatrix * aVertex;
}
```

The example for Figure 3.3 did not do one important thing that a vertex shader can do, however: modify the application-supplied vertex coordinates. As an example of geometry modification, let's start with a simple plane (represented by a 200 × 200 mesh of quads) considered as the domain of a function, and let the vertex shader apply that function. The GLIB file is essentially the same as that for the Figure 3.3 example, except that the specified geometry is a 200 × 200 set of quads in the XY-plane, instead of a sphere, specified like this:

```
QuadXY  -2.  1. 200 200
```

The vertex shader will apply the function

$$z(x,y) = 0.3 * \sin\left(x^2 + y^2\right)$$

Figure 3.4. A rippled surface generated by a vertex shader; still with simple color, ambient plus diffuse lighting, and smooth shading.

to the x and y coordinates of each vertex to calculate the z-coordinate, and will calculate the normals to each vertex by using an analytic computation, since the derivative is known. This uses the fact that the tangent vectors are given by taking the derivatives of z with respect to x and y:

$$\frac{\partial z}{\partial x} = 2.*0.3*x*\cos\left(x^2 + y^2\right),$$

$$\frac{\partial z}{\partial y} = 2.*0.3*y*\cos\left(x^2 + y^2\right).$$

After the vertices and normals are set up, the usual computations for eye coordinates (ECposition) and light intensity are done. The resulting function surface is shown in Figure 3.4.

The vertex shader for the rippled surface in Figure 3.4 is given below. The operations for the diffuse light intensity are those for standard ambient and diffuse lighting, based on the eye-space coordinates of each vertex (the ECpos variable), the normal (myNorml) computed from the analytic partial derivatives, and a fixed light position (LIGHTPOS) that would ordinarily be passed into the shader from the application as a uniform variable. The actual display coordinates gl_Position are set by multiplying by uModelViewProjectionMatrix to apply the model, view, and projection transformations. The output of this vertex shader includes two variables: the light intensity and color values defined in the vertex shader. None of this is difficult, but it requires you to work with your objects at a lower level than the usual OpenGL.

```glsl
in vec4 aVertex;
in vec4 aColor;

uniform mat4 uModelViewMatrix;
uniform mat4 uModelViewProjectionMatrix;

out float vLightIntensity;
out vec3  vMyColor;

const vec3 LIGHTPOS = vec3( 0., 10., 0. );

void main( )
{
    vec4 thisPos = aVertex;
    vMyColor     = aColor.rgb;

    // create a new height for this vertex:
    float thisX = thisPos.x;
    float thisY = thisPos.y;
    // the surface is z = 0.3 * sin (x^2 + y^2)
    thisPos.z = 0.3 * sin( thisX*thisX + thisY*thisY );

    // now compute the normal and the light intensity
    vec3 xtangent = vec3( 1., 0., 0. );
    xtangent.z = 2. * 0.3 * thisX * cos( thisX*thisX +
                                    thisY*thisY );
    vec3 ytangent = vec3( 0., 1., 0. );
    ytangent.z = 2. * 0.3 * thisY * cos( thisX*thisX +
                                    thisY*thisY );
    vec3 thisNormal = normalize( cross( xtangent, ytangent ) );

    vec3 ECpos = vec3( uModelViewMatrix * thisPos );
    vLightIntensity  = dot( normalize(LIGHTPOS - ECpos),
                            thisNormal );
    vLightIntensity = 0.3 + abs( vLightIntensity );// 0.3 ambient
    vLightIntensity = clamp( vLightIntensity, 0., 1. );

    gl_Position      = uModelViewProjectionMatrix * thisPos;
}
```

A Comment on Shader Code Efficiency

GLSL gives you some clever ways to make your code execute super efficiently on graphics hardware. As with many such things in computing, however, it often makes the code harder to read. For example, rather than creating two separate variables above, thisX and thisY, and then squaring each to compute thisPos.z as shown previously, it would be more efficient to say

```
vec2 thisXY = thisPos.xy;
thisPos.z   = 0.3 * sin( dot( thisXY, thisXY ) );
```

Similarly, the computation for the tangent vectors could be expressed more efficiently as

```
xtangent.z = 2. * 0.3 * thisX * cos( dot( thisXY, thisXY ) );
ytangent.z = 2. * 0.3 * thisY * cos( dot( thisXY, thisXY ) );
```

But, at least for some, this would make the code less readable. For this book, we have often taken our own code and re-written it to be more readable, even though that may make it less efficient. We're sure you will find lots of examples of this. Don't email us about it—we already know.

Fragment Shaders

Sometimes called *pixel shaders* (e.g., in Cg), fragment shaders operate on a fragment to determine the color of its pixel. We know that rasterization operations interpolate quantities such as colors, depths, and texture coordinates. Fragment shaders use these interpolated values, as well as many other kinds of information, to determine the color of each fragment's pixel.

The rasterizer interpolates any variables that have been defined in the geometry processing stages and passed to the fragment shader. These interpolated values may be used in any kind of fragment computation you want. These computations are performed on several fragments in parallel, with the width of the parallelization depending on the particular graphics card you use. This parallelization lets a fragment shader operate with the same kind of acceleration as graphics cards do for the fixed-function pipeline.

As we saw for vertex shaders, many operations that were automatically handled by the fixed-function pipeline are now the responsibility of the shader programmer. A GLSL fragment shader replaces or adds the following operations:

- Color computation.
- Texturing.
- Per-pixel lighting.
- Fog.
- Discarding pixels in fragments.

Figure 3.5. A sphere with a positional screen pixel-discard fragment shader.

However, a fragment shader does not replace all the operations in the rasterization process. In particular, a GLSL fragment shader does not replace several raster operations, including

- Blending.
- Stencil test.
- Depth test.
- Scissor test.
- Stippling operations.
- Raster operations performed as a pixel is being written to the framebuffer.

Figure 3.5 shows the sphere with some parts made invisible by discarding pixels in the fragment shader instead of drawing them. Its fragment shader, which is listed after the figure, takes the three input variables for light intensity, color, and model coordinates, as well as three uniform variables that were set externally to the program (in this case, in the GLIB file needed by *glman*). It also receives texture coordinates that were passed from the application. It uses the scaled and truncated texture coordinates in the model to create a screen effect, and pixels that are not within a given distance of the screen lines are discarded. If a pixel is kept, any alpha value in the color is ignored and the pixel is lit with standard diffuse lighting.

The vertex shader for this figure is straightforward. It simply calculates the normal and eye-coordinate position, from which it gets the light intensity, and then passes the attribute variable aTexCoord0 along to the fragment shader.

```
uniform mat4 uModelViewMatrix;
uniform mat4 uModelViewProjectionMatrix;
uniform mat3 uNormalMatrix;

in vec4    aVertex;
in vec4    aTexCoord0;
in vec4    aColor;
in vec3    aNormal;

out vec4   vColor;
out float  vLightIntensity;
out vec2   vST;

const vec3 LIGHTPOS = vec3( 0., 0., 10. );
```

```
void main( )
{
   vec3 transNorm  = normalize( vec3( uNormalMatrix * aNormal )
                                 );
   vec3 ECposition = vec3( uModelViewMatrix * aVertex );
   vLightIntensity = dot( normalize(LIGHTPOS-ECposition),
                          transNorm );
   vLightIntensity = clamp( .3 + abs( vLightIntensity ), 0., 1.
                                 );

   vST           = aTexCoord0.st;
   vColor        = aColor;
   gl_Position = uModelViewProjectionMatrix * aVertex;
}
```

Below is the fragment shader for Figure 3.5. It takes the *s* and *t* coordinates provided by the vertex shader and uses them to decide whether to discard a pixel.

```
uniform float uDensity;
uniform float uFrequency;

in vec4  vColor;
in float vLightIntensity;
in vec2  vST;

out vec4 fFragColor;

void main( )
{
   float sf = vST.s * uFrequency;
   float tf = vST.t * uFrequency;

   if( fract( sf ) >= uDensity && fract( tf ) >= uDensity )
      discard;

   fFragColor = vec4( vLightIntensity*vColor.rgb, 1. );
}
```

Again, a more efficient implementation that takes advantage of the parallelism in graphics hardware would be

```
vec2 stf = vST * uFrequency;

if( all( fract(stf) >= vec2(uDensity, uDensity) ) )
   discard;
```

Tessellation Shaders

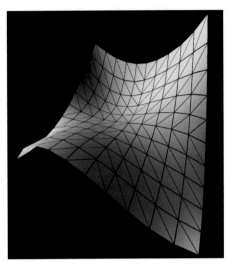

Figure 3.6. A Bézier surface interpolated from a 4 × 4 patch by tessellation shaders.

Tessellation shaders follow the vertex shader in the shader pipeline. They take vertex data and can interpolate the original vertices to create additional vertices in your geometry. (Note that this interpolation is quite different from the interpolations in fragment shaders.) Among other things, tessellation shaders let you perform adaptive subdivision of your geometry to increase the quality of your images, manage level-of-detail (LOD) image quality, or apply displacement maps without defining detailed geometry.

There are actually two kinds of tessellation shaders, as you saw in Figures 3.1 and 3.2: tessellation control shaders let you set up the parameters for the interpolations to be carried out, and tessellation evaluation shaders let you define the computation that will be used in creating the actual output geometry.

Figure 3.6 illustrates the subdivision capability of tessellation shaders. It shows a surface built from a single 4 × 4 vertex patch, with each triangle in the surface shrunken slightly so you can see how the surface is created.[1]

Two key concepts in tessellation shaders are the *patch*, or basic geometry the shader is to work on, and the *tessellation level*, or the number of subdivisions into which a patch is divided. The vertices in the patch for this figure are set in the glib file for the example using *glman*, and are available on the book's website. The tessellation control shader for the figure is shown below. It specifies the number of vertices in a patch and passes the input geometry in gl_in to the geometry gl_out for the tessellation evaluation shader to use. It also takes tessellation levels as uniform variables and sets up the required variables gl_TessLevelOuter and gl_TessLevelInner.

```
#version 400
#extension GL_ARB_tessellation_shader : enable

uniform float uOuter02, uOuter13, uInner0, uInner1;

layout( vertices = 16 )  out;
```

---

1. This example is explained in more detail in Chapter 13.

```
void main( )
{
  gl_out[ gl_InvocationID ].gl_Position =
                        gl_in[ gl_InvocationID ].gl_Position;

  gl_TessLevelOuter[0] = gl_TessLevelOuter[2] = uOuter02;
  gl_TessLevelOuter[1] = gl_TesslevelOuter[3] = uOuter13;
  gl_TessLevelInner[0] = uInner0;
  gl_TessLevelInner[1] = uInner1;
}
```

In this example, the amount of tessellation is set by uniform variables for simplicity. But, in fact, those levels could also have been set by examining the geometry's coordinate size, screen extent, zoom factors, curvature, etc. That's the advantage of placing this capability in the pipeline as a programmable shader.

The tessellation evaluation shader defines the way interpolation computations are to be done, and the tessellation evaluation shader for the figure is shown below. Part of a long set of assignments is omitted, but you should think of pij as the [i,j] entry in the 2D control points array that is passed in from the tessellation control shader. The real function of this particular shader is to set up the Bézier basis functions and the computations for position and normal for any point in an interpolated patch. This should be familiar to those who have written their own Bézier patch code. The vertices of the patch are computed with fixed-function computations based on the tessellation levels from the tessellation control shader, and the output of this shader is a set of triangle vertices that are assembled for the next piece of the pipeline.

```
#version 400
#extension GL_ARB_tessellation_shader : enable

layout( quads, equal_spacing, ccw)  in;

out vec3 teNormal;

void main( )
{
  vec3 p00 = gl_in[  0 ].gl_Position;
  ...
  vec3 p33 = gl_in[ 15 ].gl_Position;

  float u = gl_TessCoord.x;
  float v = gl_TessCoord.y;
```

```
// the Bezier basis functions and their derivatives:

float bu0 = (1.-u) * (1.-u) * (1.-u);
float bu1 = 3. * u * (1.-u) * (1.-u);
float bu2 = 3. * u * u * (1.-u);
float bu3 = u * u * u;

float dbu0 = -3. * (1.-u) * (1.-u);
float dbu1 =  3. * (1.-u) * (1.-3.*u);
float dbu2 =  3. * u *       (2.-3.*u);
float dbu3 =  3. * u *       u;

float bv0 = (1.-v) * (1.-v) * (1.-v);
float bv1 = 3. * v * (1.-v) * (1.-v);
float bv2 = 3. * v * v * (1.-v);
float bv3 = v * v * v;

float dbv0 = -3. * (1.-v) * (1.-v);
float dbv1 =  3. * (1.-v) * (1.-3.*v);
float dbv2 =  3. * v *       (2.-3.*v);
float dbv3 =  3. * v *       v;

// finally we get to compute something

gl_Position = bu0 * ( bv0*p00 + bv1*p01 + bv2*p02 + bv3*p03 )
            + bu1 * ( bv0*p10 + bv1*p11 + bv2*p12 + bv3*p13 )
            + bu2 * ( bv0*p20 + bv1*p21 + bv2*p22 + bv3*p23 )
            + bu3 * ( bv0*p30 + bv1*p31 + bv2*p32 + bv3*p33 );

vec4 dpdu = dbu0 * ( bv0*p00 + bv1*p01 + bv2*p02 + bv3*p03 )
          + dbu1 * ( bv0*p10 + bv1*p11 + bv2*p12 + bv3*p13 )
          + dbu2 * ( bv0*p20 + bv1*p21 + bv2*p22 + bv3*p23 )
          + dbu3 * ( bv0*p30 + bv1*p31 + bv2*p32 + bv3*p33 );

vec4 dpdv = bu0 * ( dbv0*p00 + dbv1*p01 + dbv2*p02 +
                    dbv3*p03 )
          + bu1 * ( dbv0*p10 + dbv1*p11 + dbv2*p12 +
                    dbv3*p13 )
          + bu2 * ( dbv0*p20 + dbv1*p21 + dbv2*p22 +
                    dbv3*p23 )
          + bu3 * ( dbv0*p30 + dbv1*p31 + dbv2*p32 +
                    dbv3*p33 );

teNormal = normalize( cross( dpdu.xyz, dpdv.xyz ) );
}
```

Geometry Shaders

The geometry shader is another kind of shader available with OpenGL and the GLSL shader language. This shader's operations change or expand the original geometry sent to the shader by developing new vertices and vertex groups. As an example, each triangle in a model could be replaced by a triangle shrunk about its centroid, as shown in Figure 3.7.

The source code for this geometry shader is more complicated, and it involves more new concepts than the previous vertex and fragment shaders do, but it is still worth seeing as a way to understand where we are headed. The basic idea is that all the vertices in each triangle primitive are being passed together (vec4 gl_PositionIn[i]). From these, a centroid is computed, and all three vertices are shrunk about it and emitted to become a new triangle. A more complete discussion is found in Chapter 12.

```
layout( triangles )  in;
layout( triangle_strip, max_vertices=32 )  out;

uniform float     uShrink;
uniform mat4      uModelViewProjectionMatrix;

in vec3           vNormal[3];

out float         gLightIntensity;

const vec3        LIGHTPOS = vec3( 0., 10., 0. );
```

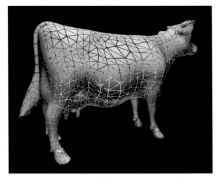

Figure 3.7. Triangles in different models shrunk with a geometry shader (this is useful for examining how fine the triangularization of a particular model is).

```glsl
vec3 V[3];
vec3 CG;

void
ProduceVertex( int vi )
{
   gLightIntensity = dot( normalize(LIGHTPOS - V[vi]), \
                          vNormal[vi] );
   gLightIntensity = abs( gLightIntensity );

   gl_Position = uModelViewProjectionMatrix *
             vec4( CG + uShrink * ( V[vi] - CG ), 1. );
   EmitVertex( );
}

void
main( )
{
   V[0]   =   gl_PositionIn[0].xyz;
   V[1]   =   gl_PositionIn[1].xyz;
   V[2]   =   gl_PositionIn[2].xyz;
   CG     =   (  V[0] + V[1] + V[2]  ) / 3.;
   ProduceVertex( 0 );
   ProduceVertex( 1 );
   ProduceVertex( 2 );
}
```

The GLSL Shading Language

The GLSL shader language is a C-like language with some extensions and some limitations. From a pure language point of view, it has some characteristics that recall features of early programming languages. For example, there are special variables that give you access to the data set by an OpenGL application into on-card registers, several special-purpose operations on vectors and matrices that are designed specifically for graphics, special variable types to reflect the different kinds of operations that will be done with variables, and shared name spaces that provide communication between applications, vertex shaders, and fragment shaders. We will describe the language in full detail in Chapter 5.

One way to think about GLSL, or any computer language, is to consider some of the basic attributes of the language. For GLSL, some of these are given in the following table.

Goals	Primary: speed; secondary: image quality
Shader Types	Vertex, Tessellation Control, Tessellation Evaluation, Geometry, Fragment
Shader Variables	Attribute, Uniform, Constant, Out, In
Coordinate Systems	Model, World, Eye, Clip
Noise	Either as a texture or using the built-in function
Compile Shaders	Done by the driver

GLSL shader code looks much like C, with the usual operators and logic. Preprocessor commands such as `#define`, `#ifdef`, and the like are available. GLSL has some extensions to support graphics operations. These include a number of new types, including some built-in vector and matrix types that are probably new to you, but that make life in graphics much easier.

- Integer scalar and vector types: `int`, `ivec2`, `ivec3`, `ivec4`.
- Real-valued scalar and vector types: `float`, `vec2`, `vec3`, `vec4`.
- Matrix types for square real-valued matrices: `mat2`, `mat3`, `mat4`.
- Matrix types for non-square real-valued matrices: `mat3x2`, etc.
- Boolean scalar and vector types: `bool`, `bvec2`, `bvec3`, `bvec4`.
- A sampler type to access textures.

The new vector and matrix types in GLSL require some new kinds of access and operations. Many familiar operators are overloaded to handle vectors and matrices . The familiar multiplication operator * has some new meanings. For the statement m*n, we have four new meanings:

- If m is a scalar and n is a vector or matrix, then m*n is a vector or matrix of the same size as n whose entries are the original vector or matrix entries, each multiplied by m.
- If m and n are both vectors of the same size, then m*n is the scalar product (component-by-component product) of the vectors, *not* their dot product.
- If m is a matrix and n is a vector of compatible size, then m*n is a vector of the appropriate size that is the usual matrix*vector product.
- If m and n are both matrices of compatible sizes, then m*n is a matrix of the appropriate size that is the usual matrix*matrix product.

A number of other operations have been added, and many operations have been extended to operate on entire vectors or matrices.

Access to components of vectors involves another set of new operations. Vector components may be accessed with the familiar [index], or they may use symbolic names, called *name sets*, that are familiar for the meanings of different vectors: `.rgba` (for vectors as color), `.xyzw` (for vectors as geometry), and `.stpq` (for vectors as texture coordinates). You can also use any subset of the symbolic names to access parts of a vector. For example, `avertex.xyz` gets you the first three components of a vertex. `avertex.rgb` looks wrong, but would get you the same thing. Another new kind of vector access involves rearranging their components, or "swizzling" them. Components can be swizzled by giving the symbolic names of the components in changed order (e.g., `c1.rgba = c2.abgr`) to rearrange their order.

GLSL shaders also extend the normal C functionality in adding new kinds of type qualifiers for variables. The new qualifiers, and their meanings, are

- `const`—a variable that is a compile-time constant and cannot be referenced outside the shader that defines it. These variables cannot be used on the left-hand side of an assignment operation under any circumstances. (This is the same as the C++ const.)
- `attribute`—a variable, only used in a vertex shader, that is set by the application per-vertex and is generally sent from the application to the graphics card by OpenGL functions. Attribute variables may include the traditional per-vertex values of model coordinates, color, normal, normal matrix, or texture coordinates, but an application may define additional attribute variables when needed.
- `uniform`—a variable that is set outside a shader and can be changed at most once per primitive.
- `in` or `out`—variables used to communicate results from one shader to another. An `out` variable is to get its value in the shader where it is defined and be passed from that shader to the next shader further along in the shader pipeline. It is a write-only variable in the shader where it is defined. An `in` variable is to be received from a previous shader in the shader pipeline and used in the shader where it is defined. It is a read-only variable in the shader where it is defined. An `in` variable in a fragment shader will be interpolated across the fragments in a graphics primitive. This interpolation will be done in a perspective-corrected fashion; see [14].

Shaders can create their own functions, just like in C/C++, with their own parameters and local variables. Another set of type qualifiers is used for function parameters for shaders. These are keyed to the role of the parameters in the function, and are

- `in`—a parameter of this type is intended to have a value when it is passed into a function but is not to be changed in the function. It functions much as a const variable would. Such parameters are intended to communicate only from the calling function to the called function.

- out—a parameter of this type is not assumed to have an initial value the first time it appears in the function, but it is assumed that a value will be assigned before the function returns. Such parameters are intended to communicate only from the called function to the calling function.

- inout—a parameter that is intended to have a value when it is passed into a function and to have a value, possibly different, when the function returns. Such parameters are intended to provide two-way communication between the called function and the calling function.

One final additional capability in fragment shaders that should be mentioned is the *discard* operator. This is used to discard pixels so they will not be passed to the framebuffer. Note that this is quite different from having the pixels made transparent by setting their alpha color value to zero. Pixels with zero alpha still have a depth value and are recorded in the depth buffer, so they mask any pixel that might lie behind them. As you can clearly see in Figure 3.5, discarded pixels do not mask anything.

The GLSL shader language is missing some of the properties of C that you may be used to using. Remember that shaders operate in the graphics processor, not in a general-purpose processor, and that this limits the operations that it makes sense for the language to support. Many of these can be worked around (type casts) and some do not fit the concept of graphics processing (no enums or strings)—and some you simply will need to live without or will need to do outside the shader. Some of the differences include

- No type casts (use constructors instead).
- No automatic promotion (although some GLSL compilers handle this).
- No pointers.
- No strings.
- No enums.
- Can only use 1D arrays (no bounds checking).
- No file-based pre-processor directives.

There are several attribute variables that you will use a lot in your vertex shaders. These variables are defined in your application and give you access to per-vertex OpenGL state information for your shader. In the examples above, you saw some key values taken from these attribute variables, such as model coordinates, normals, and color, and these values (possibly modified) were turned into out variables so they could be used by tessellation or geometry shaders or interpolated later by a fragment shader. Using our variable name convention, and noting that you may use other names instead of those we chose here, these variables include

- `vec4 aVertex`—the coordinates of the current vertex in model coordinates.
- `vec3 aNormal`—the coordinates of the current vertex normal in the original coordinates.
- `vec4 aColor`—the color defined for the current vertex, if one has been defined.
- `vec4 aTexCoordi` (i = 0, 1, 2, ...)—the level i texture coordinates associated with the vertex.

There are also some uniform variables that you will use a lot. These variables are also defined in your application and are available to all your shaders. In the examples above you saw some of these variables involved in the coordinate computations. Again, these use our name convention and, noting that these names are chosen for clarity of presentation, we have

- `mat4 uModelViewMatrix`—the ModelView matrix, the product of the viewing and modeling transformation matrices, that is active for the particular vertex.
- `mat4 uProjectionMatrix`—the matrix of the projection transformation that is active for the particular vertex.
- `mat4 uModelViewProjectionMatrix`—the product of the ModelView matrix and the Projection matrix.
- `mat3 uNormalMatrix`—the normal matrix that is active for the particular vertex (as we will see, this is the inverse transpose of the ModelView matrix).

Other important uniform variables you will define in your application define lights and materials. These are described in the discussion of uniform variables below.

The built-in vertex shader output variable `gl_Position` is a particularly key variable, because you set it as the final vertex position for the remaining geometry processing. Another vertex shader output variable you may use is `gl_PointSize`.

There are two fragment shader variables you will use a lot. These are, in a sense, the primary output variables from a fragment shader; you give them values to set the properties of each pixel as the fragment is processed. They let you set the color and depth for a pixel, respectively.

Technically, none of the coordinate systems are part of GLSL, but they are available by applying GLSL operations. World space is not available with fixed-function OpenGL but requires the ability to define your own transformations, which, of course, shaders let you do.

All the operations of a fragment shader—color computation, texturing, color arithmetic, and fog—come together to set these variables. They are

- `vec4 fFragColor`—the color of the pixels.
- `float gl_FragDepth`—the depth of the pixels.

Passing Data from Your Application into Shaders

As you write any program with the OpenGL API, even if you don't intend that program to use GLSL shaders, you create data that the system will use in creating a scene. This is generally graphical data that describes the scene. For example, you can specify the color for each vertex, or you can create an array of vertices and a parallel array with data such as elevations, temperature, or any measured data. The data could be used in fixed-function operations by manipulating primitives based on your data, or with shader-based operations by putting the data into user-defined attribute or uniform data that you can access within the shader function(s). In these sections, we describe how you can create attribute or uniform data for shaders, and we give some examples that show these in action. In Chapter 9, we describe how you can create sampler data for shaders.

Defining Attribute Variables in Your Application

Attribute variables are a way to provide per-vertex data to a vertex shader. These are only available to a vertex shader. If any vertex-specific attribute data needs to be used by a later shader, the vertex shader must first convert it to an out variable so the later shader can take it as an `in` variable. Here we describe the general approach to defining variables that describe properties of an individual vertex in your model.

Besides the usual attribute data such as the coordinates, normal, color, or texture coordinates of a vertex, you may also need to define other data to associate with a vertex. OpenGL lets applications define custom attributes to pass to a vertex shader. Each vertex attribute has an indexed location and can contain up to four values.

As with uniform variables, you need to determine the symbol table location of an attribute variable before you can set it:

```
GLuint glGetAttribLocation( GLuint program,
                            GLchar * attribName );
```

where `attribName` is a character string of the name of the variable.

An application can set a per-vertex attribute using one of the functions:

```
void glVertexAttrib{i}{t}{v}(GLuint index, TYPE val)
```

The value of `i` can be 1, 2, 3, or 4, depending on the dimension of the data to be given to that attribute. The value of `t` specifies the data type for the data to be given to the attribute; this can be b (byte), s (short), i (int), f (float), d (double), ub (unsigned byte), us (unsigned short), or ui (unsigned int). The suffix v means that the data is in vector form rather than as a list of scalars. These are consistent with the format of the `glvertex*` functions.

Notice that the `glVertexAttrib*` routines do not take a program handle as one of their arguments. Since you set the attribute variables as you do the drawing, it is assumed that the intended shader program has already been made active when `glVertexAttrib*` is called.

The parameter `index` is the particular symbol table index of the attribute variable you are setting, and the parameter or parameters `val` are the value(s) to be written to the attribute variable at that index. All the `glVertexAttrib` functions are expected to be used between `glBegin` and `glEnd`, just as the built-in attribute setting functions are.

The type of the data `val` is expected to match the type specified in the function name. However, since the vertex attributes are always stored in an array of type vec4, any byte, short, int, unsigned byte, unsigned short, or unsigned int will be converted into a standard `GLfloat` before it is actually stored.

In the short application code fragment below, which uses compatibility mode for clarity, we assume that the attribute named abArray has been defined in the vertex shader as, say,

```
vec3 aMyArray[N]:
```

and we want to set the values of that attribute for each vertex of a triangle. The values to be assigned to that attribute for the vertices are the values of a0, b0, and c0 (respectively a1, b1, and c1, or a2, b2, and c2). The role of the `glVertexAttrib3f( )` function is to set these values for the attribute.

```
GLint myArrayLoc = glGetAttribLocation( program, "aMyArray" );
if(myArrayLoc < 0 )
    fprintf( stderr, "Cannot find Attribute variable
                      'aMyArray'\n" );
else
{
```

```
    glBegin( GL_TRIANGLES );
      glVertexAttrib3f( myArrayLoc, a0, b0, c0 );
      glVertex3f( x0, y0, z0 );
      glVertexAttrib3f( myArrayLoc, a1, b1, c1 );
      glVertex3f( x1, y1, z1 );
      glVertexAttrib3f( myArrayLoc, a2, b2, c2 );
      glVertex3f( x2, y2, z2 );
    glEnd( );
}
```

A very simple visualization per-vertex attribute example would display pressure data on a surface. The usual way this would be programmed with the fixed-function OpenGL would be to use the pressure to define the color at each vertex in the surface, and then—assuming a continuous pressure function on the surface—to send the surface's graphics primitives into the rendering stages, to be drawn with smooth shading color interpolation. However, we could also define pressure to be an attribute variable with each vertex, and use that directly for drawing the surface, giving us more options in using color to present the pressure data.

Attribute Variables in Compatibility Mode

In compatibility mode, GLSL defines a number of built-in attribute variables for a vertex shader to use directly or to pass along to other shaders. Each of the standard OpenGL functions that define a vertex (those you can call within a `glBegin`-`glEnd` pair) defines a built-in attribute variable that can be used by a vertex shader. Each time one of these functions is invoked, the corresponding attribute variable's value is updated. These variables are defined fully in Chapter 5 on the GLSL language, and are shown in Table 3.1.

```
    attribute vec4 gl_Color;;
    attribute vec3 gl_Normal;
    attribute vec4 gl_Vertex;
    attribute vec4 gl_MultiTexCoord0;
```

Standard OpenGL Function	Built-in Attribute Variable	Our Name
glVertex*(...)	gl_Vertex	aVertex
glColor*(...)	gl_Color	aColor
glNormal*(...)	gl_Normal	aNormal
glMultiTexCoord*(i, ...)	gl_MultiTexCoordi, i=1..N	aTexCoord0

Table 3.1. Attribute variables defined by compatibility-mode OpenGL vertex functions.

The steps in doing this are as follows:

- Define the attribute variable in the application and set the variable to its appropriate value for each vertex as you define the vertex geometry.
- Pick up the value of the attribute variable in the vertex shader and write it to an `out` variable so it can be interpolated smoothly across each graphics primitive.
- Use the variable as an `in` variable to any shader that needs it and, if appropriate, use its value to determine the color to be used in filling pixels.

This could let us add pressure contour lines, or could let us color different pressure regimes in distinct colors, or create other displays as needed. This idea will be explored more fully in Chapter 15.

Defining Uniform Variables in Your Application

GLSL uniform variables contain information that can change at most with each graphics primitive. You can think of these uniform variables as a sort of "global variables" that are available to all the shaders currently being used. If you want a shader to have data and that data isn't directly available from OpenGL, you can define your own uniform variables to give that data to a shader. Uniform variables are used within a shader, and their values are set by the application. Uniform variables can hold any kind of data, including structs and arrays, as we saw with the built-in uniform variables.

The mechanism for defining and using your own uniform variables is indirect and somewhat unusual. When you define a uniform variable in your shader program, you simply declare the variable in the usual way:

```
uniform type name;
```

This associates a name and a type with the variable, but does not associate an address. An address is only assigned when the shader program is linked. Once linking has been done, an address is available for each variable. You query the address and then use it to set the variable from your application.

But how does the application get the address for a variable it does not know about? The application must know the name of the uniform variable in a linked shader program. It can then get the location (or address) with the function

```
GLint glGetUniformLocation(GLuint program, const GLchar *name);
```

Here `program` is the value returned from the `glCreateProgram( )` function, and `name` is the name (a text string) of the uniform variable. This function returns the address of the named variable within the named program object, so it can be used in the application. The uniform variable must be a simple variable, not an array or struct; these are handled differently. A uniform variable (either built-in or user-defined) is called *active* if the link operation finds that it can be accessed during program execution; a link operation must have been done (though it might not have succeeded) before the uniform variables in the shader program can be active.

You can think of this as creating a pipe from your application to the shader. The location you get from glGetUniformLocation( ) is the place the pipe goes. You then use one of the glUniform*( ) functions to put data into the pipe to get it to the shader.

The application can set the value of a uniform variable whose location is known in three ways. The first way sets scalar or simple vector data with the function

```
glUniform{i}{t}(GLint location, TYPE val)
```

where i can be 1, 2, 3, or 4, depending on the dimension of the variable, and t can be either f or i, depending on whether the type's base is floating-point or integer. The function causes the value of the parameter val to be loaded into the location indicated. This parameter can be a simple vec1, vec2, vec3, vec4, ivec1, ivec2, ivec3, or ivec4, but not an array of these types.

The second way sets array (vector) data with

```
glUniform{i}{t}v( GLint location, GLuint length, const TYPE
                  *val )
```

where the meanings i and t are the same, but the data in val is a vector of the specified type (including vec* and ivec*) whose length is length.

Finally, the third way sets matrices, and is

```
glUniformMatrix{i}fv( GLint location, GLuint count,
                      GLboolean transpose, const GLfloat *val )
```

If i has the value 2, *val must be a 2×2 matrix; if 3, a 3×3 matrix; and if 4, a 4×4 matrix. If transpose has value GLfalse, the matrix is taken to be in standard OpenGL column matrix order, while if transpose has value GLtrue, the matrix is taken to be in row-major order. The value of count is the number of matrices that are being passed, so if you are only passing a single matrix, that value is 1.

When you develop vertex shaders, it is sometimes nice to be able to separate the Model and the Viewing matrices, instead of having them precombined into one ModelView matrix, as OpenGL does. If you are willing

Notice that none of these glUniform* routines take a program handle as one of its arguments. Those routines set uniform variables in the currently active shader program. So be sure that you call glUseProgram( ) on the correct program before setting that program's variables.

However, there is another set of GLSL API routines that let you specify the program. They look like this:

```
glProgramUniform*( program,
   loc, count, value(s) );
```

to manipulate the contents of those matrices yourself, then you can accomplish this using matrix uniform variables.

If you have defined a struct as a uniform variable, you cannot set the entire struct at once; you must use the functions above to set each field individually.

As an example, suppose you wanted to pass a light location into your shaders. The following very short code fragment, to be used in your application, wants to store a value in your shader's vec3 uniform variable named uLightPos.

The glGetUniformLocation function lets you find the location of the uniform variable in the shader program's symbol table. The glUniform3fv function lets you set that uniform variable. Note also how location is checked to ensure that the variable is actually found.

```
float LightPos[3] = { 0., 100., 0. }; // values to store

GLint lightPosLoc = glGetUniformLocation( program,
                                    "uLightPos" );
             // where in the shader symbol table to store them
if( lightPosLoc < 0 )
   fprintf(stderr, "Uniform variable 'uLightPos' not found\n");

   . . .

glUseProgram( program );

if( lightPosLoc >= 0 )
   glUniform3fv( lightPosLoc, 3, lightPos );
```

A Convenient Way to Transition to the Newer Versions of GLSL

The GLSL specification has been in transition. Many (most) of the built-in GLSL variables have been deprecated in favor of defining and using your own variable names. Although it is not clear if the GLSL deprecated features will completely go away, it is clear that they might. We believe that graphics programmers should start transitioning to the new way of doing things. This is further supported by that fact that OpenGL ES 2.0 *requires* the transition

Uniform Variables in Compatibility Mode

In compatibility mode, GLSL defines a number of built-in uniform variables that give you access to OpenGL states for primitives, as we describe fully in Chapter 5 on the GLSL language. There are a number of built-in uniform variables, including the ModelView, Projection, and Normal matrices and all texture, light, and materials data. Your applications set these values through standard OpenGL functions and can use the associated uniform variables in your shaders. These give you access to all the OpenGL state values or values derived from these states. When a program object is made current, the built-in uniform variables that track the OpenGL state are initialized to the current value of those states, and any later OpenGL calls that modify state values update the built-in uniform variable that tracks those states. The most commonly-used of these are shown in Table 3.1.

Standard OpenGL Function	Built-in Uniform Variable

transformations	`mat4 gl_ModelViewMatrix`
	`mat4 gl_ModelViewProjectionMatrix`
	`mat4 gl_ProjectionMatrix`
	`mat3 gl_NormalMatrix`

materials	`struct gl_MaterialParameters {`
	    `vec4  emission;`
	    `vec4  ambient;`
	    `vec4  diffuse;`
	    `vec4  specular;`
	    `float shininess;`
	`} gl_Frontmaterial; gl_BackMaterial;`

lights	`struct gl_LightSourceParameters {`
	    `vec4  ambient;`
	    `vec4  diffuse;`
	    `vec4  specular;`
	    `vec4  position;`
	    `vec4  halfVector;`
	    `vec3  spotDirection;`
	    `float spotExponent;`
	    `float spotCutoff;`
	    `float spotCosCutoff;`
	`} gl_LightSource[gl_MaxLights];`

Table 3.2. Some common uniform variables defined by OpenGL functions in compatibility mode.

to the new approach. Compare the installed base for OpenGL desktop to the installed base for OpenGL ES (mobile), and you realize that developing applications that run only on OpenGL desktop is short-sighted. As the standard continues to evolve, you will have a huge advantage if you develop applications that can run both on the desktop and on the ubiquitous mobile devices.

For our own work, we have developed a way to start a smooth transition to the new approach through the use of a set of #defines in a file called *gstap.h*, shown here and also available at this book's website:

```
#ifndef GSTAP_H
#define GSTAP_H


// gstap.h -- useful for glsl migration
// from:
//  Mike Bailey and Steve Cunningham
//  "Graphics Shaders: Theory and Practice",
//  Second Edition, AK Peters, 2011.


// we are assuming that the compatibility #version line
// is given in the source file, for example:
// #version 400 compatibility


// for OpenGL-ES compatibility:

precision highp          float;
precision highp          int;


// uniform variables:

#define uModelViewMatrix           gl_ModelViewMatrix
#define uProjectionMatrix          gl_ProjectionMatrix
#define uModelViewProjectionMatrix
        gl_ModelViewProjectionMatrix
#define uNormalMatrix              gl_NormalMatrix
#define uModelViewMatrixInverse    gl_ModelViewMatrixInverse
```

---

2. "gstap" stands for the book title, *Graphics Shaders: Theory and Practice*.

```
// attribute variables:

#define aColor          gl_Color
#define aNormal         gl_Normal
#define aVertex         gl_Vertex

#define aTexCoord0      gl_MultiTexCoord0
#define aTexCoord1      gl_MultiTexCoord1
#define aTexCoord2      gl_MultiTexCoord2
#define aTexCoord3      gl_MultiTexCoord3
#define aTexCoord4      gl_MultiTexCoord4
#define aTexCoord5      gl_MultiTexCoord5
#define aTexCoord6      gl_MultiTexCoord6
#define aTexCoord7      gl_MultiTexCoord7


#endif   // #ifndef GSTAP_H
```

These #defines allow you to use new names for things, without having to (yet) define them and pass them in yourself. Then, when the time comes to complete your migration to the new approach, you don't need to make massive code changes to your shaders. Note that these names use our variable naming standard descsribed earlier in this chapter.

To make life even easier for you, the gstap.h code has been built-in to the *glman* software, so that every shader source that you load automatically has it included. Just include a line in your .glib file with the word *gstap.h* on it. If you use *glman*, there is no reason not to transition away from the deprecated built-in variables right away.

Exercises

The code for all the shaders discussed in this chapter is available on the book's website, and this chapter's exercises are mostly concerned with experiments on this code using the *glman* application. Details on *glman* are discussed in the next chapter, so you may want to use it as a reference while you work on these exercises.

1. Experiment with shape: in this chapter we only used spheres for our examples, but *glman* allows you to use a number of other kinds of shapes. In the GLIB file for any of these examples, replace the sphere by other

shapes, and see how the effects change. Other shapes you may use are cylinders, boxes, cones, tori, and teapots.

2. Experiment with color: change the color of the simple figures in these examples to other colors. You may do this with the GLIB file, or you may add color as a uniform variable set through the *glman* parameter interface described in the next chapter.

3. Compute with color: you can use color as data and base your computations on it. For example, in a fragment shader you can include a statement like

```
if (color.b > 0.5) color.r = 1.0;
```

This can be a very useful technique for debugging shaders, since you cannot instrument your shader code with print statements or other familiar techniques.

4. Compare pixel blending with pixel discarding: instead of discarding pixels as in the example of Figure 3.5, change the alpha value of the color of each pixel that would have been discarded to zero and see what happens. Don't be satisfied to observe the results from a single viewpoint; rotate the sphere (or other object) to view it from all angles, and note when an alpha of zero has, and when it does not have, the same effect as a discard.

5. Figure 3.5 showed a very regular pattern of discards because of the logic in the fragment shader. Change that logic and see what kind of patterns you can make on the sphere. For example, apply a trigonometric function to some combination of coordinates, and see if you can discard sinusoidal ribbons around the sphere.

6. Get the GLIB file for the tessellation shader example in Figure 3.6, and experiment with this example by changing the vertices in the patch and by changing both the inner and outer tessellation levels. (Use any convenient fragment shader to finish creating the image.)

7. Add the geometric shrink shader to the previous exercise so you can see the individual triangles in the patch you produce, as was done in Figure 3.6.

4

Using glman

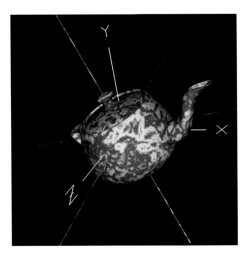

Shaders, like many other areas in graphics, have many complexities in their structure and options, and one of the best ways to learn them is simply to try out ideas, choices, and different parameters in the shaders you write. However, exploring shaders in this way can be time-consuming when you have to go through the entire edit-compile-link-run cycle for each change you want to test in the shader. In order for you to try out many options and ideas for shaders with a very short turnaround cycle, the *glman* tool provides a handy OpenGL program substitute that lets you change shader code and see the results very quickly, especially since it also lets you experiment with the values of uniform variables as shader parameters. The cycle of experimentation for developing shaders with and without *glman* is shown in Figure 4.1.

To use *glman*, you need to create a GLIB file. The name *GLIB* stands for "GL Interface Bytestream," and a GLIB file is a scene description script whose

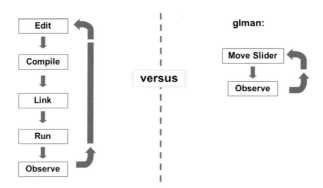

Figure 4.1. The cycle of experimentation without *glman* (left) and with *glman* (right).

details are described later in this chapter. This is an ASCII-encoded input file inspired by the Photorealistic RenderMan RIB file. You need to have both a vertex shader and a fragment shader to use *glman*; you can also have a tessellation shader or a geometry shader if you want, and if your system supports it.

You start by writing a GLIB file that describes your geometry and specifies your vertex, tessellation, geometry, and fragment shaders. The GLIB file can define uniform variables, including variables that can be changed using sliders or color pickers. You can edit GLIB and shader files from within *glman*, so you can start adding effects to the shaders, or geometry to the GLIB file, to get incremental results. The *glman* system will return error messages if you have compile errors in your shaders, which is very helpful as you begin to learn to develop them. This experimental approach and incremental development of shaders gives you good feedback on what works and lets you create some very interesting images along the way.

While *glman* will let you make some very interesting images that illustrate how your shaders work, you should realize that it is not a production tool for creating general graphics applications. There were conscious design decisions to support only a limited geometry and interaction set, for example. What it does is give you a tool to develop shaders easily and fairly quickly and to experiment with shader parameters, and it does that very well.

When you are satisfied that the shaders you have developed do the things you want, you can be confident that they will be useable for your other work. Later chapters discuss how to use shaders for applications, so the shaders you develop here will be useful there.

You can get *glman* from this book's website at http://www.cgeducation.org/glman. It runs on Windows, even if you do not have a compiler and programming environment on the system. Linux and Macintosh versions are being worked on and will be announced on the book's webapge when ready. It does, however, require that the OpenGL system be available on your computer and that your system graphics card supports programmable shaders. The *glman* distribution includes some additional files that you need to have on your system and has instructions on how to install them. If your computer and OpenGL systems have the geometry shader capability, those are also supported by *glman*. Our plans are to keep *glman*'s capabilities up with wherever the GLSL shader specification goes.

Using glman

The *glman* application is started in the usual way an application is started on your machine. When it begins, it presents a user interface window, as shown in Figure 4.2. (All of these figures are from a Windows environment.) This window has several parts that will be discussed as we go through the chapter. The key parts are loading a GLIB file, editing files, handling screen dumps, supporting scene and eye transformations, enabling object picking and transformations, and a few others; the interface is not particularly complex and is easy to understand.

The first thing *glman* does is query your graphics card's driver to see what shader types it supports. There will be up to six user interface "Edit a XXX File" buttons, depending on what is supported. If a button is left out, it means your system can't handle that type of shader anyway.

Following OpenGL's standard, *glman*'s eye position is at the origin looking in the −Z direction. When your scene is loaded, you should push it back a little bit in the −Z direction using the Eye Transformation *Trans Z* widget to make it visible.

In addition to this interface window, *glman* opens a small console window on the screen. This window gives you some information about your system, as well as the operation of the application and your shaders, but most of the time it can be safely ignored—or even minimized. On the other hand, you may want to get very detailed information about your operations through this window by using verbose mode. Other program windows may also be opened up if you request them, as described later in this chapter.

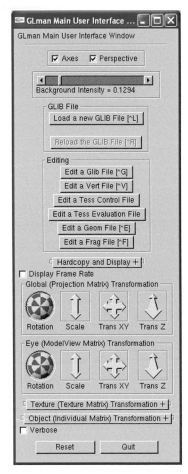

Figure 4.2. The full *glman* interface window.

Loading a GLIB File

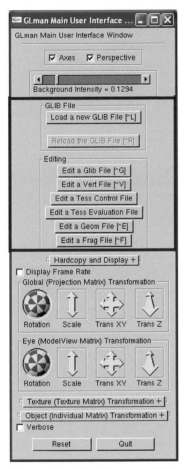

Figure 4.3. The file area of the interface panel

The file areas of the *glman* interface are shown in Figure 4.3. You load a GLIB file with the load or reload buttons; the load button brings up a file browser to select the file. This area lets you load a new file or reload the file you have been using; the latter is how you would reload an image when you had been experimenting with the shaders or changing the geometry. It also shows the full path name of the file you have loaded, although sometimes this is really too long for appropriate display.

The GLIB file supports a modest set of geometry and texture specifications. The full set of commands available in GLIB files is listed below, along with their parameters. The commands themselves are case-insensitive, but any text arguments are case-sensitive. Numbers in square brackets [ ] show the default values if the parameters are not set. If no default is given, then this command does not do anything without parameters.

Editing GLIB and Shader Source Files

The .glib, .vert, .tcs, .tes, .geom, and .frag files can be edited any way you want. If you want to open a WordPad (on Windows) or TextEdit (on Macintosh) editing window on a file, click on one of the buttons in the Editing section of the interface, and then select the file from the given file browser. You can have as many of these editing windows open at one time as you wish, and this can be a good way to copy functionality from one shader to another.

GLIB Scene Creation

GLIB includes a number of commands that you will use to control your display. These include commands about the window and viewing, about transformations, about creating geometry to display, about textures, about the shaders to use and their uniform variables, and about a few miscellaneous things. While we always write commands with an initial capital letter, they are case-insensitive. Some commands have default parameters. These are given with the command description.

Window and Viewing

`WindowSize wx wy`	Specify the initial graphics window size in pixels. [600. 600.]
`Ortho xl xr yb yt`	Set the current projection to orthographic with the given parameters. [-1. 1. -1. 1.]
`Persp fov`	Set the current projection to perspective with the given field of view (angle in degrees). [50.]
`Color r g b a`	Set the current rendering color to (r, g, b, a). If no alpha value is given, alpha is set to 1.0. $0. \leq r, g, b, a \leq 1$. (*glman* can also take `Colour` to make it look more international.)

Transformations

Like OpenGL itself, these transformations take effect in the reverse order in which they are listed; the one nearest to the geometry is performed first.

`Translate tx ty tz`	Pre-concatenate a translation by the given translation values onto the current matrix.
`Rotate angle ax ay az`	Pre-concatenate a rotation by the given angle around the line with the given direction onto the current matrix (angle in degrees).
`Scale sx sy sz`	Pre-concatenate a scale by the given scale factors onto the current matrix.
`Scale s`	Uniformly scale by (s, s, s,)
`PushMatrix`	Push the current matrix on the matrix stack.
`PopMatrix`	Pop the current matrix from the matrix stack.

Defining Geometry

The geometry options let you select enough shapes to see how your shaders will perform on a variety of different objects. The .obj file option lets you use a large number of shapes that you can get from different sources.

`Box dx dy dz`	Create a 3D box. If specified, (dx, dy, dz) are the lengths of the sides. [2. 2. 2.]
`Cylinder radius height`	Create a solid cylinder. [1. 1.]
`Cone radius height`	Create a solid cone. [1. 1.]
`DiskXY`	Create a unit disk parallel to the *XY* plane and passing through *Z* = 0.
`LinesAdjacency [v0] [v1] [v2] [v3]`	Create an instance of the OpenGL geometry shader GL_LINES_ADJACENCY primitive. This only works with geometry shaders. Each vertex consists of an *x*, *y*, and *z*, given in square brackets. So, for instance, [*v0*] might be: [1. 2. 3.]
`glBegin topology` `glVertex x y z` `...` `glEnd`	Specify the vertices for different OpenGL tropologies, including LinesAdjacency, TrianglesAdjacency, and the new GL_PATCHES topology, discussed in Chapter 13.
`Linewidth N`	Set the width of individual lines to `N` pixels.
`PointCloud numx numy numz`	Create a 3D point cloud, a regular point grid in three dimensions. The parameters num* are the number of points to use in each direction.
`JitterCloud numx numy numz`	Create a 3D point cloud as above, with the position of each point jittered (moved randomly) from its regular position.
`Pointsize size`	Define the size of points in your scene.
`QuadBox numquads`	Create a series of `numquads` (quadrilaterals parallel to the *XY* plane). The *XYZ* coordinates run from (-1.,-1.,-1.) to (1.,1.,1.). The 3D texture coordinates run from (0.,0.,0.) to (1.,1.,1.). This is a good way to test 3D textures. [10]
`QuadXY z size nx ny`	Create a quadrilateral parallel to the *XY* plane, passing through *Z* = z. If given, `size` is the quadrilateral's dimension, going from (-size, -size) to (size, size) in *X* and *Y*. If given, `nx` and `ny` are the number of sub-quads this quadrilateral is broken into. This is a good way to test 2D textures. [0 1 4 4]
`QuadXZ y size nx nz`	Creates a quadrilateral parallel to the *XZ* plane, passing through *Y* = y. If given, `size` is the quadrilateral's dimension, going from (-size, -size) to (size, size) in *X* and *Z*. If given, `nx` and `nz` are the number of sub-quads this quadrilateral is broken into. [0 1 4 4]

QuadYZ x size ny nz	Creates a quadrilateral parallel to the YZ plane, passing through $X = x$. If given, size is the quadrilateral's dimension, going from (-size, -size) to (size, size) in Y and Z. If given, ny and nz are the number of sub-quads this quadrilateral is broken into. [0 1 4 4]
Soccerball radius	Creates a geometric soccer ball from 12 pentagons and 20 hexagons. As part of this, two uniform variables are defined: FaceIndex: which face are we on right now. 0–11 are the pentagons, 12–31 are the hexagons. Tangent: vec3 pointing in a consistent tangent direction, same as the Sphere uses. In addition, the s and t texture coordinates are filled with good values for mapping an image to each face. The p value is filled with a normalized radius from the center. The seam is located at $p = 1$. [1.]
Sphere radius slices stacks	Create a solid sphere. This primitive sets the vertex coordinates, the vertex normals, and the vertex texture coordinates. In order to align bump-mapping, it also sets a vec3 called Tangent at each vertex. The vectors Tangent are all tangent to the sphere surface and always point in a consistent direction, towards the North Pole. [1. 60. 60.]
Teapot	Create a solid teapot. The default teapot is approximately 1.6 units high and 3 units long.
Torus innerradius outerradius	Create a solid torus. [.2 1.]
Wiresphere radius	Create a wireframe sphere. [1.]
Wirecylinder radius height	Create a wireframe cylinder. [1. 1.]
Wirecone radius height	Create a wireframe cone. [1. 1.]
Wirecube L	Create a wireframe cube [1.]
Wiretorus innerradius outerradius	Create a wireframe torus. [.2 1.]
Wireteapot	Create a wireframe teapot.
Xarrow numslices	Create an arrow along the X-axis, from $X = 0.$ to $X = 1.$ If specified, numslices is the number of individual slices to use along the arrow. [100]

The .obj file format was developed by Wavefront years ago to store geometric information, including lines and polygons (and more). The *glman* application supports a subset—but a very useful subset—of the format. A full description of the file format is found in [30], and there are various public-domain sources for .obj files that you can import. You will find several .obj files in the book's Web resources. If you have a particular geometry on which you want to test your shader(s), creating an .obj version of the geometry could be useful, and it is not difficult to create.

`Obj filename`	Reads a list of `GL_TRIANGLES` from an .obj file named *filename*. If a filename is not given, *glman* will prompt you for it. The full .obj format can be quite complex, but *glman* just supports vertices, normals, texture coordinates, and faces.
`WireObj filename`	Same as `Obj`, but creates a wireframe object.
`ObjAdj filename`	Reads a list of `GL_TRIANGLES_ADJACENCY` from an .obj file named *filename*. Triangles with adjacency are described in Chapters 5 and 12, and this command is useful for working with geometry shaders. If you don't have a real need to use triangle adjacency, use `Obj` instead of `ObjAdj`. The file will read faster, and the resulting geometry will display faster. If no filename is given, *glman* will prompt you for it. As with the `Obj` command, this feature just supports vertices, normals, texture coordinates, and faces.

In order to work with tessellation shaders, *glman* must support the concept of a patch. This requires one new command and a construction to define the patch geometry.

`NumPatchVertices N`	Specify the number of vertices in a patch.

`glBegin gl_patches`
  `glVertex X Y Z`
  `...`
  `glVertex X Y Z`
`glEnd`
	Define the vertices that make up the patch. The total number of `glVertex` statements must match the number of vertices specified for the patch.

Specifying Textures

These commands let you load a 1D, 2D, or 3D texture from a file to use with your shaders.

`Texture1D texture_unit` `filename`	Read a 1D texture from a file in a raw format, which consists of one 4-byte integer giving the dimension of the texture and then four components per texel specifying the red, green, blue, and alpha of that texel as either unsigned bytes or 32-bit floating point numbers.
`Texture2D texture_unit` `filename`	Read a 2D texture from a file. Don't use texture units 2 or 3 unless you want to override the 2D and 3D noise textures. If the filename ends in a `.bmp` suffix, an uncompressed BMP image file is assumed, with red, green, and blue read from the file (no alpha). Any other filename pattern implies a "raw" file format, which is described later. The four components can be all unsigned bytes or all 32-bit floating point.
`Texture3D texture_unit` `filename`	Read a 3D texture from a file in a raw format, which consists of three binary 4-byte integers giving the X, Y, and Z dimensions of the volume, and then four components per texel specifying the red, green, blue, and alpha of that texel. The four components can be all unsigned bytes or all 32-bit floating point.

`CubeMap texture_unit \`
`posxfile    negxfile`
`posyfile    negyfile`
`poszfile    negzfile`
	Generate a cubemap texture on texture unit `texture_unit` with the six BMP image face files, as specified

Specifying Shaders

These commands specify the shaders that are to be compiled and linked with your geometry to produce the image. For geometry shaders they also include specifications of the input and output geometry types they will use.

`Vertex`	`file.vert`	Specify a vertex shader filename.
`TessControl`	`file.tcs`	Specify a tessellation control shader filename.
`TessEvaluation`	`file.tes`	Specify a tessellation evaluation shader filename.
`Geometry`	`file.geom`	Specify a geometry shader filename.
`Fragment`	`file.frag`	Specify a fragment shader filename.

| Program programname uniformvariables ... | Compile and link the vertex, fragment, and possibly geometry (see below), shaders into a program, and specify the uniform variables for that program (see below). The program command must come last in this group. It links together the current vertex shader, the current fragment shader, and possibly the current tessellation shaders and geometry shader. This lets you reuse a shader in another shader program by simply not redefining another shader of that type. If you want to unspecify a shader in a program (that is, no longer use it), just give its vertex, fragment, tessellation, or geometry command with no arguments. |

If you use a geometry shader, you can also use the geometry commands in the table below in your GLIB file before the Program statement.

| Geometryinputtype | Specify what type of topology this geometry shader expects to find as input. This can be: GL_POINTS, GL_LINES, GL_LINES_ADJACENCY, GL_TRIANGLES, or GL_TRIANGLES_ADJACENCY. |
| Geometryoutputtype | Specify what type of topology this geometry shader will be emitting. This can be GL_POINTS, GL_LINE_STRIP, or GL_TRIANGLES_STRIP. |

Like the vertex, tessellation, geometry, and fragment shader specifications, these must come before the program command.

Miscellaneous

The miscellaneous information for GLIB files includes two important functions—creating noise textures and setting a timer for animations. It also includes several commands that are useful in defining the presentation to the user.

Noise2d res	Create a 2D noise texture (see below).
Noise3d res	Create a 3D noise texture (see below).
Timer numsecs	Set the timer period from the default of 10 seconds per cycle to numsecs per cycle.
Background color	Define the background color for your image. This duplicates the function of the background slider in the interface window.

MessageBox An informative text message	Put up a Message Box with the text message in it so you can show an informative message to the user.
verbose	Sets the system to output all actions to the console window, overriding the function in the interface window.

The text conventions in GLIB files are

- Multiple whitespace characters in a row are treated as a single whitespace character.
- A # causes the rest of the line to be treated as a comment and ignored.
- A / causes the rest of the line to be treated as a comment and ignored (so that // will act as expected).
- A backslash (\) at the end of a line causes the carriage return to be ignored. The current line is continued onto the next line. This must be the last character on that line before the return.

You can see that the available geometry in *glman* is good, but it is probably not rich enough to support many real applications. That is deliberate—*glman* is only intended to give you a testbed to support your experimentation with shaders. From the experience of students and others who have used it, it does that well.

Specifying Uniform Variables

Uniform variables are specified on the Program command line in a tag-value pair format. The values may be scalars, arrays, range variables, or colors.

- Scalar variables are just listed as numbers.
- Array variables are enclosed in square brackets, as [ ].
- Range variables are enclosed in angle brackets, as < >. These are scalar variables, and *glman* automatically generates a slider in the Uniform Variable user interface for each range variable, so that you can then change this value as *glman* executes. The three values in the brackets are <min current max>, e.g., <0. 5. 10.>. To decide if this range variable should be a float or an int, *glman* will look into your shader program's symbol table, and will create a slider of the appropriate type.
- Boolean variables can also end up in your user interface as well. In the GLIB file, a Boolean variable has a name, and then the word true or the word false inside angle brackets, e.g., "<true>." The *glman* user interface will automatically create a checkbox in the user interface window. The value in the brackets is the initial setting of the checkbox.

Most OpenGL shader compilers are heavily optimizing, so if you define a uniform variable but don't use it to make some part of the scene display, the variable will likely be eliminated and not seen by the loader. This can generate an error that will make no sense to you because you are pretty sure you actually typed the uniform variable name into your shader. The message looks like this:

Message

Cannot find Range variable 'Twist'

OK

So be careful to use all the uniform variables you define!

- Color variables are enclosed in curly brackets, as { }. Color variables may be either RGB or RGBA, as

  {red green blue}

  or

  {red green blue alpha}

  This will generate a button in the UI panel that, when clicked, brings up a color selector window. The color selector allows you to change the value of this color variable as *glman* executes.

- Multiple vertex-geometry-fragment-program combinations are allowed in the same GLIB file. If there is more than one combination, they will appear as separate rollout panels in the user interface. The first program rollout will

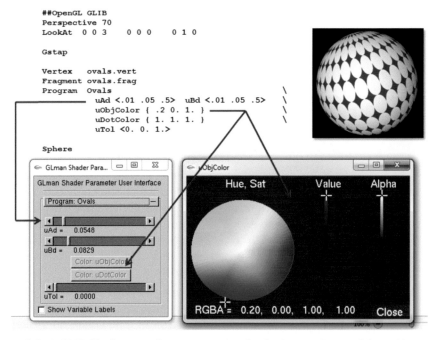

Figure 4.4. A GLIB file that specifies parameter and color interaction, and the uniform variable interface window and color picking window it creates.

be open, and all the others will be closed. Open the ones you need when you need them.

As an example of how the uniform variable selectors are presented, the parameter interface window and color selection window shown in Figure 4.4 were created as a result of the lines in the GLIB file shown in that figure.

Examples of GLIB Files

In Chapter 3 we saw some examples of vertex and fragment shaders and the images they create with *glman*. In this section we present the GLIB files that correspond to these examples, so you can see how they were set up. These example GLIB files are pretty simple, but they will help you get started on writing your own as you start developing shaders using *glman*.

We'll see the example GLIB file from the screen shader example of the previous chapter. In this example, you will see the following features:

- The perspective is identified, with a field of view.
- Eye position information is provided (eye position, look-at position, up-vector).
- The vertex and shader files ovalnoise.vert and ovalnoise.frag are specified.
- Uniform variables are set up.
- The geometry is a standard teapot.

```
##OpenGL GLIB
Perspective 70
LookAt 0 0 3  0 0 0  0 1 0

Vertex  ovalnoise.vert
Fragment ovalnoise.frag
Program OvalNoise \
  uAd <.05 .1 .5> uBd <.05 .1 .5>  \
  uNoiseAmp <0. 0. 3.> uNoiseFreq <0. .25 1.> \
  uAlpha <0. 1. 1.> \
  uTol <0. 0. .25> \
  uUseChromaDepth <false> \
  uChromaBlue <-5. -2.4 -1.> \
  uChromaRed <-3. 1.1 2.> \
  uDotColor {1. .5 0.}

Teapot
```

Another example GLIB file comes from the function graphing shader of Chapter 2; in this example, you will see the following features:

- Perspective is identified, with a field of view of 70°.
- The vertex and fragment shaders `ripple.vert` and `ripple.frag` are specified.
- The color is specified with RGB of (1.0, 0.5, 0.0).
- A `QuadXY` is specified with range –5 to 5 and with 200 sub-quads in each direction (this makes the function graph show up very smoothly).

You should be able to see something of these in Figure 3.4 in the earlier chapter.

```
##OpenGL GLIB
Perspective 70

Vertex  ripple.vert
Fragment ripple.frag
Program Ripple

Color 1. 0.5 0
QuadXY .2 5. 200 200
```

More on Textures and Noise

Textures and noise are two important concepts for fragment shaders, and *glman* gives you good access to them. This section covers a few important ideas in working with them.

Using Textures

As indicated above, there are two ways to input a 2D texture in *glman*: as a BMP file or as a raw texture file. If you input the texture as a BMP file, the file must be 24-bit RGB, uncompressed. If you want this texture to be useable on any graphics card, even an older one,, be sure the image dimensions are powers of two. Some graphics cards quietly don't require this to be true, but many still do.

The 2D raw texture format is very simple. The first 8 bytes are two 4-byte integers, declaring the S and T image dimensions. The next bytes are the RGBA values for each texel. These RGBA values can be unsigned bytes or floats. Either way, *glman* will look at the size of the file and do the right thing.

Do not confuse this format with the raw format from Photoshop; that is simply a list of colors that does not include any dimensions.

If you write code to produce a raw 2D floating point texture file, it should be organized like this:

```
int nums, numt;

. . .

fwrite( &nums, 4, 1, fp ); // nums is the S dimension of the file
fwrite( &numt, 4, 1, fp ); // numt is the T dimension of the file

for( int t = 0; t < numt; t++ )
{
  for( int s = 0; s < nums; s++ )
  {
    float red, green, blue, alpha;
    . . .
    // set red, green, blue, and alpha for the texel at
    // (s, t)
    fwrite( &red, 4, 1, fp );
    fwrite( &green, 4, 1, fp );
    fwrite( &blue, 4, 1, fp );
    fwrite( &alpha, 4, 1, fp );
  }
}
```

The 3D texture raw format is analogous to this and is just as simple. The first 12 bytes are three 4-byte integers, declaring the S, T, and P volume dimensions. The following bytes are the RGBA values for each texel. These RGBA values can be unsigned bytes or floats. Again, *glman* will look at the size of the file and do the right thing.

If you write code to produce a raw 3D texture file, it should be organized like this:

```
int nums, numt, nump;
. . .

fwrite( &nums, 4, 1, fp ); // S dimension
fwrite( &numt, 4, 1, fp ); // T dimension
fwrite( &nump, 4, 1, fp ); // P dimension

for( int p = 0; p < nump; p++ )
{
  for( int t = 0; t < numt; t++ )
  {
    for( int s = 0; s < nums; s++ )
    {
```

```
        float red, green, blue, alpha;
        . . .
        fwrite( &red, 4, 1, fp );
        fwrite( &green, 4, 1, fp );
        fwrite( &blue, 4, 1, fp );
        fwrite( &alpha, 4, 1, fp );
    }
  }
}
```

Note that *glman* expects the binary byte-ordering in a raw texture file to be consistent with the Intel x86 architecture. If you write raw texture files from a pre-Intel Macintosh, you must reverse the byte ordering yourself.

The second argument in the `Texture2D` and `Texture3D` commands is the OpenGL texture unit to assign this texture to. You then need to tell your shaders what that texture number is. For example, the GLIB `Texture` command might specify that a texture is to use texture unit 7 by

```
Program Texture uTexUnit 7
```

and your fragment shader might include code that picks up the value of uTexUnit as the unit for the `sampler2D` texture with

```
uniform sampler2D uTexUnit;
in vec2 vST;    // from the vertex shader
out vec4 fFragColor;

void
main( )
{
   vec4 rgba  = texture( uTexUnit, vST );
   fFragColor = vec4( rgba.rgb, 1. );
}
```

You should not hard-code the value 7 in the `Texture2D` function call—the compiler won't let you! Furthermore, don't use texture units 2 and 3 yourself; *glman* uses these as default values to tell your shaders about its built-in 2D and 3D noise textures.

Using Noise

As we will see in Chapter 10, *glman* automatically creates a 3D noise texture and places it into Texture Unit 3. Your vertex, tessellation, geometry, or fragment shader can get at it through the pre-created uniform variable called Noise3. You can reference it in your shader as

```
uniform sampler3D Noise3;
. . .
vec3 stp = ...
vec4 nv = texture( Noise3, stp );
```

The noise texture is a vec4 whose components have separate meanings, described in Table 4.1. The [0] component is the low frequency noise. The [1] component is twice the frequency and half the amplitude of the [0] component, and similarly for the [2] and [3] components. Each component is centered around a value of .5, so that if you want a plus-or-minus effect, subtract .5 from each component. To get a nice four-octave noise value between 0 and 1 (useful for noisy mixing), add up all four components, subtract 1, and divide the result by 2, as shown in the following table and GLSL code. More details on this can be found in Chapter 10.

Component	Term	Term Range	Term Limits
0	nv.r	$0.5 \pm .5000$	$0.0000 \rightarrow 1.0000$
1	nv.g	$0.5 \pm .2500$	$0.2500 \rightarrow 0.7500$
2	nv.b	$0.5 \pm .1250$	$0.3750 \rightarrow 0.6250$
3	nv.a	$0.5 \pm .0625$	$0.4375 \rightarrow 0.5625$
	sum	$2.0 \pm \sim 1.0$	$\sim 1.0 \rightarrow 3.0$
	sum -1	$1.0 \pm \sim 1.0$	$\sim 0.0 \rightarrow 2.0$
	(sum -1) / 2	$0.5 \pm \sim 0.5$	$\sim 0.0 \rightarrow 1.0$
	(sum -2)	$0.0 \pm \sim 1.0$	$\sim -1.0 \rightarrow 1.0$

Table 4.1. The range of the four octaves of noise and some useful combinations.

```
float sum = nv.r + nv.g + nv.b + nv.a;   // range is 1. -> 3.
sum = (sum - 1.) / 2.;                    // range is now 0. -> 1.
```

By default, the *glman* 3D noise texture has dimensions $64 \times 64 \times 64$. You can change this by putting a command in your GLIB file of the form

```
Noise3D 128
```

to get size 128, or choose whatever resolution you want (up to around 400). Remember that for the most general use, the resolution should be a power of two. The first time *glman* creates a 3D noise texture for you, it will take a few seconds. But *glman* then writes it to a file, and the next time this 3D texture is needed it is read from the file, which is a lot faster.

A 2D noise texture works the same way, except you get at it with

```
uniform sampler2D Noise2;
. . .
vec2 st = ...
vec4 nv = texture( Noise2, st );
```

Functions in the glman Interface Window

The *glman* user interface window includes a number of other functions besides loading GLIB files, which we saw at the beginning of this chapter. In this section, we will look at them so you can use them easily in your work.

Generating and Displaying a Hardcopy of Your Scene

Generating a hardcopy. Because you will be doing cool things with *glman*, you will often want to write your output to an image file. The Hardcopy and Display button shown in Figure 4.2 expands as shown in Figure 4.5. This gives you a Create Hardcopy File button that will write output (at the resolution you specify in the resolution window) to a BMP file and will bring up a file browser window that lets you specify the name of the BMP file to write into. This does not just do a raw pixel dump of the graphics window area; it generates the scene into a separate framebuffer and writes that buffer into the file, which means you can ask for a hardcopy image that has higher resolution than your screen has. This is useful when generating hardcopy for high-quality publications and large posters.

Figure 4.5. The expanded screen capture and display area.

Display the hardcopy file. To confirm the hardcopy file you got, and perhaps to send it to a printer, click on the Display the Hardcopy File button.

Global Scene Transformation

The Global Scene Transformation widgets at the top of the transformation group in Figure 4.6 let you transform the entire scene in the graphics window. There are mouse button shortcuts; the scene can be rotated by holding down the left mouse button and moving the cursor in the graphics window, or it can be scaled by holding down the middle mouse button (if you have one) and moving the cursor in the graphics window.

It is important to realize that, unlike what is normally done in an OpenGL program, these transformations do not end up in the ModelView matrix. In *glman*, they end up in the Projection matrix, so they have no impact on anything your shaders do in eye coordinates. For example, these scene transformations can be used to see the back side of a scene without changing the eye coordinate behavior of the shaders.

Eye Transformation

These widgets are the second set of transformation widgets in Figure 4.6. They let you transform the entire scene in the graphics window. Unlike the Global Scene Transformation widgets above, however, these transformations *do* end up in the ModelView matrix, just as if the OpenGL gluLookAt( ) routine had been called. That is, these scene transformations change the Eye Coordinate behavior of the shaders.

To repeat something we said at the start of this chapter, unless you initially translate your geometry in the negative *Z* direction in the GLIB file, your first move upon opening up a new GLIB scene is probably to use the "Trans Z" widget in the Eye Transformation group to push the scene back into the viewing volume, where it is more visible. You can use the .glib LookAt command to do this as well.

Object Picking and Transformation

Individual objects in the scene can be picked and independently transformed. This is a good way to test shaders that operate in eye coordinates rather than in model coordinates. In order to use this functionality, just click on the "+" sign in the "Object (Individual Matrix) Transformation" button to bring it up. To remove it, click on the "−" sign in the button.

To be able to select an object, you must enable object picking by turning on the Enable Object Picking checkbox shown in Figure 4.7. Then clicking on a 3D object in the scene with the left mouse button will cause that object to be selected, as shown in Figure 4.8. A large 3D cursor becomes centered on the object to show that it is selected.

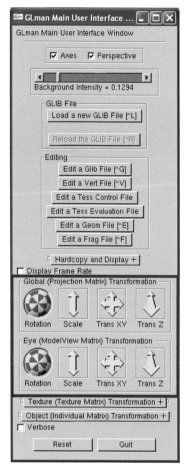

Figure 4.6. The interface window with the transformation functions.

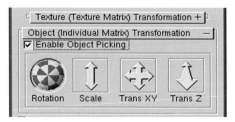

Figure 4.7. The expanded Texture and Object Transformation area in the interface window.

When an object has been selected, the Object Transformation widgets shown in Figure 4.7 will become active. These widgets will apply transformations to the selected object separately from all other objects in the scene. The object transformations go into the *ModelView* matrix for the one picked scene object, where they will impact any

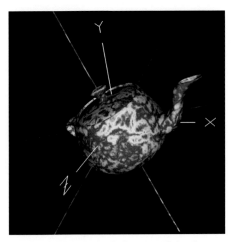

Figure 4.8. A picked object with both axes and the 3D cursor.

shader that performs operations in eye coordinates. When object picking has been enabled, mouse motions in the window noted above are applied only to the selected object.

To deselect an object, click in an open area of the graphics window, uncheck the Enable Object Picking checkbox, or close the object transformation area by clicking on the "−" sign in the button.

Texture Transformation

In addition, *glman* gives you a way to change the texture transformation matrix (mat4 gl_TextureMatrix[0]). As this is not something that is done often, *glman* has hidden it in a user interface "rollout." Just click on the "+" sign in the "Texture (Texture Matrix) Transformation" button to bring it back out. The Texture Transformation widgets work the same as the Global Scene Transformation, Eye Transformation, and Object Transformation coordinate transforms. Note that using these widgets will not automatically transform texture coordinates as in the fixed-function OpenGL pipeline. These widgets just set the gl_TextureMatrix[0] matrix. What you do with that is up to you.

Monitoring the Frame Rate

It is sometimes useful to get an idea of how much certain shader operations affect the overall speed of the graphics pipeline. For example, certain math functions are implemented in hardware, some in software; if-tests often cause a slowdown; and low-count for loops often give better performance if they are unrolled. To see what your current frame rate is, click the Display Frame Rate checkbox in the middle of the user interface window. This makes *glman* time your display as you interact with it. After you turn this option on, you will see two things: (1) a frames-per-second (FPS) number will be presented in the graphics window, and (2) your display speed will drop sharply. This speed drop is caused by *glman* looping through multiple instances of your display to get more precise timing. Your speed will go back to normal once you turn off this option. The timing does not include the initial setting and clearing of the framebuffers, nor does it include swapping of double buffers. It measures the display speed of just your scene.

Miscellaneous

At the top of the user interface window there are two checkboxes and one slider, shown in Figure 4.9.

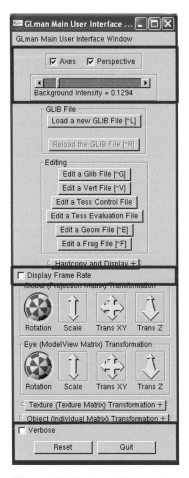

- *Axes.* When this checkbox is selected, the three coordinate axes in eye space are shown. Each of the axes is labeled and is two units long in the appropriate direction.

- *Perspective.* When this checkbox is selected, you are toggled between perspective and orthogonal viewing, irrespective of your specification in the GLIB file.

- *Background Intensity.* This slider lets you set the background intensity for your image.

At the bottom of the user interface window you will see an area with a checkbox and two buttons, also shown in Figure 4.9. The options given in this area are described below.

- *Verbose.* Normally, the messages in the console window are things that you might really need to know. If you would like to see more of what is really going on behind the scenes, click this checkbox on—but at times this can be voluminous, so be sure you really want to see all this. Don't say we didn't warn you!

- *Reset.* This button returns the scene to its original form before any global or eye transformations have been made, and before any selections. However, any changes that were made in the uniform variables declared in the GLIB file are retained.

There is one more checkbox in another window that you should know about:

- *Show Variable Labels.* This checkbox shows up at the bottom left of the Uniform Variable user interface window shown in Figure 4.4. When you click it, the values of the uniform variables will be superimposed on top of your graphics scene. This is very handy for doing screen cap-

Figure 4.9. The Axes, Perspective, and background color sections (top), the Display Frame Rate box (middle), and the Verbose checkbox and Reset and Quit buttons (bottom).

tures of your graphics scene and documenting the uniform variable value settings that made this scene.

Exercises

The exercises in this chapter will give you some experience in working with the *glman* application, which should make it easier for you to do the work on shaders in later chapters. Exercises in later chapters will ask for you to do things in *glman* to work with the functionality of different shader types.

1. In the previous chapter we gave some examples of shaders to create some of the chapter's figures, and in this chapter we showed the GLIB files that worked with them to create the figures. For at least one of these, identify each of the GLIB file commands and show how it led to features of the figure(s) it helped create.

2. The *glman* interface panel has a number of functions, and you should take a moment to exercise as many of those as you can. In particular, use the eye transformation, hardcopy, object selection and manipulation, and frame rate options, and analyze and note what each of these does.

3. Use the editing functions of *glman* to make small changes in the GLIB file and the vertex and fragment shader files and note the effect of the changes. Do this by first loading a GLIB file and noting the image, and then editing one or more of the files and using the Reload function. This cycle should become very familiar to you as you develop your shaders.

4. The *glman* tool provides a number of different graphics primitives. Use several primitives in a single scene (described in a GLIB file) to see how each looks. Use translations so they won't all be drawn on top of each other, and use a different color for each.

5. Create a scene with at least two objects whose color is set by a *glman* uniform color variable. (You can do this as part of Exercise 4.)

6. Create a scene with an object whose properties (for example the density and frequency of the screen in the pixel-discard shader in the previous file) are set by a *glman* uniform slider variable. (You can do this as part of Exercise 4.)

7. Create a scene that includes a graphics object defined by an .obj file. You can get such files from the book's website, or you can get such files from the book's website http://www.cgeducation.org.

8. Create a scene that uses texturing on a graphics primitive. You may need to refer to Chapter 8 for some details.

5

The GLSL Shader Language

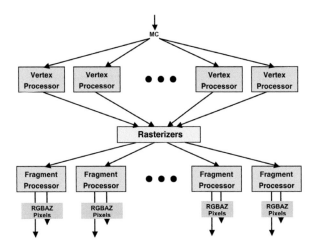

As shader capabilities in graphics hardware have become more flexible, shader languages have been developed to give the graphics programmer access to these capabilities. The GLSL shading language was designed to be device independent and has been part of the OpenGL standard from OpenGL 2.0 forward. It accomplishes its device independence by having compilers built into the graphics card driver translate the GLSL code into the specific device instructions for that card. The actual process of attaching shaders to shader programs, compiling them, and linking them to be downloaded into the graphics card is part of the GLSL API, covered in Chapter 14.

GLSL is a very C-like language, with most of the same fundamental code structure and operators that are found in that language. Thus, there are no challenges to the graphics programmer in understanding the control flow, basic operations, or basic data types in the language. However, there are some areas where GLSL extends the capabilities of C, some areas where

GLSL shader capabilities are very much a moving target. This chapter and all our examples are based on GLSL 4.1. However, we also include many features that are deprecated in that standard but are available in compatibility mode, because they may be helpful to someone learning to work with shaders for the first time.

In order to keep current on GLSL, you should consult [32] from time to time.[1] You will not need a new copy of *glman*, however, because OpenGL will compile only the GLSL shaders, but you may need to get a new OpenGL driver.

GLSL omits some of the capabilities of C, and some areas where GLSL has language features that remind us of the best of earlier generations of computer languages. This chapter focuses on these differences and discusses why they are needed for the shader environment. There is a tendency for any discussion like this to have a strong flavor of a language manual, and you might find that you use this chapter more as a reference than as general reading.

We introduced a number of GLSL language features in Chapter 3, but here we take a more thorough approach to the language and describe it more formally. We are working from the GLSL language specification [23] and include those features and capabilities that we believe are most useful to you, but we are not absolutely complete in our coverage. Once you are familiar with a good working set of GLSL, you probably should read the GLSL specification to see what else is there—especially since the language will continue to evolve over time.[1]

We are indebted to the GLSL Shader Language Specification document both for the overall information it contains and for its excellent tables of GLSL functions and operations that we have borrowed from extensively.

Factors that Shape Shader Languages

Shader languages operate in a different environment and with different goals than general-purpose languages. Their environment is the processing capability of graphics cards, which differs in some important ways from the capability of a general CPU, and their goals are tightly focused on supporting graphics operations, rather than more general kinds of computations. These capabilities shape the language in significant ways, and it is important that you understand their impacts as you write shaders.

---

1. Good resources: "OpenGL." *Khronos.* Available at http://www.khronos.org/opengl/.
   "OpenGL 4.2 API Quick Reference Card." *Khronos.* Available at http://www.khronos.org/files/opengl42-quick-reference-card.pdf, 2010.
   "OpenGL Shading Language." *OpenGL.* Available at http://www.opengl.org/documentation/glsl/, 2011.

Graphics Card Capabilities

The first thing we should understand when we think of a language to support graphics shaders is that graphics cards, or GPUs, are not like standard CPUs in several ways. In some ways they are much more advanced than most processors, and in some ways they are more restricted. GPUs are meant to operate on streaming data, transforming it and passing it along a pipeline of processing stages. They hate exceptions, and exceptions can force a whole pipeline to be flushed and restarted. The GLSL shader language has added features that take advantage of graphics card capabilities, especially features that come from the increasingly general-purpose architecture of these cards. These changes are described throughout this chapter.

Parallelism in Graphics Cards

One of the main differences between graphics cards and standard processors is that graphics cards can be parallel processors. Certainly there are some kinds of data-level parallelism in modern processors and, in fact, it has become common for systems to offer parallelism through multiple processors or cores. But these are different kinds of parallelism. Today's graphics cards typically perform parallelism at four levels:

1. Device-Level Parallelism—multiple processors or multiple graphics cards can exist in the same system.
2. Core-Level Parallelism—each processor typically has multiple cores that are capable of independent execution.
3. Thread-Level Parallelism—each core can run multiple threads, that is, can have multiple instruction streams.
4. Data-Level Parallelism— many instructions can act on multiple data elements at once.

Much of the time, the details of these modes of parallelism are abstracted away from the application programmer, and are used as shown in Figure 5.1. This is a good thing. Most of the time, we don't care where or how the processing takes place, just that it happens with sufficient parallelism to handle the increasing demands of today's complex rendering tasks.

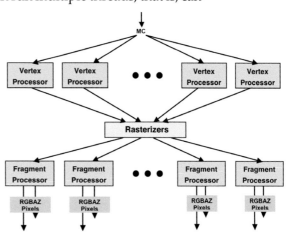

Figure 5.1. Abstracted parallelism in graphics processors.

The Need to Support Graphics Operations

Another key fact about graphics cards is that they must carry out a large number of matrix operations at high speeds, so matrix and vector operations are native to the language, and most likely supported at some level in your hardware. Thus, the GLSL language is shaped by its goal of supporting the operations needed for computer graphics. This is done by adding specific support for matrix and vector data types and operations, including both operations and useful functions; supporting functions that are frequently used for geometric operations; adding language support for noise functions; and adding functions for texture and fragment operations. Some of these are included so they can be optimized, and some are included in anticipation of higher-level operations moving onto graphics cards. GLSL developments so far have extended the original scope of the language, and there is every reason to believe that when additional graphical capabilities are available, such as the recent development of geometry shaders, the language will be extended to support them.

Built-In Data

General-purpose processors have registers that can be used for many kinds of variables, so each must be capable of any kind of operation. Graphics cards designed as OpenGL 2.1 was being released, on the other hand, have a number of special-purpose registers that are loaded with specific data when information is received from the general OpenGL application program. This gives these graphics cards known environments that can be read or written by a shader program, leading to the use of specific names for variables that have particular information.

This aspect of the graphics environment is primarily handled in GLSL by a number of built-in variables that let you access standard data passed to the graphics card from the OpenGL API. This data describes geometry, lighting, transformations, and textures. By using the appropriate GLSL variables, you can use this information for computation in your shaders.

More recently, however, graphics cards have become much more general processors, and these special-purpose registers have been deprecated. A few specific variables have been retained, but the task of building the graphics environment has been passed to the graphics programmer. This increases the programmer's task, but returns significant improvements in performance and in the generality of graphics operations you can create. These changes are described below and in the chapters on each kind of shader.

General GLSL Language Concepts

GLSL is designed to be similar to C and maintains many of the familiar conventions of that language. The overall syntax is the same, with the same conventions for literals and identifiers, and the same preprocessor capabilities. You have have the full set of integer and unsigned integer operations, most of the same operators, and the same operator precedence. The looping and conditional structures are the same, including the switch statement. Overall, if you know C, you will find the basic nature of GLSL to be quite comfortable.

However, there are differences between GLSL and C that are driven by the differences in the special environment and the goals of the language, rather than by limitations of C. There are five fundamental ways in which GLSL differs from most conventional languages:

1. The range of conventional operators and functions is extended beyond those usually found in C or similar languages.
2. The language contains some capabilities, such as name sets and shared data namespaces that are implicit in the language, rather than explicitly specified.
3. Data passing between shaders is handled by specifically declaring which variables are input and which are output, and some variables must be explicitly passed along from a shader to subsequent shaders.
4. Function parameters are passed by value-return, rather than by value alone.
5. Some general-purpose language capabilities are omitted.

In GLSL, some conventional operators and functions have extended capabilities, and some new functions and operations are introduced that are convenient for graphics. GLSL has two new implicit capabilities that come from extending the variable types to include types that carry specific capabilities and from using a shared namespace to communicate between shaders. The GLSL function parameters and omitted capabilities from C come from changes in the processing environment. All these differences are described fully later in this chapter, but are briefly discussed in the sections below.

Shared Namespace

Shaders operate independently of each other, so an application can use any shader independently of any other. In order for shaders to communicate, they must use memory on the graphics card, so the application and its shaders must create names for variables in on-card memory. Sharing these names between shaders that are linked into a single shader program then creates the between-shader communication that shaders need. The set of names of variables used by a set of shaders is called a *shared namespace*.

A namespace may hold *attribute variables*, created by the appliction to define per-vertex data and available only to the vertex shader as `in` variables; *uniform variables*, created by the application to be used as read-only variables by any shader; and *shader-defined variables*, created as `out` variables to pass on as `in` variables to later shaders. (The concept of `out` and `in` variables is discussed later in this chapter.) Some variables created in vertex-processing shaders are intended to be used by fragment shaders by being interpolated across a fragment as a geometric primitive is processed.

You can define attribute variables in your application through the OpenGL API function `glVertexAttrib*( )` and make them accessible to the vertex shader. This lets you define per-vertex data that can be used to define colors or other properties of vertices. You can also define uniform variables to communicate from your OpenGL application to vertex or fragment shaders. Because of limitations on the memory on the graphics card, there is a limit to the total amount of uniform data available to you. Defining and accessing user-defined attribute and uniform variables will be discussed when we present the GLSL API in Chapter 14.

The types and initializers of variables with the same name must match across all shaders that are linked into a single executable. It is legal for some shaders to provide an initializer for a particular variable, while other shaders do not, but all provided initializers must be equal. This is checked as the program is linked.

There are a few specific variables that GLSL uses for very specific capabilities; these may be seen as basic parts of the namespace for one or more kinds of shader. These are described in the chapters on the different shaders.

Extended Function and Operator Capabilities

GLSL extends some of the operators and functions of C to act on vectors and matrices. The standard scalar arithmetic operators are extended to vectors by applying the original operation componentwise. The additive operators are also extended to componentwise operations on matrices, but the multiply operator is taken to mean the standard linear algebra matrix multiplication. Many familiar functions on scalars are similarly extended to vectors by acting componentwise.

GLSL also adds several new vector and matrix operators. There are name set conventions for vectors that let you name components in computer-graphics ways, and there are operations to construct vectors and matrices, and to reorder vector components that give you much more flexible control over these data objects. Overall, GLSL treats vectors and matrices much more like data primitives than does C.

New Functions

GLSL includes many numeric functions that might be relatively easy to write for yourself, but that when included, make their capabilities more standardized across the developer world. These include `floor`, `ceil`, `fract`, `mod` (a generalized version of the familiar function), `min`, `max`, `clamp`, `mix`, `step`, and `smoothstep`. GLSL also includes several vector and matrix functions to support common operations in a uniform way. These include the dot and cross product for vectors, functions for the reflection and refraction vectors, and the transpose and outer product for matrices. These are described fully later.

New Variable Types

GLSL introduces some new variable types: `const`, `attribute`, and `uniform`. Const variables act as constants, much as if they were set with a #define statement, only more strongly typed as they are in C and C++. Attribute variables are per-vertex values passed to the vertex shader. Uniform variables let you define graphics variables that do not vary across a primitive and make them accessible to all shaders.

Shaders create a shared namespace, described above, by specifying the variables to be included in the namespace. They do this by declaring out variables, treated as write-only and used to give variables values to be used in the next shader in the pipeline, and in variables, treated as read-only and used to read values in from the previous shader in the pipeline. An out variable declared in, say, a vertex shader, can be used to set a value to be read in an in variable of the same name declared in, say, a fragment shader.

There are some keywords that modify the behavior of in variables for a fragment shader; these are `flat`, `noperspective`, and `centroid`. The keyword `flat` indicates that values of the input variables are not to be interpolated across a primitive. The usage is

```
flat in float variable_name;
```

as discussed in Chapter 8. The keyword `noperspective` indicates that these variables are interpolated in screen space, rather than being interpolated in a perspective-correct way. The usage is

```
noperspective in float variable_name;
```

The keyword `centroid` indicates that values are to be centroid sampled, that is, sampled at an implementation-defined position in the intersection of a pixel and a primitive, for the purpose of determining what value to apply to the pixel. This is an advanced topic, but it could be useful if you are applying functions across a primitive that may be discontinuous or highly non-linear.

New Function Parameter Types

GLSL function parameters are passed by *value-return*, rather than by value. This allows two-way communication between the calling function and the called function by copying values into and out of function parameters. Parameters are modified by the keywords `in`, `out`, and `inout`. The parameter keyword `in` describes the traditional pass-by-value of C, while the parameter keywords `out` and `inout`, described later in this chapter, replace the need for reference parameters. GLSL does not use pointers.

Language Details

In the sections below, we discuss specific features of the GLSL shader language. In most cases, it should be clear how these features support the kinds of computation needed for shaders. In a few cases, however, we will briefly discuss some examples, such as swizzle operations where the language features make capabilities possible that go beyond those implicit in the nature of the language.

Omitted Language Features

Because GLSL is not a general-purpose language, it does not have some capabilities we are used to seeing in C and other languages. In fact, it cannot have some of these features because the graphics processor does not support all the operations that a general-purpose processor must. The features that are omitted are probably less important for most processing than they are convenient, so you will probably not miss them too much. They include

- There are no char, char *, or string data types, and GLSL has no string-manipulation functions.
- There is no sizeof( ) operator, because there is no need to deal with data in various sizes. There are standard constructors for arrays and matrices of all needed sizes.
- No implicit type conversions are allowed in GLSL. Conversions are supported by explicit type constructors.

Instead of implicit conversions, or type casts, there are three explicit constructors for simple types, as follows:

- int(arg): converts the argument to an int; the argument may be a float or a bool.
- float(arg): converts the argument to a float; the argument may be an int or a bool.
- bool(arg): converts the argument to a boolean; the argument may be a float or an int.

The usual conversion operations are used: conversions from float to int simply drop the fractional part, nonzero floats or ints convert to the Boolean *true*, etc. This is a different syntax from the familiar cast operations, but it gives you the same functionality if you need it.

New Matrix and Vector Types

GLSL supports a number of predefined data types for vectors and matrices. Vectors may have a real, integer, or Boolean base type, but matrices must be real. Many familiar vector and matrix operations and functions can be applied to variables of these types, and a number of useful new functions are also provided. These are discussed in several sections later in this chapter.

GLSL's built-in floating-point scalar and vector types are float, vec2, vec3, and vec4. The storage for a variable of type vecN is simply that of a traditional array, but you want to use the built-in type rather than the traditional array type. Using the vecN types explicitly makes a much larger number of operations available for the data, and these operations can then take advantage of graphics card parallelism to work at a much higher speed.

GLSL's built-in integer, scalar, and vector types are int, ivec2, ivec3, and ivec4. Again, the storage for an ivec variable is the same as that for a traditional array, but the explicit ivec type can take a much larger set of operations.

GLSL's built-in Boolean scalar and vector types are bool, bvec2, bvec3, and bvec4. The main value in Boolean vectors is their ability to support logical operations on vectors, and thus to parallelize some logical tests.

GLSL supports a number of matrix types. For square matrices, mat2, mat3, and mat4 can be used for square floating-point matrices of dimension 2×2, 3×3, or 4×4, respectively. Using explicit matrix types rather than simple arrays lets you take advantage of GLSL's many matrix operations and functions.

There are also matrix types that define the dimensions explicitly by listing both dimensions in the declaration. Thus, GLSL has mat2x2, mat2x3, mat2x4, mat3x2, mat3x3, mat3x4, mat4x2, mat4x3, and mat4x4 floating-point matrix types. When the two dimensions are equal, this is the same as the declarations above (mat2x2 is the same as mat2, for example). Using these matrix types lets you use GLSL's matrix operations on non-square matrices. Note that there is no declaration of mat1xN or matNx1 arrays; when a one-dimensional array is needed, you can usually use a simple vecN in its place.

Name Sets

GLSL supports some standard name sets for vector components that are used for notational convenience. For a vec4 variable, you can use (x, y, z, w) if you want to refer to components for geometry, (r, g, b, a) if you want to refer to components for color, or (s, t, p, q) if you want to refer to components for texture coordinates. The name set you choose need not depend on the context; you can use (x, y, z, w) to refer to colors if you like, for example. (Note that the letter r for texture coordinates has been replaced by p to avoid confusion with the letter r for red.) In general, you should be careful to avoid name sets that imply such meanings when choosing name sets for vectors other than geometry, RGBA color, or texture.

The component selection syntax allows multiple components to be selected by appending their names (which must be from the same name set) after the period (.). So with a declaration vec4 v4, for example, we have the examples given in the table below.

v4.rgba	Is a vec4 and is the same as just using v4.
v4.rgb	Is a vec3 made from the first three components of v4.
v4.b	Is a float whose value is the third component of v4; also v4.z or v4.p.
v4.xz	Is a vec2 made from the first and third components of v4; also v4.rb or v4.sp.
v4.xgba	Is illegal because the component names do not come from the same set.

Vector Constructors

GLSL has a number of constructors that let you create new vectors from a mix of scalars and other vectors. These constructors have the same name as the vector types and serve to construct a vector of the named type. Some examples are given in the table below.

`vec3(float, float, float)`	Initializes each component of a vector with the explicit floats provided.
`vec4(ivec4)`	Makes a vec4 with component-wise conversion.
`vec2(float)`	Initializes a vec2 with the float value in each position.
`ivec3(int, int, int)`	Initializes an ivec3 with three ints.
`bvec4(int,int,float,float)`	Performs four Boolean conversions.
`vec2(vec3)`	Drops the third component of a vec3.
`vec3(vec4)`	Drops the fourth component of a vec4.
`vec3(vec2, float)`	`vec3.xy = vec2` `vec3.z = float`
`vec3(float, vec2)`	`vec3.x = float` `vec3.yz = vec2`
`vec4(vec3, float)`	`vec4.xyz = vec3` `vec4.w = float`
`vec4(float, vec3)`	`vec4.x = float` `vec4.yzw = vec3`
`vec4(vec2a, vec2b)`	`vec4.xy = vec2a` `vec4.zw = vec2b`

To initialize a matrix by using specified vectors or scalars, we recall that matrices are stored in column-major order (unlike in C), so the components are assigned to the matrix elements in that order.

`mat2(vec2, vec2)`
`mat3(vec3, vec3, vec3)`
`mat4(vec4, vec4, vec4, vec4)`
`mat3x2(vec2, vec2, vec2)`
	Each matrix is filled using one column per argument.

`mat2(float, float, float, float)`	Rows are first column and second column, respectively.

mat3(float, float, float,
      float, float, float,
      float, float, float)
	Rows are first column, second column, and third column, respectively.

mat4(float,float,float,float,
      float,float,float,float,
      float,float,float,float,
      float,float,float,float)
	Rows are first column, second column, third column, and fourth column, respectively.

mat2x3(vec2, float, vec2, float)	Rows are first column and second column, respectively.

Even though GLSL offers these 2D matrix formats, it is sometimes convenient to use simpler 1D arrays. For example, we can represent a 3×3 matrix M as three separate vec3 variables and then multiply M by a matrix V by using three dot products.

There are many other ways to construct a matrix from vectors and scalars, as long as there are enough components to initialize the matrix. The construction acts as though the matrix begins as an identity matrix (or a subset of an identity matrix), and the new elements that are specified replace the originals. For example, to construct a matrix from a matrix we might have the possibilities given in the following table.

mat3x3(mat4x4)	Uses the upper-left 3×3 submatrix of the mat4x4 matrix.
mat2x3(mat4x2)	Takes the upper-left 2×2 submatrix of the mat4x2, and sets the last column to vec2(0.).
mat4x4(mat3x3)	Puts the mat3x3 matrix in the upper-left submatrix and sets the lower right component to 1 and the rest to 0.

Functions Extended to Matrices and Vectors

Standard programming languages tend to have a number of numeric functions and operators, including trigonometric functions, exponential functions, number manipulation functions, and relational operators. In GLSL, most of these can operate on vectors, as well as on scalar values.

The familiar bitwise integer functions <<, >>, %, &, |, ^, and ~ are all available in GLSL and apply to both simple integer and ivecN data.

In the lists of functions below, we use the term genType to refer to any scalar or vector data type that is appropriate for each function. In general, these functions use float or vecN data, but you can use an integer type anywhere a float type is needed, because GLSL allows that implicit type conversion.

GLSL supports the familiar set of trigonometric and inverse trigonometric functions. As with all the other functions, these can operate componentwise on vectors. Arguments identified with *angle* are assumed to be in radians.

`genType radians( genType degrees)`	Converts degrees to radians: $(\pi/180)$*degrees*.
`genType degrees( genType radians)`	Converts radians to degrees: $(180/\pi)$*radians*.
`genType sin( genType angle)` `genType cos( genType angle)` `genType tan( genType angle)`	The standard trigonometric sine, cosine, and tangent functions, with the argument *angle* in radians.
`genType asin(genType x)`	Arc sine. Returns the primary radian value of the angle whose sine is x. The range of returned values is $[-\pi/2,\pi/2]$. Undefined if $|x|>1$.
`genType acos(genType x)`	Arc cosine. Returns the primary radian value of the angle whose cosine is x. The range of returned values is $[0,\pi]$. Results are undefined if $|x|>1$.
`genType atan(genType y, genType x)`	Arc tangent. Returns the primary radian value of the angle whose tangent is y/x. The signs of x and y determine the angle's quadrant. The range of returned values is $[-\pi,\pi]$. Undefined if x and y are both 0.
`genType atan( genType y_over_x)`	Arc tangent. Returns the primary radian value of the angle whose tangent is y_over_x. The range of returned values is $[-\pi/2,\pi/2]$.

GLSL also supports the full range of hyperbolic trigonometric functions, sinh, cosh, and tanh, and their inverses.

GLSL has the usual exponential, logarithmic, and square root functions, including exponential and logarithmic functions of base 2. These can also operate componentwise on vectors.

`genType pow(genType x, genType y)`	Power function. Returns x raised to the y power, x^y. Undefined if $x < 0$, or if $x = 0$ and $y \leq 0$.
`genType exp(genType x)`	Returns the natural exponentiation of x, e^x.
`genType log(genType x)`	Returns the natural logarithm of x, the value y for which $x = e^y$. Undefined if $x \leq 0$.
`genType exp2(genType x)`	Returns 2 raised to the x power: 2^x.
`genType log2(genType x)`	Returns the base 2 logarithm of x, the value y for which $x = 2^y$. Undefined if $x <= 0$.
`genType sqrt(genType x)`	Returns the nonnegative square root of x. Undefined if $x < 0$.
`genType inversesqrt( genType x)`	Returns $1/\sqrt{x}$. Undefined if $x \leq 0$.

Don't use inversesqrt( ) to normalize a vector! Use normalize( ) instead.

GLSL supports a familiar set of common functions, as well as some that are not as familiar. Among the less-familiar functions are some that are very useful in combining colors or geometry. These functions can all operate componentwise on any vector. Note that the mod function is generalized to real numbers as well as integers. The functions abs, clamp, min, max, and sign can be applied to integers as well as to real numbers.

genType abs(genType x)	Returns x if $x \geq 0$, otherwise returns $-x$.
genType sign(genType x)	Returns 1.0 if $x > 0$, 0.0 if $x = 0$, or -1.0 if $x < 0$.
genType floor(genType x)	Returns a value equal to the nearest integer that is less than or equal to x.
genType ceil(genType x)	Returns a value equal to the nearest integer that is greater than or equal to x.
genType fract(genType x)	Returns the fraction part of x: $x - floor(x)$.
genType truncate (genType x)	Returns the integer closest to x whose absolute value is not larger than $abs(x)$.
genType round(genType x)	Returns the integer closest to x.
genType mod(genType x, float y) genType mod(genType x, genType y)	Generalized modulus. Returns $x - y * floor(x/y)$.
genType min(genType x, genType y) genType min(genType x, float y)	Minimum. Returns y if $y < x$, otherwise returns x.
genType max(genType x, genType y) genType max(genType x, float y)	Maximum. Returns y if $x < y$, otherwise returns x.

genType clamp(genType x,
        genType minVal,
        genType maxVal)
genType clamp(genType x,
      float minVal,
      float maxval)
	Clamped value; Returns $min(max(x, minVal), maxVal)$. Undefined if $minVal > maxVal$.

genType mix(genType x,
      genType y,
      genType a)
genType mix(genType x,
      genType y,
      float a)
	Proportional mix. Returns a linear combination of x and y: $a * x + (1 - a) * y$.

genType mix(genType x,
      genType y,
      bool b)
	Select the value of either x or y, depending on the value of b.

`genType step(genType edge,`
`        genType x)`
`genType step(float edge,`
`        genType x)`
	Step function at the value of edge. Returns 0.0 if $x < edge$, otherwise returns 1.0.

`genType smoothstep( genType edge0,`
`            genType edge1,`
`            genType x)`
`genType smoothstep( float edge0,`
`            float edge1,`
`            genType x)`
	Returns 0.0 if $x <= edge0$ and 1.0 if $x >= edge1$, and performs smooth Hermite interpolation between 0. and 1. when $edge0 < x < edge1$. This is useful in cases where you would want a threshold function with a smooth transition. This is equivalent to
	`  genType t;`
	`  t = clamp((x - edge0)/`
	`  (edge1 - edge0), 0., 1.);`
	`  return 3.*t*t - 2.*t*t*t;`
	Results are undefined if $edge0 > edge1$.

Operations Extended to Matrices and Vectors

The traditional primitive operators, sum (+), difference (–), product (*), and quotient (/), operate only on scalar data in most languages. In GLSL, this is extended in a natural way to vector and matrix data. There are two different cases to consider here.

Sums, differences, and quotients act componentwise when

- One operand is a scalar and one is either a vector or matrix, or
- Both are vectors or matrices.

Products act componentwise when

- One operand is a scalar and one is either a vector or matrix, or
- Both are vectors.

Note that if u and v are vectors, u*v is *not* a dot product! This product u*v is just a componentwise product and is still a vector. If you are trying to get a dot product, use dot( ) instead. In order to compute a product of vectors or matrices, of course, both operands must have the same dimensions and appropriate types. The result is a vector or matrix of the appropriate size and type.

Products of a vector and a matrix, or of two matrices, are different; they do not perform scalar operations, but perform the correct linear algebra operations on their operands. For vectors u, v and matrices m, n, r (always assuming appropriate dimensions so the operations make sense),

- We can write u = v * m; this treats v as if it were a $1 \times d$ matrix and performs the correct operation of the dot product of v with each column of m.
- We can write u = m * v; this treats u and v as if they were $d \times 1$ matrices and performs the correct operation of the dot product of v with each row of m.
- We can write r = m * n; this performs the dot product of each row of m with each column of n to produce the matrix r.

In addition, the assignment operator = and relational equality and inequality operators == and != can be applied to entire arrays or structs, but the operands must be of the same size and, for structs, the same declared types. Other relational functions are available for vectors, but they differ from the familiar built-in relational operators. These are described later in this chapter.

Other familiar vector operations, the dot and cross products, are available through the built-in dot and cross product operations that are described fully later in this chapter when we present GLSL's matrix functions. These include several other useful capabilities. For example, if you should want the componentwise scalar product of two matrices, you will need to use the new matrix function matrixCompMult. Or if you should want to do an outer product of two vectors (the outer product of two vectors u, v of dimension n is defined as though u has dimension $n \times 1$ and v has dimension $1 \times n$ and you are computing the matrix product [u times v]), you can use the new matrix function outerProduct.

New Functions

As described in previous sections, many common functions from C are also available in GLSL. However, languages such as C do not focus on graphics and so have few functions to handle geometry and matrix data. GLSL provides several new functions to do this. The list here is long, but is broken out into several different areas, as they are in the language specification.

Geometric Functions

GLSL supports a number of functions to support geometric operations. These have an obvious application for graphics, since many of the basic graphical operations basically manipulate geometry. These functions include the familiar scalar functions for length and dot product, and the familiar vector operations for cross product and normalization. They also include less familiar vector operations for reflection, refraction, and faceforward that can be very useful.

`float length(genType x)`	Returns the length of the vector x, $\sqrt{(x[0]^2 + x[1]^2 + ...)}$.
`float distance(genType p0, genType p1)`	Returns the distance between $p0$ and $p1$: `length(p0 - p1)`.
`float dot(genType x, genType y)`	Returns the dot product of x and y: `x[0]*y[0]+x[1]*y[1]+... .`
`vec3 cross(vec3 x, vec3 y)`	Returns the cross product of x and y, $$\begin{bmatrix} x[1]y[2] - y[1]x[2] \\ x[2]y[0] - y[2]x[0] \\ x[0]y[1] - y[0]x[1] \end{bmatrix}.$$
`genType normalize(genType x)`	Returns a vector in the same direction as x, but with a length of 1, or $\dfrac{x}{\|x\|}$.
`genType faceforward( genType N, genType I, genType Nref)`	Make N face in the direction of $Nref$. If $dot(Nref, I) < 0$ return N, otherwise return $-N$.
`genType reflect(genType I, genType N)`	For the incident vector I and surface orientation N, returns the reflection direction: $I - 2 * dot(N,I) * N$. The normal vector N must already be normalized in order to achieve the correct result.

`genType refract(genType I, genType N, float eta)`	For the incident vector I and surface normal N, and the ratio of indices of refraction *eta*, return the refraction vector. The result is computed by
	
	`k=1.0-eta*eta*(1.0-dot(N,I)*dot(N,I))`
	`if (k < 0.0)`
	    `return genType(0.0)`
	`else`
	    `return eta*I-(eta*dot(N,I)+sqrt(k))*N.`
	
	The incident vector I and the normal vector N must already be normalized in order to achieve the correct result.

Matrix Functions

GLSL has several useful functions for matrices, including componentwise multiplication, the outer product, and the transpose. If no matrix type is otherwise specified, mat is used for any matrix type.

`mat matrixCompMult(mat x, mat y)`	Multiply matrix x by matrix y component-wise, so that *result[i][j]* is the scalar product of *x[i][j]* and *y[i][j]*. Note: to get linear algebraic matrix multiplication, use the multiply operator (*).

`mat2 outerProduct(vec2 c, vec2 r)`
`mat3 outerProduct(vec3 c, vec3 r)`
`mat4 outerProduct(vec4 c, vec4 r)`
`mat2x3 outerProduct(vec3 c, vec2 r)`
`mat3x2 outerProduct(vec2 c, vec3 r)`
`mat2x4 outerProduct(vec4 c, vec2 r)`
`mat4x2 outerProduct(vec2 c, vec4 r)`
`mat3x4 outerProduct(vec4 c, vec3 r)`
`mat4x3 outerProduct(vec3 c, vec4 r)`
	Treats the first parameter c as a column vector (matrix with one column) and the second parameter r as a row vector (matrix with one row) and does a linear algebraic matrix multiply $c * r$, yielding a matrix whose number of rows is the number of components in c and whose number of columns is the number of components in r.

`mat2 transpose(mat2 m)`
`mat3 transpose(mat3 m)`
`mat4 transpose(mat4 m)`
 	
`mat2x3 transpose(mat3x2 m)`
`mat3x2 transpose(mat2x3 m)`
`mat2x4 transpose(mat4x2 m)`
`mat4x2 transpose(mat2x4 m)`
`mat3x4 transpose(mat4x3 m)`
`mat4x3 transpose(mat3x4 m)`
	Returns a matrix that is the transpose of m; m need not be square, as is shown. The input matrix m is not modified.

Relational Functions for Vectors

GLSL extends the familiar relational operators for scalars to a set of relational functions for vectors. These compare vectors componentwise and return a bvec result that can be used for parallel comparisons. There are also several functions that can convert a bvec result to a single Boolean scalar. In these descriptions, *vec* is a real vector, *ivec* is an integer vector, and *bvec* is a Boolean vector, and their lengths are arbitrary except that in each case the lengths are equal.

`bvec lessThan(vec x, vec y)` `bvec lessThan(ivec x, ivec y)`	Returns the component-wise compare of $x < y$.
`bvec lessThanEqual(vec x, vec y)` `bvec lessThanEqual(ivec x, ivec y)`	Returns the component-wise compare of $x <= y$.
`bvec greaterThan(vec x, vec y)` `bvec greaterThan(ivec x, ivec y)`	Returns the component-wise compare of $x > y$.
`bvec greaterThanEqual(vec x, vec y)` `bvec greaterThanEqual(ivec x, ivec y)`	Returns the component-wise compare of $x >= y$.

`bvec equal(vec x, vec y)`
`bvec equal(ivec x, ivec y)`
`bvec equal(bvec x, bvec y)`
	Returns the component-wise compare of $x == y$.

`bvec notEqual(vec x, vec y)`
`bvec notEqual(ivec x, ivec y)`
`bvec notEqual(bvec x, bvec y)`
	Returns the component-wise compare of $x\ != y$.

`bool any(bvec x)`	The vector equivalent of the logical *or*, | —returns true if any component of x is true.
`bool all(bvec x)`	The vector equivalent of the logical *and*, & —returns true only if all components of x are true.
`bvec not(bvec x)`	The vector equivalent of the logical *not*, ! —returns the component-wise logical complement of x.

Texture Lookup Functions

The built-in texture lookup functions give you access to textures through samplers, as set up through the OpenGL API. A texture sampler is a GLSL uniform variable that has been previously associated with a particular texture unit. The texture unit acts as a pointer to the texture data itself and its sampling information, such as size, pixel format, number of dimensions, filtering methods, and number of mip-map levels. These texture properties are taken into account as the texture is accessed.

Texture lookup functions can be used by both vertex and fragment shaders. However, level of detail is not computed by fixed functionality for vertex shaders, so there are some differences in operation between vertex and fragment texture lookups.

The additional functions support texture lookups for shadow textures or for *level-of-detail* ("LOD") in shaders. Functions whose names include Lod are allowed only in vertex shaders. The bias term is optional for fragment shaders, but is not accepted for vertex shaders. If it is included, it is added to the level of detail before the texture access.

```vec4 texture(sampler1D sampler,\n float coord [, float bias])\nvec4 textureProj(sampler1D sampler,\n vec{2,4} coord [, float bias])\nvec4 textureLod(sampler1D sampler,\n float coord, float lod)\nvec4 textureProjLod(sampler1D sampler,\n vec{2,4} coord, float lod)```	Use the texture coordinate coord to do a texture lookup in the 1D texture currently bound to sampler. For the projective (Proj) versions, the texture coordinate coord.s is divided by the last component of coord.
```vec4 texture(sampler2D sampler,\n vec2 coord [, float bias])\nvec4 textureProj(sampler2D sampler,\n vec{3,4} coord [, float bias])\nvec4 textureLod(sampler2D sampler,\n vec2 coord, float lod)\nvec4 textureProjLod(sampler2D sampler,\n vec{3,4} coord, float lod)```	Use the texture coordinate coord to do a texture lookup in the 2D texture currently bound to sampler. For the projective (Proj) versions, the texture coordinate (coord.s, coord.t) is divided by the last component of coord. The third component of coord is ignored for the vec4 coord variant.
```vec4 texture(sampler3D sampler,\n vec3 coord [, float bias])\nvec4 textureProj(sampler3D sampler,\n vec4 coord [, float bias])\nvec4 textureLod(sampler3D sampler,\n vec3 coord, float lod)\nvec4 textureProjLod(sampler3D sampler,\n vec4 coord, float lod)```	Use the texture coordinate coord to do a texture lookup in the 3D texture currently bound to sampler. For the projective (Proj) versions, the texture coordinate is divided by coord.q.
```vec4 texture(samplerCube sampler,\n vec3 coord [, float bias])\nvec4 textureLod(samplerCube sampler,\n vec3 coord, float lod)```	Use the texture coordinate coord to do a texture lookup in the cube map texture currently bound to sampler. The direction of coord is used to select in which face to do a two-dimensional texture lookup.

```
vec4 shadow1D( sampler1DShadow sampler,
               vec3 coord [, float bias])
vec4 shadow2D( sampler2DShadow sampler,
               vec3 coord [, float bias])
vec4 shadow1DProj( sampler1DShadow sampler,
                   vec4 coord [, float bias])
vec4 shadow2DProj( sampler2DShadow sampler,
                   vec4 coord [, float bias])
vec4 shadow1DLod( sampler1DShadow sampler,
                  vec3 coord, float lod)
vec4 shadow2DLod( sampler2DShadow sampler,
                  vec3 coord, float lod)
vec4 shadow1DProjLod( sampler1DShadow sampler,
                      vec4 coord, float lod)
vec4 shadow2DProjLod( sampler2DShadow sampler,
                      vec4 coord, float lod)
```

Use the texture coordinate coord to do a depth comparison lookup on the depth texture bound to sampler, as described in Section 3.8.14 of Version 1.4 of the OpenGL specification. The third component of coord (coord.p) is used as the R value. The texture bound to sampler must be a depth texture, or results are undefined. For the projective (Proj) version of each built-in, the texture coordinate is divided by coord.q, giving a depth value R of coord.p/coord.q. The second component of coord is ignored for the 1D variants.

Fragment Processing Functions

GLSL fragment shaders can antialias procedural textures using a variety of techniques, including analytic prefiltering. To support this, GLSL includes functions that let you calculate the gradient of any parameter in screen space, and a function that gives you a value for the upper bound of the width of the sampling filter needed to eliminate aliasing.

genType dFdx(genType p)	Returns the derivative in x using local differencing for the input argument p.
genType dFdy(genType p)	Returns the derivative in y using local differencing for the input argument p.

These two functions are commonly used to estimate the filter width used to antialias procedural textures. It is assumed that the expression is being evaluated in parallel on a SIMD array, so that at any given point in time the value of the function is known at the grid points represented by the array. Local differencing between array elements can therefore be used to derive dFdx, dFdy, etc.

genType fwidth(genType p)	Returns the sum of the absolute derivative in x and y using local differencing for the input argument p, abs(dFdx(p)) + abs(dFdy(p));

Noise Functions

The GLSL language specification defines the noise functions shown here, but at this writing, it has not actually been implemented in all GLSL systems. While everyone agrees that there need to be built-in noise functions available, not everyone agrees on what would be the best specific implementation. This is why *glman* builds them in using 2D and 3D textures.

GLSL includes the built-in noise functions below, which can be used by both fragment and vertex shaders. The noise functions are pseudo-random stochastic functions that are C^1 continuous with range [–1., 1.] and mean 0.0, and they are deterministic for a given input. The output has the same statistical character if the domain is rotated or translated. The noise functions can readily be used to create textures that add to the visual complexity of a scene.

`float noise1(genType x)`	Returns a 1D noise value based on the input value x. At this time, this function is not available in GLSL.
`vec2 noise2(genType x)`	Returns a 2D noise value based on the input value x. At this time, this function is not available in GLSL.
`vec3 noise3 (genType x)`	Returns a 3D noise value based on the input value x.
`vec4 noise4 (genType x)`	Returns a 4D noise value based on the input value x.

Swizzle

An operation that is probably new to you is the *swizzle* operation. This lets you rearrange or reorganize the components of a vector in any way you want. This operation is specified by simply writing the components of a vector in any order you want, using one of the component name sets. For example, if m is a vec4, you can reverse the order of the components of m by writing m.wzyx, or you can duplicate some of the components of m by writing m.rrbb.

New Function Parameter Types

GLSL function parameters differ from the standard C "pass by value" approach. GLSL parameters are passed by *value-return*. This means that parameters' values may be copied into a function or may be returned by the function, or both, but unlike with "pass by reference" variables, there is no change to any of the actual parameters until the function returns. The function parameters are preceded by one of the keywords in, out, or inout; this comes before the type of the parameter.

The keywords' meanings are

- const: The value of the input parameter is copied to the formal parameter, but no change to the formal parameter is allowed in the function.
- in: The value of the actual parameter is copied to the formal parameter, but no changed value will be returned. The actual parameter may be an expression that sets the value to be copied into the function. The formal parameter may be changed during the execution of the function. The keyword in may be preceded by const, in which case the formal parameter will be treated as a const in the function.
- out: The formal parameter must be an lvalue and will have no value until it is set inside the function. Any function operations may use this parameter, but a value must be set in the function. The value of the formal parameter in the function is copied to the actual parameter when the function terminates.
- inout: The formal parameter must be an lvalue and is assumed to have a value when it is copied to the function, and this value may be used or changed during the function execution. When the function terminates, the value of the formal parameter is copied to the actual parameter.

Const

The *const* data type lets you declare named compile-time constants. Any variables qualified by const are read-only variables for that shader and must be initialized when declared; the initial values must be constant expressions. The const qualifier can be used with any of the basic data types. As in C++, using const is good programming style because it is strongly typed and it will cause the compiler to throw an error if you attempt to re-assign a value to something you originally expected should never get reassigned.

GLSL has several built-in const variables for vertex and fragment shaders. The values given for initialization are implementation-dependent and are the minimum values allowed.

```
const int gl_MaxLights = 8;
const int gl_MaxClipPlanes = 6;
const int gl_MaxTextureUnits = 2;
const int gl_MaxTextureCoords = 2;
const int gl_MaxVertexAttribs = 16;
const int gl_MaxVertexUniformComponents = 512;
const int gl_MaxVaryingFloats = 32;
const int gl_MaxVertexTextureImageUnits = 0;
const int gl_MaxCombinedTextureImageUnits = 2;
const int gl_MaxTextureImageUnits = 2;
const int gl_MaxFragmentUniformComponents = 64;
const int gl_MaxDrawBuffers = 1;
```

Compatibility Mode

OpenGL 4.1 has replaced a number of features of the 2.x and 3.x standards with much more general functionality. This has increased the power, efficiency, and generality of the standard, but requires much more planning and setup than the earlier standard. If you are maintaining OpenGL code that was based on the 2.x and 3.x standards, or if you simply want to write quick shaders to test out some ideas, you may want to work in what is called *compatibility mode*: a mode in which you can use the earlier OpenGL functionality.

Defining Compatibility Mode

It is quite straightforward to specify that a shader is to be run in compatibility mode. If you are working in OpenGL 4.x, you can simply put the line

```
#version 400 compatibility
```

at the top of any shader source. If you are working in OpenGL 3.3, a similar command can be used:

```
#version 330 compatibility
```

Then you can use any functionality you like from the OpenGL 2.1 standard.

Among the things you might find most useful from the earlier standard is the set of built-in data. These let you pick up attribute and uniform variables that are defined by OpenGL 2.1 functions so you can use them easily in your shaders.

OpenGL 2.1 Built-in Data Types

GLSL originally included some completely new data types that correspond to functions needed to manage data flow across the spectrum of an application, the OpenGL API, the onboard data on a graphics card, and the needs of vertex and fragment shaders. These types are available in OpenGL 2.1 or in compatibility mode for later versions, and are named *attribute*, *uniform*, and *varying*. Their function is described in this section.

In general, you can differentiate these data types by how often the data they represent change. *Uniform* data changes infrequently and never within a graphics primitive; *attribute* data changes frequently, often as frequently as each vertex; and *varying* data changes most frequently, with each fragment as it's interpolated by the rasterizer.

Attribute

The *attribute* data qualifier lets you access per-vertex data passed to the graphics card by the OpenGL API functions. Attribute variables have only *float*, *vec*, and *mat* data types, and cannot be declared as arrays or structs. Attribute variables are only accessible in a vertex shader and are read-only for that shader. They must have global scope and must be declared outside of function bodies before they are first used.

Originally, GLSL had built-in variable names for all the standard OpenGL vertex attributes to give you easy access to data defined by OpenGL vertex functions. These are

```
attribute vec4 gl_Color;
attribute vec3 gl_Normal;
attribute vec4 gl_Vertex;
attribute vec4 gl_MultiTexCoordi; // i = 0..7
```

Uniform

The *uniform* qualifier identifies global variables whose values are constant across a graphics primitive. This can be used with any of the basic data types, or when declaring a variable whose type is a structure, or an array of any of these. Uniform variables are read-only for all shaders and are initialized externally either at link time or through the OpenGL API.

GLSL has a large set of built-in uniform variables that let you access the graphics states set by the OpenGL API in your application. These are listed below in groups that access similar states.

Primary matrices. OpenGL maintains four primary matrices that are available to your shaders:

```
uniform mat4 gl_ModelViewMatrix;
uniform mat4 gl_ProjectionMatrix;
uniform mat4 gl_ModelViewProjectionMatrix;
uniform mat4 gl_TextureMatrix[gl_MaxTextureCoords];
```

Derived matrices. OpenGL computes a number of other matrices that are used in various geometry processing steps. Some of these are inverses or transposes of the primary matrices, and you should be aware that if the primary matrix is poorly conditioned, the inverses may have unpredictable values. These derived matrices are available to your shaders:

```
uniform mat3 gl_NormalMatrix; // transpose of inverse of
                              // the upper leftmost 3x3 of
                              // gl_ModelViewMatrix
uniform mat4 gl_ModelViewMatrixInverse;
uniform mat4 gl_ProjectionMatrixInverse;
uniform mat4 gl_ModelViewProjectionMatrixInverse;
uniform mat4 gl_TextureMatrixInverse[gl_MaxTextureCoords];
uniform mat4 gl_ModelViewMatrixTranspose;
uniform mat4 gl_ProjectionMatrixTranspose;
uniform mat4 gl_ModelViewProjectionMatrixTranspose;
uniform mat4 gl_TextureMatrixTranspose
   [gl_MaxTextureCoords];
uniform mat4 gl_ModelViewMatrixInverseTranspose;
uniform mat4 gl_ProjectionMatrixInverseTranspose;
uniform mat4 gl_ModelViewProjectionMatrixInverseTranspose;
uniform mat4 gl_TextureMatrixInverseTranspose
   [gl_MaxTextureCoords];
```

Normal scaling. If your application does its own normal scaling instead of relying on the normalization operation, you can access that normal scaling factor:

```
uniform float gl_NormalScale;
```

Front and back clipping planes. When you specify your projection in OpenGL, you specify the front and back clipping planes, and hence the depth of these planes. This data is available to your shaders:

```
struct gl_DepthRangeParameters
{
  float near; // n
  float far; // f
  float diff; // f - n
};
uniform gl_DepthRangeParameters gl_DepthRange;
```

Clip planes. OpenGL allows you to define clipping planes in your scene by specifying the equation of the plane as four real numbers. This data is available to your shaders:

```
uniform vec4 gl_ClipPlane[gl_MaxClipPlanes];
```

Point parameters. In OpenGL you can specify the properties of a geometric point. This data is available to your shaders:

```
struct gl_PointParameters
{
   float size;
   float sizeMin;
   float sizeMax;
   float fadeThresholdSize;
   float distanceConstantAttenuation;
   float distanceLinearAttenuation;
   float distanceQuadraticAttenuation;
};
uniform gl_PointParameters gl_Point;
```

In the items below, we introduce some shortcut names for a number of properties of materials and lights. These are used to show how the later derived materials states are computed.

Materials. When you use the OpenGL lighting model, you specify properties of the materials that make up a graphics primitive. This data is available to your shaders:

```
struct gl_MaterialParameters
{
   vec4 emission;        // Ecm
   vec4 ambient;         // Acm
   vec4 diffuse;         // Dcm
   vec4 specular;        // Scm
   float shininess;      // Srm
};
uniform gl_MaterialParameters gl_FrontMaterial;
uniform gl_MaterialParameters gl_BackMaterial;
```

Lights. When you specify a light in OpenGL, you specify a number of properties, from the light's colors to the light's position, to the type of light it is to be. You also specify the kind of light model to be used. This data is available to your shaders:

```
struct gl_LightSourceParameters
{
   vec4 ambient;         // Acli
   vec4 diffuse;         // Dcli
   vec4 specular;        // Scli
```

```
    vec4 position;     // Ppli
    vec4 halfVector;        // Derived: Hi
    vec3 spotDirection;     // Sdli
    float spotExponent;     // Srli
    float spotCutoff;       // Crli

// (range: [0.0,90.0], 180.0)
    float spotCosCutoff;  // Derived: cos(Crli)
// (range: [1.0,0.0],-1.0)
    float constantAttenuation; // K0
    float linearAttenuation;   // K1
    float quadraticAttenuation;  // K2
};
uniform gl_LightSourceParameters gl_LightSource
    [gl_MaxLights];

struct gl_LightModelParameters
{
    vec4 ambient;           // Acs
};
uniform gl_LightModelParameters gl_LightModel;
```

Derived materials state. These states are products of the light and material that are used for actual color computations:

```
struct gl_LightModelProducts
{
    vec4 sceneColor;  // Derived. Ecm + Acm * Acs
};
uniform gl_LightModelProducts gl_FrontLightModelProduct;
uniform gl_LightModelProducts gl_BackLightModelProduct;

struct gl_LightProducts
{
    vec4 ambient;       // Acm * Acli
    vec4 diffuse;       // Dcm * Dcli
    vec4 specular;      // Scm * Scli
};
uniform gl_LightProducts gl_FrontLightProduct
    [gl_MaxLights];
uniform gl_LightProducts gl_BackLightProduct[gl_MaxLights];
```

Texture environment. This set of GLSL built-in uniform variables gives you the colors that are produced by each texture unit and the coordinates of the eye plane or object plane for eye-linear or object-linear textures, respectively.

```
uniform vec4 gl_TextureEnvColor[gl_MaxTextureUnits];
uniform vec4 gl_EyePlaneS[gl_MaxTextureCoords];
      // eye linear
uniform vec4 gl_EyePlaneT[gl_MaxTextureCoords];
uniform vec4 gl_EyePlaneR[gl_MaxTextureCoords];
uniform vec4 gl_EyePlaneQ[gl_MaxTextureCoords];
uniform vec4 gl_ObjectPlaneS[gl_MaxTextureCoords];
      // object linear
uniform vec4 gl_ObjectPlaneT[gl_MaxTextureCoords];
uniform vec4 gl_ObjectPlaneR[gl_MaxTextureCoords];
uniform vec4 gl_ObjectPlaneQ[gl_MaxTextureCoords];
```

Fog. All the GLSL fog parameters set by the graphics API are available to your shaders:

```
struct gl_FogParameters
{
  vec4 color;
  float density;
  float start;
  float end;
  float scale; // Derived: 1.0 / (end - start)
};
```

Varying

GLSL's varying variables provide communication from vertex shaders to fragment shaders. Vertex shaders compute information for each vertex and write them to varying variables to be interpolated across a graphics primitive and then used by a fragment shader. GLSL specifies that default interpolations of varying variables must be done in a perspective-correct manner, so the problems of perspective correction that we saw in Chapter 1 are not part of GLSL. Only those varying variables used in the fragment shader must be written by the previous shader in the shader pipeline, but that previous shader may also declare other varying variables. A fragment shader cannot write to a varying variable.

The varying qualifier can be used only with float variables, floating-point vectors, matrices, or arrays of these. Structures cannot be varying. Varying variables must have global scope and must be declared outside of function bodies.

Varying variables may be defined using a modifier that describes how they are interpolated across a fragment. These modifiers are flat, noperspective, and centroid, and were discussed earlier in this chapter.

Summary

We have seen that GLSL is a language that looks familiar enough to be used easily, but that it has a significant number of new features that make writing shaders possible—and that are easy enough to use that it's straightforward to get started by writing shaders that do interesting things. Like OpenGL, it has enough capability that you will likely never run out of ways to add sophistication and new features to your shaders, or to create every effect that it can give you. This chapter should familiarize you with the basic operation of GLSL and should be a useful reference for you, but only when you actually begin to use the language to write shaders will you really understand the graphical power it gives you.

Exercises

1. For the following table of operator and operand type, indicate which operator can legally operate on the operands given. For each one that is legal, create an example of the two operands and show the result of the operation.

Operator	Left Operand	Right Operand	Result
+	mat2	float	:
+	vec3	ivec3	:
*	vec2	mat2	:
*	mat3x4	mat4x3	:

2. For the following table of functions and parameter type(s), indicate whether the function can legally act on the parameter(s) given. For each case where the function can legally act, identify the type of the return value, give an example of the function applied to the parameter(s) and show the returned value of the function.

	Function name	Parameter(s)
a.	pow	vec4, vec4
b.	mod	vec3, float
c.	cross	vec3, vec3
d.	outerProduct	mat2x3, mat3x4
e.	notEqual	float, vec4

3. Use GLSL operators to write three different ways to calculate the distance between two points.

4. Diagram the data flow that describes how geometric data gets from an application, through the OpenGL API, to the graphics card, to a vertex shader, to a fragment shader, and finally to a single pixel that is output to the graphics color buffer.

5. Write constructors to create new variables from old ones, using either the scalar, vector, or matrix constructors described in this chapter.

   a. Construct an integer I from a float F.

   b. Construct a vec3 from three ints.

   c. Construct a vec2 as the middle two components of a vec4.

   d. Construct a mat4 with the first row a set of four floats and with the remaining part of each column given by a vec3.

6. Write statements you could use in a GLSL shader to convert a vec4 color to a grayscale color with the same alpha value. Is there a difference in how you would do this for a vertex shader and for a fragment shader?

6

Lighting

The simplest way to perform lighting is by computing it per-vertex, which would place responsibility for most of the work squarely on the shoulders of the vertex shader. If lighting is performed this way, the color is computed based on light and material properties that determine the color of each vertex based on the standard *ambient-diffuse-specular* (*ADS*) lighting model. This per-vertex color can be used for either flat or smooth shading. However, if a more complex shading model is to be used, such as Phong or anisotropic shading, the color computation will probably be deferred until the fragment shader, where per-pixel color can be computed.

In this chapter, we will discuss both per-vertex and per-fragment lighting methods.

The ADS Lighting Model

This lighting model is the basis for fixed-function OpenGL lighting, and we want to see how to handle this in shaders you write yourself. You were probably introduced to this in your beginning computer graphics course, but let's review it to be sure we're all using the same terminology and notation. The three kinds of light used in this model are

- *Ambient* light, or light that is always present at all points in a scene.
- *Diffuse* light, or light that comes directly from a light source.
- *Specular* light, or light that is reflected in a "shiny" way from a light source by an object.

Each of these kinds of light contributes to the overall lighting at any point in a separate way. The general context for these contributions is shown in Figure 6.1, which illustrates a point on a surface with normalized (unit) vectors from the point to the eye, $\hat{E}$; from the point to a light source, $\hat{L}$; the normal to the surface at the point, $\hat{N}$; and the reflected light direction $\hat{R}$.

Ambient light contributes to the lighting as a product of the ambient light itself L_A and the ambient light color of the material being lighted M_A:

$$A = L_A * M_A.$$

Diffuse light contributes to the lighting as a product of the diffuse light itself L_D, the diffuse light color of the material being lighted M_D, and the cosine of the angle Θ between the light and the normal, $(\hat{L} \bullet \hat{N})$:

$$D = L_D * M_D * (\hat{L} \bullet \hat{N}).$$

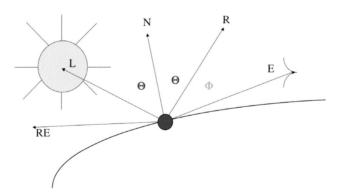

Figure 6.1. The setup for ADS lighting.

Specular light contributes to the lighting as a product of the specular light itself L_S, the specular light color of the material being lighted M_S, and a power (the "shininess" coefficient SH) of the cosine of the angle Φ between the eye vector and the light reflection vector, $(\hat{R} \bullet \hat{E})^{SH}$:

$$S = L_S * M_S * (\hat{R} \bullet \hat{E})^{SH}.$$

Then the total lighting at the point is the sum of these:

$$A + D + S = L_A * M_A + L_D * M_D * (\hat{L} \bullet \hat{N}) + L_S * M_S * (\hat{R} \bullet \hat{E})^{SH}.$$

The reflection vector R is calculated by $R = 2(\hat{N} \bullet \hat{L})\hat{N} - \hat{L}$. Details on how these individual formulas are derived may be found in any introductory graphics text, such as [14]. Also, GLSL has a built-in function called `reflect( )`, which will do this for you.

This model can also take into account attenuation, or the reduction in light intensity with distance. OpenGL models this with three factors: a constant attenuation A_C, a linear attenuation A_L, and a quadratic attenuation A_Q. If a point is at a distance D from a light, the overall attenuation A is calculated as

$$A = \frac{1}{A_C + A_L D + A_Q D^2}.$$

The distance can be calculated from the light and vertex positions in eye space, and this value of A then multiplies the diffuse and specular terms above.

In the ADS lighting function in the next section, we use the reflected-light formulation because we have access to the reflection for each pixel, using the GLSL function `reflect( )` to compute the reflection vector. However, fixed-function OpenGL uses the half-angle formulation for specular light because it is easier to compute for each vertex.

The ADS Lighting Model Function

Below is a function that computes the color at a vertex based on the ADS lighting model with standard light and material definitions. It is intended for use with *glman*, so it uses stubs for the values it would get from another source. These stubbed values would come from system uniform variables, as noted in the function's comments.

You can use this function in a vertex shader if you are computing the color at each vertex, as you would if you were planning to interpolate the color across the graphics primitive, as in smooth shading, or you can use it in a fragment shader if you are computing the color at each pixel for Phong shading. These two kinds of shading were discussed earlier in this chapter. Because we have not yet talked about the GLSL programming API, we have stubbed in the light and materials definitions in the function, indicating where they would come from if this were part of a graphics application.

```
//Assumed context:
//uniform variables uLightsource[i] and uFrontMaterial are
//stubbed with constant values below. These would probably be
//passed into the shader function if used in an application.
//
//variables myNormal and myPosition are passed in; in a vertex
//shader these would be computed and used directly, while in a
//fragment shader these would be set by the associated vertex
//shader.
//
//the ADS color is returned from the function

vec3 ADSLightModel( in vec3 myNormal, in vec3 myPosition )
{
  const vec3 myLightPosition       = vec3( 1. , 0.5, 0.  );

  const vec3 myLightAmbient        = vec3( 0.2, 0.2, 0.2 );
  const vec3 myLightDiffuse        = vec3( 1. , 1. , 1 . );
  const vec3 myLightSpecular       = vec3( 1. , 1. , 1.  );

  const vec3 myMaterialAmbient     = vec3( 1. , 0.5, 0.  );
  const vec3 myMaterialDiffuse     = vec3( 1. , 0.5, 0.  );
  const vec3 myMaterialSpecular    = vec3( 0.6, 0.6, 0.6 );

  const float myMaterialShininess = 80.;

//normal, light, view, and light reflection vectors
  vec3 norm   = normalize( myNormal );
  vec3 lightv = normalize( myLightPosition - myPosition);
  vec3 viewv  = normalize( vec3(0.,0.,0.) - myPosition );
  vec3 refl   = reflect( vec3(0.,0.,0.) - lightv, norm );
//ambient light computation
  vec3 ambient = myMaterialAmbient*myLightAmbient;

//diffuse light computation
  vec3 diffuse = max(0.0, dot(lightv, norm)) * myMaterialDiffuse
                 *myLightDiffuse;

//Optionally you can add a diffuse attenuation term at this
//point
```

```
//specular light computation
  vec3 specular = vec3( 0.0, 0.0, 0.0 );
  if( dot(lightv, viewv) > 0.0)
  {
    specular = pow(max(0.0, dot(viewv,refl)),
                   myMaterialShininess)*myMaterialSpecular*
                   myLightSpecular;
  }
  return clamp( ambient + diffuse + specular, 0.0, 1.0);
}
```

This calculation does not take into account lighting attenuation. If you want to include attenuation, you can enhance this computation by computing the distance to the light and getting the light's constant, linear, and quadratic attenuation terms as uniform variables, and then computing

```
1./(constant + linear*distance + quadratic*distance*distance)
```

as a multiplier of the diffuse and specular components, as described above. (Attenuation does not act on the ambient light component.)

These computations use simple vector addition and subtraction, not homogeneous addition and subtraction, because we want to keep this simple. If you want to make them fully general, you would need to replace these with homogeneous vector addition and subtraction, as we discussed in Chapter 1. This would be necessary, for instance, if you have a directional light source (which acts as if it were placed at infinity).

Types of Lights

Since the fixed-function pipeline does all the color computations at the vertex processing stage, whenever you use shaders to replace fixed-function operations, you must handle lighting yourself. Besides the full ADS lighting model, there are other issues in lighting because OpenGL supports spot lights and directional lights, as well as positional lights. To be able to replace fixed-function lighting computations, you must have ways to handle all the options that you plan to use. If you are using lighting, you are probably using material properties as well.

Overall, the OpenGL API gives you ways to define color, lights, and material properties that are treated globally in the graphics system. So you may define a light position, a color, etc. using the API calls to set their global properties, so that any shader can pick them up. We have often used an alternate approach of

Recall our assumption that in our example shader code, we use general attribute and uniform variables with our first-letter naming convention instead of the built-in OpenGL variable names. These names are close enough to the built-in variable names that you can easily convert them if you are working in compatibility mode.

setting discrete uniform variables in our examples, because we can then put them on sliders so that you can experiment with them. In applications, though, you should probably take the more global OpenGL API approach. This will be described in Chapter 14.

Positional Lights

The most common kind of lighting in OpenGL scenes is with positional lights. Each light has position, color, and a number of other values.

For positional lights, the primary consideration is the direction from a vertex to the light source, and you can get that by a simple vector subtraction so you can make it an out vector in the vertex shader and pass it to the fragment shader. Alternately, you can make the vertex position in eye space an out variable so the fragment shader can use the ADS lighting function. Your choice will probably depend on the effect you are trying to achieve. As we will see in examples below, you can get traditional smooth shading by computing the light direction at each vertex and defining the color as an out variable in a vertex (or tessellation) shader, while you can get Phong shading by defining the normal as an out variable and interpolating either the vertex position or the light direction for each pixel.

Lighting Method	Vertex Shader Does	Rasterizer Interpolates	Fragment Shader Does
Per-vertex	Lighting model	Color	Applies color
Per-fragment	Setup	Normal and EC position	Lighting model

Directional Lights

If you use directional lights or spot lights, the necessary data for using these kinds of lights can be found in the components of the built-in uniform uLightSource[i] struct. Directional lights, also called *parallel light sources*, are treated in almost the same way as positional lights, except that the direction to the light is always the same, regardless of the position of a point. This simplifies the light direction in any lighting computation by letting you use the light direction directly, instead of computing the direction between the point and the light position. Conceptually, for a directional light, you simply treat the light as a homogeneous point at infinity.

Spot Lights

Spot lights include specifications for the direction, cutoff, and attenuation. To use a spot light, you must compute the angle between the light direction and the direction from the light to the vertex. By comparing that to the light's cutoff angle and using the light's attenuation, you can then determine the value of the light at the vertex. This requires the vertex shader to send both the light

position and the light direction to the fragment shader, and the fragment shader must calculate the angle between the light direction and the vector from the light to the point in order to see whether to use the light in the color computation.

In the vertex shader example below, you can see the kind of computation that is needed to compute the light intensity for a spot light. The color always includes the ambient light, and it uses diffuse and specular light for the particular light source only if the point is close enough to the light direction. The effect of spot lighting is shown in Figure 6.2, where the light shines on only part of the geometric primitive, but we omit the specular contribution in this case to simplify the computation.

A vertex shader for lighting with a spot light or directional light (or both) requires us to manage that lighting function ourselves. The fixed-function OpenGL spot light on the standard teapot is shown in Figure 6.2 (top), while we can use the capabilities of GLSL and the vertex shader to create the "fuzzy" spot light shown in Figure 6.2 (bottom). The vertex shader for this example has only three things to do:

Figure 6.2. The effect of a spot light on a teapot that lies on the edge of the light's illumination area. Traditional OpenGL spot light (top) and a spot light with a fuzzy edge (bottom).

- Copy the color from the attribute variable aColor to an out variable such as vColor.
- Set an out variable such as vLightIntensity with the light intensity based on diffuse lighting computations at this vertex.
- Set an out variable such as vECposition with the eye coordinates of the vertex.

The fragment shader carries out all the interesting computations that simulate spot lighting for *glman* use. The positions of the light, the eye, and a focal point of the light are set in eye space to define two vectors that meet at the focal point, and uniform slider variables are used to set the angle of the light and the horizontal location (the variable LeftRight) of the light focal point. The cosine of the angle set by the vectors is compared with the cosine of the cutoff angle in a smoothstep( ) function to determine the amount of diffuse light to include for each pixel. The simulation uses a number of parameters that would normally be taken from the uniform lighting variables provided by the system. See the GLSL API for more details.

```
uniform float uAngle;
uniform float uLeftRight;
uniform float uWidth;

in vec4   vColor;
in float  vLightIntensity;
in vec3   vECposition;

out vec4 fFragColor;

const vec4  LIGHTPOS   = vec4(0.,0.,40.,1.);
const float AMBCOEFF   = 0.5;
          // simulate ambient reflection coefficient
const float DIFFCOEFF = 0.6;
          // simulate diffuse reflection coefficient

void main( )
{
  // stubs for data in system attribute variables
  // simulate MC light position

  vec3   ECLightTarget  = vec3( uModelViewMatrix *
                    vec4( uLeftRight, 0., 1.5, 1. ) );
  vec3   LightDirection = normalize( ECLightTarget - LIGHTPOS );
  vec3   EyeDirection   = normalize( vECposition   - LIGHTPOS );

  // Ambient only
```

```
    fFragColor = vLightIntensity*AMBCOEFF*vColor;

    // Add diffuse light based on spotlight
    float myAngleCosine  = dot( LightDirection, EyeDirection );
    float CutoffCosine   = cos( radians(uAngle) );
    float BlendFactor    = smoothstep( CutoffCosine - uWidth,
                     CutoffCosine + uWidth, myAngleCosine);

    fFragColor += DIFFCOEFF*BlendFactor*vColor*vLightIntensity;
}
```

Of course, in an application, uAngle and uWidth would be passed to the shader as uniform variables from the application, and it would be better to compute the value of CutoffCosine there, instead of for each pixel. We do it as above in order to take advantage of *glman*.

Setting Up Lighting for Shading

Shading is the process of determining the color of each pixel in each primitive in your scene. This is actually carried out in the fragment processing part of the graphics processor that we described in Figure 1.5, but the vertex processor must set up the right environment for the kind of shading that you will implement. In this section, we will discuss some kinds of shading and how they are set up. In our discussion, we will draw on several shader concepts from Chapter 2.

The standard shading models available in fixed-function OpenGL are limited. They are *flat shading*, where a polygon is given a single color, and *smooth shading*, where the colors at the vertices of the polygon are interpolated to fill its interior. These are far from the only kinds of shading that have been used in the graphics field, but they are enough for many kinds of graphics work. More sophisticated shading is discussed later in this chapter and in Chapter 8.

Recall from the discussions in Chapter 1 that the fixed-function vertex processor must set a color for each vertex, and that the fragment processor can only interpolate vertex colors. This gives us our first two kinds of shading: flat shading and smooth shading. However, if we have vertex and fragment shaders, we can set up out variables in the vertex shader so that the fragment shader can interpolate other information and compute each pixel's color directly. This gives us two other kinds of shading: Phong shading and anisotropic shading.

Flat Shading

Flat shading is a type of per-vertex color computation. In order to use flat shading for a graphics primitive, the vertex shader will determine a color for a particular vertex (called the *provoking vertex*) and pass it forward to the fragment processor. The color will not be interpolated across the fragments. The color can come from an aColor attribute variable, or it could come from a lighting calculation, as described below.

In early versions of GLSL, it was not possible to specify flat shading, and flat shading was seen as an operation that would be done by fixed-function processing outside the GLSL shaders. However, GLSL has added a keyword flat to the GLSL language, defining a variable type called *flat out variables*. These variables may be passed to a fragment shader and call for the variable's value not to be interpolated across a graphics primitive during fragment processing. Our familiar teapot is shown in Figure 6.3 with flat shading, a look that may be familiar from your own beginning graphics work.

Figure 6.3. The familiar teapot with flat shading.

Vertex shaders that use flat out varying variables differ little from those you are already familiar with. An example vertex shader is shown below, which computes light intensity from the standard diffuse technique and passes this intensity to a fragment shader through the flat out variable vLightIntensity. Compare this with the vertex shader you saw early in the book to create Figure 2.2.

```
uniform vec3 uLightPos;

flat out float vLightIntensity;

void main( )
{
    vec3 transNorm  = normalize( uNormalMatrix * aNormal );
    vec3 ECposition = ( uModelViewMatrix * aVertex ).xyz;
    vLightIntensity = dot(normalize(uLightPos-
                                      ECposition),transNorm);
    vLightIntensity = abs(vLightIntensity);
    gl_Position     = uModelViewProjectionMatrix * aVertex;
}
```

Smooth (Gouraud) Shading

Smooth shading is another kind of per-vertex color computation. In order to use smooth shading (also known as *Gouraud shading*) for a graphics primitive, the vertex shader must determine a color for each vertex as above and pass that color as an out variable to the fragment processor. The color can be determined from the ADS lighting model by using the function we gave earlier in this chapter, or it can simply be defined in an application through a color attribute variable. Because the color is passed to the fragment shader as an in varying variable, it is interpolated across the fragments that make up the primitive, thus giving the needed smooth shading. Below, we see a very simple vertex shader that computes the out variable vColor using the ADSLightModel function and makes it available to a fragment shader. Figure 6.4 shows the familiar teapot with Gouraud shading; it is clear that this is the smooth shading we are used to seeing in fixed-function shading.

Figure 6.4. The familiar teapot with smooth (Gouraud) shading.

```
out vec3 vColor;

// use vec3 ADSLightModel here

void main( )
{
   vec3 transNorm = normalize( uNormalMatrix * aNormal );
   vec3 ECpos     = ( uModelViewMatrix * aVertex ).xyz;

   vColor         = ADSLightModel( transNorm, ECpos );

   gl_Position    = uModelViewProjectionMatrix * aVertex;
}
```

The specular highlight in Gouraud-shaded figures are often not smooth, but show the typical smooth-shading effect of differing interpolations across neighboring primitives that leads to Mach banding on polygon edges. We will see much better results in the next section when we develop Phong shading.

Phong Shading

Phong shading is a per-fragment color computation, and is a capability missing from the fixed-function OpenGL system. In true Phong shading, the vertex normals are interpolated across a graphics primitive, and the ADS lighting model is applied separately at each individual pixel. In order to do that, the

lighting model's key variables must be evaluated and set up as out variables during vertex processing. The vertex shader code below sets up the normal and position data for the ADS lighting model function in out variables, so that a fragment shader can interpolate these variables and use them in the ADSLightModel( ) function to compute the color. The actual fragment shader that implements this lighting is shown in Chapter 8. In Figure 6.5, you can see the smooth specular highlight that you expect from Phong shading.

Figure 6.5. The familiar teapot with Phong shading.

```
out vec3 vNormal;
out vec3 vECpos;

void main( )
{
   vNormal    = normalize( uNormalMatrix * aNormal );
   vECpos     = ( uModelViewMatrix * aVertex ).xyz;
   gl_Position = uModelViewProjectionMatrix * aVertex;
}
```

This specular computation uses the unit reflection vector, $\hat{R}$, which changes with each pixel. An alternative approach computes the "half angle" — the vector $\hat{H}$ halfway between the light $\hat{L}$ and the eye $\hat{E}$ vectors — and uses the cosine of the angle Φ between $\hat{H}$ and the normal $\hat{N}$. If the angle Φ is zero, the cosine is 1 and the light is reflected directly to the eye. As the angle increases, the cosine decreases. Again, a power of that cosine is used to control the size of the specular highlight. So we could replace the specular term in the model by the expression

$$S = L_S * M_S * (\hat{N} \bullet \hat{H})^{SH}.$$

The half angle vector $\hat{H}$ is computed as the average of the unitized L and E vectors, which in GLSL is expressed as normalize(L + E), and the term $(\hat{N} \bullet \hat{H})^{SH}$ that provides the shiny appearance of specular light is slightly differ-

Figure 6.6. Specular lighting with the half-angle formulation (left) and full-angle formulation (right).

ent from the similar term in the reflection vector formulation. In general, the half-angle formulation for specularity gives a slightly less-focused specular highlight than the reflected-light version. Since the shininess coefficient *SH* is simply an approximation that is adjusted for visual effect anyway, the difference is only qualitative. You can see this qualitative difference in Figure 6.6, which shows the half-angle formulation on the left, and the full-angle formulation on the right.

In fact, it is sometimes possible to get even better shading than Phong shading. For some kinds of applications, it is possible to compute exact normals at each pixel instead of simply interpolating vertex normals. We call this *exact shading*, and we discuss it further in Chapter 8.

Anisotropic Shading

Anisotropic shading is another per-pixel color computation that is not available in fixed-function OpenGL. Anisotropic shading is shading in which specular light is not reflected equally in all directions from the surface. An example of this is shown in Figure 6.7, which simulates a sphere for which light is reflected more strongly in a direction perpendicular to the arc from the poles through the point. Note that the bright spot in the figure is not circular because the material has different properties in different directions. Materials such as fur, hair, and brushed metal behave this way [22].

If you are writing shaders to implement anisotropic shading, the vertex shader must send the usual information, such as the normal, the eye position, and the light position, into the fragment shader, in the same way as would be done for Phong shading. In addition, the fragment shader must get whatever extra information is needed to describe the directional reflection; in this case, that is the tangent vector to the sphere normal to the polar arc through the point. The fragment shader then carries out the ambient and diffuse light computations for regular ADS lighting and computes the specular part of the light based on the new light direction.

The particular kind of anisotropic shading shown in Figure 6.7 is a computer graphics "classic," going back to the late 1980s. The specular reflection is not given by the usual term

$$S = L_S * M_S * (\hat{R} \bullet \hat{E})^{SH},$$

but by the term

$$dl = \hat{T} \bullet \hat{L},$$

$$de = \hat{T} \bullet \hat{E},$$

$$S = L_S * M_S * (dl * de + (\sqrt{1 - dl * dl}) * (\sqrt{1 - de * de}))^{SH},$$

where $\hat{T}$ is the tangent vector (the direction of the brushing or hair), $\hat{L}$ is the light vector, $\hat{E}$ is the eye vector, and SH is the shininess. In the code snippet below, taken from the fragment shader, the values of the tangent, light, and eye vectors, and the value of vColor, are assumed to have been computed separately in the associated vertex shader. The anisotropic shading parameters uKa, uKd, and uKs are assumed to be passed into the shader, and the color vColor is used for all three components of the ADS lighting model.

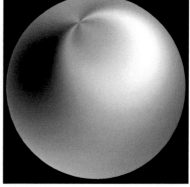

Figure 6.7. Anisotropic lighting in human hair (left); a sphere with anisotropic shading (right).

```
vec3 ambient = vColor.rgb;

float dl = dot( That, Lhat );
vec3 diffuse = sqrt( 1. - dl*dl ) * vColor.rgb;

float de = dot( That, Ehat );
vec3 spec = uLightColor * pow(dl * de +
    sqrt(1. - dl*dl) * sqrt(1. - de*de), uShininess);

fFragColor = vec4( uKa*ambient + uKd*diffuse + uKs*spe, 1. );
```

Exercises

1. Compare the tradeoffs between granularity and shading quality, specifically between smooth and Phong shading. Create a model with a granularity you can adjust, and see if you can identify the granularity of smooth shading that is indistinguishable from Phong shading.

2. In the text, we say that the specular light computation using the reflection vector gives you a smaller specular highlight than the computation using the half-angle vector when the same specularity exponent is used. Modify the ADS lighting function in the text to use the half-angle formulation, and verify this statement. Add a slider for the shininess exponent to the GLIB file for the Phong shader, and see if you can quantify the relation between the exponents for the two formulations that give the same look.

3. Modify the ADS light function to use homogeneous vector computations throughout. Is this enough to make it work with directional as well as positional lights? If not, modify it further to support directional lights.

4. In the spotlight example in the text, we simply used ambient and diffuse light. Modify this shader to use the ADS light function and compute specular light as well.

5. Suppose that you had a material that reflected light from a sphere differently from the anisotropic example above: the light is reflected in a direction tangent to the sphere toward the poles. Write a shader to implement this kind of lighting.

7

Vertex Shaders

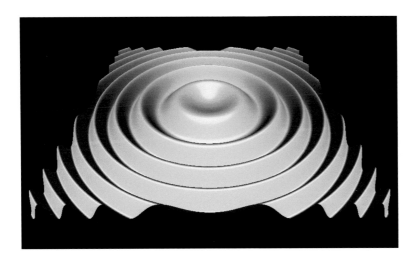

In fixed-function OpenGL, the vertex processing in the graphics pipeline is responsible for taking the model-space geometry you define, along with whatever color, lighting, materials, shading, and texture information you specify, and creating a set of vertices in clip space that have color, depth, normal, and texture associated with each. The role of the vertex shader is shown in Figure 7.1. The vertex shader replaces much of the fixed-function vertex processing, and possibly changes the vertex coordinates as well. It also sets up the shader environment for any further vertex processing by tessellation and geometry shaders and for the rasterization and fragment shader processing.

In this chapter, we will discuss the vertex shader from a functional approach: what it does, what its inputs are, what its outputs are, and what kind of operations it can perform. We will also see several examples of vertex shaders that carry out many of these shaders' different operations.

Vertex Shaders in the Graphics Pipeline

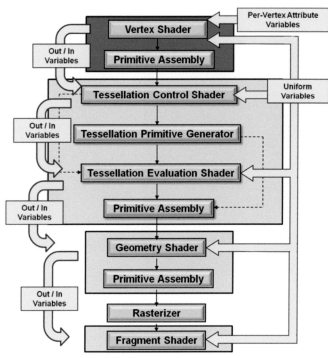

Figure 7.1. The place of vertex shaders in the pipeline.

As we consider in detail how the vertex shader works in the graphics pipeline, we need to look at the inputs to a shader and the outputs from a shader, as well as the kinds of processing that can go between the input and the output.

In the discussions below, we will often refer to aspects of the GLSL shader languages that were presented in Chapter 5, because vertex processors deal with attribute variables, uniform variables, and variables that are passed to other shaders for their work. If you are working through this book in chapter order, this material should be fresh, but if you are picking it up bit by bit, you should at least skim Chapter 5 to understand the basic ideas of GLSL variables.

Input to Vertex Shaders

Vertex shaders take the inputs that would ordinarily go to the vertex processing stage of the graphics pipeline, along with other data that the application might want to send to the shaders. This lets the vertex shader replace key parts of the standard vertex processing. Vertex shaders can take attribute and uniform variables as inputs, and produce other variables as outputs. Both attribute and uniform variables are treated as read-only variables by vertex shaders. (Vertex shader *out* variables are treated as write-only variables destined for the next stage in the pipeline.)

Attribute variables can take on a different value for each vertex in your model and are considered to be read-only to the vertex shader. Some of the attribute variables are built-in to GLSL, such as vertex coordinates, vertex color, vertex normal, and vertex texture coordinates.

You can also create your own per-vertex attribute variables. These can be used to send per-vertex data values, as well as geometry, into the graphics pipeline so that the graphics functions can use the data in developing images. This might include per-vertex application-specific data such as elevation, temperature, density, or speed, which can be used in computing the image. We will see some examples of the use of application-defined attribute variables in Chapter 15.

Uniform variables are constant across a graphics primitive and are read-only to all shader types. As with attribute variables, uniform variables come from the OpenGL application program.

The GLSL built-in uniform variables reflect the kind of information that an application would specify, including such items as

- The primary OpenGL matrices, such as the ModelView matrix, the Projection matrix, and the Texture matrix.
- The derived OpenGL matrices, such as the Normal matrix, the ModelViewProjection matrix, and the ModelViewInverse matrix.
- The front and back clipping planes and the user-defined clipping planes.
- The material properties: ambient, diffuse, specular, shininess, and emission.
- The full set of light properties, including colors, position, direction, cutoff, and attenuation properties.
- The texture environment.
- The fog data, such as color, density, start, and end.

Besides the built-in uniform variables, an application can provide user-defined uniform variables as needed through the GLSL API. The mechanics of defining and initializing these variables will be described in Chapter 14. These variables can be used in similar ways as the system-defined attribute variables if you are working with data that is constant over a graphics primitive.

Another vertex shader input can come from texture coordinates that are defined in modeling operations. Textures can be used in vertex shaders for a variety of applications, such as displacement maps. However, the most common use of texture coordinates in a vertex shader is to pass them along as *out* variables so they can be interpolated by the rasterizer for use by the fragment shader, as we see in the next section.

Vertex shaders can also accept uniform sampler variables to access several kinds of textures. We discuss sampler variables in more detail in Chapter 9.

The inputs to the vertex shader are not just data but can also affect the kind of processing that will be done. Those that determine different kinds of processing include the choice of projection, the shading to be used, whether color is specified or computed, and what kind of lighting and material will be used to set the color of a vertex.

Output from Vertex Shaders

The output from a vertex shader is much the same kind of output as would come from the vertex processing in the fixed function graphics pipeline. A vertex shader can create and set variables for later use in tessellation, geometry, or fragment shaders. The vertex shader must also create certain variables that are needed for rasterization and fragment processing.

The primary responsibilities for the vertex shader in the fixed-function environment are to compute and pass forward the coordinates of the model, transformed into clip space, and to compute and pass forward the color of each vertex.

The special variables that are output for the geometry of the model include the required variable gl_Position (which holds the 4D vertex position in clip coordinates), and gl_PointSize (which optionally holds a point size in pixels). If texturing is to be used, the texture coordinate attribute variables gl_MultiTexCoord*i* must be converted into *out* variables so that they can be used in subsequent pipeline stages, including being interpolated by the rasterizer for the fragment shader.

The vertex shader can also compute the color of each vertex and pass it along to the fragment processor to use.

A uniform variable could contain any information that should be constant across a geometric primitive. That is a uniform variable's *scope*. Uniform variables may be read in the vertex shader, in a tessellation shader, in a geometry shader, or in a fragment shader. Examples of such variables include *glman's* range variables, which you define in GLIB files.

Other variables may be defined by the vertex shader to transfer any kind of per-pixel data to the tessellation, geometry, or fragment processing stage. These may include transferring the value of user-defined attribute variables to variables defined in the vertex shader, for example. It may also include creating appearance information such as pixel colors, or geometric information such as normals or light direction, which can later be used in tessellation, geometry, or fragment processing.

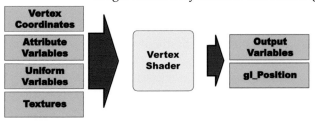

Figure 7.2. The inputs and outputs for a vertex shader.

These inputs and outputs for the vertex shader are summed up in Figure 7.2.

Geometry

If you are planning to use computed colors or textures for your final image, based on the vertex coordinates of your graphical objects, it can be important for your vertex shader to enable these coordinates to be passed to your fragment shader so they can be used there. There are two kinds of geometry that you can use for this: *model-space geometry* or *eye-space geometry*. We use a prefix convention to show these; the MC prefix corresponds to model-space geometry while the prefix EC corresponds to eye-space geometry. These are, of course, two of the main 3D spaces you work with in computer graphics. We can compute these primary kinds of geometry as follows.

- For model-space geometry, you simply use the space in which your model was defined: `vec3 MCposition = aVertex.xyz;`
- For eye space coordinates, you want to work with the geometry after all modeling has been applied. This is straightforward using the ModelView matrix: `vec3 ECposition = (uModelViewMatrix*aVertex).xyz;`

In Figure 7.3, we see how a shader can use the model coordinate (left) or eye coordinate (right) values to generate colors. The fragment shaders for both images create stripes that are parallel to the YZ plane, but the vertex shaders differ in sending either model coordinates or eye coordinates to the fragment shader to be used to determine the colors. The geometry in both cases has been

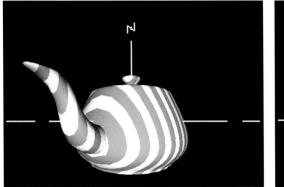 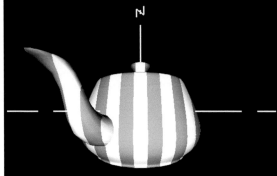

Figure 7.3. The teapot with model coordinates determining the colors (left) and with eye coordinates determining the colors (right).

rotated to show that the model coordinates stay with the object's geometry, but the eye coordinates stay fixed relative to the viewing space. That is, on the left, the stripes are parallel to the *YZ* plane of the model coordinates, and on the right, the stripes are parallel to the *YZ* plane of the rotated (eye) coordinate space.

Below is the vertex shader for Figure 7.3, with a Boolean switch to choose whether you want to send the eye-space or model-space coordinates on to the fragment shader. The lighting computation in this shader is very simple, merely handling the diffuse light intensity that would be part of a full lighting model, as we will discuss later in this chapter. In Chapter 8, we will show a simple fragment shader that handles the coordinates that this vertex shader develops.

```
uniform bool    uUseModelCoords;
out vec4        vColor;
out float       vX, vY, vZ;
out float       vLightIntensity;

void
main( )
{
    vec3 TransNorm  = normalize( uNormalMatrix * aNormal );
    vec3 LightPos   = vec3( 0., 0., 10. );
    vec3 ECposition = ( uModelViewMatrix * aVertex ).xyz;
    vLightIntensity = dot(normalize(LightPos - ECposition),
                          TransNorm);
    vLightIntensity = abs( vLightIntensity );

    vColor = aColor;
    vec3 MCposition = aVertex.xyz;
    if( uUseModelCoords )
    {
        vX = MCposition.x;
        vY = MCposition.y;
        vZ = MCposition.z;
    }
    else
    {
        vX = ECposition.x;
        vY = ECposition.y;
        vZ = ECposition.z;
    }
    gl_Position = uModelViewProjectionMatrix * aVertex;
}
```

OpenGL and World Coordinates

World Coordinates are what you get when Model Coordinates are transformed into the scene but are not yet transformed into the eye's coordinate space. Why don't we have an example here of colors determined by world-space coordinates? Because OpenGL doesn't capture world coordinates in a way that shaders can get access to them through built-in variables. We can use the model coordinates because we can access the vertex coordinates through the OpenGL variable `aVertex`, and we can use the eye coordinates because we can access the model view matrix through the OpenGL variable `uModelViewMatrix`. But the world coordinates are not available to us using OpenGL fixed-function matrices. However, you can manage your own model transformations and create world-space vertices in your vertex shader using code such as

```
uniform mat4 uWorldMatrix;    // created and passed in by app
. . .
vec3 WCposition = ( uWorldMatrix * aVertex ).xyz;
```

This vertex shader shows other useful techniques. It picks up the object's color from the attribute `aColor` variable and passes it on as a new variable to be used by the fragment shader, computes the light intensity using a standard diffuse lighting technique and passes that on as well, so that the lighting can be used in the fragment shader. However, if you want to use the full ADS lighting model, you must take into account much more than just the light intensity. This is covered in Chapter 6.

Fixed-Function Processing after the Vertex Shader

Some parts of the graphics pipeline usually associated with the vertex processing are not subsumed by a vertex shader. These include

- all clipping, including view volume clipping and user-defined clipping,
- homogeneous division,
- viewport processing,
- depth range scaling.

Finally, primitive assembly is done after all vertex processing is finished and before the assembled vertices are sent to later shaders (such as tessellation or geometry shaders) and finally to the rasterization stage.

The Relation of Vertex Shaders to Tessellation Shaders

Tessellation shaders can optionally follow vertex shaders in the shader pipeline Their primary function is to expand an original geometric primitive into a set of primitives that expresses the geometry in more detail. This can be done by, for example, performing adaptive subdivision, refining coarse models into finer ones, applying displacement maps, and carrying out level-of-detail adaptations to improve the visual quality of an image.

The input to the tessellation shaders consists of the assembled primitives from a vertex shader together with data that controls the subdivision to be performed. The output from the tessellation shaders consists of the collection of vertices for the new geometry, ready for the next primitive assembly step. This is all discussed more fully in Chapter 13.

The Relation of Vertex Shaders to Geometry Shaders

Geometry shaders have many of the same capabilities as tessellation shaders, but with two very important differences:

1. Besides some standard primitives, they may take as input a different kind of graphics primitive, which includes not only vertices in the primitive but also vertices adjacent to the primitive—the "geometry with adjacency" primitive type—and they produce standard graphics primitives as output.

2. In creating the output, they are allowed to create new topologies. For example, a geometry shader can take points in and produce triangles out, or can take triangles in and produce lines out.

In either case, both tessellation and geometry shaders can rely on vertex shaders to preprocess vertices and manage attribute variables for the benefit of the rest of the pipeline This is all discussed more fully in later chapters.

Replacing Fixed-Function Graphics with Vertex Shaders

On general principle, it should be possible to write a vertex shader to carry out any of the non-reserved vertex processing functions of the fixed-function graphics pipeline. This is underscored by the fact that some graphics devices are starting to use OpenGL ES 2.0, which omits all fixed-function operations. In this section, we will look at some familiar functionality and develop vertex shaders to carry out those functions. We will look at standard kinds of operations, including several kinds of lighting and shading, and will show a vertex shader for each. In Chapter 8, we will develop fragment shaders to go with many of these vertex shaders, so that you can see a full solution. The full solution will be included with the materials available for the book.

Standard Vertex Processing

The vertex and primitive grouping information for a vertex shader comes directly from the graphics application as attribute variables or as user-defined uniform or other variables, as described above. The original vertex geometry is in model space, so the normal and vertex position need to be set into world space and then eye space, the built-in gl_Position variable needs to be defined, and the light intensity and color need to be defined as new variables and made available to later fragment shader processing. This is very straightforward, as shown in the simple vertex shader below. This shader comes from a *glman* example that defines the light position in the vertex shader, rather than taking it as an attribute variable from the application. It also does not compute the fragment colors itself, but sends the variables vColor and vLightIntensity to be used to determine the pixel colors in the fragment shader, as we have seen in earlier examples.

```
out vec4 vColor;
out float vLightIntensity;

void
main( )
{
  const vec3 LIGHTPOS = vec3( 3., 5., 10. );
  vec3 TransNorm = normalize( uNormalMatrix * aNormal );
  vec3 ECposition = ( uModelViewMatrix * aVertex ).xyz;
  vLightIntensity = dot(normalize(LIGHTPOS - ECposition),\
                    TransNorm);
  vLightIntensity = abs( vLightIntensity );

  vColor         = aColor;
  gl_Position    = uModelViewProjectionMatrix * aVertex;
}
```

Going Beyond the Fixed-Function Pipeline with Vertex Shaders

So far, we have focused on how you can use vertex shaders just to replace fixed-function capabilities. While that may seem redundant, it may have helped you to understand how to keep some of the kinds of graphics you want when you move to using shaders. It may also become the only way to get your graphics on devices that do not support the fixed-function pipeline in their built-in graphics systems.

Shaders have the capability to add new functionality to the standard fixed-function kind of graphics. We have seen that techniques such as Phong shading, long missing from OpenGL graphics, are now possible using the combined capabilities of vertex and fragment shaders. Similarly, the vertex shader can be set up to take user-defined per-vertex attribute data to a vertex shader, so that an image can be directly derived from application data.

When we discussed the inputs to the vertex shader, we noted that an application can define its own attribute variables for use by shaders. As we pointed out earlier, however, only a vertex shader can read an attribute variable, so one of a vertex shader's tasks is to transfer the necessary attribute values to other variables, so they can be used in whatever ways the application has in mind. Of course, a vertex shader can modify the values in the process. These attribute variables may also be used in the vertex shader itself. This lets you define shaders that respond to data in different ways, a critical capability that will be exploited when we discuss scientific visualization in a later chapter.

Vertex Modification

A vertex shader can modify the coordinates it receives. The vertex shader is a one-vertex-in, one-vertex-out process, and it cannot create more vertices — that's what tessellation and geometry shaders are for. The main application of vertex shaders is to change the vertices of the primitives you already have defined, and to set up variables such as lighting that depend on the vertices. Some of this could take user-defined attribute or uniform variables and use them to define the changes to be made.

Dome Geometry Example

The fixed function pipeline is limited to performing linear transformations on vertices. A very interesting use for vertex shaders is to transform vertices in ways that the fixed function pipeline cannot. One such application is to perform the transformations needed to display a 3D scene on a dome. A dome projector is capable of expanding the displayed image to nearly a 180º field of view, using a large fisheye lens. From a graphics point of view, there is a circle on the display screen that the lens maps to the dome circumference. If you look directly at the center of projection, the circumference of the circle is what you see when you look 90º to the left, right, down, and up, as shown in Figure 7.4.

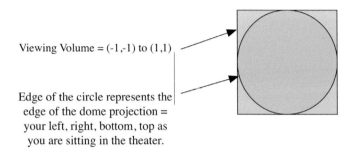

Viewing Volume = (-1,-1) to (1,1)

Edge of the circle represents the edge of the dome projection = your left, right, bottom, top as you are sitting in the theater.

Figure 7.4. The dome projection viewing volume.

Imagine a line drawn out from the center of the dome projector to the center of the dome wall. Now imagine a line drawn from the dome projector to the (x,y,z) point being plotted. The angle between these two lines is Φ, and the angle around that center line is Θ. The dome projection strategy is to leave Θ alone and treat Φ as a radius, with $\Phi = \pi/2$ representing the maximum radius of 1.0. This situation is shown in Figure 7.5 [3].

The dome projection can be demonstrated with *glman*. Here is the dome GLIB file:

```
##OpenGL GLIB
Ortho -1. 1. -1. 1. .1 1000.
Vertex dome.vert
Fragment dome.frag
Program Dome
Color 1. .5 0.
```

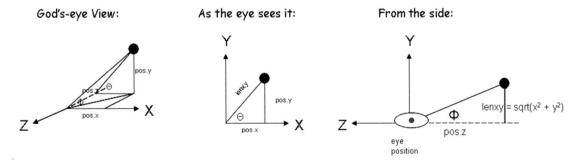

Figure 7.5. Dome projection diagrams.

```
PushMatrix
   Rotate -90 1 0 0
   WireTeapot
PopMatrix
```

Notice that this uses an orthographic projection. That seems strange, because we would expect to use perspective for most of the images we would want to display. The perspective is actually here—it is created as part of the dome equation in the vertex shader. This happens through the use of the point's z-coordinate in computing the angle Φ. That dome equation makes geometry appear to reach a vanishing point as it gets farther away and maps everything to be inside the unit circle. This orthographic projection is there to handle the display of the unit circle and to set up the depth clipping.

The dome vertex shader code actually does all the work of converting spaces that is shown in Figure 7.5. As is often the case when working with *glman*, we have hardcoded a variable, the light position that would be picked up from the OpenGL environment in a real application.

```
const float      PI = 3.14159265;
out vec4         vColor;

void
main( void )
{
   vColor = aColor;

   vec4 pos = uModelViewMatrix * aVertex;
   float lenxy = length( pos.xy );

   if( lenxy != 0.0 )
   {
      float phi = atan( lenxy, -pos.z );
      pos.xy = normalize( pos.xy );
   // pos.xy is now equal to (cos theta, sin theta)
      float r = phi / (PI/2.); // radius <= 1.
      pos.xy *= r;        // same theta, different radius
   // pos.z is left alone so that it can participate in depth
   // clipping
   }

   gl_Position = uProjectionMatrix * pos;
}
```

 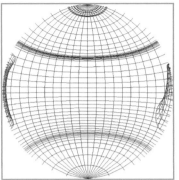 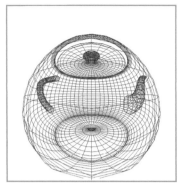

Figure 7.6. Zooming in on a dome projection.

Figure 7.6 shows the effect that this shader gives vertices as you zoom into the object. These images are from the monitor and so will look distorted, but they will look correct when projected through the projector's fisheye lens. As you can see in the left-hand image of Figure 7.6, from a distance the teapot looks about the same as it always does. But as you get closer, you can see in the middle image of the figure that the geometry starts to get squeezed against the unit circle. This makes sense in the dome world, because as you zoom through a scene, objects never actually disappear to the left, right, bottom, or top, as they would in a normal Cartesian zoom. If you think of yourself as sitting in the center of the dome and flying through a scene, objects close to you just get more even with you. Finally, in the right-hand image of Figure 7.6, you are in the exact center of the teapot. From there, you can see the handle, spout, lid, and base of the teapot all at the same time. But objects can get behind you or too far in front, and so the only clipping that actually takes place in a dome projection is Z clipping.

Issues in Vertex Shaders

There are always some things in any new capability that can trip people up. This is also true of vertex shaders. Here, we talk about a few of those potential pitfalls you might run into.

Creating Normals

First, when you change the geometry that came from your model, how do you create accurate normals? You may have defined the normals in your original model, but now the geometry has changed, and you need to compute the new model's normals. How you can do this depends on the way your geometry is defined.

In case you have an analytic description of the modified surface or graphical object, you can compute the surface normal by analytic means. If you have any two non-collinear vectors in the tangent plane to the surface at a point, then their cross product (in the right order) is normal to the surface. So if you have the surface as an explicit function surface, $z(x,y)$, the two partial derivatives define tangent vectors $dx = \langle 1 \quad 0 \quad \partial z/\partial x \rangle$ and $dy = \langle 0 \quad 1 \quad \partial z/\partial y \rangle$ that lie in the plane, and their cross product $dx \times dy$ can be computed and normalized to get an analytic normal. Figure 7.7 shows the function surface of Figure 3.4 with specular lighting added as discussed in the previous chapter. An exercise at the end of this chapter encourages you to explore this idea more generally.

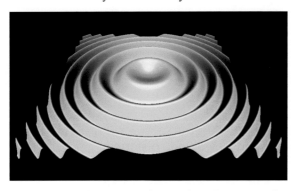

Figure 7.7. A function surface with analytic normals.

An even more interesting case of this is the general surface, defined on a rectangular domain with points in 3D space. As an example, consider Enneper's surface, defined by

$$x(u,v) = u - u^3/3 + uv^2,$$
$$y(u,v) = -v - u^2v + v^3/3,$$
$$z(u,v) = u^2 - v^2.$$

It's nice to create exact normals at vertices of analytic objects, but it's even better to do that for each pixel in the object. This exact shading is discussed in Chapter 8.

We will omit the shader code here, but it is straightforward to compute the u and v partial derivatives of each component, build the tangent vectors in the u and v directions, and use the cross product to compute the normal to the surface at any point. A full set of application and shader code is available for this on the book's website. Figure 7.8 shows the surface.

If the surface is analytic, but implicit rather than explicit, so that the surface equation is given by $S(x,y,z) = 0$, then its normal vector is given by $N = \langle \partial S/\partial x \quad \partial S/\partial y \quad \partial S/\partial z \rangle$ and again, this needs to be normalized. The overall computation is not otherwise significantly different.

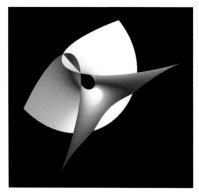

Figure 7.8. Enneper's surface.

On the other hand, if your surface or object is given by simply setting vertex values, the normal cannot be found analytically, and we must resort to computations based on cross products of edges at vertices. This may be made difficult, because the vertex shader can only access coordinates of the vertex being processed; it cannot access the coordinates of other vertices in the primitive. In case all the vertex computations can be known without the actual coordinates, this can be sidestepped. An example would be when a texture map is used to compute vertex offsets, because adjacent texture coordinates can be read from the vertex being processed, so the adjacent vertex coordinates can be inferred.

But what if the computation does not let us infer coordinates? There really is nothing the vertex shader can do in that case. However, geometry shaders give you a way around this. In Chapter 12, we will show how you can access the data from all the vertices in a primitive so you can compute a vertex normal based on the cross product of edges, and at least get flat shading. If your primitives also have adjacency information, you can get access to some adjacent primitives as well, so you may be able to do just a bit better than flat shading. See Chapter 12 for more information.

Summary

You can do several kinds of computation in either the vertex or fragment shader. For example, you can calculate the direction from a vertex to a light in a vertex shader and make it a variable to be interpolated in the fragment shader, or you can use the interpolated pixel position and calculate the direction from that in a fragment shader. How do you decide exactly what you do in the vertex shader and what you do in the fragment shader?

As you write vertex shaders, it can be tempting to write a separate shader for each application. However, the lessons of code reuse suggest that you should think about creating very general vertex shaders that can be used with several different fragment shaders. This offers a very good place to include appropriate `#ifdef` statements, so you can turn specific shader operations on or off very easily. This might mean that you would need to create more variables in your vertex shader than you would need for any one particular fragment shader, because other versions of the same shader might need them. Most shader compilers are fiercely optimizing, and you will likely not find that there is a penalty for including variables that don't affect the generation of the scene detail.

Exercises

1. Replace the simple fixed-function vertex processing for a straightforward example with a vertex shader. Use the shader to compute each vertex position and vertex color, and pass on the color values as new variables to a fragment shader to get smooth shading. If your implementation of GLSL supports flat shading, implement that as well.

2. Take a straightforward vertex shader such as one you would use for smooth shading, and design two different ways to organize information that you would pass on to a fragment shader to complete an image. Sketch out the fragment shader you would use, and discuss how your choices would affect the design of the fragment shader.

3. Look at the section of Chapter 14 that covers user-defined attribute and uniform variables. Think of an application that can use this kind of attribute or uniform data, and assuming that these have been designed, write a vertex shader that takes this data and prepares it for a fragment shader's use. Sketch how the fragment shader would use that data in setting pixel colors.

4. Create a simple scene that is made up of a few primitives, each with its own modeling transformation. Create a model-space shader similar to that used for Figure 7.3, applying the appropriate modeling transformations to each vertex as it is used.

5. Implement the Cartesian hyperbolic vertex shader, described in the Hyperbolic Geometry section of the Scientific Visualization shader. Do it using *glman*, so that you can make the parameter K a uniform slider variable and experiment with the effect of different values of K.

6. As we did in the discussion in Chapter 3 around Figure 3.4, define a 2D grid on a plane, and display any surface defined by analytic expressions by writing a vertex shader to compute the position and normals at the domain points. The vertex shader shown with the example in Chapter 3 will be a good starting point, and you might consider implementing the Enneper surface whose equations are given in this chapter.

7. Your goal is to simulate wringing out a sponge object. Design an object with a texture that easily shows deformation, and write a glib file that provides a uniform Twist slider variable. As the Twist slider goes from 0. to 1., the object should

- twist about the Y (vertical) axis,
- get squished to zero in the Y direction, and
- shrink by 30% in the horizontal (X and Z).

It should look something like the example below.

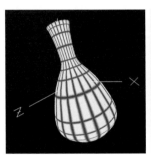 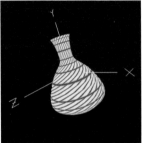 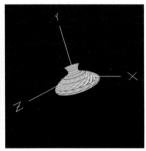

8

Fragment Shaders and Surface Appearance

Just as with vertex shaders, there are specific roles for fragment processing in the fixed-function graphics pipeline. Their task is to take state variables, plus the values that are interpolated across a polygon, and produce a final color for each pixel. In the fixed-function world there are few things to interpolate: position, depth, color, and texture coordinates. The classical graphics literature contains many more things that can be done with interpolations, however, and the fragment shader in GLSL can do a great number of them. This chapter describes the basics of fragment shaders, including some fun techniques you can't do with fixed-function OpenGL graphics.

Once again, we consider the role of fragment processing in the graphics pipeline, just as we did for the role of the vertex shader. The general place of this functionality is shown in Figure 8.1, which recalls Figure 7.1. We see that fragment processing takes the interpolated values within a graphics primitive in screen space and produces pixels with color and depth to be incorporated into the framebuffer.

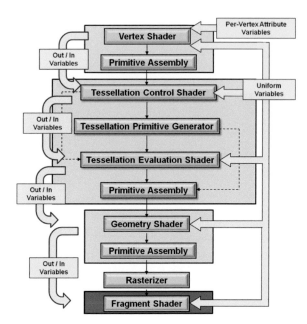

Figure 8.1. The place of the fragment shader in the pipeline.

Basic Function of a Fragment Shader

The basic function of a fragment shader is to take uniform variables and the output from the rasterizer and compute the color of the pixel for each fragment. Figure 8.2 illustrates this process, showing first how the distinct vertices of a primitive are processed by the rasterizer to form the set of fragments that make up the primitive.

Of course, many other built-in properties of vertices besides color and light intensity can be interpolated in fragment processing. The two most important of these are texture coordinates and pixel depth. If you are using texturing, as the texture coordinates are interpolated, you can use these coordinates to sample a texture (or multiple textures) to help determine the colors of each pixel. We will focus on textures and their contribution to fragment processing in the chapter on texturing, and will keep our focus on other fragment processing here.

Inputs to Fragment Shaders

There are many different kinds of inputs to a fragment shader from an application, from the OpenGL system, or from a vertex shader. By now, these are quite familiar, but we want to remind our-selves of them in the fragment shader context.

Uniform Variables

Fragment shaders can use uniform variables that are provided by the system or by the application. Because uniform variables do not change within a graphics primitive, they will not change during the interpolations that the rasterizer performs. However, they can be used for any computations that might be needed in fragment processing.

As a preview, there is a special kind of uniform variable for textures that is available to both vertex and fragment shaders, but which is particularly important for fragment shaders: the uniform sampler variable. The uniform sampler variables correspond to textures, so with the 1D, 2D, and 3D textures, we have sampler types `sampler1D`, `sampler2D`, and `sampler3D`. Since GLSL also allows cube mapping textures, we have the additional sampler type `samplerCube`. The particular sampler type that you use must correspond to the texture type that was defined in your application. The value associated with a sampler variable is the texture image number associated with the texture it represents, which is also set up in the texture definition functions in your application. The `texture( )` function will be used with the texture unit and texture coordinates to return the texture value at those coordinates, as in the line

```
vec4 textureValue = texture( TexUnit, coordinateVector );
```

We will see examples of this use in texture-based fragment shader code later in this chapter.

Input and Output Variables

Perhaps the most important inputs to fragment shaders are the variables that are passed to the fragment shader as `out` variables by the pipeline stage that occurs right before the rasterizer and fragment processor. This could be a vertex, geometry, or tessellation shader. These variables are the data that are interpolated across a graphics primitive in order to give the fragment shader enough information to set the colors of each pixel.

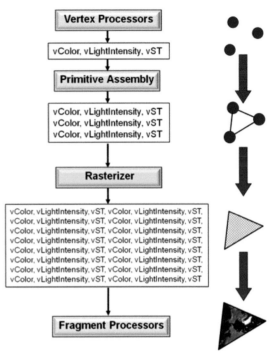

Figure 8.2. The vertices of a graphics primitive and the fragments that are processed to make up the primitive being displayed.

The fragment shader must use an output `vec4` variable to declare what color should be placed in its pixel. In OpenGL 3 and beyond, you declare this yourself, something like

```
out vec4 fFragColor;
```

In pre-OpenGL 3 systems, there is a built-in vec4 variable, called `gl_FragColor`, for this purpose. Our examples here will use the standard in OpenGL 3 and beyond.

You can declare other `out  vec4` variables in your fragment shader and write color data to it in order to send your graphics output to another buffer or a texture. You simply declare these variables to be the appropriate kind.

Other variables can also be provided by the previous pipeline stage to give the fragment shader any data or information that could be used in developing the pixel colors. Among the things these variables might provide are

- Light intensity, for scenes that use per-vertex lighting.
- Geometric coordinates in model or eye coordinates, as discussed later in this chapter.
- Texture coordinates, used as indices into the texture array to a per-fragment lighting model.
- Per-vertex reflection vectors, for use in environment mapping, cube mapping, or any other computation that involves reflections.
- Per-vertex refraction vectors, for use in cube mapping or any other computation that involves refractions.
- Vectors from vertices to the light source(s), for dealing with spot lighting or Phong shading.
- Data, for other computations that may depend on application-specific information that has been passed through the vertex processor.
- The coordinates $(x, y, z, 1/w)$ of each fragment in window-relative space, from the built-in variable `gl_FragCoord`.

These variables are not required, but they might be written by the previous shader in the pipeline in case the application using the shaders needs them for its particular use.

The overall input and output operations of fragment shaders are shown in Figure 8.3.

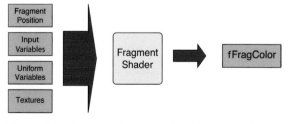

Figure 8.3. Inputs and outputs for a fragment shader.

Additional Output Variables

A fragment shader program can also write a value to the built-in variable float gl_FragDepth so that the depth can be used in later depth processing. Setting this overrides the fragment depth that the graphics pipeline keeps around for use in the depth buffer. This would be a way, for example, for you to offset pixels' depth values to alter the scene's z-fighting behavior.

Particularly Important "In" Variables for the Fragment Shader

The most important of the varying variables are those that give the position, color, texture coordinates, depth, and user-defined values. These are described in more detail below.

Colors

Computing the color for each fragment can be done in many different ways. The fixed-function role includes operations to interpolate colors that are passed in for each vertex, to interpolate texture coordi-

If you are working in compatibility mode, there are built-in versions of several of the input variables we discuss in this chapter:

> gl_Vertex
> gl_Normal
> gl_MultiTexCoord*i*
> gl_NormalMatrix
> gl_ModelViewMatrix

Here we use the variable name conventions we introduced earlier, but the conventions are basically the same as the built-in names without the gl_ prefix.

nates and use textures to calculate colors, and to use the interpolated color and texture color to develop a final pixel color. Once the color is developed, it is written to your output vec4 color variable (fFragColor in our case) to store the pixel's color for further work before the fragment is written to the color buffer.

From now on, we are going to use the vec4 variable fFragColor to indicate we are assigning the final pixel RGBA to. You, of course, are free to use whatever variable name you want, or to continue to use gl_FragColor in the compatibility profiles.

Texture Coordinates

If your graphics primitives have been assigned texture coordinates, you can get the texel coordinates for each vertex from whatever texture coordinates variable you have interpolated through the rasterizer. As most of our examples in this chapter use just a vertex and fragment shader, we will call this vec2 variable vST.

Once you have the texture coordinates interpolated through the rasterizer, you get the actual texel color from the texture( ) function. You can then use that color for any further texture processing, including multitexturing or managing the texture mode. This is described fully in the chapter on texture mapping.

Other Data

In the previous chapter, we saw that an application can create attribute data for each vertex, and that a vertex shader can take this attribute data and create variables for the tessellation and geometry shaders that eventually pass them on to be used in creating colors. Later in this chapter, we will see some examples showing how this can be done. This is a particularly important capability for visualization that will be discussed in more detail in the visualization chapter.

Coordinate Systems

If you will be using geometric information that has been passed into the fragment shader as in variables, as we discussed in the last chapter, you will get different effects, depending on the coordinate system that is used to develop the geometric information for your fragment shader's use. In the next few sections, we will talk about how some of these coordinate systems affect your images.

Model Coordinates

Model coordinates are directly available to the vertex shader from the per-vertex variable we called aVertex (or gl_Vertex in compatibility mode), but must be moved into output variables in the vertex shader before they can be passed along to the tessellation or geometry shader and finally used in a fragment shader. Similarly, the model-coordinate normal is available from the attribute variable we called aNormal (or gl_Normal) but must be moved into an output variable by a vertex shader before it can be used in a fragment shader.

You are most likely going to want to use model coordinates for developing an appearance for your objects when you want that appearance to depend on the object itself, and not on the location or orientation of the object in space. For example, this could be the basis for a procedural texture that moved with the object, as we will discuss later in this chapter. Another example of model-coordinate textures could come from building a rectangular space with the same dimensions as a 3D data texture and using slices of the space to view the data in the texture, yielding a kind of volume visualization. Another example of the use of model coordinates could be to create an object-linear one-dimensional texture. This is discussed in the stripes example later in this chapter.

Eye Coordinates

Eye coordinates are what model coordinates become when they have been transformed into the scene where they belong and then transformed so that they are given with respect to the eye's viewing coordinate system. The eye coordinates for a vertex can be computed from the per-vertex variable aVertex by

```
uModelViewMatrix * aVertex
```

and the eye coordinate version of the normal vector is computed from aNormal by

```
uNormalMatrix * aNormal
```

Both of these computations were used in early *glman* examples in the chapter on shader concepts.

You might use eye coordinates in case you want to present information from the viewer's point of view, and in that case you might develop a procedural texture based on eye-coordinate information. Textures based on eye coordinates can include eye-linear one-dimensional textures, discussed in the ChromaDepth example later in this chapter. This idea will also be used to create a 3D "data probe" in the visualization chapter.

Fragment Shader Processing

Outputs from Fragment Shaders

The primary output from the fragment shader is the same as that from the fragment-processor in the fixed-function pipeline: pixel color, ready to be processed by the remaining pixel operations and then written into the framebuffer. The fragment shader can also produce a depth value for each pixel, which can be useful if you want to compute a depth that is different from the usual interpolation of the vertex depths.

Replacing Fixed-Function Processing with Fragment Shaders

Before we start thinking of developing sophisticated kinds of fragment shading, we should stop to ask how we would implement the fixed-function kinds of shading we get from ordinary OpenGL. Sometimes this is easy, but sometimes it involves more computation than we might expect. In these sections, we will review the primary kinds of work of the fixed-function fragment processor and ask how we can do them with a fragment shader.

Shading

In the world of fixed-function OpenGL, *shading* means one of the standard ways to apply colors to the pixels in a graphics primitive. For fixed-function operations, all the processes that develop a color from lighting models are done during vertex processing, so if we simply replace the fixed-function processing with fragment shaders, we can assume that the key inputs to the fragment shader are the color values, depths, and texture coordinates of each vertex in each graphics primitive. The simple flat and Gouraud shading were described in the earlier chapter on lighting.

Flat Shading

Flat shading is a standard, and very simple, way to give a color to a polygon. It takes a single color and applies it identically to each pixel in the polygon. To use flat shading, we usually specify a single color first and then define the vertices of the primitive. If you should specify a separate color for each vertex but still specify flat shading, the color that is used will be the color of the last vertex specified in the primitive.

We noted in the chapter on vertex shaders that GLSL did not originally support non-interpolating rasterization behavior, but that it has now added the keyword flat for output variables headed to the fragment shader as well as for the corresponding input variables in the fragment shader, so that those variables are *not* interpolated across the polygon. In the previous chapter, we introduced this concept and gave an example of a vertex shader to support flat shading. Below, we show some fragment shader code that does this.

```
in flat float   vLightIntensity;
uniform  vec4   uColor;
out      vec4   fFracColor;

void main( )
{
   fFragColor= vec4( vLightIntensity * uColor.rgb, 1. );
}
```

The effect of this code is to use the familiar diffuse lighting computation that computes the light intensity in the vertex shader and sends it as a flat variable instead of as a regular variable. The light intensity then is treated as a constant for the primitive, yielding the same color for the entire primitive.

Note that `flat` variables can also be used as a way for a vertex shader to pass "global" values down to a fragment shader.

Smooth (Gouraud) Shading

Smooth shading (or Gouraud shading) is a very helpful tool in creating attractive images with OpenGL, but it has some rather severe shortcomings. It does not handle specular highlights well, because specular highlights do not linearly interpolate well on the interior of a polygon. Also, smooth shading is vulnerable to Mach bands, meaning it shows the boundaries of polygons more than it should. Its implementations may also do strange things for quads and polygons that have very different colors at their vertices, because it is usually implemented by breaking the object into triangles and handling each triangle separately. Unfortunately, implementing smooth shading in a fragment shader will likely not solve these problems, but it may well be something you would want to have in your shader arsenal.

An extremely simple fragment shader to do smooth shading is shown below. This simply takes the color that has been computed for each vertex, using whatever process the vertex shader has needed and saved there as vmyColor. A vertex shader that does this was shown in the chapter on lighting, and a Gouraud-shaded teapot was shown in Figure 5.4. The computed color is passed to the fragment shader and is interpolated across the primitive and saved as the fragment color in fFragColor. Of course, this is a very simple example, but it does everything that fixed-function smooth shading does.

```
in   vec3   vmyColor;
out  vec4   fFracColor

void main( )
{
    fFragColor = vec4( vmyColor, 1.0 );
}
```

Traditional Texture Mapping

Texture mapping is another fixed-function operation that can be readily handled by fragment shaders. Texture coordinates are easily set up as input variables, so they are interpolated for each fragment, and sampler functions can look up coordinates in a texture map to get the actual texels to be used in determining each pixel's color. Rather than covering texture mapping in this chapter, we discuss it fully in the next chapter.

False Coloring

Color is important in creating realistic images, but it has other functions as well. If you want to display information that has more than three dimensions, for example, you can use traditional geometry to show up to three dimensions and then use color for the fourth. You can also use color to emphasize the third

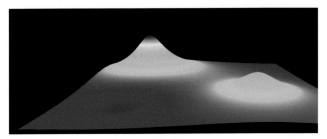

dimension when your geometry is projected to the two dimensions of a screen or of paper. This use is shown in Figure 8.4; this same figure was used in the discussion of false coloring (or pseudocolor) in [14], but here the figure has been generated using vertex and fragment shaders and is much more effective. The technique is much more general than this, of course. We will examine this approach and the more general concept of transfer functions in the later chapter on shaders in scientific visualization.

Figure 8.4. A surface whose elevation is coded with color.

The vertex shader is much like the one we illustrated when we created Figure 6.7 in the previous chapter, so we won't include it here. The function in the figure is a Coulomb function. If we have an array of vec3 data and each entry's x- and y-coordinates represent a position in the plane, while the z-coordinate represents the charge at that point, the function is

$$value(x, y) = \sum \frac{Q[i].z}{\sqrt{\left(\left(x - Q[i].x\right)^2 + \left(y - Q[i].y\right)^2\right)}},$$

where the sum is over all the entries in the plane. This function is written in the vertex shader as

```
float Value = 0.0;
for(int i=0; i<3; i++ )
{
    float dist=sqrt((x-Q[i].x)*(x-Q[i].x)+(y-Q[i].y)*(y-
                                                    Q[i].y));
    Value += Q[i].z/dist;
}
```

Note that the dist computation could have been expressed, probably more efficiently, as

```
float dist = distance( vec2(x,y), Q[i].xy );
```

The fragment shader simply uses the z-coordinate of the interpolated model-space coordinates for each vertex, computed in the fragment shader, as the input to a color-determining function, and colors the pixel accordingly. This use of data to determine color is known as a *transfer function*. We use it here, and will use it a lot more in the chapter on visualization.

```
in float vLightIntensity;
in float vMyHeight;
out vec4 fFragColor;

uniform float uVertical;
uniform float uScale;

vec3 Rainbow( in float zval )
{
  vec3 myColor;

  if (zval < 0.)                    // black if below bound
    { myColor.r = 0.; myColor.g = 0.; myColor.b = 0.; }

  else if ((zval >= 0.) && (zval < 0.2))     // purple to blue
                                             // ramp
    { myColor.r=0.5*(1.0-zval/0.2); myColor.g=0.0;
      myColor.b=0.5+(0.5*zval/0.2); }

  else if ((zval >= 0.2) && (zval < 0.40))   // blue to cyan
                                             // ramp
    { myColor.r= 0.0; myColor.g=(zval-0.2)*5.0;
          myColor.b = 1.0; }

  else if ((zval >= 0.40) && (zval < 0.6))   // cyan to green
                                             // ramp
    { myColor.r= 0.0; myColor.g= 1.0;
          myColor.b = (0.6-zval)*5.0; }

  else if ((zval >= 0.6) && (zval < 0.8))    // green to yellow
                                             // ramp
    { myColor.r= (zval-0.6)*5.0; myColor.g= 1.0;
          myColor.b = 0.0; }

  else if (zval >= 0.8)                      // yellow to red
                                             // ramp
    { myColor.r= 1.0; myColor.g= (1.0-zval)*5.0;
          myColor.b = 0.0; }
```

```
    else                                // white if above bound
       { myColor.r = 1.; myColor.g = 1; myColor.b = 1.; }

    return myColor;
}

void main( )
{
   vec3 color = Rainbow(vMyHeight);

   fFragColor = vec4( color, 1.);
}
```

Another example of using false color is to provide contour lines for surface displays. To do that, you would create and display the surface however you like, but if the model-space elevation at a particular pixel is within a certain tolerance of one of the contour line elevations, you color the pixel with the contour line color, instead of the ordinary surface color. If you are already using false coloring for your figure, you can include this contour information in your transfer function; if you are not, you can make a special contour-only transfer function and apply it in your fragment shader after your other coloring operations. See Chapter 15 for more details. This kind of application is similar to the model-space coloring example shown in Figure 6.3 and is left as an exercise for the reader.

What Follows a Fragment Shader?

The fragment shader is not the last word on the color of pixels that are written to the color buffer. Several steps in the fixed-function graphics pipeline follow the fragment shader. These include depth comparisons if depth testing is enabled, alpha blending, stencil testing, masking, dithering, and logical raster operations. Because these are standard fixed-function operations, we won't go into them further. These operations use information that is not available to the fragment shader, such as the existing contents of the color and depth buffers, and are tightly controlled as pixels are finally written to the color buffer. The fragment shader has some role in these operations, even if it does not perform them. Depth testing uses the depth output from the fragment shader, for example, and alpha blending uses the alpha channel that is the fourth coordinate of the fFragColor value.

Additional Shader Effects

The main value in fragment shaders, of course, lies in the capabilities that go beyond the functionality that is available from the fixed-function graphics pipeline. In the sections below, we'll talk about some of these capabilities and give examples of fragment shaders that support them.

Discarding Pixels

A unique capability of fragment shaders (that is, unavailable with standard fixed-function processing) is the ability to discard pixels. This function is much stronger than simply setting the alpha value of pixels to zero, because it makes the pixel disappear in any view. We mentioned this in the earlier chapter on general shader concepts, so here we simply remind ourselves of this capability, shown in Figure 8.5. The key factor is the discard keyword in the fragment shader that instructs the shader to stop processing the pixel and not record it in the framebuffer.

Figure 8.5. The standard teapot with some pixels discarded by a noise process.

Phong Shading

In the previous chapter we introduced a function that computes the ambient-diffuse-specular lighting model from a set of light and material properties. In that chapter, we showed how that function could be used in a vertex shader to set colors for each vertex, so that the rasterizer could smoothly interpolate the colors or intensities across a polygon. Here, we want to see how to do lighting at each fragment, instead of at each vertex. This is known as *Phong shading*.

    A Phong shading fragment shader takes the normal as a varying variable from the vertex shader, has it interpolated in the rasterizer, and uses the interpolated normals to compute the ADS color at each fragment. The fragment shader that created the right hand image in Figure 8.6 is shown below. This uses the ADSLightModel( ) function introduced in the lighting chapter.

```
in vec3 vNormal;    // interpolated from the vertex shader
in vec4 vPos;       // interpolated from the vertex shader
out vec4 fFragColor;
```

Figure 8.6. The smooth- (left) and Phong-shaded (right) teapots from Chapter 5.

```
//Assumed context:
//
//variables myNormal and myPosition are passed in and
//the ADS color is returned from the function

vec3 ADSLightModel( in vec3 myNormal, in vec4 myPosition )
{
// use the function from the Lighting chapter
}

void main( )
{
   vec3 color = ADSLightModel( vNormal, vPos);
}
```

The figures from the lighting chapter showing how Phong shading differs from smooth shading are repeated here as Figure 8.6. Notice that the jagged per-vertex artifacts in the smooth-shaded example are eliminated by using Phong shading.

The specular highlight in the right image is much more effective than that in the left image. The reason is that in the left image, the specular highlight is computed at each vertex and interpolated across the polygon. If a polygon's vertices don't get much specular lighting, then the pixels in that polygon won't have much either, even if the specular lighting is supposed to be high in the interior.

Shading with Analytic Normals

As good as Phong shading is, it is still not exact, because it interpolates normals linearly across each primitive, so if there is any nonlinear variation in that region, it is not seen. Sometimes we can do better. In the previous chapter, we showed that we could create an analytic height-field function surface with a vertex shader, computing the normal at each vertex by using partial derivatives. We can also create the normals at each pixel in a fragment shader by the same technique.

Figure 8.7. The rippled surface with exact shading.

We begin by interpolating the points in the horizontal plane of the function in the rasterizer. It is straightforward to get these from the aVertex values in the vertex shader, and then create a vec2 varying variable for the fragment shader's use. You also need to pass the actual pixel position as a varying variable, because that is needed in the ADSLightModel( ) function. You then compute the normal from the interpolated domain coordinates and pass that value and the position to the lighting function to get the pixel color.

The result is shown in Figure 8.7, which should be compared with Figure 7.7 in the previous chapter. Notice how much more smoothly this surface moves from one primitive to another, especially in the area along each of the foreground ridges. Is this better than Phong shading? Theoretically, yes, because it is analytic. Visually, it will probably depend on the nature of the surface. This is explored in an exercise.

The fragment shader for this figure is shown below. It uses the ADSLightModel( ) function given above, so that function has been abridged. The surface is given by the function $f(x,y) = 0.3*\sin(x^2 + y^2)$ with partial derivatives

$$\frac{\partial f}{\partial x} = 2.*0.3*x*\cos(x^2 + y^2),$$

$$\frac{\partial f}{\partial y} = 2.*0.3*y*\cos(x^2 + y^2).$$

You will see these in the fragment shader code below, where we assume that the two input variables vMyXY and vPos come from a vertex shader.

```
in vec2 vMyXY;
in vec4 vPos;
out vec4 fFragColor;
```

```
vec3 ADSLightModel( in vec3 myNormal, in vec4 myPosition )
{
   ...
}

void main( )
{
   float dfdx = 2.*0.3*vMyXY.x*cos(vMyXY.x*vMyXY.x +
                                   vMyXY.y*vMyXY.y);
   float dfdy = 2.*0.3*vMyXY.y*cos(vMyXY.x*vMyXY.x +
                                   vMyXY.y*vMyXY.y);
   vec3 xtangent = vec3( 1., 0., dfdx );
   vec3 ytangent = vec3( 0., 1., dfdy );
   vec3 thisNormal = normalize( cross( xtangent, ytangent ) );

   vec3 color = ADSLightModel( thisNormal, vPos);
   fFragColor = vec4( color, 1. );
}
```

As a quick aside, the code above was written to correspond closely to the equations that it represents. But one could be a little more cryptic, and a little more efficient, by coding the expression

```
vMyXY.x*vMyXY.x + vMyXY.y*vMyXY.y
```

as

```
dot( vMyXY.xy, vMyXY.xy )
```

Anisotropic Shading

The examples of shading above have all been *isotropic*, that is, the light reflected from the surface at a point has been assumed to be the same in all directions. However, this is not true of all surfaces. Anisotropic shading models light that is reflected differently in different directions [19]. This is a property of a surface, and examples include hair (see the left image in Figure 8.8), brushed metallic surfaces, scored surfaces, or surfaces made up of oriented threads. A fur-covered surface can also be treated as an isotropic surface.

Anisotropic shading does not simply use the usual angles, the angle from the normal of the diffuse reflection and the angle from the reflected light in the specular reflection. Instead, it computes the angle with which light is reflected from a surface. This may be a direct calculation, as it is in the example below, or it may use a function called the *bidirectional reflection distribution function* (or *BRDF*) to determine how much light is reflected toward the eye. This function typically depends on both the latitude Θ and longitude Φ angle of the eye and

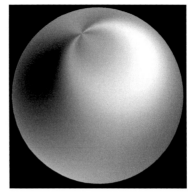

Figure 8.8. Anisotropic lighting in human hair (left); a sphere with procedural anisotropic shading (right).

of the light from the point being lighted: $\rho\left(\Theta_e, \Phi_e, \Theta_l, \Phi_l\right)$. The BRDF may also take into account behaviors that differ for different wavelengths (or different colors) of light.

None of the shading models in the fixed-function graphics pipeline of OpenGL handle anisotropic shading at all, but we can do this within a fragment shader, as described in the chapter on lighting. In the right image in Figure 8.8, we see an example of a sphere that uses an anisotropic fragment shader, discussed below. The light returned by the surface is clearly not the circular spot we would have expected to see from normal (that is, isotropic) shading; its shape reflects the behavior of brushed metal or threads that all go through the poles of the sphere.

Data-Driven Coloring

One of the really significant capabilities that GLSL shaders give you is the ability to pass data to the shaders, where it can be used to derive the colors of individual pixels. We have already alluded to the fact that an application can provide data to shaders by defining uniform and attribute variables that can be used freely in developing an image. This idea is also important in scientific visualization and will be covered in detail in that chapter, but we describe it briefly here because this capability is an important part of the idea of the fragment shader.

As an example of using data to color an image, we can get a number of different kinds of weather data. Say that we want to be able to draw some conclusions about the weather from this data. Figure 8.9 shows three images from the GOES (Geostationary Operational Environmental Satellites) system, displaying a visible light image at the left, a data map of infrared (temperature) in the center, and a data map of water vapor concentration at the right.

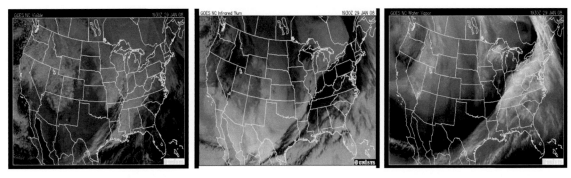

Figure 8.9. Three GOES satellite views from space: visible light (left); infrared (center); water vapor concentration (right).

Suppose we wanted to ask for the areas in which snow is most likely. We would infer that these areas are where the water vapor concentration is high and the infrared is low. It is difficult to eyeball this from the images in Figure 8.9, but if you read the visible, infrared, and water vapor from three textures into visibleLightColor, infraredInten and watervaporInten, and read two thresholds, InfraRedThreshold and WaterVaporThesold, as uniform variables, it is straightforward to write these criteria into a fragment shader, as shown in the fragment shader here:

```
vec3 rgb = visibleLightColor;
. . .
if( infraredInten < InfraRedThreshold &&      // cold
    watervaporInten > WaterVaporThreshold )   // damp
        rgb = vec3( 0., 1., 0. );    // "likely snow" = green

fFragColor = vec4( rgb, 1. );
```

The image generated from this shader is shown in Figure 8.10. Note that this gives a fairly obvious representation of the three major storm systems that were moving through the United States that day. Making this a real weather forecasting tool would require applying more science to determine what the appropriate cutoff values for moisture and infrared should be, along with studying other factors that might be included. But this image by itself is very useful.

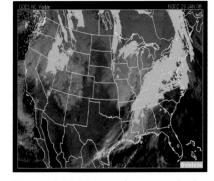

Figure 8.10. Using a fragment shader to locate all areas with high water vapor concentration and low infrared.

Images Using Other Data

An important use of computer graphics is to create images that show how data or other information is distributed over some concrete or abstracted geometry. This use, and how it is facilitated by shaders, is discussed in the later chapter on scientific visualization. Here we want to give a simple example of how the eye coordinates can be used to modify the colors in an image.

The example we present is ChromaDepth coloring [2]. This computes the color for each vertex in your model by the depth of the vertex in your scene; that is, by the distance from the vertex to the eye plane. The purpose of this is to give the illusion of depth when the scene is viewed while wearing special ChromaDepth glasses.

Because we are working with shaders, we can obtain a vertex's eye coordinate depth easily as the z-coordinate of its eye coordinate, and can map that distance into a range that the ChromaDepth( ) function below can use: typically 0 to 1, though the function will clamp the value into that range. The ChromaDepth( ) function implements a *transfer function*, a function that computes a color from a real number. This can be called from a fragment shader to set the color of each fragment as it is interpolated. This function was used to create the image shown in Figure 8.11.

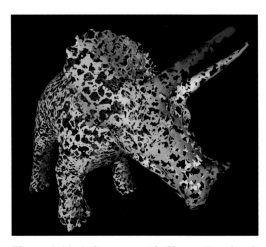

Figure 8.11. A dinosaur with ChromaDepth coloring and erosion.

```
uniform float uChromaBlue;   // z-depth corresponding to blue
uniform float uChromaRed;    // z-depth corresponding to red

in float vLightIntensity;    // from lighting model
in float vZ;                 // depth in eye coordinates
out vec4 fFragColor;

vec3
ChromaDepth( float t )
{
    t = clamp( t, 0., 1. );

    float r = 1.;
    float g = 0.0;
    float b = 1. - 6. * ( t - (5./6.) );
```

```glsl
if( t <= (5./6.) )
{
    r = 6. * ( t - (4./6.) );
    g = 0.;
    b = 1.;
}

if( t <= (4./6.) )
{
    r = 0.;
    g = 1. - 6. * ( t - (3./6.) );
    b = 1.;
}

if( t <= (3./6.) )
{
    r = 0.;
    g = 1.;
    b = 6. * ( t - (2./6.) );
}

if( t <= (2./6.) )
{
    r = 1. - 6. * ( t - (1./6.) );
    g = 1.;
    b = 0.;
}

if( t <= (1./6.) )
{
    r = 1.;
    g = 6. * t;
}

    return vec3( r, g, b );
}



void
main( )
{
    float t = ( vZ - uChromaRed ) / ( uChromaBlue - uChromaRed );
    vec3 theColor = ChromaDepth( t );
    fFragColor = vec4( vLightIntensity*theColor, 1. );
}
```

Exercises

1. Hand-code a polygon with different colors at each vertex and draw it, specifying flat shading using only the fixed-function pipeline. Describe the result, and discuss why this result may happen.

2. Hand-code a polygon having more than three vertices with different colors at each vertex and draw it, specifying smooth shading using only the fixed-function pipeline. Describe the result, and discuss why this result may happen. It may help to try several examples where the vertex order or the color at each vertex is changed.

3. Create a simple surface of your choosing and color it, based on the model-space elevation of each pixel. You may either color the whole surface based on elevation, or you may use a lighting model to display the surface and create contour lines based on elevation.

4. Write the necessary shaders to create a Phong-shaded version of the ripple surface of Figure 8.7, and compare it to the exact-shaded surface shown there. Can you see a difference? What if you zoom in very closely to the surface?

5. Take the fragment shader for round bumps on a sphere and adapt it from a purely diffuse lighting and shading model to a Phong lighting and shading model.

6. Identify another analytic surface besides that of Figure 8.7; you may find examples from mathematics, physics, chemistry, or other sources. Create the surface and calculate exact shading for it as described in this chapter. Compare that with smooth or Phong shading for the surface.

7. Add the ChromaDepth( ) function to any program you have written, such as the surface of the previous exercise, in order to use the ChromaDepth coloring to present a three-dimensional image to the viewer.

9

Surface Textures in the Fragment Shader

Texture mapping is a special activity within shader programs. In can be used in vertex, geometry, tessellation, or fragment shaders, although most of the time it seems to find its most fun use in fragment shaders. In texture mapping, texture coordinates from the original model are used as an index into a 1D, 2D, or 3D texture. Textures can hold any piece of information. Most of the time, they hold information related to determining the color of a pixel during fragment processing. However, more and more, textures are finding themselves being used to hold general-purpose data for a variety of shader-based computations. However, in this chapter, we will discuss the use of textures for image creation. While this should be familiar from your introduction to graphics, you have much more control over the use of textures when you're using fragment shaders. We will go well beyond the traditional texture mapping and will cover other techniques, such as bump mapping and cube mapping, that take texture coordinates as their starting point. And later, in Chapter 15 on scientific visualization, we will show how textures can be used to pass data to shaders.

Texture Coordinates

Texture coordinates specify the coordinates in texture space for each vertex of a graphics primitive. Texture coordinates are not part of the basic geometry of a primitive, but rather are an attribute attached to each vertex. In the vertex shader, the per-vertex texture coordinates are typically assigned to variables that can be interpolated by the rasterizer across the entire polygon and then given to the fragment shaders.

In the previous chapter on fragment shaders, you saw that you access the interpolated texture coordinates with the texture coordinate variables we have been calling vST in the vertex shader, and that you can get the RGBA color of a texel from one of the texture( ) functions. You are not limited to using just the single texels at those given texture coordinates, however. You can also use any texture coordinates you need in developing the color of the pixel. As an example, in the chapter on scientific visualization, we will describe the *line integral convolution (LIC)* process that probes the texture map along specific function streamlines to compute the color of each pixel. You can use a great deal of creativity in how you use textures.

Traditional Texture Mapping

Traditional OpenGL texture mapping uses a number of functions that define the way a texture is read, stored, accessed, and processed. The apparent complexity comes mostly from the flexibility that a generalized graphics API must have in order to be used so widely. If you are writing your own texture functions in a fragment shader, you can implement just those operations you need, which should make the task less intimidating than it might appear.

Your experience is that fixed-function OpenGL supports four kinds of textures: 1D, 2D, and 3D textures, and cube maps. It also supports multitexturing. Our goal is to see how you can create each of these standard functionalities with fragment shaders.

When you first encounter texturing in OpenGL, you find that to use textures, you must first set up a number of texture properties. You must associate

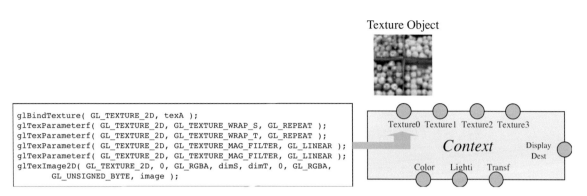

Figure 9.1. Docking texture parameters with the OpenGL system.

a texture identifier (an integer generated by glGenTextures( ); this is texA in Figure 9.1) with a texture, you must set a number of texture parameters (such as texture wrap and filter), and you must set the texture image parameters that interpret the texture (color model, dimensions, size of texture component, and texture data). This is illustrated in Figure 9.1, which shows how the usual set of texture functions specify texture properties. The texture unit is the number of the "docking port" in the graphics context, with default zero, and the texture identifier texA acts as a pointer to a specific area in GPU memory.

In a fixed-function program, you must also associate a texture name with the texture identifier, enable textures, and specify the texture environment. Overall, the setup for a single fixed-function texture that has been loaded into an array texImage looks like this:

```
GLuint texA;

glGenTextures( 1, &texA );
glEnable( GL_TEXTURE_2D );
glBindTexture( GL_TEXTURE_2D, texA );

glTexParameteri(GL_TEXTURE_2D,GL_TEXTURE_WRAP_S,GL_REPEAT);
glTexParameteri(GL_TEXTURE_2D,GL_TEXTURE_WRAP_T,GL_REPEAT);
glTexParameteri(GL_TEXTURE_2D,GL_TEXTURE_MIN_FILTER,GL_LINEAR);
glTexParameteri(GL_TEXTURE_2D,GL_TEXTURE_MAG_FILTER,GL_LINEAR);
glTexImage3D(GL_TEXTURE_2D,0,GL_RGB8,TEX_WIDTH,TEX_HEIGHT,
          0,GL_RGB,GL_UNSIGNED_BYTE,texImage);

glTexEnvi(GL_TEXTURE_ENV, GL_TEXTURE_ENV_MODE, GL_BLEND);
```

As we will see in a moment, the setting of the texture image and the sampling parameters still need to happen when using shaders. However, the setting of the texture environment is replaced by your fragment shader.

GLSL Texture Mapping

With GLSL, your application still needs to set up the texture array `texImage` and the associations from Figure 9.1, but you must create your own association of the texture with the texture unit. You must set up the uniform variable `texLoc`, give it the name `uImageUnit` that you will see throughout this chapter's examples, and set its value to to something (0, in this example). This associates the name `uImageUnit` with the texture `GL_TEXTURE0`, and you can use any of the fragment shaders in this chapter with your application.

```
glActiveTexture( GL_TEXTURE0 );

glBindTexture( GL_TEXTURE_2D,texA );
glTexParameteri(GL_TEXTURE_2D,GL_TEXTURE_WRAP_S,GL_REPEAT);
glTexParameteri(GL_TEXTURE_2D,GL_TEXTURE_WRAP_T,GL_REPEAT);
glTexParameteri(GL_TEXTURE_2D,GL_TEXTURE_MIN_FILTER,GL_LINEAR);
glTexParameteri(GL_TEXTURE_2D,GL_TEXTURE_MAG_FILTER,GL_LINEAR);
glTexImage2D(GL_TEXTURE_2D,0,GL_RGB8,TEX_WIDTH,TEX_HEIGHT,
             0,GL_RGB,GL_UNSIGNED_BYTE,texImage);

GLuint texLoc = glGetUniformLocation(program, "uImageUnit");
glUniform1i( texLoc, 0 );
```

The GLSL built-in texture lookup functions give you access to textures through *samplers*, set up through the OpenGL API. A texture sampler is a GLSL uniform variable that has been previously associated with a particular texture unit (e.g., `Texture0` in Figure 9.1). The texture unit acts as a "docking port" for the texture object itself. The texture object contains sampling information, such as size, pixel format, number of dimensions, filtering methods, and number of mip-map levels. These texture properties are taken into account as the texture is accessed. Regardless of all of these settings, though, texture sampler functions in GLSL always return a `vec4` (RGBA) value.

The actual look of the texture mapping result is familiar, but seeing some straightforward texture mapping code and the resulting image is instructive.

Figure 9.2. A texture and the familiar teapot with this texture.

An example texture, and that texture applied to the familiar teapot, are shown in Figure 9.2. The fragment shader code for this image follows.

In the shader code below, the linking of the uImageUnit sampler with the actual texture object has already happened in the application, and the mapping from the original texture attribute to the variable vST has been done in the vertex shader. In this example we are using the multitexture at index 0, or glTexCoord2f in traditional OpenGL API. The 2D texture coordinates for the individual texture have been interpolated as the .st components of the texture variable, and the texture( ) function has returned the value from the texture unit at those coordinates. Finally, we note that the texture has been set up to wrap.

Below we give the GLIB file, the vertex shader, and the fragment shader for this example. The GLIB file sets the texture object to come from the apples.bmp file and links that to texture unit 5. It also assigns a value of 5 to a uniform variable called uImageUnit and tells the shader program about it. The vertex shader sets the texture coordinate and the value of gl_Position, and the fragment shader reads the color of the texture from uImageUnit and assigns it to the pixel.

Here we use the function texture( ) in place of the texture1D, texture2D, texture3D, and textureCube functions used in compatibility mode. In the newer versions of OpenGL, the texture( ) function takes its dimension from the dimension of the sample variable.

GLIB File

```
##OpenGL GLIB
Perspective 70

Texture 5 apples.bmp

Vertex   brightness.vert
Fragment brightness.frag
Program  Brightness uImageUnit 5

Teapot
```

Vertex Shader

```
out vec2        vST;

void main( )
{
  vST           = aTexCoord0.st;
  gl_Position = uModelViewProjectionMatrix * aVertex;
}
```

Fragment Shader

```
uniform sampler2D uImageUnit;
in vec2           vST;
out vec4          fFragColor;

void main( )
{
  vec3 color = texture( uImageUnit, vST ).rgb;
  fFragColor = vec4( color, 1.);
}
```

The Texture Context

In Figure 9.1, we saw an area identified as "Context" without much explanation. In fact, this is an important idea, and when working with textures, it can be very helpful to look at the idea of the OpenGL rendering context in more detail.

When you set up a texture in fixed-function OpenGL, you first get the identifier for the texture, representing the location where the texture information will be. This is done by the two statements

```
GLuint texA;
glGenTextures( 1, &texA );
```

You can then assign a number of values to properties of the texture, as is also shown in the functions in Figure 9.1. The set of values to be assigned is the same for each texture. If you were implementing this in C++, you could use a class as a way to envision it:

```
class TextureObject
{
   enum minFilter, maxFilter;
   enum storageType;
   int numComponents;
   int numDimensions;
   int numS, numT, numP;
   void *image;
};
```

When you want to make that texture object current, you can dock the texture with the texture port in the context as shown in Figure 9.1. That is, in C++ you would make that port in the context point to the address of the proper texture object. The texture parameters would then "flow" from your program through the context to the actual texture object. From then on, any time you want to use that texture, the values in its texture object will have been retained, so you only need to bind ("dock") it again:

```
glActiveTexture( GL_TEXTURE0 );
glBindTexture( GL_TEXTURE_2D, texA );
```

Texture Environments in the Fixed-Function World

Fixed-function OpenGL includes several standard texture operations to determine how a texture is used in deciding colors for each fragment. Some of the standard OpenGL options include the texture modes *blend*, *decal*, *modulate*, and *replace*. In the OpenGL documentation or standard textbooks (for example [14]) you will see the exact operation that is required for each of these texture modes, depending on the kind of data the texture represents. For example, if the texture is RGB color and the mode is *blend*, then you would

1. Compute the color of the pixel C_f without texture considerations.
2. Compute the color of the pixel C_t from pure texture operations.
3. Compute the color component product $C_f * (1 - C_t)$ as the color of the pixel.

If you are using multitexturing, more than one texture is used to compute the texture color C_t.

The other texture operations are similar. If the mode is *modulate*, you would replace the third step by

3. Compute the color component product $C_f * C_t$ as the color of the pixel.

And finally, if the mode is either *decal* or *replace*, the third step is replaced by

3. Use the color C_t as the color of the pixel.

There are other definitions of these texture modes for RGBA color, alpha, or luminance, but the examples above are enough to show you that the computations for these modes are simple. In the fixed-function world, you need to know what all of these options are. In the shader world, you set this yourself by what you write in the shader.

Texture Sampling Parameters

Texture sampling parameters are an intrinsic part of using textures, whether you are in the fixed-function world or the shader world. For example, what do you do if your texture coordinates lie outside the normal [0., 1.] range? The options are to wrap or clamp these coordinates. Computing a wrapping or clamping operation is straightforward; if you want to use clamp operations, any value larger than 1 is simply replaced by 1, while any value smaller than 0 is simply replaced by 0. If you want to use wrap operations, replace any texture coordinate c out of the standard range by $c - floor(c)$ to get only the fractional part of the coordinate.

Also, what do you do if an individual pixel's texture coordinates don't correspond to exact integer indices of a texel in your texture? This can happen if you have many texels within one pixel (minification) or if you have many pixels that correspond to one texel (magnification). You need to define the filter operations that OpenGL is to perform when this happens. The two filter options are to use nearest (GL_NEAREST) or linear interpolation (GL_LINEAR) with neighboring texels to get the particular pixel color. The actual operations are straightforward for either minification or magnification. The nearest filter is defined by simply picking the texel that is nearest the texture coordinates (in $|x| + |y|$ measure), while the linear filter is defined by taking the weighted average of the four texels that are nearest (in the same measure) to the texture coordinates.

Samplers

Samplers are special kinds of functions that are used to access a particular texture map using the sampling parameters that you have set. Typically, they are implemented in hardware for speed. The values passed into the sampler should be the number of the texture unit to be used to access the texture and the texture coordinates. The type of the sampler defines the kind of texture map that will be accessed. The available types are

- `sampler1D`, `sampler2D`, and `sampler3D` are used to access standard 1D, 2D, and 3D textures, respectively.
- `samplerCube` is used to access textures in a cube map.
- `sampler1DShadow` or `sampler2DShadow` are used to access 1D or 2D shadow textures when depth comparisons are enabled.

Samplers should be considered an opaque data type within a shader. The suffix on the sampler type indicates the texture type to be accessed: 1D, 2D, 3D, cube map, 1D shadow, or 2D shadow. In OpenGL, a texture object of each of the first four texture types can be bound to a single texture unit. This suffix allows the desired texture object to be chosen. A 1D shadow sampler is used to access the 1D texture when depth comparisons are enabled, and a 2D shadow sampler is used to access the 2D texture when depth comparisons are enabled, but we do not discuss shadow textures here. If two uniform variables of different sampler types contain the same value, an error is generated when the next rendering command is issued.

The function `glUniform1i` loads a uniform variable defined as a *sampler type* with a texture unit number. Attempting to load a sampler with any other function is an error. All shader types (vertex, tessellation, geometry, and fragment) can use texture samplers.

Procedural Textures

We can use the term *procedural texture* for any process of developing textures by programming rather than by getting textures as data arrays, and is a standard computer graphics technique. In the fixed-function OpenGL graphics API, texture techniques are limited to computing data arrays to be used as textures. With the advent of fragment shaders, however, we can *compute* color values for each pixel during the fragment processing stage.

Computing the color value for each pixel has several advantages. One advantage is resolution. When you use fixed-size data arrays for textures, the texture dimensions are limited to the size of the data array. If you zoom into your geometry enough, the fixed-size texture runs out of resolution and starts looking "blocky." However, if you compute the texture values for each pixel in the fragment processor, you compute as much resolution as your equations can create, and you avoid any blockiness. Another advantage of computing texture values is that you need not use precious texture memory to store the texture, since you are computing the values on the fly.

In this section, we give some examples of procedural texturing that take advantage of this per-pixel computation, showing some techniques that you will find useful. You can take different approaches to this process. In one approach, you do not use any texture coordinates at all, but work directly from the geometry and use model, world, or eye coordinates as the basis for your computation. Examples of this kind of texturing include computing level lines or geodesic lines as textures. In another approach, you include texture coordinates in your modeling, but rather than serving as indices into a texture, the texture coordinates are used as the input to the texture computation function. Examples of this approach can include computed brick and checkerboard textures, such as are often found in beginning graphics texts, as well as more exotic kinds of textures. We use one of the more exotic examples in this section.

Using Model or Eye Coordinates

In the chapter on vertex shaders, we saw how different coordinate systems could be used to determine object coloring using both model-space and eye-space coordinates, and we saw a vertex shader that could send either set of coordinates to the fragment shader. These colorings weren't treated formally as texture operations, but because their computations can determine the color of individual pixels, they can be thought of in that way. The figure in the vertex shader chapter showing the results of these two colorings is repeated as Figure 9.3, and the fragment shader for these two figures is shown below.

Notice how the fragment shader below simply picks up the varying variable vx from the vertex shader, without caring which set of geometry produced

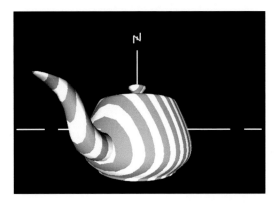
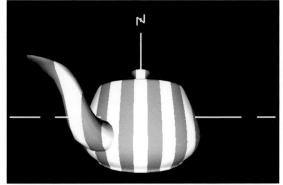

Figure 9.3. The teapots with model-space (left) and eye-space (right) colors, repeated from Chapter 7.

it. In the left-hand image, you see that the stripes follow the value of vX in model space (running from the tip of the spout to the handle), while in the right-hand image, you see that the stripes follow the value of vX in eye space (from right to left). It then uses these variables to compute the color of each pixel, either the original color of the object or the color white, based on a simple calculation—essentially computing the texture based only on the object's geometry in the space that is passed to it. This fragment shader function is designed for *glman* and uses three uniform slider variables, uA, uP, and uTol, that let you experiment with the frequency and width of the stripes, and the blurring of the stripe edges, respectively.

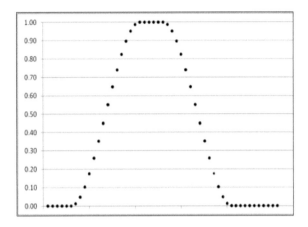

Figure 9.4. The graph of the smoothpulse function.

```
uniform float uA;
uniform float uP;
uniform float uTol;

in float vX;
in vec4  vColor;
in float vLightIntensity;

out vec4 fFragColor;

const vec4 WHITE = vec4( 1., 1., 1., 1. );

void
main( )
{
   float f = fract( uA*vX );

   float t = smoothstep( 0.5-uP-uTol, 0.5-uP+uTol, f )
               - smoothstep( 0.5+uP-uTol, 0.5+uP+uTol, f );
   fFragColor = vec4(vLightIntensity*mix( WHITE, uColor, t ).rgb,
                       1.);
}
```

Combining two smoothstep( ) functions like this

```
smoothstep( 0.5-uP-uTol, 0.5-uP+uTol,f )
 - smoothstep( 0.5+uP-uTol, 0.5+uP+uTol,f );
```

is known as a *smooth pulse* function and is very useful in smoothly blending a new color or value in a given tolerance (here uTol) of a given value range (here $0.5 - uP$ to $0.5 + uP$). This function is shown in Figure 9.4.

Using Texture Coordinates

The texture coordinates that you define with your model can be used for more than simple texture lookup. In the fragment processor, they appear as interpolated variables whose values can be used to compute a procedural texture directly. One example of doing this is a simple brick texture, in which the values of the texture coordinates are scaled up and tested for position. The code that determines the color of a pixel might look like that below. (This example assumes that a test for position is done in the Boolean colorTest( ) function.)

```
vec3 theColor;
vec2 st = vST;
st.s = fract( st.s * s_Mag_Factor );
st.t = fract( st.t * t_Mag_Factor );
if ( colorTest( st ) )
   theColor = vec3( 0.8, 0.3. 0.0 ); // color of brick
else
   theColor = vec3( 0.9, 0.6, 0.4 ); // color of mortar
fFragColor = vec4( theColor, 1. );
```

And, as before, we quickly note that the lines

```
st.s = fract( st.s * s_Mag_Factor );
st.t = fract( st.t * t_Mag_Factor );
```

could be written more efficiently as

```
st = fract( st * vec2(s_Mag_Factor,t_Mag_Factor) );
```

A more sophisticated example of a procedural texture computes the Mandelbrot function [28] given by the texture coordinates of each vertex, using an iterative process. For a particular complex number c, we can define a sequence $\{f_k(z)\}$ recursively by setting $f_0(z) = z^2 + c$ and $f_{n+1}(z) = f_n(z)^2 + c$ for a complex number z. If we start with the initial value $z = 0 + 0i$, this sequence will converge for some values of c and not for others. If it converges, the number c is said to be in the Mandelbrot set. Of perhaps more interest are those numbers c for which the sequence does not converge. Because the sequence will always converge if it is bounded, the usual computational approach is to iterate it a large number of times to see if the magnitude of $f_k(z)^2$ ever exceeds some limit. If it does, the number of iterations it takes to reach that magnitude is said to be the *Mandelbrot number* of c. The sketch below shows the way this is computed and used to color a space.

```
// Initial input is a complex number (real, imag)
// Set x = real and y = imag

Iterate until we reach a max # of iterations or x*x+y*y >= some
limit
{
   float newx = x*x - y*y + r;
   float newy = 2.*x*y + c;
   x = newx; y = newy;
}

if x*x+y*y < some limit        // the process has converged
   color the fragment blue
else
   color the fragment based on the number of iterations
```

You see this implemented in the fragment shader code below. In this code, you see two variables that are set by the vertex shader; one provides the 2D texture coordinates from the graphics primitive's surface, and the other is the light intensity, so that diffuse lighting can be used. The 2D texture coordinates are used as the real and imaginary parts of the complex number above, and are adjusted to get the texture centered and sized correctly for effect. In the vertex shader, the 2D varying variable ST is created by taking the texture coordinates for the vertices, originally in [0., 1.], and mapping them into the standard Mandelbrot complex domain [-1., 1.] where they can be interpolated by the fragment shader. All the uniform variables are set in the GLIB file, and most are *glman* slider variables, so you can experiment with the parameters for the texture.

```
uniform int uMaxIters;
uniform float uTS;      // texture coordinate scaling
uniform float uCS;      // color scaling
uniform float uS0;      // starting texture value in S
uniform float uT0;      // starting texture value in T
uniform float uLimit;   // how large before stop iterations
uniform vec3 uConvergeColor;
uniform vec3 uDivergeColor1;
uniform vec3 uDivergeColor2;

in vec2 vST;
in float vLightIntensity;
out vec4 fFragColor;

void main( )
{
```

```
float real = vST.s * uTS + uS0;
float imag = vST.t * uTS + uT0;
float real0 = real;
float imag0 = imag;
float newr;
int numIters;
vec4 color = vec4( 0., 0., 0., 1. );

for( numIters = 0; numIters < uMaxIters; numIters++ )
{
  float newreal = real0 + real*real - imag*imag;
  float newimag = imag0 + 2.*real*imag;
  newr = newreal*newreal + newimag*newimag;
  if( newr >= uLimit )
    break;
  real = newreal;
  imag = newimag;
}

// choose the color
if( newr < uLimit )
  color = uConvergeColor;
else
  color = mix( uDivergeColor1, uDivergeColor2,
            fract(numIters/uCS) );

color.rgb *= vLightIntensity;
fFragColor = color;
}
```

This works by choosing the color for each pixel in the fragment based on the way the Mandelbrot sequence converges at the point in texture space, vST, offset into the teapot's surface. If the pixel is in the area where the Mandelbrot process converges (i.e., newr < uLimit), it is colored with uConvergeColor; if it does not converge it is colored by a color that blends two other colors, using the built-in mix( ) function, depending on the number of iterations needed. Notice that the resolution just keeps increasing as the image is zoomed. An advantage of procedural texturing in fragment shaders is that the texture can be computed at the pixel level, no matter what size that pixel actually represents in the model. The potentially large number of iterations for the Mandelbrot sequence gives us the opportunity to illustrate the power of double precision in shaders. Figure 9.5 shows two views of a highly-zoomed region of the Mandelbrot set. The top figure shows this region with single-precision computation, while the bottom figure shows it with double precision.

Similar kinds of textures can be created with other iterative processes [36]. An example would be a Julia set texture that uses a slightly different kind of computation. For the function sequence as defined above,

$$f_0(z) = z^2 + c \ \text{ and } \ f_{n+1}(z) = f_n(z)^2 + c,$$

we change the focus and start with the point z as the input and some fixed complex number c as a constant. This yields a rather different kind of image, but one related to the Mandelbrot set image by whether the complex number c is in the Mandelbrot set, and if so, where it is. The fragment shader code to implement this is quite similar to the code given above, and is left as an exercise to the reader.

Bump Mapping

Bump mapping is a technique that simulates variations in a surface by manipulating the surface normals, allowing the lighting process to create the appearance of the variations. The key is to think about normals, not vertices, and to realize that in a fragment shader, you are touching each pixel individually. This technique can use an analytic approach and compute normals as function derivatives, as we will see with the ripple example below, or it can use a more geometric approach and compute normals based on location and the slopes of the shape of the bump pattern, as we will see in the pyramid map example.

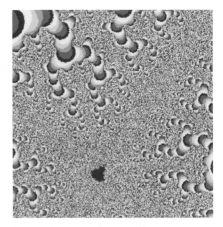

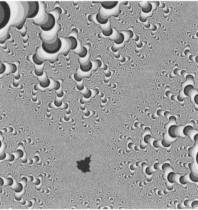

Figure 9.5. A region of the Mandelbrot set computed with single precision (top) and double precision (bottom).

Height Fields with Bump Mapping

Many effects can be created by bump mapping. One important use is in displaying *height fields*. For example, bump mapping can create the ripples on a surface, as shown in Figure 9.6; the figures also include a coordinate system for a particular pixel on the surface. Notice the difference between the ripples made by bump mapping, where the ripples do not, in fact, have any height, and ripples made in a vertex shader, as shown in Figure 3.4 of Chapter 3.

To analyze these bumps so that we can design appropriate mappings of normals, let's start working in 2D, where we can draw figures more easily. If a

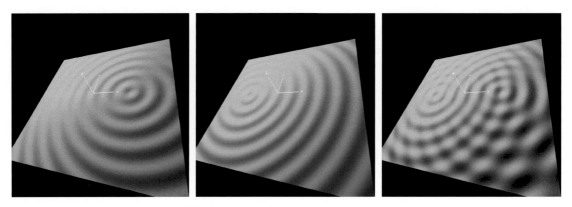

Figure 9.6. Ripples by bump mapping.

line segment has slope $m = \dfrac{dy}{dx}$, we can express the slope as the vector $[1, m]$, as shown in the diagrams below.

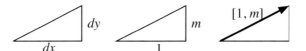

The normal to any line with slope m has slope $\dfrac{1}{-m}$ (the negative reciprocal of the original slope), so the normal can be expressed as the vector $(-m, 1.)$. Notice that the dot product is $(1,m) \times (-m,1) = 0$, as must be true if the vectors are perpendicular. So if we want to model a moving "bump" on the surface with height a, period P_d, and time t, we have

$$z = -a * \cos\left(\frac{2\pi x}{P_d} - 2\pi t\right)$$

and its slope, or derivative with respect to x, is

$$\frac{dz}{dx} = a * \frac{2\pi}{P_d} * \sin\left(\frac{2\pi x}{P_d} - 2\pi t\right)$$

so the vector slope, s, is

$$s = \left[1., 0., a * \frac{2\pi}{P_d} * \sin\left(\frac{2\pi x}{P_d} - 2\pi t\right)\right].$$

Following the same pattern as before, we see that the normal vector, n, is

$$n = \left[-a * \frac{2\pi}{P_d} * \sin\left(\frac{2\pi x}{P_d} - 2\pi t \right), 0., 1. \right].$$

This is true along just the X axis. Because the ripples are propagating out in a circular pattern, we need to rotate the normal vector into where it really is. Because we are just talking about a rotation, the transformation is the same as if we were rotating a vertex. Noting that the unrotated N_y is equal to 0., we get

$$Nx' = Nx * \cos\Theta - Ny * \sin\Theta = Nx * \cos\Theta$$
$$Ny' = Nx * \sin\Theta + Ny * \cos\Theta = Nx * \sin\Theta$$
$$Nz' = Nz = 1.$$

As we said at the beginning, so far we have been working in 2D, not 3D; for the final version of the fragment shader in the ripples case above, you need to think in polar coordinates, so you need to substitute R, the polar coordinate radius, for x in the slope equation.

```
uniform  float  uTime;
uniform  float  uAmp0, uAmp1;
uniform  float  uPhaseShift;
uniform  float  uPd;
uniform  float  uLightX, uLightY, uLightZ;
uniform  vec4   uColor;

in vec3 vMCposition;
in vec3 vECposition;

out vec4 fFragColor;

const float TWOPI = 2.*3.14159265;

void main( )
{
   const vec3 C0 = vec3( -2.5, 0., 0. );
   const vec3 C1 = vec3(  2.5, 0., 0. );

   // first set of ripples:

   float rad0 = length( vMCposition - C0 );  // ripple center 0
   float H0 = -uAmp0 * cos( TWOPI*rad0/uPd - TWOPI*uTime );

   float u = -uAmp0 * (TWOPI/uPd) * sin(TWOPI*rad0/uPd -
                                   TWOPI*uTime);
```

```
float v = 0.;
float w = 1.;

float  ang = atan(vMCposition.y - C0.y,
                  vMCposition.x - C0.x );
float  u1 = dot( vec2(u,v), vec2(cos(ang), -sin(ang)) );
float  v1 = dot( vec2(u,v), vec2(sin(ang),  cos(ang)) );
float  w1 = 1.;

// second set of ripples:

float rad1 = length( vMCposition - C1 );  // ripple center 1
float H1   = -uAmp1 * cos( TWOPI*rad1/uPd - TWOPI*uTime );

u = -uAmp1*(TWOPI/uPd)*
    sin(TWOPI*rad1/uPd-TWOPI*uTime-uPhaseShift);
v = 0.;
ang = atan( vMCposition.y - C1.y, vMCposition.x - C1.x );
float u2 = dot( vec2(u,v), vec2(cos(ang), -sin(ang)) );
float v2 = dot( vec2(u,v), vec2(sin(ang),  cos(ang)) );
float w2 = 1.;

// the sum is the normal:

vec3 normal = normalize( vec3( u1+u2, v1+v2, w1+w2 ) );

float LightIntensity =
  abs(dot(normalize(vec3(uLightX,uLightY,uLightZ)-
    vECposition),normal));
if( LightIntensity < 0.1 )
  LightIntensity = 0.1;

fFragColor = vec4( LightIntensity*uColor.rgb, uColor.a );
}
```

And, of course, there is the usual comment about the efficiency thing. The lines

```
float ang = atan( vMCposition.y - C0.y, vMCposition.x - C0.x );
float up = dot( vec2(u,v), vec2(cos(ang), -sin(ang)) );
float vp = dot( vec2(u,v), vec2(sin(ang),  cos(ang)) );
```

were written for clarity, but could have been written more efficiently by just using x and y components for the trigonometric functions:

```
vec2 d = vMCposition.xy - C0.xy;
vec2 cossin = normalize( d );
```

```
float up = dot( vec2(u,v), vec2(cossin.x, -cossin.y) );
float vp = dot( vec2(u,v), cossin.yx) );
```

In fact, this is a good programming lesson in general. Don't ever call the atan function and then turn around and use the resulting angle to compute a sine or cosine. You already had the sine and cosine when you called the atan function (albeit, possibly with a little manipulation).

Generalized Bump Mapping

Height fields are a special, and simplified, case of bump-mapping. Now, let's look at it in the general case. For this, we will define a *surface local coordinate system* at each fragment with components N, T, B (Normal, Tangent, and Bitangent $B = T \times N$). Figure 9.7 shows the pyramid map example, and the vertex and fragment shaders used to create it are shown below.

The pyramid bump map example needs special vertex and fragment shaders. The vertex shader sets up the surface coordinate system discussed above, taking the tangent and normal from the geometric object and computing the varying variable vLightDir that is used in the fragment shader, along with the computed normal, to determine the diffuse light component for the pixel. In this example, we convert everything into the eye coordinate system. It can also work to convert everything into the surface local coordinate system, but the surface local coordinate system changes at each location in the geometry. By using a "universal" coordinate system, such as eye coordinates, we can make surface coordinates, light positions and directions, reflection directions, and refraction directions all interoperate.

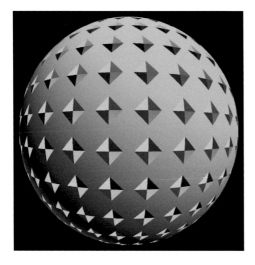

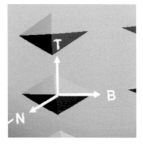

Figure 9.7. A sphere with pyramid bump mapping (left) and the right-handed *BTN* coordinate system for one particular location (right).

```
attribute vec3 aTangent;          // from glman Sphere primitive
                                  // points towards north pole

uniform float uLightX, uLightY, uLightZ; // from sliders

out vec3 vBTNx, vBTNy, vBTNz;
out vec3 vLightDir;               // light direction in TNB coords
out vec2 vST;

// N is the direction of the surface normal
// T is the direction of "Tangent", which is (dx/dt, dy/dt,
//                                            dz/dt)
// B is the TxN, which is the direction of (dx/ds, dy/ds, dz/ds)

void main( )
{
  vST = aTexCoord0.st;

  // B-T-N form an X-Y-Z-looking right handed coordinate system:
  vec3 N = normalize( uNormalMatrix * aNormal );
  vec2 T = normalize( vec3( uModelViewMatrix*vec4(aTangent,0.)
                      ) );
  vec3 B = normalize( cross(T, N) );

  // the light direction, in eye coordinates:
  vec3 lightPosition = vec3( uLightX, uLightY, uLightZ );
  vec3 ECpos = ( uModelViewMatrix * aVertex ).xyz;
  vLightDir = normalize( lightPosition - ECpos );

  // Produce the transformation from Surface coords to
  // Eye coords:

  vBTNx = vec3( B.x, T.x, N.x );
  vBTNy = vec3( B.y, T.y, N.y );
  vBTNz = vec3( B.z, T.z, N.z );

  gl_Position = uModelViewProjectionMatrix * aVertex;
}
```

The fragment shader is shown below. This uses several uniform *glman* slider variables to experiment with the surface appearance. The primary function of the shader code is to take the value of the variable vLightDir and develop the normal based on the normal that's developed by pixel position to create the appearance of the pyramids. The angle uAng is used to rotate the pyramids in place.

```
uniform  float  uAmbient;
uniform  float  uBumpDensity; // glman slider uniform variables
uniform  float  uBumpSize;
uniform  vec4   uSurfaceColor;
uniform  float  uAng;
uniform  float  uHeight;

in vec3 vBTNx, vBTNy, vBTNz;
in vec3 vLightDir;
in vec2 vST;

out vec4 fFragColor;

const float PI = 3.14159265;

float Cang, Sang;

vec3
ToXyz( vec3 btn )
{
   float xp = btn.x*Cang - btn.y*Sang;    // rotate by +Ang
   btn.y    = btn.x*Sang + btn.y*Cang;
   btn.x    = xp;
   btn = normalize( btn );

   vec3 xyz;
   xyz.x = dot( vBTNx, btn ); // convert surface local to
                              // eye coords
   xyz.y = dot( vBTNy, btn );
   xyz.z = dot( vBTNz, btn );
   return normalize( xyz );
}

void main( )
{
   vec2 st = vST;   // locate the bumps based on (s,t)

   float Swidth = 1. / uBumpDensity;
   float Theight= 1. / uBumpDensity;
   float numInS = floor( st.s / Swidth );
   float numInT = floor( st.t / Theight );

   vec2 center;
   center.s = numInS * Swidth + Swidth/2.;
   center.t = numInT * Theight + Theight/2.;
   st -= center;        // st is now wrt the center of the bump

   Cang = cos(uAng);
```

```
   Sang = sin(uAng);
   vec2 stp;              // st' = st rotated by -Ang
   stp.s = st.s*Cang + st.t*Sang;
   stp.t = -st.s*Sang + st.t*Cang;
   float theta = atan( stp.t, stp.s );

   // this is the normal of the parts of the object
   // that are not in a pyramid:
   vec3 normal = ToXyz( vec3( 0., 0., 1. ) );

   // figure out what part of the pyramid we are in and
   // get the normal there; then transform it to eye cords
   if( abs(stp.s) > Swidth/4. || abs(stp.t) > Theight/4. )
   {
      normal = ToXyz( vec3( 0., 0., 1. ) );
   }
   else
   {
      if( PI/4. <= theta && theta <= 3.*PI/4. )
      {
         normal = ToXyz( vec3( 0., uHeight, Theight/4. ) );
      }
      else if( -PI/4. <= theta && theta <= PI/4. )
      {
         normal = ToXyz( vec3( uHeight, 0., Swidth/4. ) );
      }
      else if( -3.*PI/4. <= theta && theta <= -PI/4. )
      {
         normal = ToXyz( vec3( 0., -uHeight, Theight/4. ) );
      }
      else if( theta >= 3.*PI/4. || theta <= -3.*PI/4. )
      {
         normal = ToXyz( vec3( -uHeight, 0., Swidth/4. ) );
      }
   }

   float intensity = uAmbient + (1.-uAmbient)*
                     dot(normal, vLightDir);
   vec3 litColor = uSurfaceColor.rgb * intensity;
   fFragColor = vec4( litColor, uSurfaceColor.a );
}
```

Cube Maps

Cube maps are textures that simulate the effect of an environment that surrounds the 3D scene, and are usually used to create reflection or refraction effects. Textures developed using cube maps operate differently from standard textures on the surface of an object. A cube map consists of six 2D textures, each one corresponding to the face of a cube (+X,−X,+Y,−Y,+Z,−Z) surrounding the scene. A cube map is indexed with three texture coordinates: s, t, and p. You can think of (s,t,p) as being a vector that points toward one wall of the cube map, as shown in Figure 9.8.

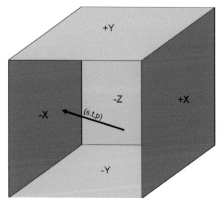

When you index into a cube map with (s,t,p), the texture-mapping hardware does the following:

1. Determines which of s, t, and p has the largest absolute value:

$$Val = \max\left(|s|,|t|,|p|\right).$$

Figure 9.8. A cube map and the (s,t,p) vector that indexes into it.

This determines which face image (+X,−X,+Y,−Y,+Z,−Z) of the cube map to index into. In Figure 9.8, this would be s, corresponding to the −X face.

2. Divides the remaining two coordinates (called a and b here) by that largest absolute value:

$$s' = \frac{a}{Val},$$

$$t' = \frac{b}{Val}.$$

In Figure 9.8, a and b would be the texture coordinates p and t.

3. Uses (s',t') as the 2D texture coordinates to use for the lookup on that face image.

To use cube maps, you must create six square texture maps of the same size that correspond to the sides of a cube. These individual texture maps are often visualized as a flattened or folded-up cube, as shown in Figure 9.9. The cube map images are created by rendering or photographing each of the six principle directions from the center of the cube, each with a 90° field of view.

Cube maps can be used to create reflection effects using the built-in GLSL reflect( ) function to compute an (s,t,p) reflection vector to look up in the cube map. Cube maps can also be used for refraction; for example, with a lens or a glass object in a scene. To do this, you use the built-in GLSL function refract( ) to compute the (s,t,p) refraction vector, and use it to look up in the cube map.

Figure 9.9. The six faces of a cube that can be used for cube mapping: unfolded (top) and folded (bottom).

Figure 9.10. A reflecting (left) and refracting (right) teapot.

Figure 9.10 shows what you can do with this: a view of both a reflective teapot in the cube (left), using reflection maps, and a glass teapot in the cube, using refraction maps (right). These figures use the NVIDIA lobby cube map. (A rich source of other cube maps can be found at [9].)

A single fragment shader will produce both these images, which come from *glman* and use the uniform slider variable uMix to control whether reflection or refraction is to be computed. They assume that a vertex shader has already computed the eye position and has set up the normal and normal matrix, and that all are varying variables, so they can be interpolated. The other computations simply use the reflection and refraction functions from GLSL and mix the color components in a familiar way.

```
uniform float       uMix;
uniform samplerCube uTexUnit;
uniform float       uIofR;      // index of refraction

in vec3  vECposition;
in vec3  vTheNormal;

out vec4 fFragColor;

const vec4 WHITE = vec4( 1., 1., 1., 1. );

void main( )
{
   vec3 normal = normalize( uNormalMatrix * vTheNormal );
```

```
// the reflect and refract functions assume the normal is
// pointing toward the eye, that is, normal.z > 0.
// if that's not true, make it true:

if( normal.z < 0. )
{
    normal = -normal;
}

vec3 ReflectVector  = reflect(normalize(vECposition),normal);
vec3 RefractVector  = refract(normalize(vECposition),
                              normal,uIofR);

vec4 reflectcolor = texture( uTexUnit, ReflectVector );
vec4 refractcolor = mix(texture(uTexUnit,RefractVector),
                        WHITE,0.2);

fFragColor=vec4(mix(reflectcolor.rgb,
                    refractcolor.rgb,uMix),1.);
}
```

Note that both the reflect( ) and refract( ) functions use the argument

```
normalize( vECposition )
```

What is this? The GLSL reflect( ) and refract( ) functions want that argument to be the incoming vector from the eye to the point that is being reflected from or refracted through. Remember that in OpenGL, once the viewing transformation has been applied, the eye ends up at the origin. So, those arguments could have been listed more clearly by making it obvious that we were creating that vector as a difference between two points, like this:

```
normalize( vECposition - vec3(0.,0.,0.) )
```

Also, note that the refraction result mixes in some white. This is because most refractive-transparent objects have a small amount of "milky" appearance to them, as light is somewhat attenuated as it passes through the material.

The second mix( ) is blending the refraction with some reflection, as is usually the case with real objects.

Are these accurate reflections and refractions? They look good, but they are not perfect, at least not in the ray-tracing sense. For one thing, each of the six images in the cube map is determined from an eye position at the center of the cube, thus forever "baking in" that direction's spatial relationships from just a single eye position. This imperfection is true for both cube map reflections and refractions. Also, when doing cube map refractions, the refraction only takes place at the front surface of the object, not both front and back, as would be the case with a real object. In 3D graphics, the back surface's behavior gets z-buffered out.

Note that you can also combine cube mapping with bump mapping, as shown in Figure 9.11. This is one of the reasons that, when doing bump mapping, it is better to convert the surface local coordinates of the bumps to eye space, instead of the other way around. This allows the bump mapping normals to interoperate with the cube map `reflect( )` and `refract( )` functions.

Render to Texture

Textures need not come only from files or from computation, as our previous examples have done. You can also render an image into a texture and then use that image as a texture. For example, you could render a wireframe teapot into a texture and use that on a moving surface, as shown in Figure 9.12.

Figure 9.11. A reflecting (left) and refracting (right) bump-mapped teapot.

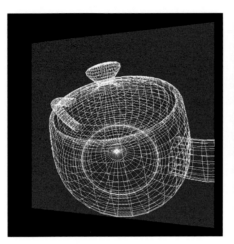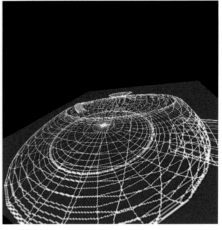

Figure 9.12. Two views of a rotating teapot on a rotating plane.

The render-to-texture operation uses the framebuffer extension, that is, `GL_framebuffer_object`, so you need to be sure this is supported on your system.

The steps to render an image to a texture involve creating the formal buffers needed for output, creating a texture, and assigning the output buffers to the texture. You then carry out a set of bindings of properties to the buffers and texture and render a scene; this scene is then a texture, and you can use it in rendering another scene. The details are below.

1. You will be changing the display destination. Generate a handle for a framebuffer object, and generate handles for a (depth) renderbuffer object and for a texture object. (These will later be attached to the framebuffer object.)

2. Bind the framebuffer object to the context.

3. Bind the depth renderbuffer object to the context.
   Assign storage attributes to it.
   Attach it to the framebuffer object.

4. Bind the texture object to the context.
   Assign storage attributes to it.
   Assign texture parameters to it.
   Attach it to the framebuffer object.

5. Render as normal.

6. Un-bind the framebuffer object from the context.

To implement these operations, our code closely follows the outline above. The code is presented in three groups. The first code group implements the first four points and would typically be found in your InitGraphics( ) function. This is independent of the particular teapot and quad example of the figure.

```
// generate FrameBuffer handle, RenderBuffer handle, Texture
// handle
GLuint FrameBuffer;
GLuint DepthBuffer;
GLuint Texture;

glGenFramebuffers(  1, &FrameBuffer );
glGenRenderBuffers( 1, &DepthBuffer );
glGenTextures(      1, &Texture );

// set up the size for the rendered texture
int sizeX = 2048;
int sizeY = 2048;

// Bind the offscreen framebuffer to be the current output
// display
glBindFramebuffer( GL_FRAMEBUFFER, FrameBuffer );

// Bind the Depth Buffer to the context, allocate its storage,
// and attach it to the Framebuffer
glBindRenderbuffer( GL_RENDERBUFFER, DepthBuffer );
glRenderbufferStorage( GL_RENDERBUFFER,
                       GL_DEPTH_COMPONENT, sizeX, sizeY );
glFramebufferRenderbuffer( GL_FRAMEBUFFER, GL_DEPTH_ATTACHMENT,
                           GL_RENDERBUFFER, DepthBuffer );

// Bind the Texture to the Context
glBindTexture( GL_TEXTURE_2D, Texture );

// Set up a NULL texture of the size you want to render into
// and set its properties
glTexImage2D(    GL_TEXTURE_2D, 0, 4, sizeX, sizeY, 0, GL_RGBA,
                 GL_UNSIGNED_BYTE, NULL );
glTexParameteri( GL_TEXTURE_2D, GL_TEXTURE_WRAP_S, GL_CLAMP );
glTexParameteri( GL_TEXTURE_2D, GL_TEXTURE_WRAP_T, GL_CLAMP );
glTexParameteri( GL_TEXTURE_2D, GL_TEXTURE_MAG_FILTER,
                 GL_LINEAR );
glTexParameteri( GL_TEXTURE_2D, GL_TEXTURE_MIN_FILTER,
                 GL_LINEAR );
glTexEnvf(       GL_TEXTURE_ENV, GL_TEXTURE_ENV_MODE,
                 GL_REPLACE );
```

```
// Tell OpenGL that you are going to render into the color
// planes of the Texture

glFramebufferTexture2D( GL_FRAMEBUFFER, GL_COLOR_ATTACHMENT0,
                        GL_TEXTURE_2D, Texture, 0 );

// see if OpenGL thinks the framebuffer is complete enough to
// use:

GLenum status = glCheckFramebufferStatus( GL_FRAMEBUFFER );
if( status != GL_FRAMEBUFFER_COMPLETE )
        fprintf( stderr, "FrameBuffer is not complete.\n" );
```

The next code group implements the last two points in the list above, and would typically be found in the Display( ) callback function. The first part of this code is very familiar modeling code, but it renders the wireframe teapot into the texture framebuffer. After that is finished, the rendering is returned to the usual hardware framebuffer. This is the last point in the list above. We have highlighted two points in the code to remind you that the dimension of the texture you are creating must be the same as the size you defined, and to note that framebuffer 0 is the standard hardware buffer.

```
// render as normal; be sure to set the viewport to match the
// size of the color and depth buffers
glClearColor( 0.0, 0.2, 0.0, 1. );
glClear( GL_COLOR_BUFFER_BIT | GL_DEPTH_BUFFER_BIT );
glEnable( GL_DEPTH_TEST );
glShadeModel( GL_FLAT );
glViewport( 0, 0, sizeX, sizeY );

glMatrixMode( GL_PROJECTION );
glLoadIdentity( );
gluPerspective( 90., 1., 0.1, 1000. );

glMatrixMode( GL_MODELVIEW );
glLoadIdentity( );
gluLookAt( 0., 0., 3., 0., 0., 0., 0., 1., 0. );

glTranslatef( TransXYZ[0], TransXYZ[1], TransXYZ[2] );
glMultMatrixf( RotMatrix );
glScalef( scale, scale, scale );
glColor3f( 1., 1., 1. );

glutWireTeapot( 1. );
```

```
// Tell OpenGL to go back to rendering to the hardware
// framebuffer:

glBindFramebuffer( GL_FRAMEBUFFER, 0 );

// if you want, have OpenGL create the multiple mipmap layers
// for you
glGenerateMipmap( GL_TEXTURE_2D );
```

The third code group is straightforward graphics programming with textures , using the vertex coordinate and texture coordinate functions in compatibility mode for clarity's sake. The texture that was just computed is used in rendering the scene (here, the simple textured quad).

```
// now render the rest of the scene as normal, using the Texture
// as you normally would:
. . .

glEnable( GL_TEXTURE_2D );
glBindTexture( GL_TEXTURE_2D, Texture );
glBegin( GL_QUADS );
    glTexCoord2f( 0., 0. );
    glVertex2f( -1., -1. );
    glTexCoord2f( 1., 0. );
    glVertex2f( 1., -1. );
    glTexCoord2f( 1., 1. );
    glVertex2f( 1., 1. );
    glTexCoord2f( 0., 1. );
    glVertex2f( -1., 1. );
glEnd( );

glDisable( GL_TEXTURE_2D );
. . .
```

Render to Texture for Multipass Rendering in glman

One of the main reasons to do render-to-texture is for multipass rendering algorithms. To make this easier to experiment with, *glman* has setup a mechanism make it easy to ask for. The following .glib file shows you how this is done:

```
##OpenGL GLIB
Perspective 90
```

```
Texture 6 1024 1024

RenderToTexture 6

Background 0. 0.1 0.
Clear

Vertex   filter.vert
Fragment filter.frag
Program  Filter1                                    \
 uAd <.01 .2 .5> uBd <.01 .2 .5>                    \
 uNoiseAmp <0. 0. 1.> uNoiseFreq <0. 1. 2.> \
 uTol <0. 0. 1.>

Teapot

RenderToTexture


Background 0. 0.0 0
Clear
LookAt 0 0 2.5 0 0 0 0 1 0

Vertex image.vert
Fragment image.frag
Program Filter2   uInUnit 6               \
                  uEdgeDetect <true>      \
                  uTEdge <0. 0. 1.>       \
                  uTSharp <-3. 1. 10.>

Translate 0 0 0.
QuadXY .2 2.
```

For once, the interesting detail is in the .glib file. The vertex and fragment files used here (two of each) are standard effects that you have already seen. The steps in the .glib file are as follows:

1. The Texture2D glib command normally looks for a file name, but it can also take an s and t resolution. In this case, it sets up an empty texture of that size in graphics memory and assigns it to the given texture unit.

2. The RenderToTexture sets up the rendering output mechanism (just discussed) to that texture unit.

3. The teapot is rendered with a shader program that creates a procedural noisy-ellipse texture.

4. The empty RenderToTexture returns rendering to go to the normal screen framebuffer.

5. Another shader program is made current. This one is a 2D image filtering program like we have seen before. It can do blur-sharpen or edge detection. The texture unit into which we just rendered the 3D scene is supplied to this program as uInUnit.

6. A quad is drawn. You know that it is drawing a 2D quad, but because it is using the results of the previous 3D render as the quad's texture, the user thinks that a 3D object is being drawn here.

7. The Filter2 shader changes the appearance of the 3D render.

Figure 9.13 shows this shader in action.

Figure 9.13. Render-to-texture and multipass in action: the original, unmodified, teapot (top left); teapot with the noise turned on (top right); noise teapot, sharpened (bottom left); noise teapot, edge detected (bottom right).

Exercises

1. Duplicate the work shown in Figure 9.5 above for Mandelbrot sets to create a texture via a Julia set computation.

2. Fixed-function OpenGL has its own texture environment functions, but when you write your own shaders for textures you implement what you need. In the chapter, we mentioned the four standard texture modes. Ignoring for now the effect on the alpha channel, implement these modes:

   a. For *replace* or *decal* mode, the color of a pixel is replaced by the color of the texel.

   b. For *modulate* mode, the color of a pixel is replaced by the product of the color of the object pixel and the color of the texel.

   c. For *blend* mode, the color of a pixel is replaced by the product of the color of the object pixel and 1 – the color of the texel.

3. Continuing with texture modes, which of these modes would probably be the most useful if you were applying more than one texture to an object? Why? Might this be different if you were including the alpha channel in your textures?

4. Develop vertex and fragment shaders for a bump map that simulates small partial spheres placed regularly on a surface, much like the pyramid shader simulates pyramids.

5. One of the problems in cube mapping is creating a good set of textures for the faces of the cube. You can do this from digital photographs if you are careful to match the edges of the faces. Do this for some familiar environment, such as your room or a campus quad.

6. Create a combined bump-map / cube-map image as shown in Figure 9.11.

7. Add other image processing effects to the multipass rendering example.

8. Find an excuse to change the two-pass example above to a three (or more) pass example.

10

Noise

One of the perpetual challenges of computer graphics has been to create images that are not only geometrically correct, but are also visually interesting. Texture mapping of real images is commonly used in this way. Another technique involves adding procedural "random" effects such as are seen in natural phenomena (clouds, fire, smoke), natural materials (marble, wood, granite, sand), small-scale randomness (random textures in materials), and many other things, through the use of *noise* functions. In this chapter we discuss noise functions and their use in shaders, specifically fragment shaders, in creating images.

The topic of noise is not necessarily associated with shaders, and you may have encountered it in another computer graphics course. We describe it separately from the details of shaders because it has interest on its own, and we will certainly find that it adds very interesting opportunities for shaders to use in creating some very attractive images.

The GLSL specification lists a built-in noise function. However, at the time of this writing, its exact behavior has not yet been universally decided upon. So, while it is in the spec, you might not be able to use it. This chapter will discuss the fundamentals of noise for graphics shaders, and will show how *glman* uses 2D and 3D textures to get around the absence of a working GLSL noise function. Even if you are not using *glman*, you will see how to computationally generate noise, which you can then use by embedding it in your own texture.

Fundamental Noise Concepts

A *noise function* is a real-valued function that takes on values between 0. and 1. over some domain.[1] A noise function is often generated by determining *pseudo-random numbers* (*PRNs*) at each of a number of fixed points in a domain and processing those values to generate a function across the entire domain. If the domain is an interval, we have one-dimensional noise; if the domain is a plane region, we have two-dimensional noise; if the domain is a region in three-dimensional space, we have three-dimensional noise. The values of the noise function can be used to modify values of such things as the pixel properties in a fragment shader. In this section we will briefly introduce some kinds of noise functions and their properties, based on one-dimensional noise operations for simplicity.

There are some choices we will need to make as we design a shader that is to use noise functions. Below we discuss some of those choices. If you are using *glman* with your study of shaders, you will find the *noisegraph* application as part of the distribution, and you can use that to experiment with many of the noise concepts you will find in this chapter. All the 1D noise function graphs that you will see as figures in this chapter were developed with *noisegraph*.

Three Types of Noise: Value, Gradient, and Value+Gradient

One choice you will need to make is whether you want to use *value noise* or *gradient noise*. The value and gradient noise functions produce results that have qualitative differences. Both kinds of noise functions are based on piecewise interpolating their definitions at a fixed set of points in their domain, usually regularly spaced. Both kinds of noise need values at each point; these are given by using system-generated pseudo-random numbers. In *value noise*, the pseudo-random values at each fixed point are used as the noise function values, and the

---

1. Some noise functions prefer the range –1. to 1. It doesn't really matter. It just means that you will transform the noise return values differently.

slope of the function at each point is set to be zero or to a natural slope (more on this later). These properties are directly interpolated to generate a piecewise cubic or quintic function across the entire domain. In *gradient noise*, the function value is set at each fixed point, and the pseudo-random values at that fixed point are used as the gradient (slope) of the curve through the point. Gradient noise with the fixed values set to zero is the type of noise originally defined for the Photorealistic RenderMan package [37]. It is also popular to set both the value and the gradient at the fixed points with pseudo-random numbers, the *value+gradient noise*. Noise that is based on pseudorandom number (PRN) gradients is often called *Perlin noise* [34], [35]. For both kinds of noise, these values are used to determine the equation of a piecewise cubic noise function between the two points, as described later in this chapter.

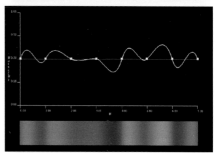

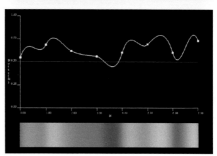

The *noisegraph* application is a tool that lets you test out these different noise types and parameters for yourself. It produces line graphs of 1D noise functions and pseudocolor regions for 2D noise. The application is driven by a menu with choices for the kind of noise, the number of octaves, and the kind of pseudocolor display; it also lets you make other choices for options discussed in this chapter.

All three types of continuous noise functions are illustrated by *noisegraph* displays in Figure 10.1. As you can tell from these graphs, value noise can, by chance, have regions of similar values, while gradient-only noise always passes through zero at regular points. This affects the kind of control you would have with

Figure 10.1. A one-dimensional value-only noise function (top), a gradient-only function (middle), and value+gradient noise function (bottom).

each. This distinction forms a kind of dual relationship between the functions and is the key to how they are defined. We will see how it affects the actual function expressions when we consider those a little later in the chapter.

Cubic and Quintic Interpolation

We can use several different options as we create the piecewise interpolation of the initial pseudo-random values that is needed to create the overall noise function. Two common ones are to use a *cubic interpolation* or to use a *quin-*

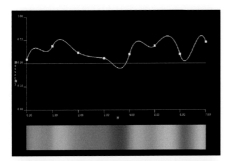

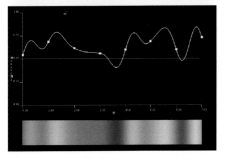

Figure 10.2. Cubic (top) and quintic (bottom) value+gradient interpolations on the same basis.

tic interpolation. Quintic interpolations are similar, but they use a fifth-degree polynomial basis rather than a cubic polynomial basis. The difference between the two interpolations may be subtle; you will need to look closely at the two value+gradient noise functions from *noisegraph* in Figure 10.2 to see any difference. Cubic interpolations are C^1 continuous (the curve has continuous slope), while quintic interpolations are C^2 continuous (the curve has both continuous slope and continuous curvature) and thus are smoother. One way to think of the difference is that quintic functions maintain the curvature continuity at each connection point by enlarging the overshoot there, not unlike racing past second base in baseball. See [35] for a more complete discussion.

Noise Equations

The key to understanding the derivation of the noise functions is realizing that they are polynomial functions whose coefficients are determined by the noise properties you are using. Let's begin with cubic noise functions and then go on to quintic functions.

Any cubic function of a single variable is given by a general cubic expression as

$$N(t) = A + Bt + Ct^2 + Dt^3.$$

This expression gives the value, or position, of the function for any parametric value t. Because this expression has four unknowns, we need four known quantities to determine them.

Now if we take the derivative of this expression, we get the gradient

$$G(t) = \frac{dN}{dt} = B + 2Ct + 3Dt^2.$$

If we consider the values of the function and gradient at the endpoints of the interval [0,1] in the parameter t,

$$N_0 = N(t=0) \quad N_1 = N(t=1)$$
$$G_0 = G(t=0) \quad G_1 = G(t=1)$$

then you can see that you have four values that you can use to compute the four unknown coefficients for the noise function. We can put these values into a system of four equations in the four unknowns, and we get

$$\begin{Bmatrix} N_0 \\ N_1 \\ G_0 \\ G_1 \end{Bmatrix} = \begin{bmatrix} 1 & 0 & 0 & 0 \\ 1 & 1 & 1 & 1 \\ 0 & 1 & 0 & 0 \\ 0 & 1 & 2 & 3 \end{bmatrix} \begin{Bmatrix} A \\ B \\ C \\ D \end{Bmatrix}.$$

We can invert this matrix and get an exact matrix expression for A, B, C, and D:

$$\begin{Bmatrix} A \\ B \\ C \\ D \end{Bmatrix} = \begin{bmatrix} 1 & 0 & 0 & 0 \\ 0 & 0 & 1 & 0 \\ -3 & 3 & -2 & -1 \\ 2 & -2 & 1 & 1 \end{bmatrix} \begin{Bmatrix} N_0 \\ N_1 \\ G_0 \\ G_1 \end{Bmatrix}.$$

This will give us the values of the coefficients in terms of the positions and gradients. To simplify this, we gather the coefficients and get an expression like this:

$$N(t) = B_{N0} N_0 + B_{N1} N_1 + B_{G0} G_0 + B_{G1} G_1.$$

When we do this, the coefficients are

$$B_{N0} = 1 - 3t^2 + 2t^3,$$
$$B_{N1} = 3t^2 - 2t^3 = 1 - B_{N0},$$
$$B_{G0} = t - 2t^2 + t^3,$$
$$B_{G1} = -t^2 + t^3.$$

Some value-only noise functions choose to set the gradients to zero at each of the noise points, but this is highly arbitrary. A better approach is to choose the gradients intelligently, based on the positions of the surrounding points. A good way to do this is with the gradients that one would use for a Catmull-Rom spline [8]. Because the noise points are all unit-spaced, the Catmull-Rom gradient simplifies to

$$G_i = \frac{1}{2}\left(N_{i+1} - N_{i-1}\right).$$

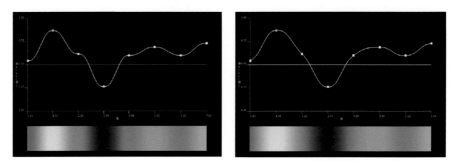

Figure 10.3. Forcing the gradients to zero (left) and computing the gradients from the distribution of points (Catmull-Rom, right). Notice how much more natural the curve appears as it passes through the connections when a reasonable slope is computed instead of artificially set to zero.

That is, to get the parametric slope at noise point i, draw a vector from the previous point to the next point, and take half of it. Figure 10.3 shows how this changes the overall shape of the noise curve, making it a lot smoother.

Since all four coefficients are spelled out above, you now have the full cubic polynomial functions for any combinations of values and gradients you want in a noise function. Using the same conditions for $t = 1$ at the end of one segment and $t = 0$ at the beginning of the next segment will ensure that the functions are differentiable at the point between them, giving you an overall C^1 noise function.

What about *quintic* noise functions? Here we need to place additional conditions on the function at the given points in order to derive the six coefficients on the general quintic polynomial function

$$N(t) = A + Bt + Ct^2 + Dt^3 + Et^4 + Ft^5.$$

We already have the function value N and the gradient G at each point, giving us four conditions. The two additional necessary conditions are given by specifying the curvature C of the function at the points. The curvature is given by the second derivative, so we now have three expressions to evaluate. Besides the $N(t)$ function above, we have

$$G(t) = \frac{dN}{dt} = B + 2Ct + 3Dt^2 + 4Et^3 + 5Ft^4,$$

$$C(t) = \frac{d^2N}{dt^2} = 2C + 6Dt + 12Et^2 + 20Ft^3.$$

As we did before, we substitute the end values at $t=0$ and $t=1$ to get the six conditions

$$N_0 = N(t = 0), \quad N_1 = N(t = 1),$$
$$G_0 = G(t = 0), \quad G_1 = G(t = 1),$$
$$C_0 = C(t = 0), \quad C_1 = C(t = 1).$$

As before, this gives us a system of six equations in six unknowns, and we can express that in matrix form as

$$\begin{Bmatrix} N_0 \\ N_1 \\ G_0 \\ G_1 \\ C_0 \\ C_1 \end{Bmatrix} = \begin{bmatrix} 1 & 0 & 0 & 0 & 0 & 0 \\ 1 & 1 & 1 & 1 & 1 & 1 \\ 0 & 1 & 0 & 0 & 0 & 0 \\ 0 & 1 & 2 & 3 & 4 & 5 \\ 0 & 0 & 2 & 0 & 0 & 0 \\ 0 & 0 & 2 & 6 & 12 & 20 \end{bmatrix} \begin{Bmatrix} A \\ B \\ C \\ D \\ E \\ F \end{Bmatrix}.$$

As above, we can invert this matrix and gather all the coefficients of N_0, N_1, G_0, G_1, C_0, and C_1 together. In the end, this lets us express the quintic noise function as

$$N(t) = B_{N0} N_0 + B_{N1} N_1 + B_{G0} G_0 + B_{G1} G_1 + B_{C0} C_0 + B_{C1} C_1$$

as we did for the cubic case. The coefficients are quintic functions of t:

$$B_{N0} = 1 - 10t^3 + 15t^4 - 6t^5,$$
$$B_{N1} = 10t^3 - 15t^4 + 6t^5 = 1 - B_{N0},$$
$$B_{G0} = t - 6t^3 + 8t^4 - 3t^5,$$
$$B_{G1} = -4t^3 + 7t^4 - 3t^5,$$
$$B_{C0} = \frac{1}{2}\left(t^2 - 3t^3 + 3t^4 - t^5\right),$$
$$B_{C1} = \frac{1}{2}\left(t^3 - 2t^4 + t^5\right).$$

These equations define a quintic function for any combination of value, gradient, and curvature at the two endpoints of the parameter interval.

As with the cubic case, if we ensure that these six conditions are the same at the $t = 1$ end of one interval and at the $t = 0$ end of the next interval, the combined function is not only differentiable at the point, but is also C^2 at the point, that is, has a continuous second derivative. We can actually simplify this further if we artificially choose to have the C^2 continuity be flat (that is, have zero curvature).

Both here and for cubic noise, we have left the final function expressions in symbolic form; for either the cubic or quintic case, and for either value or gradient noise, it is a simple matter to put back in the polynomials for the B_{XX} coefficients and complete the function expressions. You can do this easily if you want to work out the details or code these functions yourself.

Other Noise Concepts

Now that we have the fundamental concepts of noise in hand, let's look at some other very useful concepts in noise functions. These are derived from the basic noise functions discussed above, and in practice, are probably used more often than pure noise functions.

Fractional Brownian Motion (FBM, 1/f, Octaves)

Fractional Brownian motion, or *1/f noise*, is useful because it models an operation that has many different frequencies and magnitudes. It is relatively easy to obtain this from simple noise functions. For each of several simple noise functions that are defined at different frequencies, the magnitude of the noise is divided by the frequency multiplier. It is usual to use powers of two for the frequency multipliers, so in a given domain you would have multipliers of 2, 4, 8, 16, and so on. Each of these frequency doublings is called an *octave*. The division of the magnitude by the frequency is the source of the name *1/f noise*. Code to create such a noise function is shown below, and Figure 10.4 shows the *noisegraph* presentation of the effect as noise at different scales is summed to get the final values.

```
float sum = 0.;
float size = 1.;
for( int i = 0; i < 4; i++ )
{
   sum += noise( size * PP ) / size;
   size *= 2.0;
}
float y = P.y + Amplitude * sum;
```

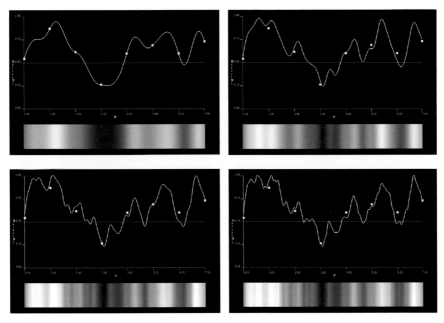

Figure 10.4. Four types of 1D piecewise cubic value+gradient noise functions: one octave (top left); two octaves (top right); three octaves (bottom left); four octaves (bottom right).

Noise in Two and Three Dimensions

For two-dimensional noise, we define a function on the $[0, 1] \times [0, 1]$ unit square with values between zero and one. Figure 10.5, from the *noisegraph* application, shows this in pseudocolor. You can see the same kind of differences in

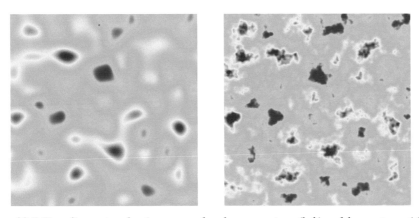

Figure 10.5. Two dimensional noise as pseudocolor; one octave (left) and four octaves (right).

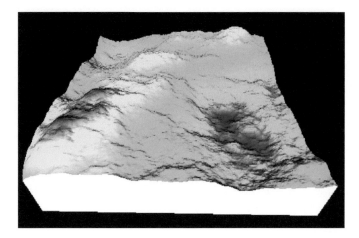

Figure 10.6. Four octaves of 2D noise represented as a pseudocolored height field.

the 2D image that you saw in the simple 1D noise graphs: the four-octave noise has the same general shape, but much more high-frequency variation. (The noise is quintic value+gradient type.) The appearance is that the higher-octave noise has more detail and is consequently visually richer. Figure 10.6 shows a 4-octave 2D noise function represented as a height field.

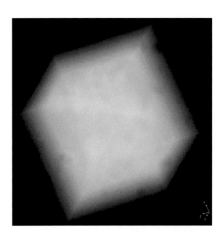

Figure 10.7. Three-dimensional one-octave noise viewed as pseudocolor in a direct volume rendering.

When we look at 3D noise, we have a little more difficult visualization problem. A 3D noise function is visualized as a pseudocolored volume in Figure 10.7. Even without seeing specific interior details, you can still see that there is some familiar-looking variation in color within the cube.

We could look at this in several ways, including explorations through some standard visualization techniques, as shown in Figure 10.8. This shows an isosurface with its isovalue equal to the midrange value of the 3D noise, and we can easily see the greatly increased complexity that comes with the additional octaves of noise.

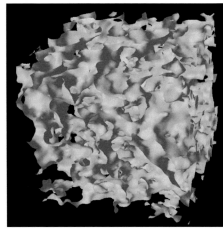

Figure 10.8. Three-dimensional noise visualized by isosurfaces through the middle value; one octave (left) and four octaves (right).

Using Noise with glman

The *glman* tool automatically creates a 3D noise texture and places it into Texture Unit 3. Your vertex, geometry, or fragment shader can access it through the pre-created uniform variable called `Noise3`. You can reference it in your shader as

```
uniform sampler3D Noise3;
. . .
vec3 stp = ...
vec4 nv = texture( Noise3, stp );
```

The "noise vector" texture `nv` is a `vec4` whose components have separate meanings. We will access these components through the rgba nameset, though you can use indices or any other nameset if you wish. The .r component is the low frequency noise. The .g component is twice the frequency and half the amplitude of the .r component, and so on for the .b and .a components. Each component is centered around the middle value of .5, so that if you want a plus-or-minus effect, subtract .5 from each component. To get a nice four-octave noise value between 0 and 1, useful for features such as noisy color mixing, add up all four components, subtract 1, and divide the result by 2, as shown in Table 10.1.

Component	Term	Term Range	Term Limits
0	nv.r	$0.5 \pm .5000$	$0.0000 \rightarrow 1.0000$
1	nv.g	$0.5 \pm .2500$	$0.2500 \rightarrow 0.7500$
2	nv.b	$0.5 \pm .1250$	$0.3750 \rightarrow 0.6250$
3	nv.a	$0.5 \pm .0625$	$0.4375 \rightarrow 0.5625$
	sum	$2.0 \pm \sim 1.0$	$\sim 1.0 \rightarrow 3.0$
	sum $-$ 1	$1.0 \pm \sim 1.0$	$\sim 0.0 \rightarrow 2.0$
	(sum $-$ 1) / 2	$0.5 \pm \sim 0.5$	$\sim 0.0 \rightarrow 1.0$
	(sum $-$ 2)	$0.0 \pm \sim 1.0$	$\sim 1.0 \rightarrow 1.0$

Table 10.1. The range of the four octaves of noise and some useful combinations.

So, if you would like to have a four-octave noise function that ranges from 0. to 1, then do this:

```
float  sum = nv.r + nv.g + nv.b + nv.a;
            // range is 1. -> 3.
    sum = ( sum - 1. ) / 2.;
            // range is now 0. -> 1.
```

If you would like to have a four-octave noise function that ranges from -1 to 1, then do this instead:

```
float sum = nv.r + nv.g + nv.b + nv.a;
            // range is 1. -> 3.
    sum = ( sum - 2. );
            // range is now -1. -> 1.
```

By default, the *glman* 3D noise texture has dimensions 64 × 64 × 64. You can change this by putting a command in your GLIB file of the form

```
Noise3D 128
```

to get dimension 128 × 128 × 128, or choose whatever resolution you want (up to around 400 × 400 × 400). Remember that for the most general use, the resolution should be a power of two. The first time *glman* creates a 3D noise texture for you, it will take a few seconds. But *glman* then writes it to a local file, and the next time this 3D texture is needed it is read from the file, which is a lot faster.

A 2D noise texture works the same way, except you get at it with

```
uniform sampler2D Noise2;
...
vec2 st = ...
vec4 nv = texture( Noise2, st );
```

Note that the table above still applies to convert the values from the noise texture into something useful. The only difference is that a 2D noise texture is indexed by a vec2 while the 3D noise texture is indexed by a vec3. But both return a vec4.

Using Noise with the Built-In GLSL Functions

If you are using a system where the GLSL built-in noise functions work, here is how you would use them. There are four built-in GLSL noise functions: noise1( ), noise2( ), noise3( ), and noise4( ). They each return a float, vec2, vec3, and vec4 , respectively, whose values are between −1. and 1. They each can accept as their single argument *any* of those four types of inputs, depending on how you want to index into the noise. Thus, where we might have said

```
uniform sampler3D Noise3;
. . .
vec3 stp = ...
vec4 nv = texture( Noise3, stp );
float sum = nv.r + nv.g + nv.b + nv.a;
sum = ( sum - 2. );
```

for *glman*, using the GLSL built-in noise functions we could accomplish the same thing by saying

```
float sum = 0.;
float size = 1.;
for( int i = 0; i < 4; i++ )
{
    sum += noise1( size*stp ) / size;
    size *= 2.;
}
```

Turbulence

Turbulence is a special effect created from a noise function.[2] It can give you a "sharper" appearance than a simple noise function. Turbulence is created by taking the absolute value of each noise octave about the midpoint before summing them. It is simple to produce if you have a good noise function. Introducing the absolute value operation can add sharp changes in the func-

---

2. Turbulence is the term used in computer graphics for what we are about to describe. Note, however, this is not the same as fluid turbulence. The overloading of the term is unfortunate.

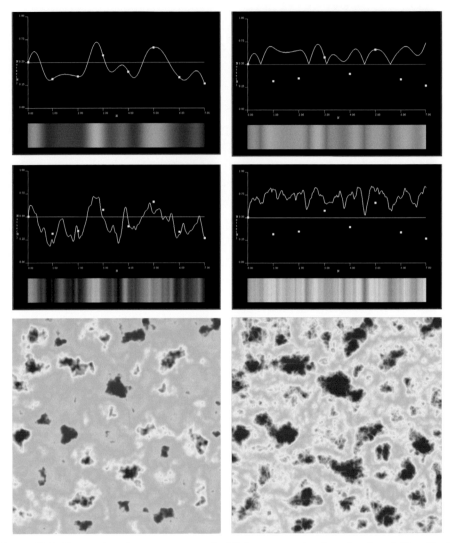

Figure 10.9. Comparing the appearance of a 1D 1-octave noise function (top left), with the turbulence function derived from it (top right); a 1D 4-octave noise function (middle left), with the turbulence function derived from it (middle right); and the same comparison with a 2D 4-octave noise function (bottom left and right).

tion. For example, the noise functions shown by *noisegraph* in Figure 10.9, a one-octave and a four-octave 1D cubic noise+gradient noise function and their absolute values, along with the four-octave 2D examples, illustrate the difference between these two kinds of noise. It is possible to have more than four octaves of noise, and *noisegraph* can provide up to eight octaves. Because the

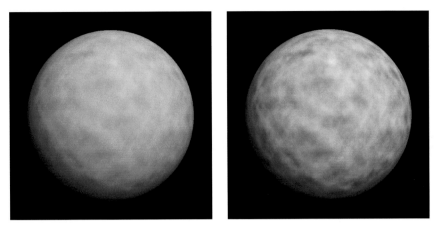

Figure 10.10. Noise as a surface texture on the simple sphere (left) and the same noise treated as turbulence on the sphere (right).

glman noise comes from a texture, we will only be using four octaves here, which will be plenty for our discussion.

As we noted for two- and three-dimensional noise, the real effect of turbulence does not lie in the pure 1D functions shown in Figure 10.9, but in the appearance of images that use it. In Figure 10.10, we show the simple sphere with ordinary noise (left) and turbulence (right) to illustrate the additional complexity that turbulence usually presents.

To get a turbulence function in *glman*, take the absolute value of each of the four components minus the mid-value 0.5. This gives us Table 10.2.

Component	Term[3]	Term Range
0	abs(nv.r − .5)	0.0000 → 0.5000
1	abs(nv.g − .5)	0.0000 → 0.2500
2	abs(nv.b − .5)	0.0000 → 0.1250
3	abs(nv.a − .5)	0.0000 → 0.0625
	sum	0.0000 → ~ 1.0000

Table 10.2. The four noise octaves converted to turbulence.

3. In GLSL, the abs( ) function is overloaded to take either the integer or floating point absolute value depending on what type was passed in. There is no fabs( ) function for floating point absolute value like there is in C and C++.

The terms can be summed and the sum used directly, as shown in the following fragment shader code that was used to produce the images in Figure 10.10.

```
uniform sampler3D Noise3;
uniform float     uNoiseScale;
uniform float     uNoiseMag;
uniform vec4      uColor1;
uniform vec4      uColor2;

in   float  vLightIntensity;
in   vec3   vMCposition;

out vec4 fFragColor;

void main( )
{
   vec4 nv = texture( Noise3, vMCposition * uNoiseScale );

   float sum =   abs(nv.r-.5) + abs(nv.g-.5) +
                 abs(nv.b-.5) + abs(nv.a-.5);

   sum   =   clamp( uNoiseMag * sum, 0.0, 1.0 );
   vec3 color = mix( uColor1.rgb, uColor2.rgb, sum )*
                 vLightIntensity;

   fFragColor = vec4( color, 1.0 );
}
```

Note that, unlike C and C++, GLSL overloads the abs( ) function name for taking the absolute value of both integers and floats.

Some Examples of Noise in Different Environments

A traditional use of noise is to provide interesting textures, often mimicking natural phenomena, to use in our images. These use several different techniques, including using only one or two of the available octaves of noise, or manipulating noise or turbulence so that the function values lie in only a limited range or are shifted. We include code for these examples, so you can see examples of some manipulations you might use.

As a first example of the use of noise to create a rich image, we illustrate noise to simulate surface erosion using pixel discards. In Chapter 3, we used the texture coordinates directly to determine the pixels to discard, and the result

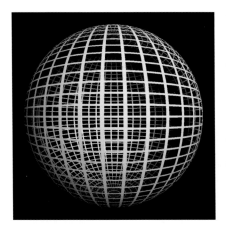 

Figure 10.11. The discard-based screen of Chapter 2 (left) and noise-based discard to simulate erosion (right).

was shown in Figure 3.5, repeated here as the left-hand image in Figure 10.11. We can take a different approach by using 2D texture coordinates to generate a noise value that will determine which pixels should be discarded. When this is applied to a sphere, the resulting figure is shown as the right-hand image in Figure 10.11—a very different kind of image. The erosion shader operates by generating a pattern from a noise function, but instead of using it to change the color of the surface, the values are used to decide whether or not to discard pixels. The shader uses two uniform variables, Min and Max, that determine the range of values that allow pixels to be kept, and the kept pixels are colored as if the sphere had no texture.

The fragment shader for the erosion example is given below. The two uniform variables for the noise frequency and cutoff values would probably be defined as slider variables in the *glman* GLIB file, and you can experiment with them to achieve the look you want.

```
uniform sampler3D Noise3;
uniform float    uMin, uMax;
uniform float    uNoiseScale;

in vec4 vColor;
in float vLightIntensity;
in vec3 vMCposition;

out vec4    fFragColor;

void main( )
```

```
{
   vec4   nv   = texture( Noise3, uNoiseScale*vMCposition );
   float  sum = nv.r + nv.g + nv.b + nv.a;
   sum = ( sum - 1. ) /2.; // range: 0. -> 1.

   if( sum < uMin )
      discard;

   if( sum > uMax )
      discard;

   fFragColor = vec4( vLightIntensity*vColor.rgb, 1. );

}
```

We look at some other examples of using noise in the sections below. These show the use of noise to simulate some natural materials, where a noise texture can add some of the complexity that is found in nature. This is a very rich subject, and our relatively simple examples can only suggest how much can be done.

Noise effects begin by choosing the domain that is to be used for the noise function, and the way the noise is to be used. The domain can be 1D, 2D, or 3D, depending on whether you want linear, surface, or solid effects. It can also be chosen to come from model space, eye space, or texture space. So you have a variety of choices that can affect the way the noise effects are generated. There are also several ways to use the noise values that you generate. You can use them directly, as we saw in the erosion example above, or you can use them to select how different colors are to be blended; the examples below all use noise to determine how blends are to be done.

Marble Shader

Figure 10.12. The teapot with a marble texture.

Marble is a material that exhibits noisy-looking veins in a base-color stone, and the nature of the veins makes it a natural material to model with a noise-based texture. The marble fragment shader whose effects are shown in Figure 10.12 implements this kind of modeling. Its domain is the 3D model coordinates of the geometry being textured, and it uses all four octaves of noise. The resulting value, along with the position of the point in model space, is then taken as input to a sine function, making the texture somewhat periodic, as the veins in marble tend to be.

The fragment shader below implements this modeling approach to simulate a marble texture. It uses three uniform variables: two colors, the color of the marble base and the color of the marble vein, and one scale that changes the general texture of the noise values that could be set up with *glman*, so you could experiment with the texture to get the effect you want.

```
uniform sampler3D Noise3;
uniform vec4      uMarbleColor;
uniform vec4      uVeinColor;
uniform float     uNoiseScale;
uniform float     uNoiseMag;

in float vLightIntensity;
in vec3  vMCposition;

out vec4 fFragColor;

void main( )
{
   vec4 nv    = texture( Noise3, vMCposition * uNoiseScale );
   float sum  =   abs(nv.r - 0.5) + abs(nv.g - 0.5)
                + abs(nv.b - 0.5) + abs(nv.a - 0.5);
   sum = clamp( uNoiseMag * sum, 0.0, 1.0 );

   float sineval  = sin(vMCposition.y*6.0+sum*12.0)*0.5 + 0.5;
   vec3 color     = mix(uVeinColor.rgb, uMarbleColor.rgb,
                        sineval) * vLightIntensity;
   fFragColor    = vec4( color, 1.0 );
}
```

Cloud Shader

Clouds are another effect that can be readily created using a fragment shader. There are so many different kinds of clouds that one shader cannot begin to capture them, but a very simple model is that clouds occur in the sky with a noise-like pattern that mixes cloud color and sky color, with gradations between them. A cloud shader might produce effects like those shown in Figure 10.13, with a parameter determining the way the clouds thin out so the sky color can be seen. Other kinds of cloud models might assume a particular geometry for cloud patterns and density and then use noise to determine what happens at the cloud region boundaries, but they could have similarities to this shader if you use the geometry to drive the mix( ) function and use the noise effects at the boundaries.

 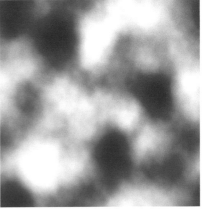

Figure 10.13. The teapot shown with a cloud texture (left) and a cloud texture on a plane (right) as it might be done for a sky background.

A fragment shader for cloud effects is given below. The noise octaves are not uniformly weighted, because clouds seem to have more structure at a larger scale, and the intensity is modified with a cosine function to achieve even wider cloud and sky regions. This shader uses four uniform variables that set the foreground and background colors for clouds and that control the scale of the domain and shift the noise either toward the foreground or the background color. If you use this shader with *glman*, the uniform variables would need to be defined as slider or color chooser variables in a GLIB file, so that you can adjust the values to tune the look of the cloud effect.

```
uniform vec4     uSkyColor;
uniform vec4     uCloudColor;
uniform float    uBias;
uniform float    uNoiseScale;
uniform sampler3D Noise3;

in float      vLightIntensity;
in vec3       vMCposition;

out vec4    fFragColor;

const float PI = 3.14159265;

void main( )
```

```
    {
        vec4 nv = texture( Noise3, uNoiseScale * vMCposition );
        float sum = ( 3.* nv.r + nv.g + nv.b + nv.a - 2. ) / 2.;
        sum = ( 1. + cos(PI * sum) ) / 2.;
        float t = clamp( uBias + sum, 0., 1. );

        vec3 color = mix( uSkyColor.rgb, uCloudColor.rgb, t );
        color *= vLightIntensity;

        fFragColor = vec4( color, 1.0 );
    }
```

Wood Shader

Wood is characterized by the rings that form as trees grow. These rings are something like the veins in marble, but rings have clearly defined edges between the light and dark wood, and the variation lies in the shape of the rings themselves. These are approximately cylindrical, with variation in their width and spacing. A wood fragment shader must try to capture those kinds of variations. In Figure 10.14, we see an example of a wood shader applied to a teapot. This solid-texture wood shader operates by adding a noise value (based on the model-space coordinates of a point) to the distance from the modeling Y-axis, and uses that distance to mix the light and dark wood colors.

Figure 10.14. The teapot shown with a wood texture.

A wood fragment shader that implements this approach is shown below. This uses five uniform variables, three shader parameters and two color variables that control the ring colors and the parameters that simulate the rings. These could be used with *glman* as slider or color selection variables in a GLIB file to let you experiment with the colors and parameters to achieve the look you want in your shader. For example, you could use light colors and wide and fairly regular ring spacing to simulate pine.

```
uniform sampler3D Noise3;
uniform vec4      uLightWoodColor;
uniform vec4      uDarkWoodColor;
uniform float     uRingFreq;
uniform float     uNoiseScale;
uniform float     uNoiseMag;
```

```
in float vLightIntensity;
in vec3 vMCposition;

out vec4  fFragColor;

void main( )
{
    vec4 nv = uNoiseMag * texture( Noise3, uNoiseScale*vMCposition
);
    vec3 location = vMCposition + nv.rgb;

    float dist = length( location.xz )
    dist *= uRingFreq;

    // create an up-down ramp:
    float t = fract( dist + nv.r + nv.g + nv.b ) * 2.0;
    if( t > 1.0 )
        t = 2.0 - t;

    vec4 color = mix( uLightWoodColor, uDarkWoodColor, t );
    color *= vLightIntensity;
    fFragColor = vec4( color.rgb, 1. );
}
```

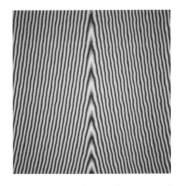

Figure 10.15. The wood shader applied to a flat surface.

One of the most common uses of a wood shader is to create wood surfaces that model the look of wooden furniture or the like. We can see in Figure 10.15 that we can modify this shader to create the texture of a wood surface (or, more precisely, a bookmatched veneer surface). This is done by changing the expression for the dist variable by adding terms as

```
sqrt(location.x*location.x+location.z*location.z)+
    sqrt(8.+location.y)+sqrt(8.+abs(location.x));
```

and, as before, note that

```
sqrt( location.x*location.x + location.z*location.z )
```

can be written more efficiently as

```
length( location.xz )
```

This gives roughly parallel structures on each side of the middle of the surface. Other techniques for surfaces would consider the surface as a side of a board (a modified cube) and would pick up the texture of the side as part of the wood-textured solid.

Advanced Noise Topics

The topic of noise in computer graphics is a very large one. We have just touched on it here in order to give you enough information to appreciate these functions and to get started using them. However, there are many more advanced issues that have not been covered here. One of the biggest is the issue of band limiting noise functions. Value, gradient, and value+gradient noise functions in two and three dimensions have problems with high frequencies creeping in to them. This can result in aliasing problems in the final image. Some solutions have been proposed, including an elegant approach using wavelets. See [11] for more details.

Using Noisegraph

The *noisegraph* tool has been designed to let you experiment with a number of different parameters used to generate computer graphics noise, and to give you a qualitative feel for how those parameters affect the nature of the noise function. The *noisegraph* tool is controlled by a user interface panel (shown in Figure 10.16), which is fairly simple to use, and it displays both a 1D and a 2D noise function with the properties set up in the panel.

Note that *noisegraph* can produce three different types of noise: value-only, gradient-only, and value+gradient. In the example shown here, the selections in the top part of the interface panel are for a four-octave value+gradient noise function with quintic interpolation. You can see this in the 1D noise function window. Multiple octaves can be summed. Each octave is twice the frequency and half the amplitude of the octave below it, as we discussed earlier in the chapter.

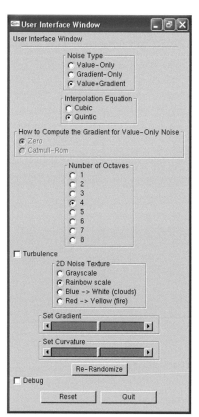

Figure 10.16. The noisegraph user interface panel.

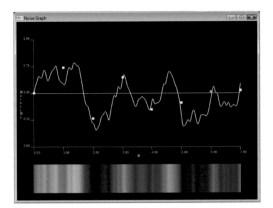

Figure 10.17. The four-octave value+gradient 1D noise function with quintic interpolation described above.

The order of the noise curve can be either cubic or quintic. The cubic curve is C^1 (slope) continuous everywhere, while the quintic curve is C^2 (curvature) continuous.

If value noise is used, the slope at each noise point can be artificially set to zero (horizontal) or can be smoothed using a Catmull-Rom slope.

Notice that one of the control points for the 1D noise function is highlighted in green in the 1D noise function shown in Figure 10.17. When a point is selected (by pointing to it and clicking the left mouse button), its information can be edited as follows:

- The point can be moved up and down using the mouse, if the type of noise is value-only or value+gradient.
- The Gradient slider can be adjusted if the noise type is gradient-only or value+gradient. If the noise uses quintic interpolation, the Curvature slider can also be adjusted.

The other important option for noise is the Turbulence check box. When this is checked, the individual octaves' absolute values are summed to determine the noise function's value.

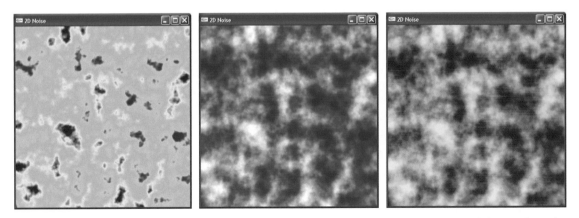

Figure 10.18. The 2D noise function defined above with rainbow (left), sky (center), and fire (right) color scales.

This 1D noise function makes up the bottom edge of the 2D noise function shown in the 2D noise window in Figure 10.18. As you interactively make changes in the 1D noise function, the changes also show up in the 2D function window. The 2D noise function can be displayed with your choice of four color transfer functions according to the 2D Noise Texture radio buttons. Figure 10.18 shows the same 2D noise function with a rainbow scale (blue-to-green-to-red), sky scale (blue-to-white), and fire scale (red-to-yellow).

Exercises

1. Experiment with noise: in the fragment shader for any of the chapter's examples, use the different octaves of noise in different ways, as we did with the cloud shader, to see how that can affect the texture. For example, you might use

   ```
   nv.r + 2.*(nv.g-.5) + 4.*(nv.b-.5) + 8.*(nv.a-.5) + 1.5
   ```

   to use all four of the octaves at the same amplitude.

2. Illustrate a 2D noise function as a surface in the same way one would develop a surface as the graph of a simple function of two variables. Use a rather fine mesh in the domain to capture the shape of the function. Do this for one-octave noise and four-octave noise, and compare the relation between the shapers to the relation between the pseudocolor 2D noise functions in Figure 10.5.

3. Use *glman* to examine the nature of the four individual octaves of noise by creating a very simple fragment shader similar to that in the turbulence shader shown in Figure 10.9. For each octave, write a shader that derives a texture from that octave and uses a uniform slider variable to discard pixels whose value is less than that slider's value. From that, determine the smallest and largest value of the octave of noise.

4. Explore the difference between transparency and pixel discarding. Instead of discarding pixels in the erosion shader, set the alpha value of the pixels you would discard to zero. Describe what happens when you rotate the scene, and why that happens.

5. Most of the examples in this chapter have used noise to set or modify the color of a fragment, but you can also use it in other ways. Modify the previous exercise to set the alpha component of each pixel with the noise function so that the "transparency" is noisy, and note the effect. (The effect might be best observed if you have two planes of different

color, draw the back plane first, and then draw the front plane with this noisy transparency.)

6. There are many places where you can find "noisy" behavior that you can simulate with noise-based shaders. In one of these, create an "asphalt" shader, based on your observation of asphalt in streets and parking lots, by starting with an appropriate gray color and darkening it randomly using noise. Apply this to a rectangle and see how close the results are to actual asphalt.

7. Of course, the random behavior of an "asphalt" shader as above doesn't really capture the nature of a street or parking lot. For these you need to show the dirtier areas where tires travel or where cars drip oil. These are also noisy, but the noise is confined to particular areas. You can take a noise function and trim it to specific areas (define a region where the noise is to be applied and use the smoothstep( ) function to handle the edges or the region). Then add this to the color from the simple asphalt shader.

11

Image Manipulation with Shaders

The OpenGL computer graphics API is primarily intended for rendering 3D synthetic scenes from geometric primitives, but some capabilities for manipulating images were built into the system from the beginning. With the addition of shader capabilities, OpenGL can now use texture access and manipulation operations to carry out a number of new image functions. In this chapter, we describe some of these functions. Our main tools will be the ability to get texels directly from a texture and the ability to do arithmetic on texel values.

The general form of the GLIB file is as below, including a uniform slider variable T, used in case you use a parameterized operation such as image blending, and variables for the resolution of the image file. Each texture needs to be assigned to a texture unit. Here we have set up the GLIB file for two textures, because some of the later examples in this chapter operate on two images. Of course there will be changes if we work on a single image (using only one file, sample.bmp), if we use a different image (replacing the name of the image file), or if we include additional uniform variables to support other computations.

```
##OpenGL GLIB

Ortho -1. 1. -1. 1.

Texture 5 sample1.bmp
Texture 6 sample2.bmp

Vertex sample.vert
Fragment sample.frag
Program Sample  uT <0. 0. 5.>   \
                  uImageUnit 5 uImage2Unit 6

QuadXY .2 5.
```

If you are using *glman*, do not use texture units 2 and 3, because *glman* uses those to hold its built-in 2D and 3D noise textures.

This GLIB file puts the two texture images on texture units 5 and 6. You can arbitrarily pick which texture units to use, up to the total number supported by your graphics card.

The vertex shader is short and uses our familiar conventions for variable names:

```
out vec2 vST;

void main( )
{
   vST = aTexCoord0.st;
   gl_Position = uModelViewProjectionMatrix * aVertex;
}
```

Throughout this chapter we will be looking at different image manipulation functions that we can build into fragment shaders.

Basic Concepts

GLSL deals with images by treating them as textures and using texture access and manipulation to set the color of each pixel in the color buffer. This color buffer may then be displayed, letting you see the effect of your manipulation, or it may be saved as another texture or output as a file.

In Figure 11.1, we see a texture image as it might have been read from an image file. This texture file may be treated as an image raster by working with each texel individually. A built-in GLSL function textureSize( ) will tell you the resolution of the texture, called *ResS* and *ResT* in Figure 11.1.

There are two ways to access a single texel in a texture. Since any OpenGL texture has texture coordinates ranging from 0.0 to 1.0, the coordinates of the center of the image are vec2(0.5,0.5) and you can increment texture coordinates by 1./*ResS* or 1./*ResT* to move from one texel to another horizontally or vertically, respectively. Alternately, if you are working with GLSL 1.50 (OpenGL 3.2) or higher, you can access any texel with the texelFetch( ) function. We will use these GLSL texture-access capabilities in the fragment shader to identify and calculate colors for pixels in the color buffer.

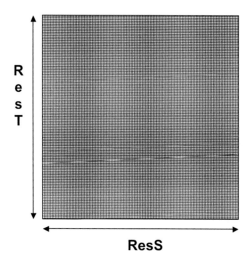

Figure 11.1. A texture raster that could be created from an image file.

In order to be as general as possible, we will address and increment texture coordinates with real numbers rather than integers, in spite of the weakness in this approach, since it can lead to some unintentional interpolations of pixel values.

Single-Image Manipulation

In the next several sections, we work with an individual image and compute the color of output pixels by using information contained in the image. This is in contrast to some later sections in this chapter, when we use two different images as textures loaded into different texture units in our computation.

Luminance

The luminance of a color is the overall brightness of the color, with no reference to the color's hue. Luminance is a more complex property than it might seem, because our eyes respond to different primary colors differently. Luminance has been studied because of the need to give luminance cues to persons who have deficient color vision, as described in [15, Chapter 5], and because it was necessary to consider luminance when creating a color system that could support both black-and-white and color television.

The sRGB specification (also known as IEC 61966-2-1) is emerging as a standard way to define colors across various monitors and applications [42]. In sRGB, luminance is defined as a linear combination of red, green, and blue. The weight vector for luminance in sRGB is

```
const vec3 W = vec3( 0.2125, 0.7154, 0.0721 );
```

We use this set of weights in much of the upcoming sample vertex shader code to compute the luminance of a pixel by taking the dot product of the vector .rgb with this weighting vector as follows:

```
vec3 irgb = texture( uImageUnit, vST ).rgb;
float luminance = dot( irgb, W );
```

Note that these numbers in the weight vector W sum to 1.0000 so that dotting this vector with a legitimate RGB vector will produce a luminance between 0 and 1. We will find luminance to be an important concept in several image manipulation techniques, such as grayscale. Grayscale conversion of an image is accomplished by replacing the color of each pixel with its luminance value. When you compute each pixel's luminance, as shown in the code fragment above, you can create a grayscale representation of the image by setting the pixel color to a vector of the luminance value:

```
fFragColor = vec4( luminance, luminance, luminance, 1.);
```

A conversion from a color image to grayscale in this way is shown in Figure 11.2.

Figure 11.2. A supermarket fruit image (left) and its grayscale equivalent (right).

CMYK Conversions

A common function when you are doing graphics that will be published using standard printing process is converting your RGB-color images to CMYK-color. The RGB color model is based on emissive colors, adding color components to black, as used by computer monitors. The CMYK color model is a transmissive model, created by subtracting color components from white. Standard printing uses four subtractive color components: cyan, magenta, yellow, and black. Converting RGB colors to CMYK colors and outputting the four single-color images is called creating CMYK separations. The single-color images are used to create four printing plates. The conversion from the RGB color space to the CMYK color space is straightforward, although there are different approaches. The examples shown here are taken from [5].

RGB to CMYK conversion works like this. First, convert RGB to CMY by subtracting the RGB color from white. Then calculate the amount of black in each color and segregate it out as the K value, then adjust each of the CMY colors to reflect the fact that this K is present. Sample fragment shader code to convert a variable vec3 color to a variable vec4 cmykcolor is shown here.

```
vec3 cmycolor = vec3(1., 1., 1.) - color;
float K = min( cmycolor.x, min(cmycolor.y, cmycolor.z) );
vec3 temp = (cmycolor - vec3(K,K,K,) )/(1.0 - K);
vec4 cmykcolor = vec4(temp, K);
```

A more complex, but much more satisfactory, conversion scales the values of cmycolor above by modifying the value of K used to convert to cmykcolor. This approach, which yields a good approximation of the Adobe Photoshop CMYK conversion, is given by

$$\begin{pmatrix} C' \\ M' \\ Y' \\ K' \end{pmatrix} = \begin{pmatrix} C - f_{UCR}(K) \\ M - f_{UCR}(K) \\ Y - f_{UCR}(K) \\ f_{BG}(K) \end{pmatrix}$$

where the functions f_{UCR} and f_{BG} are given by

$$f_{UCR}(K) = S_K * K$$

$$f_{BG}(K) = \begin{cases} 0 & K < K_0 \\ K_{max} * \dfrac{K - K_0}{1 - K_0} & K \geq K_0 \end{cases}$$

Figure 11.3. A color image (top) and the four CMYK separations (shown in grayscale) in C-M-Y-K order.

where $S_K = 0.1$, $K_0 = 0.3$, and $K_{max} = 0.9$. This approach is used in developing Figure 11.3.

A separation is a grayscale image that captures one of the C, M, Y, or K components of the image. These are output as files to be used in printing either on film or digitally. To create a separation, you use code such as that above and replace each pixel's color with the single-color grayscale. For example, to create the magenta separation, we could use

```
fFragColor = vec4( cmykcolor.yyy, 1.);
```

Since there is no "cmyk" nameset, and since namesets pay no attention to the meaning of the components, we have used the xyzw nameset for the vec4 cmykcolor in this example.

An example of creating separations is shown in Figure 11.3, which shows an original color image and four separations created with this technique. The separations are shown in grayscale to emphasize the amount of ink that would be required to print each; darker values in the separations indicate that more ink of that color will be used at that point. The most obvious effect in this fruit image is the yellow tones in the fruits and the foliage, along with the magenta tones from the red fruit colors.

The fragment shader for this CMYK conversion is shown below, with the variables in the discussion hard-coded for this example.

```
#define CYAN
#undef   MAGENTA
#undef   YELLOW
#undef   BLACK

uniform sampler2D uImageUnit;

in vec2 vST;

out vec4 fFragColor;

void main( )
{
   vec3 irgb = texture( uImageUnit, vST ).rgb;

   vec3 cmycolor = vec3( 1., 1., 1. ) - irgb;
   float K = min( cmycolor.x, min(cmycolor.y, cmycolor.z) );
   vec3 target = cmycolor - 0.1 * K;
   if (K < 0.3) K = 0.;
   else K = 0.9 * (K - 0.3)/0.7;
   vec4 cmykcolor = vec4( target, K );

#ifdef CYAN
   fFragColor = vec4( vec3(1. - cmykcolor.x), 1. );
#endif

#ifdef MAGENTA
   fFragColor = vec4( vec3(1. - cmykcolor.y), 1. );
#endif

#ifdef YELLOW
   fFragColor = vec4( vec3(1. - cmykcolor.z), 1. );
#endif

#ifdef BLACK
   fFragColor = vec4( vec3(1. - cmykcolor.w), 1. );
#endif
}
```

Hue Shifting

Along with the conversion to CMYK color, you can also convert among the other major color models. We assume that you are familiar with the HLS and HSV color models [14], and we will implement hue shifting by converting RGB to either HLS or HSV color, changing the hue in the new color model, and then shifting back to RGB. The effect of this kind of image shifting is shown in Figure 11.4.

Figure 11.4. A color image and the same image with hue shifted by 240 degrees.

Some sample fragment shader code to do this is shown below, using the HSV color model. This color model is used because the hue is an angular function, and you can shif color easily by adding a numeric value to the hue and taking the result mod 360. The color conversions from RGB to HSV and back from HSV to RGB use two functions from [18]. The hue-shifting shader is written to use the *glman* slider variable *T*, with range [0., 360.], to control the amount of the hue shift.

```
uniform float uT;
uniform sampler2D uImageUnit;

in vec2 vST;

out vec4 fFragColor;

vec3
convertRGB2HSV( vec3 rgbcolor )
```

```
{
  float h, s, v;

  float r = rgbcolor.r;
  float g = rgbcolor.g;
  float b = rgbcolor.b;
  float v = float maxval = max( r, max( g, b ) );
  float minval = min( r, min( g, b ) );
  if (maxval==0.) s = 0.0;
  else s = (maxval - minval)/maxval;

  if (s == 0.)
    h = 0.; // actually h is indeterminate in this case
  else
  {
    float delta = maxval - minval;
    if ( r == maxval ) h = (g - b)/delta;
    else
      if (g == maxval) h = 2.0 + (b - r)/delta;
      else
        if (b == maxval) h = 4.0 + (r - g)/delta;
    h *= 60.;
    if (h < 0.0) h += 360.;
  }
  return vec3( h, s, v );
}

vec3
convertHSV2RGB( vec3 hsvcolor )
{
  float h = hsvcolor.x;
  float s = hsvcolor.y;
  float v = hsvcolor.z;
  if (s == 0.0) // achromatic- saturation is 0
  {
    return vec3(v,v,v); // return value as gray
  }
  else // chromatic case
  {
    if (h > 360.0) h = 360.0; // h must be in [0, 360)
    if (h < 0.0) h = 0.0; // h must be in [0, 360)
    h /= 60.;
    int k = int(h);
    float f = h - float(k);
    float p = v * (1.0 - s);
    float q = v * (1.0 - (s * f));
    float t = v * (1.0 - (s * (1.0 - f)));
```

```
      if (k == 0) return vec3 (v, t, p);
      if (k == 1) return vec3 (q, v, p);
      if (k == 2) return vec3 (p, v, t);
      if (k == 3) return vec3 (p, q, v);
      if (k == 4) return vec3 (t, p, v);
      if (k == 5) return vec3 (v, p, q);
   }
}

void main( )
{
   vec3 irgb = texture( uImageUnit, vST ).rgb;
   vec3 ihsv = convertRGB2HSV( irgb );
   ihsv.x += uT;
   if (ihsv.x > 360.)  ihsv.x -= 360.; //add to hue
   if (ihsv.x < 0.)    ihsv.x += 360.; //add to hue
   irgb = convertHSV2RGB( ihsv );
   fFragColor = vec4( irgb, 1. );
}
```

This example includes an implicit conversion between the RGB color representation and the HSV color representation, showing how more general color conversions may be done.

Image Filtering

A number of image manipulations are based on filtering images. A filter is a process that convolves a pixel with its neighbors by using a matrix to weight neighboring pixels. The size of the filter, the values in the filter, and the meaning of different values that are returned when a filter is applied, all vary from algorithm to algorithm.

As two examples of filters, consider the following. One is a three-by-three Sobel filter that is used to detect horizontal edges. The other is a five-by-five blur filter that can be used to smooth (or blur) an image:

$$
\begin{bmatrix} -1 & -2 & -1 \\ 0 & 0 & 0 \\ 1 & 2 & 1 \end{bmatrix}, \quad \frac{1}{273} * \begin{bmatrix} 1 & 4 & 7 & 4 & 1 \\ 4 & 16 & 26 & 16 & 4 \\ 7 & 26 & 41 & 26 & 7 \\ 4 & 16 & 26 & 16 & 4 \\ 1 & 4 & 7 & 4 & 1 \end{bmatrix}.
$$

The filters are used as weights in creating a weighted sum of the values in an adjacent set of pixels. For pixel values P_{ij} and filter elements F_{ij} and a filter width of $2 * n + 1$, we can express this weighted sum as

$$\sum_{i=-n}^{n}\sum_{j=-n}^{n} F_{ij} * P_{ij}$$

There are some general properties that filters may have. Filters are often square matrices, usually of odd size, so we can often talk about a 3×3 or 5×5 filter. The sum of the weights in the filter is often one, especially when the overall content of an array is to be preserved, so applying a filter usually does not change the overall magnitude of whatever the filter is applied to.

Image Blurring

Image blurring can be done by applying a simple symmetric filter to the image, so that each pixel's color is influenced by the color of each of its neighbors. You can use a simple 3×3 blur convolution filter like the one below or a larger 5×5 blur convolution filter like the 5×5 example shown above:

$$\frac{1}{16} * \begin{bmatrix} 1 & 2 & 1 \\ 2 & 4 & 2 \\ 1 & 2 & 1 \end{bmatrix}.$$

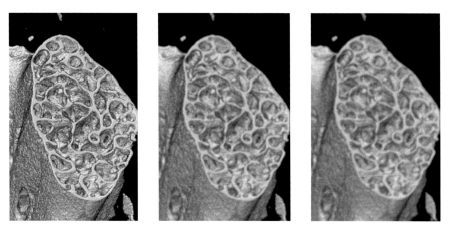

Figure 11.5. An original image (left) blurred by a 3×3 filter (center) and a 5×5 filter (right).

Examples of these two filters' effects are shown in Figure 11.5 and are compared with an original unblurred image, both to show you the blurred images and to let you compare the amount of blurring generated by each of these filters. Because blurring is not very easy to see in reduced-size naturalistic images, we have chosen an original visualization image whose edges are particularly pronounced.

Below is a fragment shader that applies the 3×3 blur convolution filter above to a set of pixels to blur an image. The computation is done without formal matrix multiplication as the pixels with weight 1.0 are gathered, as are those with weight 2.0 and the single pixel with weight 4, and the result is divided by the overall weight. The code for a 5×5 blur filter would look quite similar, and both are included with the resources for this book; the difference is that four additional pixel addresses are needed, and 25 individual pixel colors are generated, instead of the nine shown here.

```
uniform sampler2D uImageUnit;

in vec2 vST

out vec4 fFragColor;

void main( )
{
   ivec2 ires = textureSize( uImageUnit, 0 );
   float ResS = float( ires.s );
   float ResT = float( ires.t );
   vec3 irgb = texture( uImageUnit, vST ).rgb;

   vec2 stp0 = vec2(1./ResS, 0. ); // texel offsets
   vec2 st0p = vec2(0.    , 1./ResT);
   vec2 stpp = vec2(1./ResS, 1./ResT);
   vec2 stpm = vec2(1./ResS, -1./ResT);

// 3x3 pixel colors next

   vec3 i00   = texture( uImageUnit, vST ).rgb;
   vec3 im1m1 = texture( uImageUnit, vST-stpp ).rgb;
   vec3 ip1p1 = texture( uImageUnit, vST+stpp ).rgb;
   vec3 im1p1 = texture( uImageUnit, vST-stpm ).rgb;
   vec3 ip1m1 = texture( uImageUnit, vST+stpm ).rgb;
   vec3 im10  = texture( uImageUnit, vST-stp0 ).rgb;
   vec3 ip10  = texture( uImageUnit, vST+stp0 ).rgb;
   vec3 i0m1  = texture( uImageUnit, vST-st0p ).rgb;
   vec3 i0p1  = texture( uImageUnit, vST+st0p ).rgb;
```

```
        vec3 target = vec3(0.,0.,0.);
        target += 1.*(im1m1+ip1m1+ip1p1+im1p1); //apply blur filter
        target += 2.*(im10+ip10+i0m1+i0p1);
        target += 4.*(i00);
        target /= 16.;
        fFragColor = vec4( target, 1. );
}
```

Chromakey Images

Chromakey image manipulation is used in "green screen" or "blue screen" image replacement. This lets you take any image and replace any regions that have the same color as the key color or are very near the key color with a background texture or portions of another image. The chromakey replacement effect is shown in Figure 11.6.

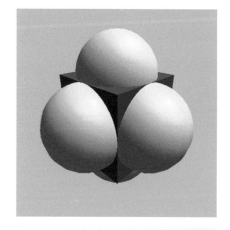

For chromakey computation, two textures are required, an "image texture" and a "before texture." The "image texture" is the one that may contain pixels in the color key that would need to be replaced, and the "before texture" is the one that would replace any color-keyed pixels. The process then is relatively simple: read the image texture, and for each pixel, either keep this pixel, or if the pixel color is sufficiently near the key color, replace the pixel with the corresponding pixel in the before texture. The code fragment below uses pure green as the color key, simulating a green-screen process. The value of uT is a tolerance, or a measure of how near a color must be to the color key before its pixel will be replaced. This is typically very small, so that only colors very near green, vec3(0., 1., 0.), will pass the limit test and will be replaced by the "before" texture color.

A fragment shader for this process is shown below, with uniform slider variables uT and uAlpha from a GLIB file. The foreground image comes from the BeforeUnit and the background image is from the AfterUnit. The uAlpha variable controls the alpha value for the foreground image as seen in the figure.

Figure 11.6. A synthetic image (top) and the result of green-screen chromakey processing to replace the green color and blend the foreground image with a background with an alpha value of 0.7 (bottom).

```glsl
uniform float uT;
uniform float uAlpha;
uniform sampler2D uBeforeUnit, uAfterUnit;

in vec2 vST;

out vec4 fFragColor;

void main( )
{
    vec3 brgb = texture( uBeforeUnit, vST ).rgb;
    vec3 argb = texture( uAfterUnit, vST ).rgb;
    vec4 color;

    float r = brgb.r;
    float g = brgb.g;
    float b = brgb.b;
    color = vec4( brgb, 1. );
    float rlimit = uT;
    float glimit = 1. - uT;
    float blimit = uT;
    if( r <= rlimit && g >= glimit && b <= blimit )
        color = vec4( argb, 1. );
    else
        color = vec4( uAlpha*brgb + (1.-uAlpha)*argb, 1. );

    fFragColor = color;
}
```

Stereo Anaglyphs

A very interesting and fun use for image-based fragment shaders is to produce *stereo anaglyphs*. These have long been used in comic books and movies, and are still popular today. These are sometimes called "red-blue stereo," although today most glasses are actually red-cyan, with the convention that the red filter is over the left eye and the cyan filter is on the right.

Before writing the shader, we need to see how the glasses actually work. Our shader will produce a composite image that incorporates both the left and right eye views. When the composite image is viewed through the red filter, we want to see just the left eye image. The right eye image needs to be blocked, or in image terms, it needs to be blacked out. Similarly, when the composite image is viewed through the cyan filter, we want to see just the right eye image, so the left eye needs to be blocked. Since a red filter passes red light and blocks cyan light, this means that the left eye image needs to be coded in red and the right eye image needs to be coded in cyan (i.e., greens and blues). The cyan filter on the right eye blocks red and passes green and blue, so the reverse needs to happen for the right eye. Thus, the final composite image needs to get its red component from the left eye image and its green and blue components from the right eye image.

An example of doing this is shown in Figure 11.7. You need to have some red-cyan glasses to see the effect.

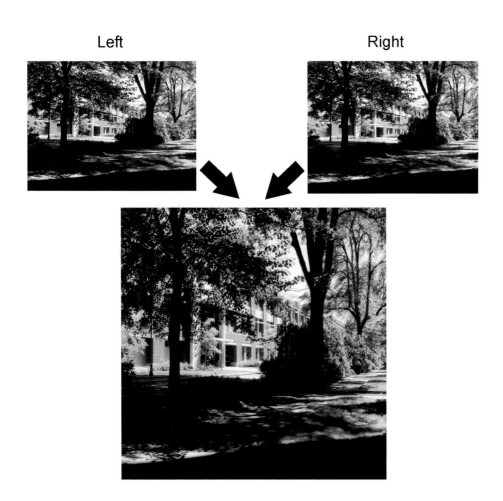

Figure 11.7. A pair of stereo images (top) and the composite anaglyph (bottom).

The strategy for creating anaglyph images, then, is this:

1. Start with left and right images of a 3D scene. These can be produced with a camera or by separately rendering two views of the same scene. Much of this is discussed in [27]. For photographs, take two pictures from points about 4 inches to 6 inches apart that frame the same area, preferably in the photos' foregrounds or middlegrounds.

2. Create a composite image using the red from the left eye image and the green and blue from the right eye image.

3. Because there is often vertical disparity between stereo images, especially when shot with a handheld camera, allow one image to be repositioned vertically.

4. Whatever objects appear in the same location in the two images will appear to live in the plane of the screen or paper. This depth is known as the plane of zero parallax. While it is cool to place the plane of zero parallax towards the back of the scene so that most of the scene seems to hover in midair, it is awkward. Here's why. In our everyday existence, things can appear in midair in front of us, a flying bird for example. Graphics scenes get clipped on the left, right, bottom, and top, but that midair bird doesn't. So, a graphics scene hovering in front of us has the potential to look rather unworldly when it gets clipped in midair for no apparent reason. A more natural-looking approach is to place the plane of zero parallax in the front, so that most of the 3D scene appears to live inside the monitor or book. If we were watching the midair bird through a window, and the bird suddenly got clipped against the window sides, we would think nothing of it. So a graphics scene that goes into the page and gets clipped will look like something we are used to seeing. So, in producing this anaglyph, it is also a good idea to allow one image to be repositioned horizontally to change the plane of zero parallax.

5. Because the red and cyan filters are not usually perfectly balanced, allow the color components to be scaled to compensate for any inequities.

The GLIB file needs to bring in both image files and set up the sliders:

```
##OpenGL GLIB

Texture 5 left.bmp
Texture 6 right.bmp

Vertex anaglyph.vert
```

```
Fragment anaglyph.frag
Program Anaglyph                        \
        uOffsetS <-.25 0. .25>          \
        uOffsetT <-.25 0. .25>          \
        uRed        <0. 1. 5.>          \
        uGreen      <0. 1. 5.>          \
        uBlue       <0. 1. 5.>          \
        uLeftUnit 5 uRightUnit 6

QuadXY .2 5.
```

Like the other examples in this chapter, most of the work is in the fragment shader:

```
uniform sampler2D uLeftUnit, uRightUnit;
uniform float uOffsetS, uOffsetT;
uniform float uRed, uGreen, uBlue;

in vec2 vST;

out vec4 fFragColor;

void main( )
{
   vec4 left = texture(uLeftUnit, vST );
   vec4 right = texture(uRightUnit,vST+vec2(uOffsetS,
                                            uOffsetT));

   vec3 color = vec3( left.r, right.gb );
   color *= vec3( uRed, uGreen, uBlue );
   color = clamp( color, 0., 1. );

   fFragColor = vec4( color, 1. );
}
```

Notice that the fragment shader uses five uniform slider variables that are set up in the GLIB file. The variables uOffsetS and uOffsetT control the offset in the right image, to make up for differences in registering the images, and the three uniform variables uRed, uGreen, and uBlue let you adjust the color balance to make up for variations in the colors in the glasses. When you create an anaglyph image, you may want to adjust the image with these variables to get the best effect.

Figure 11.8 shows another example of creating stereo anaglyphs.

Right   **Left**

Figure 11.8. An anaglyph made from stereo pairs of images of Mars, from NASA's website [7]. Note that in the top of this figure, the left eye view is on the right and the right eye view is on the left. This makes it possible to free-view these images if you are good at crossing your eyes. If you are good at parallel free-viewing, try the top of Figure 11.7.

3D TV

While we are on the subject of stereographics, let's go one step farther. One proposal for 3D television ("3DTV") has been a technique called "SmoothPicture" [21] which transmits a single stereo image by spatially interlacing the left and right images into it, as shown in Figure 11.9. Each separate image is decimated in complementary checkerboard patterns before being combined. A

3D-enabled digital television decomposes the single image back into decimated left and right images, doubles its refresh rate to 120 Hz, and alternately displays the images: left-right-left-right-... Viewers wear shutterglass stereo eyewear to channel the proper image into the proper eye.

Fortunately, existing programs can be adapted fairly easily to produce this spatially-interlaced signal. A left eye and right eye view would need to be rendered, each to its own texture. A fragment shader, shown below, would then create the checkerboard interlace pattern. A simple way to do that would be to use the built-in gl_FragCoord window-relative pixel-space coordinates, to decide whether this fragment should receive the left eye image or the right.

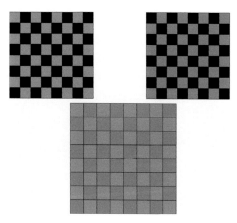

Figure 11.9. Left and right eye views being combined into a single spatially interlaced image.

```
uniform sampler2D uLeftUnit, uRightUnit;

in vec2 vST;

out vec4 fFragColor;

void main( )
{
   int row = int( gl_FragCoord.y );
   int col = int( gl_FragCoord.x );
   int sum = row + col;

   vec4 color;
   if( ( sum % 2 ) == 0 )
     color = texture( uLeftUnit, vST );
   else
     color = texture( uRightUnit, vST );

   fFragColor = vec4( color.rgb, 1. );
}
```

Here is an example of what this looks like. Figure 11.10 shows left and right eye images. (In this case they were taken with a stereo camera, but they could just have easily been computer-generated.) The spatially interlaced image is also shown as part of Figure 11.10, along with a zoomed-in view more clearly showing the checkerboard interlacing pattern.

Figure 11.10. Left and right eye images, top, and the spatially interlaced result and a zoom-in view, bottom.

Shutterglass stereo , in which each eye sees an image separately through polarized lenses, has been a visualization mainstay for many years, finding important applications in architecture, biology, chemistry, computer-aided design, geology, etc. In addition to the obvious entertainment applications, 3DTV should become an important tool for science and engineering.

Edge Detection

Edge detection is a classic image processing technique, and is relatively easy to do in a fragment shader. The edge detection process we present uses a pair of Sobel filters, one for horizontal components and one for vertical components. The horizontal Sobel filter was shown above. The vertical Sobel filter is the same, but rotated 90 degrees. Specifically, the horizontal and vertical filters are, respectively,

$$\begin{bmatrix} -1 & -2 & -1 \\ 0 & 0 & 0 \\ 1 & 2 & 1 \end{bmatrix} \text{ and } \begin{bmatrix} -1 & 0 & 1 \\ -2 & 0 & 2 \\ -1 & 0 & 1 \end{bmatrix}.$$

The effect of the Sobel filters is to compare two columns (or rows, depending on which filter you are using) that are one column (or row) apart; if there is no edge, the colors should be quite close and the filter should return a very small value. If the returned value or values are "large", the process infers that an edge is present. The test may be done on the original image or the luminance-only image.

Notice that in the rightmost image of Figure 11.11, the filter results are interpreted as colors. Where there is no edge, the output figure is very dark;

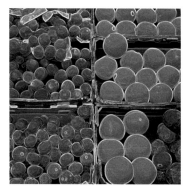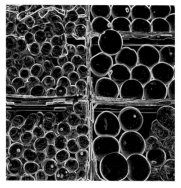

Figure 11.11. The edge detection operation, with the edge-showing image combined with the original image in proportions 0.0 (left), 0.5 (middle), and 1.0 (right).

where there is an edge, the output color is light. This visually validates the concept of detecting edges, though in many applications you would go on to make processing decisions based on these edges rather than simply displaying them.

Below, you see an example of some fragment shader code that implements these ideas. The colors of the 3 × 3 set of pixels are retrieved from the image texture, a dot product of each is done with the luminance weight vector to convert the 3 × 3 image to grayscale, and then the Sobel filters are applied and the two results combined to set a single grayscale output value. Finally, that output value is mixed with the original color according to a *glman* uniform slider variable, *uT*.

```
ivec2 ires = textureSize( uImageUnit, 0 );
float ResS = float( ires.s );
float ResT = float( ires.t );
vec3 irgb  = texture( uImageUnit, vST ).rgb;

vec2 stp0 = vec2(1./ResS, 0. );
vec2 st0p = vec2(0.    , 1./ResT);
vec2 stpp = vec2(1./ResS, 1./ResT);
vec2 stpm = vec2(1./ResS, -1./ResT);

const vec3 W = vec3( 0.2125, 0.7154, 0.0721 );
float i00    = dot( texture( uImageUnit, vST ).rgb, W );
float im1m1  = dot( texture( uImageUnit, vST-stpp ).rgb, W );
float ip1p1  = dot( texture( uImageUnit, vST+stpp ).rgb, W );
float im1p1  = dot( texture( uImageUnit, vST-stpm ).rgb, W );
float ip1m1  = dot( texture( uImageUnit, vST+stpm ).rgb, W );
float im10   = dot( texture( uImageUnit, vST-stp0 ).rgb, W );
float ip10   = dot( texture( uImageUnit, vST+stp0 ).rgb, W );
float i0m1   = dot( texture( uImageUnit, vST-st0p ).rgb, W );
float i0p1   = dot( texture( uImageUnit, vST+st0p ).rgb, W );
float h= -1.*im1p1-2.*i0p1-1.*ip1p1+1.*im1m1+2.*i0m1+1.*ip1m1;
float v= -1.*im1m1-2.*im10-1.*im1p1+1.*ip1m1+2.*ip10+1.*ip1p1;

float mag    = length( vec2( h, v ) );
vec3 target  = vec3( mag, mag, mag );
fFragColor = vec4( mix( irgb, target, uT ), 1. );
```

Embossing

We can modify the idea of edge detection to include replacing color by luminance and highlighting images differently depending on the edges' angles. The result is the emboss operation that is commonly found in image manipulation programs. The result of an emboss operation is shown in Figure 11.12, and the code for a fragment shader to accomplish this is shown below. This

Figure 11.12. An original photo (left) along with the emboss operation results (right).

code includes #define statements to create grayscale or color embossing; both are shown in the figure.

```
#define GRAY

uniform sampler2D uImageUnit;

in vec2 vST;

out vec4 fFragColor;

void main( )
{
    ivec2 ires = textureSize( uImageUnit, 0 );
    float ResS = float( ires.s );
    float ResT = float( ires.t );
    vec3 irgb  = texture( uImageUnit, vST ).rgb;

    vec2 stp0  = vec2(1./ResS, 0. );
    vec2 stpp  = vec2(1./ResS, 1./ResT);
    vec3 c00   = texture( uImageUnit, vST ).rgb;
    vec3 cp1p1 = texture( uImageUnit, vST + stpp ).rgb;

    vec3 diffs = c00 - cp1p1;  // vector difference
    float max = diffs.r;
    if ( abs(diffs.g)) > abs(max) ) max = diffs.g;
    if ( abs(diffs.b)) > abs(max) ) max = diffs.b;

    float gray = clamp( max + .5, 0., 1. );
    vec3 color = vec3( gray, gray, gray );
    fFragColor = vec4( color, 1. );
}
```

Toon Shader

There are various kinds of shader that are known as *toon shaders*. One is a shader for 3D graphics, in which the colors are quantized, and the edges are enhanced by coloring them black. This is the "toon shader" used by many commercial 3D graphics packages, so named because the resulting images look like a hand-drawn cartoon.

This shader operates in a relatively simple fashion and uses the edge-detection filtering discussed above and some color quantization. This models both kinds of enhancement seen in the 3D toon shader. At a high level, the 2D toon shader's operations are

1. Calculate the luminance of each pixel.
2. Apply the Sobel edge-detection filter and get a magnitude.
3. If magnitude > threshold, color the pixel black
4. Else, quantize the pixel's color.
5. Output the colored pixel.

This is shown in the following fragment shader, which is set up with uniform slider variables MagTol and Quantize to manipulate the image through *glman*. Notice that this gets the nine texture values needed for a 3 × 3 filter, converts each to its saturation value, and then applies both horizontal and vertical Sobel filters and tests their combination for edges The color is then quantized to simulate the behavior of hand-drawn cartoons.

Figure 11.13. The original fruit image (top) and with toon shading applied (bottom).

```
uniform sampler2D uImageUnit, uBeforeUnit, uAfterUnit;

uniform float uMagTol;
uniform float uQuantize;

in vec2 vST;

out vec4 fFragColor;
```

```
void main( )
{
  ivec2 ires = textureSize( uImageUnit, 0 );
  float ResS = float( ires.s );
  float ResT = float( ires.t );

  vec3 irgb = texture( uImageUnit, vST ).rgb;
  vec3 brgb = texture( uBeforeUnit, vST ).rgb;
  vec3 argb = texture( uAfterUnit, vST ).rgb;

  vec3 rgb = texture( uImageUnit, vST ).rgb;
  vec2 stp0 = vec2(1./uResS, 0. );
  vec2 st0p = vec2(0.    , 1./uResT);
  vec2 stpp = vec2(1./uResS, 1./uResT);
  vec2 stpm = vec2(1./uResS, -1./uResT);

  const vec3 W = vec3( 0.2125, 0.7154, 0.0721 );
  float i00  = dot( texture( uImageUnit, vST).rgb, W );
  float im1m1= dot( texture( uImageUnit, vST-stpp ).rgb, W );
  float ip1p1= dot( texture( uImageUnit, vST+stpp ).rgb, W );
  float im1p1= dot( texture( uImageUnit, vST-stpm ).rgb, W );
  float ip1m1= dot( texture( uImageUnit, vST+stpm ).rgb, W );
  float im10 = dot( texture( uImageUnit, vST-stp0 ).rgb, W );
  float ip10 = dot( texture( uImageUnit, vST+stp0 ).rgb, W );
  float i0m1 = dot( texture( uImageUnit, vST-st0p ).rgb, W );
  float i0p1 = dot( texture( uImageUnit, vST+st0p ).rgb, W );

  // next two lines apply the H and V Sobel filters at the pixel
  float h= -1.*im1p1-2.*i0p1-1.*ip1p1+1.*im1m1+2.*i0m1+1.*ip1m1;
  float v= -1.*im1m1-2.*im10-1.*im1p1+1.*ip1m1+2.*ip10+1.*ip1p1;
  float mag = length( vec2( h, v ) ); // how much change
                                       // is there?
  if( mag > uMagTol )
  { // if too much, use black
    fFragColor = vec4( 0., 0., 0., 1. );
  }
  else
  {                   // else quantize the color
    rgb.rgb *= uQuantize;
    rgb.rgb += vec3( .5, .5, .5 );      // round
    ivec3 intrgb = ivec3( rgb.rgb );    // truncate
    rgb.rgb = vec3( intrgb ) / Quantize;
    fFragColor = vec4( rgb, 1. );
  }
}
```

Artistic Effects

If you use a commercial image manipulation program such as Photoshop or a general-distribution version such as GIMP, you will find a number of "artistic filters" that you can use to make an image look more like a painting or as if any of several other kinds of thing had been done to it. It is interesting to consider how you might be able to create such artistic effects with a GLSL fragment shader.

A general approach might be to select a region of several texels from the image relative to the current texel, and apply some sort of process that results in a single color value. For example, you might choose the texel in the region that has the greatest luminance. In Figure 11.14 we have done that to create a painting effect for the familiar cherry blossom figure of this chapter. The process is fairly straightforward; we develop a full 5×5 texel rectangle R around an individual pixel, as well as a 5×5 mask rectangle M whose values are simply zero or one. We then look at the luminance values of each texel in the set $R * M$ and use the texel with the highest luminance value in the place of the particular pixel. The code is rather long because, at this writing, GLSL does not allow variables to be used as array indices, so we will not include it here. It is available with the resources for the book.

It is straightforward to choose which values are zero and which are one in the mask, and changing the "shape" of the mask will change the effect of the filter. You can use other criteria besides the maximum luminance to select the color for the pixel. There is ample ground here for fruitful experimentation!

Figure 11.14. An image (left) with a painting-effect filter applied (right).

Image Flipping, Rotation, and Warping

In the previous examples of single-image manipulation, we worked with each pixel in place. However, we can also compute the color for a pixel by manipulating the coordinates of the pixel to get that pixel's color from another place in the image.

While we create image warps to achieve particular effects on specific images, it can be useful to have some kind of uniform benchmark image for warps. There are many such benchmark images, depending on just what effects you want to see, but in Figure 11.15 we see a simple rectangular grid that we will use to examine the details of changes in the images.

We will work with images by treating them as texture maps, as we have throughout this chapter so far. When we compute the source address for a pixel, we are applying a function from the pixel address space to itself. Since the texture space is the unit square, $[0, 1] \times [0, 1]$ we are looking for functions that map that space to itself. Sometimes, however, we may want to double the size of that space and shift it so that the space we are working with is $[-1, 1] \times [-1, 1]$ to make it convenient to apply familiar functions (such as trigonometric functions) to the space. Examples and exercises will help clarify what we mean by this.

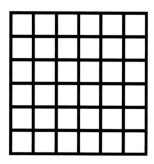

Figure 11.15. The rectangular grid image.

One of the simplest kinds of address-based image manipulation is *image flipping*. There are two kinds of flipping: horizontal and vertical. In vertical image flipping, you exchange the top pixels in the image with the bottom pixels, effectively mirroring the image around a horizontal line. In horizontal image flipping, you exchange the left and right pixels in the image, effectively mirroring it around a vertical line.

You can flip an image by a very simple calculation on the texture coordinates. Since the texture coordinates are in the interval $[0, 1]$, the function $t = 1 - t$ will reverse the order of the coordinate t in this interval. If this is applied to the texture coordinates in the fragment shader (with the common *glman* setup) as

```
vec2 st = vST;
st.t = 1. - st.t;
vec3 irgb = texture( uImageUnit, st ).rgb;
fFragColor = vec4( irgb, 1. );
```

then the resulting image will be displayed "upside down" or flipped vertically. It is quite easy to see how a horizontal flip could be implemented by manipulating the *s* texture coordinate.

Simple image rotation (that is, rotation through a multiple of 90 degrees) can be done similarly. If you want to rotate an image by 90 degrees counterclockwise, for example, you can simply replace the s-coordinate of the texture by the original texture t-coordinate, and the t-coordinate of the texture by one minus the s-coordinate. (See if you can quickly figure out why the "one minus" is needed.) In terms of functions of two variables, the function $f(st) = (t, 1 - s)$ captures this operation. The other simple rotations are similarly easy. More general rotations are straightforward applications of the usual graphics rotation operations, but are complicated by the need to preserve the rectangular form factor in the domain and are thus not considered here.

Filling a pixel with a pixel from somewhere else in the image is more interesting. You can apply any function or procedure that you like to manipulate the address of any particular pixel, so long as it stays within the unit

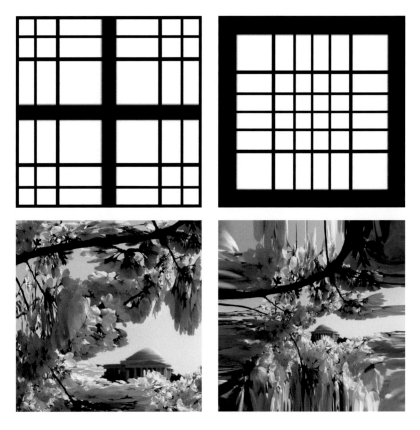

Figure 11.16. The grid (above) and cherry blossom image (below), manipulated to magnify (left) or compress (right) the center part of the image.

square of the pixel space. The process of manipulating the image by applying a function to the pixel address space is called *image warping* [46] and has many potential uses.

In most image warping applications, the effect of the function can vary quite a bit if different parameter values are used in the function. Fortunately, *glman* is easy to set up so you can create uniform slider variables for these parameters. For example, if we consider the image warping with the function $x = x + t * \sin(\pi * x)$ applied to both coordinates of the texel, we see in Figure 11.16 the effect of two different values of the parameter t for this warping on both the grid above and on the cherry blossom image.

The fragment shader that defines this effect is shown below.

```
const float PI = 3.14159265;

uniform sampler2D uImageUnit;
uniform float uT;

in vec2 vST;

out vec4 fFragColor;

void main( )
{
    vec2 st = vST;
    vec2 xy = st;
    xy = 2. * xy - 1.;          // map to [-1,1] square
    xy += uT * sin(PI*xy);

    st = (xy + 1.)/2.;          // map back to [0,1] square
    vec3 irgb = texture( uImageUnit, st ).rgb;
    fFragColor = vec4( irgb, 1. );
}
```

Other kinds of image warping apply more complex kinds of operations to pixel coordinates. The *twirl transformation* is one example, and others are explored in the exercises. For the twirl transformation, we work in pixel coordinates, so we start by transforming texture coordinates to pixel coordinates, apply the twirl transformation, and then come back to texture coordinates to select the actual pixel colors.

The twirl transformation rotates the image around a given anchor point (x_c, y_c) by an angle that varies across the space from a value α at the center, decreasing linearly with the radial distance as it proceeds toward a limiting radius $r_{\max}$. The image remains unchanged outside the radius $r_{\max}$. The notation has (x', y') as the original pixel coordinates and (x, y) as the coordinates of the pixel whose color you use; look for this in the shader code. The inverse mapping function for this transformation is given by

$$T_x^{-1} : x = \begin{cases} x_c + r\cos(\beta) & \text{for } r \leq r_{\max} \\ x' & \text{for } r > r_{\max} \end{cases}$$

$$T_y^{-1} : y = \begin{cases} y_c + r\sin(\beta) & \text{for } r \leq r_{\max} \\ y' & \text{for } r > r_{\max} \end{cases}$$

with

$$d_x = x' - x_c \qquad\qquad r = \sqrt{d_x^2 + d_y^2}$$

$$d_y = y' - y_c \qquad \beta = \arctan_2(d_y, d_x) + \alpha(\frac{r_{\max} - r}{r_{\max}})$$

The resulting image effect is shown in Figure 11.17 for the rectangular grid and for the cherry blossom image.

In the twirl transformation fragment shader below, look for the changes to and from pixel coordinates, and note the two parameters (angle α and limiting radius $r_{\max}$) that are set up as uniform variables, so they can be defined as *glman* uniform slider variables.

```
const float PI = 3.14159265;

uniform sampler2D uImageUnit;
uniform float uD, uR;

in vec2 vST;
```

Figure 11.17. The twirl transformation on the grid (left) and on the cherry blossom image (right).

```
out vec4 fFragColor;

void main( )
{
  ivec2 ires = textureSize( uImageUnit, 0 );
  float Res = float( ires.s ); // assume it's a square
                                // texture image
  vec2 st = vST;
  float Radius = Res * uR;
  vec2 xy = Res * st;          // pixel coordinates from
                               // texture coords

  vec2 dxy = xy - Res/2.;  // twirl center is (Res/2, Res/2)
  float r  = length( dxy );
  float beta = atan(dxy.y,dxy.x) + radians(uD)*
                                (Radius-r)/Radius;

  vec2 xy1 = xy;
  if (r <= Radius)
  {
    xy1 = Res/2. + r * vec2( cos(beta), sin(beta) );
  }
  st = xy1/Res;  // restore coordinates

  vec3 irgb = texture( uImageUnit, st ).rgb;
  fFragColor = vec4( irgb, 1. );
}
```

Image warping need not be uniform, of course, and you can readily use noise functions, as described in the previous chapter, to modify the address of a source pixel in an image. Some code for a fragment shader to do this is below, and the result is shown in Figure 11.18.

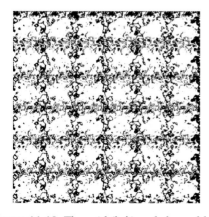 

Figure 11.18. The grid (left) and cherry blossom image (right) with noise as pixel offset.

```
uniform sampler2D uImageUnit;
uniform float uT;
uniform sampler3D Noise3;

in vec3 vMCposition;
in vec2 vST;

out vec4 fFragColor;

void main( )
{
    vec2 st = vST;
    float x = st.x;
    float y = st.y; // extract coordinates
    vec4 noisevecx = texture( Noise3, vMCposition );
    vec4 noisevecy = texture( Noise3,
                                 vMCposition+vec3(noisevecx) );
    x += uT*(noisevecx[.r]-noisevecx[.g]+noisevecx[.b]
              +noisevecx[.a]-1.);
    y += uT*(noisevecy[.r]-noisevecy[.g]+noisevecy[.b]
              +noisevecy[.a]+1.);
    st = vec2( x, y );   // restore coordinates
    vec3 irgb = texture( uImageUnit, st ).rgb;
    fFragColor = vec4( irgb, 1. );
}
```

You can also see *image morphing*, the transition over time from one image to another, as a combination of image warping and image blending. The image blending part of this is discussed in the sections below, while the image warping for morphing is a very specialized process where a fixed set of points on one image are mapped to a fixed set in another, and the image blending is parameterized so that at the beginning, the geometry of one image is fixed, and at the end, the geometry of the second image is achieved. This is well beyond the scope of our discussion here, however; you can read more in [46].

The Image Blending Process

There are several kinds of image manipulation in which you create a linear combination of the pixels from one image with those from a constant or from another image. This kind of combination is shown in Figure 11.19. In the next few sections, the base value will be a constant color or a value derived directly from each pixel, so only the image being manipulated is used. Later in this

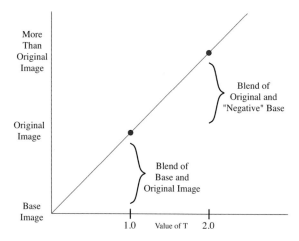

Figure 11.19. The meaning of the parameter T in the blending process.

chapter, we will present examples where one of these images is a particular base image, and the other is an image that you want to manipulate. The general form of the linear combination is

$$I_{out} = (1. - T) * I_{base} + T * I_{source}.$$

We are used to equations such as this being limited by having the parameter T restricted to the range [0., 1.]. However, for some of these applications, we don't make any such limitation, because for some effects it is easier to ask for what you don't want than to ask for what you do. Going outside the [0., 1.] range will allow us to extrapolate to the effect we want to achieve.

The parameter in the blend can be varied to get different results, and here *glman*'s ability to attach a uniform variable to a slider can be very helpful in experimenting with the effects of a parameter. The built-in GLSL mix( ) function supports the actual blending sum.

Blending an Image with a Constant Base Image

There are several image-manipulation processes that involve blending each pixel of an image with a constant value. The operations that result are quite common and are very useful. Many of the examples below have been set up for the *glman* environment with a uniform slider variable T that performs the blending operation shown in Figure 11.19.

Color Negative

The *color negative* models the way photographic negatives work. A photographic negative blocks the complement of a color from getting to photographic paper, so the negative of an image is computed by subtracting the color of each pixel from white:

```
vec3(1.0, 1.0, 1.0) - color.rgb
```

If you use that negative as the base image, you get an image that looks just like the photographic negative, as shown in Figure 11.20.

The following code for the negative fragment shader sets up a color and its negative so you can blend between them with the variable *uT*. At uT = 0 you have the original image, and at uT = 1 you have the negative.

```
uniform sampler2D uImageUnit;
uniform float uT;

in vec2 vST;

out vec4 fFragColor;

void main( )
{
    vec3 irgb = texture( uImageUnit, vST ).rgb;
    vec3 neg = vec3(1.,1.,1.) - irgb;
    fFragColor = vec4( mix( irgb, neg, uT ), 1. );
}
```

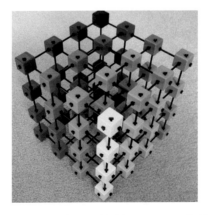 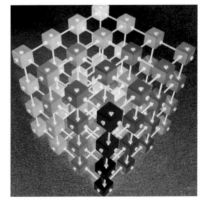

Figure 11.20. An image (left) and its color negative (right).

Brightness

Informally, brightness can be thought of as the amount of not-black in a color. For RGB color, "less" black means that the color components are nearer to 1.0, and "more" black means that the components are nearer to 0.0. To manipulate the brightness of an image, use a black image with color

```
target = vec3(0.0, 0.0, 0.0)
```

as the base. Values of uT less than 1.0 will darken each component of the color, while values greater than 1.0 will brighten each component of the color up to the point where the color is clamped. This can, of course, wash out colors if the colors are already bright or if you use uT too large. This is shown in Figure 11.21.

Sample code for a very simple fragment shader that adjusts brightness is shown below. In effect, brightening the image is done by subtracting black from it.

```
uniform sampler2D uImageUnit;
uniform float uT;
in vec2 vST;
out vec4 fFragColor;

void main( )
{
   vec3 irgb  = texture( uImageUnit, vST ).rgb;
   vec3 black = vec3( 0., 0., 0. );
   fFragColor = vec4( mix( black, irgb, uT ), 1. );
}
```

Figure 11.21. Brightness manipulation in a photograph from a prehistoric French tomb with $uT = 0.0$ (left), 1.0 (middle), and 2.0 (right).

Contrast

The contrast in an image describes how much the colors stand out from gray. To manipulate the contrast in an image, use as a base image a constant 50% gray image, which is easily computed as

```
target = vec3(0.5,0.5,0.5);
```

Parameter values of T less than 1 will move each color component toward 0.5, reducing the contrast in the image, while values greater than 1 will move each color component away from 0.5, increasing the contrast, as shown in Figure 11.22.

Sample code for a very simple fragment shader that adjusts either brightness or contrast is shown below. In effect, brightening the image is done by subtracting black from it, and contrast is increased by subtracting 50% gray from it.

```
#define BRIGHTNESS
#undef CONTRAST

uniform sampler2D uImageUnit;
uniform float uT;

in vec2 vST;

our vec4 fFragColor;

void main( )
{
    vec3 irgb = texture( uImageUnit, vST ).rgb;
```

Figure 11.22. Contrast manipulation in a photograph of a ruined French abbey with $T = 0.0$ (left), 1.0 (middle), and 2.5 (right).

```
#ifdef BRIGHTNESS
    vec3 target = vec3( 0., 0., 0. );
#else
    vec3 target = vec3( 0.5,0.5,0.5 );
#endif
    fFragColor = vec4( mix( target, irgb, uT ), 1. );
}
```

Blending an Image with a Version of Itself

Another common kind of image manipulation involves creating a base value that is computed from the image itself. This might be a grayscale image or a blurred image in the examples below. Again, these are common and very useful kinds of manipulation. And again, we show examples that have been set up for *glman* as described above.

Saturation

We think of *color saturation* as a description of the "purity" of the color, or how far the color is from gray. This is consistent with the notion of saturation in the HLS color system, where saturation is the distance from the pure grays that are at the center of the HLS double cone. If saturation is reduced, the color is more gray; if it is increased, the color is purer and more vivid.

To manipulate the saturation of an image, you create a grayscale base image by replacing the color at each point by its luminance that we defined earlier in this chapter:

```
target = vec3( luminance, luminance, luminance);
```

and mix the color with this target, as we have seen. Values of uT less than 1 will move each color component toward its luminance, making the color less saturated, while values greater than 1 will move each color component away from the luminance, making it more saturated, as shown in Figure 11.23.

A simple fragment shader to manipulate saturation is shown below.

```
const vec3 W = vec3( 0.2125, 0.7154, 0.0721 );

uniform sampler2D uImageUnit;
uniform float uT;

in vec2 vST;
```

Figure 11.23. Saturation manipulation of the supermarket fruit image with $uT = 0.0$ (left), 1.0 (middle), and 2.0 (right).

```
out vec4 fFragColor;

void main( )
{
   vec3 irgb = texture( uImageUnit, vST ).rgb;
   float luminance = dot( irgb, W );
   vec3 target = vec3( luminance, luminance, luminance );
   fFragColor = vec4( mix( target, irgb, uT ), 1. );

}
```

Sharpness

We think of sharpness as the degree of clarity in both coarse and fine image detail in an image. Alternately, you could think of sharpness as the opposite of blurred. Manipulating the sharpness of the image takes advantage of this fact by creating an extrapolation from a blurred version of the image through the image itself. The blurred image is created by the blurring process discussed earlier in the chapter. An example of sharpening an image is shown in Figure 11.24; the left and middle images are larger versions of those of Figure 11.5.

A fragment shader to manipulate sharpness would contain code something like the following. The code uses the same filter and computation described in the image blur example earlier in the chapter, except that it ends by mixing the blurred image ("target") and the original image ("irgb"). The shader files are included in the materials with this book.

```
   ...
   fFragColor = vec4( mix( target, irgb, uT ), 1. );
```

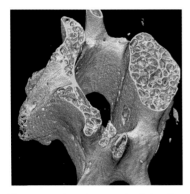 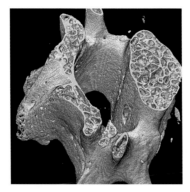 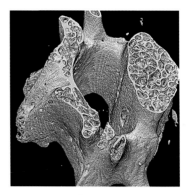

Figure 11.24. The result of the sharpness operation with the 5 × 5 blurred image ($T = 0$, left), the original image ($T = 1$, middle), and the sharpened image ($T = 5$, right).

This is a special case of unsharp masking, a standard image manipulation technique to sharpen photographic images for printing. The general technique uses a blur filter of adjustable radius and an adjustable blend; this example uses radius 1 and a limited adjustable blend.

Blending Two Different Images

The two-image manipulations in the sections above have really been about creating effects in a single image, using another reference image as a tool. However, sometimes you have two images that each have content, and you

Figure 11.25. Two sample images we will use to illustrate blending: Washington cherry blossoms (left) and Xidi, an ancient Hong village in Anhui province, China (right).

want to blend both images. There are a number of different common kinds of blends. In the sections below, we will sketch a few of them and show examples. It should be straightforward for you to complete any implementations that we do not give completely. In addition, we have included a few more blends as chapter exercises. Figure 11.25 shows two sample images that we will use to illustrate many of the blending operations we discuss.

Other Combinations

Complex and interesting interpolations of two images are possible because you can use any function that takes two RGB color values and returns another RGB color value. The function could act on entire RGB vectors or it could act on the individual color components separately. We explore a few of these below, and there are a few more in the exercises.

Cosine Interpolation

As an example, consider a cosine-based interpolation from [20] that looks interesting; Figure 11.26 shows the effect. The same pixel from both images is

read, and the color components of the two pixels are combined, using cosine multipliers. The cosine is applied to each component, so components nearer one are increased. If we take $Argb$ as the color of the "after" image and $Brgb$ as the color of the "before" image, as above, then the blended color is given by

$$color = \rho - \alpha * \cos\left(\pi * Argb\right) - \beta * \cos\left(\pi * Brgb\right)$$

where ρ is a base color, basically an overall luminance, and α and β are chosen to weight the two images (and either $|\rho| + |\alpha| + |\beta|$ cannot exceed 1 or you must clamp the result).

Figure 11.26. The cosine interpolation of the two sample images.

Sample fragment shader code for this operation is given below. Notice that we have used values of 0.5 and –0.25 as the base value and cosine multiplier, respectively; in an exercise, we encourage you to experiment with these (and we suggest that you use *glman* uniform slider variables to do so).

```
const float PI = 3.14159265;

uniform sampler2D uBeforeUnit, uAfterUnit;

in vec2 vST;
```

```
out vec4 fFragColor;

void main( )
{
    vec3 brgb = texture( uBeforeUnit, vST ).rgb;
    vec3 argb = texture( uAfterUnit,vST).rgb;
    vec3 target = 0.5 - 0.25*cos(PI*brgb) - 0.25*cos(PI*argb);
    fFragColor = vec4( target, 1. );
}
```

Multiply

The *multiply* operation does exactly as the name suggests. You read a pixel from each image and multiply the color components together to get the final color of the pixel. In this way, one image is being used as a subtractive filter for the other.

Since all the color components are less than or equal to one, the final image will likely be darker than either original. In order to account for that, you can balance the colors by computing the luminance of the original colors, *argb*, *brgb*, and *target*, and adjusting the final output color of each pixel so its luminance is the average of the two input pixels' colors. Some sample fragment shader code for this is shown below. The result, both without and with the color balancing, is shown in Figure 11.27.

```
const vec3 W = vec3(0.2125, 0.7154, 0.0721)

uniform sampler2D uBeforeUnit, uAfterUnit;

in vec2 vST;

out vec4 fFragColor;

void main( )
{
    vec3 brgb = texture( uBeforeUnit, vST ).rgb;
    vec3 argb = texture( uAfterUnit, vST ).rgb;
    vec3 target = argb * brgb;

    float alum = dot( argb, W );
    float blum = dot( brgb, W );
    float tlum = dot( target, W );
    target = (alum + blum)/(2.*tlum);
    fFragColor = vec4( target, 1.);
}
```

Figure 11.27. The results of the multiply without the color balancing (left) and with the color balancing (right) operations on our sample images.

Darken and Lighten

The *darken* and *lighten* operations are very similar, so we discuss them together. The darken operation on two images uses one image to darken the other. You read a pixel from each image, and you take the smaller of the values of each color component for each pixel. Some sample fragment shader code for this is shown below.

The lighten operation is the converse of the darken operation above; you read a pixel from each image, and you take the larger of the values for each color component for each pixel. The fragment shader code for this is left as an exercise. The result for both operations is shown in Figure 11.28.

```
uniform sampler2D uBeforeUnit, uAfterUnit;

in vec2 vST;

out vec4 fFragColor;

void main( )
{
    vec3 brgb = texture( uBeforeUnit, vST ).rgb;
    vec3 argb = texture( uAfterUnit, vST ).rgb;
    vec3 target = min( argb, brgb ); // alternately max(...)
    fFragColor = vec4( target, 1.);
}
```

Figure 11.28. The result of the darken (left) and lighten (right) operations on our sample images.

Image Transitions

In addition to combining two images into one, we should think about ways to move from one image to another over time. One example of this is the set of slide transitions in Powerpoint, but the control we have with fragment shaders lets us go well beyond the options available there.

The basic principle is that we start with each pixel from one image, which we will call the *Before* image, and we manipulate each pixel in a way that finishes with a second image, which we will call the *After* image. We can replace *Before* pixels with *After* pixels in any way we like, and we will try to create some interesting effects in doing so. In all our examples in this section, we start with the two images of Figure 11.25, the Washington cherry blossoms and the Hong village.

Horizontal Replace

The first transition we will consider moves the *Before* image off the display to the right while simultaneously moving the *After* image onto the display from the left. However, as we go through the transition, both images are displayed in their entirety; each is simply compressed into the part of the display that is available to it. An example of the transi-tion partly completed is shown in Figure 11.29.

The .glib file and vertex shader source are essentially identical to the image blending examples above, so we will focus on the fragment shader source, shown below.

```
uniform float uT; //0. <= uT <= 1.
uniform sampler2D uBeforeUnit, uAfterUnit;

in vec2 vST;

out vec4 fFragColor;

void main( )
{
    vec2 st = vST;
    vec3 brgb = texture( uBeforeUnit, st ).rgb;
    vec3 argb = texture( uAfterUnit, st ).rgb;
    vec3 color;

    if ( st.x < uT )
    {
        st = vec2( st.x/uT, st.y );
        vec3 thisrgb = texture( AfterUnit, st ).rgb;
        color = thisrgb;
    }
    else
    {
        st = vec2( (st.x-uT)/(1.-uT), st.y );
        vec3 thatrgb = texture( BeforeUnit, st ).rgb;
        color = thatrgb;
    }

    fFragColor = vec4( color, 1.);
}
```

Figure 11.29. The Hong village image replacing the cherry blossom image.

Here the two halves of the if statement represent the two halves of the display: the side where the *s*-component of the texture coordinate is less than uT and the side where it is greater than uT. For each pixel coordinate, the *s*-component of the appropriate image (i.e., texture) is calculated by a proportional computation, and the resulting texture coordinate is used to select the texel to be displayed.

As uT goes from 0. to 1., the effect in this example is to create the transition from the *Before* image to the *After* image over that same period. No static figure can capture the full effect; an exercise invites you to create your own transition and see it work.

Dissolve

The *image dissolve* operation computes a weighted average of the *Before* and *After* images that determines how much of each image's color is used in the output image. This weight can be given by a parameter that changes over time, giving the effect of moving from one image to another, as can be done for slideshows. This is shown in Figure 11.30 and in the weighted-average fragment shader code below. As the value of uT ranges from 0. to 1., the *Before* image dissolves into the *After* image.

```
uniform sampler2D uBeforeUnit, uAfterUnit;
uniform float uT;

in vec2 vST;

out vec4 fFragColor;

void main( )
{

    vec3 brgb = texture( uBeforeUnit, vST ).rgb;
    vec3 argb = texture( uAfterUnit, vST ).rgb;
    fFragColor = vec4( mix( argb, brgb, uT ), 1. );
}
```

Figure 11.30. A dissolve of the two sample images with uT = 0.5.

Burn-Through

Another transition can be made where the *After* image "burns through" the *Before* image; that is, where the parts of the *After* image with the strongest luminance replace the same parts of the *Before* image. We will leave this exact transition for the exercises, but we will consider an example where we approximate the luminance by the average of the R, G, and B colors in the *After* image. The effect of this transition is almost like the *After* image burning through the *Before* image, which is why we have chosen this name for it. In Figure 11.31 we see this transition partway through. It is not difficult to see some of the darker architectural features of the village scene coming through the cherries image.

Figure 11.31. The Hong village image burning through the cherry blossom image.

Again, the .glib file and vertex shader are essentially the same as previous ones, and the fragment shader is shown below.

```
uniform float uT;
uniform sampler2D uBeforeUnit, uAfterUnit;

in vec2 vST;

out vec4 fFragColor;

void main( )
{
  vec3 brgb = texture( uBeforeUnit, vST ).rgb;
  vec3 argb = texture( uAfterUnit, vST ).rgb;
  vec3 color;

  if ( (argb.r + argb.g + argb.b)/3. < uT )
    color = argb;
  else
    color = brgb;

  fFragColor = vec4( color, 1.);
}
```

There is even less computation in this fragment shader; the average of the *After* color components is calculated and compared with the parameter *uT*, and the *After* color is used instead of the *Before* color when the color values are low (that is, when the colors are dark). As the value of *uT* moves from 0. to 1., more and more of the texels in the *After* image satisfy the condition and become part of the final display.

Break-Through

What if we had some other way for the *After* image to replace the *Before* image over time? What if, for example, we generated a random texture with a Noise( ) function and used the values of that random texture to determine whether the *Before* or *After* image is used for each pixel? An example of this kind of transition is shown in Figure 11.32. This is something like the burn-through transition, but the image that controls the pixel selection is hidden and there is no apparent relation between this intermediate image and either of the two original images.

Because this process uses noise operations, the .glib and vertex shader are somewhat different from the ones we have seen before in this chapter. The .glib file simply selects a 3D noise texture and proceeds as in previous examples.

```
##OpenGL GLIB

Noise3D 128
Ortho -1. 1. -1. 1.

Texture 6 cherries.bmp
Texture 7 Hong.village.bmp

Vertex  transition.vert
Fragment transition.frag
Program Transition uBeforeUnit 6 uAfterUnit 7

QuadXY .2 5.
```

Figure 11.32. A break-through transition with the Hong village image replacing the cherry blossom image under the control of a noise function.

The vertex shader adds an input variable, the familiar *MCposition*, that holds the model coordinates for each vertex in the initial quad and, when it is interpolated across the quad, will hold the model coordinates for each pixel in the display.

```
out vec3 vMCposition;
out vec2 vST;

void main( )
{
   vMCposition = vec3(aVertex);
   vST      = aTexCoord0.st;
   gl_Position = uModelViewProjectionMatrix * aVertex;
}
```

Finally, the fragment shader gets the pixel colors for each image as usual, but then gets a noise value (the variable *nv*) for the pixel by querying the 3D sampler function Noise3 at a position determined by the pixel's model coordinates. Since the original quad was 10 units across, we divide the model coordinates by 10 to get the actual texture coordinate for the pixel. The octaves of the noise value are then used to compute a numeric value whose fractional value is used for the comparison that selects the image.

```
uniform float uT;
uniform sampler3D Noise3;
uniform sampler2D uBeforeUnit, uAfterUnit;

in vec3 vMCposition;
in vec2 vST;
```

```
out vec4 fFragColor;

void main( )
{
   vec3 brgb = texture( uBeforeUnit, vST ).rgb;
   vec3 argb = texture( uAfterUnit, vST ).rgb;
   vec3 color;

   vec4 nv = texture(Noise3, vMCposition/10.);
   float sum = nv.r + nv.g + nv.b + nv.a;
   sum = ( sum - 1. ) / 2.;   // 0. to 1.
   sum = fract( sum );
   if ( sum < uT )
      color = argb;
   else
      color = brgb;

   fFragColor = vec4( color, 1.);
}
```

Figure 11.33. The grayscale texture used in the break-through transition.

Although we do not save it for any other use, this numeric value *sum* actually provides a noise texture that acts as the controller for the transition; if we set

```
color = vec3( sum, sum, sum );
```

instead of setting color in the if statement, we can see that texture, shown in Figure 11.33.

There are obviously many other ways you could control which image contributes the actual value for any pixel. For example, almost any of the image blending operations that involves taking part of one image and part of another image under control of a parameter could be used to create a transition by varying that parameter. Further developments are left for the curious reader.

Notes

These sections have discussed a number of techniques that are all rather similar, but that differ in how an image is processed on its own, is compared with a reference image, or is combined with a different image. The techniques are straightforward; choosing the right one to use when you want to create a particular effect takes experience and some time.

Exercises

1. Complete the work of the CMYK separation example by presenting the four separations in their actual color, instead of in grayscale. You may use any image you like, but the file Figure-11.3.tif is included in the resources for the book so that you may compare your work to that in this chapter.

2. Create an anaglyph of a familiar scene, such as part of your home or campus, by taking two digital photographs from nearby points that frame the same portion of the middle ground of the scene, and combining them as described in this chapter.

3. Implement *image rotation* by any multiple of 90° by taking the original texture coordinates and applying trigonometric functions to them.

4. Implement *image flipping* or *image inversion*, the process where the top and bottom of an image are reversed. Do the same for reversing the left and right sides of an image.

5. Implement some different *image warping* approaches than the one we discussed in the chapter. Consider how you might use trigonometric functions in only one direction, exponential functions, or other kinds of manipulations to the texture coordinates.

6. Implement *selective coloring*. Using the luminance value, it is simple to convert an image to grayscale, but this can be done selectively. Get an image for which one thing stands out in a different color (for example, an apple on a windowsill) and make everything grayscale except that one thing. Use color testing on each pixel to decide whether or not to change it.

7. In the discussion of the interpolation operation, we use the equation below to combine the two colors we are blending:

```
vec3 target = vec3(0.5) - 0.25*cos(PI*brgb) -
    0.25*cos(PI*argb);
```

Experiment with the values used to control the blending. As a first try, you might vary the base color b and the subtractive terms s in the equation

```
vec3 target = b - s*cos(PI*brgb) - s*cos(PI * argb);
```

with the relationship $s = (1 - b)/2$. Make b a slider uniform variable in a GLIB file and use *glman* to experiment with this concept. Record and comment on your results.

8. You can combine the manipulation techniques described in this chapter to achieve other specific effects. For example, if you have a photograph of a green apple but you want an image of a red apple, you can use the technique from the chromakey to select the greens of the apple and then use the hue shifting operation to change the green to red, while retaining some of the character of the green apple. Pick one of your images that has a strong area of some color, and change that color to another color.

9. Combine some of the effects from this chapter and see what you get. For example, you can sharpen images with one technique and then make them grayscale with another. (Does it matter in which order you do that?) You can take the image output of one technique and use it as the input to the next. If you push some of the techniques beyond their logical bounds (for example, take a *very* large mixing factor for sharpness) you may get some images that could effectively be taken into another technique (for example, grayscale). See what you can do!

The next two exercises consider other examples of image warping, similar to the example shown in Figure 11.16. Like that example, these come from [6, Chapter 16].

10. The ripple transformation displaces pixels in waves in both the *x*- and *y*-directions. This transformation has four parameters: the period lengths $\tau_x, \tau_y \neq 0$ (in pixels) and the wave magnitudes a_x, a_y (in pixels) in both directions:

$$x = x' + a_x \sin\left(2\pi y'/\tau_x\right) \text{ and } y = y' + a_y \sin\left(2\pi x'/\tau_y\right).$$

Create a shader that implements the ripple transformation, and apply it to both a grid image and a natural image. In [4] an example uses the parameters (in pixels) $\tau_x = 120$, $\tau_y = 250$, $a_x = 10$, and $a_y = 15$, so you might use these.

11. The spherical transformation simulates viewing the image through a hemispherical lens. If we assume that the lens is centered on the image, the parameters of this transformation are the radius of the lens r_{max} and its refraction index η. The functions that implement this transformation are

$$x = x' - \begin{cases} z \tan(\beta_x) & \text{for } r \leq r_{max} \\ 0 & \text{for } r > r_{max} \end{cases}$$

$$y = y' - \begin{cases} z \tan(\beta_y) & \text{for } r \leq r_{max} \\ 0 & \text{for } r > r_{max} \end{cases}$$

with

$$d_x = x' - x_c, \quad r = \sqrt{d_x^2 + d_y^2}, \quad \beta_x = \left(1 - \frac{1}{\rho}\right)\arcsin\left(\frac{d_x}{\sqrt{d_x^2 + z^2}}\right)$$

$$d_y = y' - y_c, \quad z = \sqrt{r_{max}^2 - r^2}, \quad \beta_y = \left(1 - \frac{1}{\rho}\right)\arcsin\left(\frac{d_y}{\sqrt{d_y^2 + z^2}}\right)$$

Implement the spherical transformation and apply it to a grid image and to a natural image. A good value for the refraction index is $\eta = 1.8$.

The next few exercises ask you to examine some operations on pairs of images and see the results.

12. The *screen* operation is similar to the multiply operation, but you take the complement of each pixel's color components, multiply the components together, and take the complement of the result. Implement this operation. The result will be lighter than either original; explain why. As we did in the multiply example in the text, use a luminance computation to balance the screen operation results with the originals.

13. The *difference* between two images is defined by the absolute value of the color difference between the images' pixels. Implement this image operation.

14. *Negation* and *exclusion* are similar to difference, but treat the colors somewhat differently. For the negation operation, the color target is

    ```
    vec3 target = vec3(1.,1.,1.) - abs(1. - argb - brgb );
    ```

    while for the exclusion operation, the color target is

    ```
    vec3 target = argb + brgb - 2.0 * argb * brgb;
    ```

    Implement both the negation and the exclusion operations. The target for the negation operation is automatically in the legal range for color, but the target for exclusion may not be; you will probably want to clamp it to [0., 1.].

15. Color *burn* and *dodge* are two other related operations. The color burn operation is given by

    ```
    vec3 target = vec3(1.,1.,1.) - (1.-argb)/brgb;
    ```

    Since you are dividing by the value of color components that are no larger than one, you may get results greater than one, so you may need to clamp this result to [0., 1.]:

    ```
    vec3 result = clamp( target, 0., 1. );
    ```

The color dodge operation involves a divide instead of a multiply and involves the inverse rather than the original of the second image. Again, some clamping may be needed.

```
vec3 target = argb/(vec3(1. - brgb);
```

Implement both the color burn and dodge operations.

16. Modify the burn-through transition to replace the RGB average value with the computed luminance. Can you see any subjective difference between these two transitions? Discuss why you think the difference, or lack of difference, you see is reasonable.

17. In a variation on the break-through transition, create a systematic gray-scale pattern texture and use that to control the selection of the image for each pixel. Look at the selection of transitions available in Powerpoint and identify the transitions that can be implemented by this approach.

18. In the break-through transition discussion, we said that you could actually display the noise texture used to control which image is presented at each stage of the transi-tion. Do this. Then capture one frame part way through the transition and compare that capture to the noise texture to see if you can identify the texture's action in the transition.

19. In the break-through transition discussion, Figure 11.33 shows how you can create an output image from the noise texture, by assigning the same value to all three color components. What if you assign nv[0] to red, nv[1] to green, and nv[2] to blue? What do you get? Why?

20. If you declare a variable

```
uniform float Timer;
```

then *glman* will fill it with a value from 0. to 1. over the course of 10 seconds. Try using Timer instead of uT in the image transitions to create an animated effect.

12

Geometry Shader
Concepts and Examples

The geometry shader is a new capability in shaders, introduced in late 2006 with the release of Shader Model 4 to take advantage of the ever-growing capability of high-end graphics cards. It adds to the programmer's graphics capabilities by providing tools to expand the basic model geometry to include more or different graphics primitives than were initially defined. Thus, geometry shaders should really be called "geometry creators" or "geometry expanders." The place of the geometry shader in the graphics pipeline is shown in Figure 12.1, where "vertex processing" can include a vertex shader, tessellation control shader, or tessellation evaluation shader.

The geometry expansion that is provided by the geometry shader has many uses. One is in using the input geometry to create additional geometry, such as silhouette edges, shrunk triangles, or hedgehog plots. Another is in managing *level of detail* (LOD). The LOD, shrunk triangles, and silhouette edges examples are discussed later in this chapter, and hedgehog plots are discussed in Chapter 15.

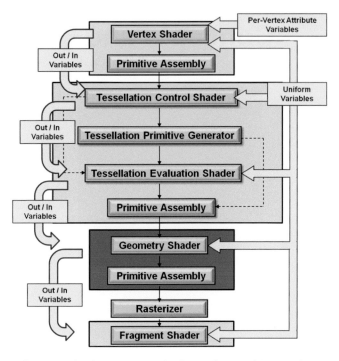

Figure 12.1. The geometry shader in the graphics pipeline.

What Does the Geometry Shader Do?

If you use a geometry shader, your application or your vertex shader can generate all the familiar topology types plus a few new ones that we will cover below:

- Points.
- Lines.
- Line strips.
- Line loops.
- Lines with adjacency.
- Line strips with adjacency.
- Triangles.
- Triangle strips.

- Triangle fans.
- Triangles with adjacency.
- Triangle strips with adjacency.
- Quads.
- Quad strips.

Any of these topologies can be used by the application, but geometry shaders have a limited number of topologies that they can accept. These are points, lines, lines with adjacency, triangles, or triangles with adjacency.

Thus, the primitives used by the application sometimes need to be internally converted. You, the application programmer, don't need to know about this. But, you, the shader writer, do.

Geometry shaders are not intended to provide a *general-purpose* LOD capability because (1) they have a limit to the number of new vertices that they can create, and (2) they have limited access to the surrounding vertex information that would be needed for, say, subdivision surfaces. *Tesselation shaders* are meant for this and are described in the Chapter 13.

On the output side, the geometry shader then generates points, line strips, or triangle strips, and feeds them on to the rest of the graphics pipeline.

There needn't be any correlation between geometry shader input type and geometry shader output type. Points can generate triangles, triangles can generate triangle strips, and so on. In the silhouette example later on in this chapter, the input is the new "triangles with adjacency" graphics primitive, while the output is simply lines. This is described more visually in Figure 12.2.

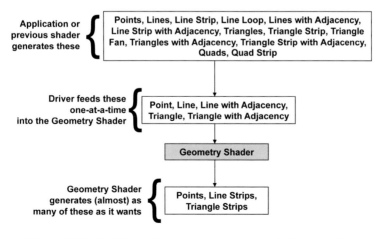

Figure 12.2. The kinds of processing geometry shaders can do.

Geometry shaders can access uniform variables, just like vertex and fragment shaders can. They can also access all of the standard OpenGL-defined variables, such as the transformation matrices. Thus, you can transform the original vertices in the vertex shader, or transform them as they are being emitted from the geometry shader, whichever is more convenient.

New Adjacency Primitives

As we saw in the brief discussion above, the geometry shader language introduces some new geometric primitives to support the expansion capabilities in this shader. These primitives add adjacency information to the fundamental primitive, so that the additional adjacent vertices can be used in the primitive expansion. At the OpenGL API level, these are reflected in additional arguments to the familiar `glBegin( )` function:

- `GL_LINES_ADJACENCY`
- `GL_LINE_STRIP_ADJACENCY`
- `GL_TRIANGLES_ADJACENCY`
- `GL_TRIANGLE_STRIP_ADJACENCY`

These arguments reflect the new adjacency primitives that are defined with geometry shaders. The additional primitives, and the number and meaning of the vertices that are used in implementing them if no geometry shader is used, are listed below. If you use a geometry shader, you will define what the vertices mean by the action of your shader.

- *Lines with adjacency.* 4N vertices are given (where N is the number of line segments to draw). For each set of four vertices, a line segment is drawn between vertex 1 and vertex 2. Vertices 0 and 3 are not part of the drawing, but provide adjacency information.
- *Line strip with adjacency.* N+3 vertices are given (where N is the number of line segments to draw). A line segment is drawn between vertices 1 and 2, vertices 2 and 3, ..., and vertices N and N+1. Vertices 0 and N+2 are not part of the drawing, but provide adjacency information.
- *Triangles with adjacency.* 6N vertices are given (where N is the number of triangles to draw). For each triangle, vertices 0, 2, and 4 define the triangle, while vertices 1, 3, and 5 tell where adjacent triangles are.
- *Triangle strip with adjacency.* 4+2N vertices are given (where N is the number of triangles to draw). Vertices 0, 2, 4, 6, 8, 10, ... define the triangles, while vertices 1, 3, 5, 7, 9, 11, ... tell where adjacent triangles are.

These primitives are described graphically in Figure 12.3. This shows the sets of input vertices and the way those vertices define the primitives for lines,

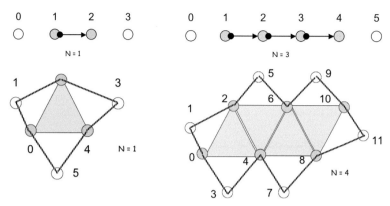

Figure 12.3. The four new geometric primitives with their adjacent points: lines with adjacency (top left), line strip with adjacency (top right), triangles with adjacency (bottom left), and triangle strip with adjacency (bottom right).

line strips, triangles, and triangle strips. In all these cases, the vertices are listed in the order given, and are interpreted as described above. Notice that for the line primitives, the first and last vertices are the adjacent primitives, while for the triangle primitives, the vertices begin with one in the actual primitives and the adjacent vertices are interleaved with the vertices in the primitive.

There is also a new GLSL built-in variable for geometry shaders. The variable

```
int gl_PrimitiveIDIn
```

holds the number of primitives processed since the last time `glBegin( )` was called. Its value is zero for the first primitive after the `glBegin( )` function, and calling a vertex array function counts as an implied `glBegin( )`. Geometry shaders can set the value of `gl_PrimitiveID` to send a primitive number to the fragment shader.

Layouts for Input and Output Variables

A geometry shader must be told something about its input and output variables. As you can see in Figure 12.1, a geometry shader is always preceded by a primitive assembly step, which groups multiple vertices into a single topological primitive before handing them to the geometry shader. Thus, on the input side, geometry shaders need to know what that topology is. This is done with a GLSL `layout` statement, which goes at the top of the code:

```
layout( topology ) in;
```

where *topology* must be one of the following:

```
points
lines
lines_adjacency
triangles
triangles_adjacency
```

Figure 12.1 also shows you that the geometry shader is followed by another primitive assembly step. Thus, on the output side, a geometry shader needs to tell that step what topology to use to assemble the emitted vertices. To do this, a second `layout` statement is included at the top of the code:

```
layout( topology, max_vertices=num ) out;
```

where *topology* must be one of the following:

```
points
line_strip
triangle_strip
```

and *num* is the maximum number of vertices that this geometry shader will emit. All graphics cards have a maximum that *num* can be, usually around 1024.

New OpenGL API Functions

It is a little clumsier, but you can also choose not to use the layout identifiers and instead use `glProgramParameteri( )` calls. The OpenGL function `glProgramParameteri( )` sets various parameters concerning the operation of the geometry shader. There are three primary uses of this function

1. The number of vertices the geometry shader will be emitting is given by

```
glProgramParameteri( progname,
        GL_GEOMETRY_VERTICES_OUT, intvalue)
```

where `intvalue` is that number. For many of the current graphics boards (as of this writing), `invalue` can be as much as 1024. (1024 sounds like a lot, but if you are trying to smooth a pyramid into a hemisphere, it isn't nearly enough. This is one of the reasons that geometry shaders are not intended for general level-of-detail work.)

2. The primitive type that is to be sent to the geometry shader is given by

```
glProgramParameteri( progname,
        GL_GEOMETRY_INPUT_TYPE, intvalue)
```

where intvalue is a symbolic parameter for the primitive type that this geometry shader will be receiving. This parameter can take on any one of the five symbolic values

- GL_POINTS
- GL_LINES
- GL_LINES_ADJACENCY
- GL_TRIANGLES
- GL_TRIANGLES_ADJACENCY

The kind of graphics primitive that can be passed to the geometry shader depends on the kind of geometry that the shader is to emit.

- If GL_LINES is chosen, the lines could actually come from GL_LINES, GL_LINE_STRIP, or GL_LINE_LOOP.
- If GL_LINES_ADJACENCY is chosen, the lines with adjacency could actually come from GL_LINES_ADJACENCY or GL_LINE_STRIP_ADJACENCY.
- If GL_TRIANGLES is chosen, the triangles could actually come from GL_TRIANGLES, GL_TRIANGLE_STRIP, GL_TRIANGLE_FAN, GL_QUADS, or GL_QUAD_STRIP.
- If GL_TRIANGLES_ADJACENCY is chosen, the triangles with adjacency could actually come from GL_TRIANGLES_ADJACENCY or GL_TRIANGLE_STRIP_ADJACENCY.

3. The actual primitive type that is to be emitted from the geometry shader is given by

```
glProgramParameteri(progname,
        GL_GEOMETRY_OUTPUT_TYPE, intvalue)
```

where intvalue is a symbolic parameter for the primitive type that the geometry shader will be emitting. This parameter can take on the symbolic values

- GL_POINTS
- GL_LINE_STRIP
- GL_TRIANGLE_STRIP

There is an issue about using the function glProgramParameteri( ) in a display list, which may not be obvious but which can cause some difficulties. Consider the following example of using a geometry shader within a display list:

```
GLuint dl = glGenLists( 1 );
glNewList( dl, GL_COMPILE );
. . .
program = glCreateProgram( );
. . .
glProgramParameteriEXT( program,GL_GEOMETRY_INPUT_TYPE,
  inputGeometryType);
glProgramParameteriEXT(program,GL_GEOMETRY_OUTPUT_TYPE,
  outputGeometryType);
glProgramParameteriEXT(program,GL_GEOMETRY_VERTICES_OUT,101);
glLinkProgram( program );
glUseProgram( program );
. . .
glEndList( );
```

These glProgramParameteri( ) and glUseProgram(program) function calls will be deferred until the list is executed by the execution of glCallList(1), but the glCreateProgram( ) and glLinkProgram(program) calls that are highlighted will be executed *immediately* when they are processed, even though the rest of the list is deferred. So while the parameter setting function can be placed inside a display list definition, this is usually a bad idea, because that would defer the execution of the function until glCallList( ) is called for the list you are defining. Then the geometry shader would be called with the wrong parameters, giving incorrect results. Our advice is to defer both the setting of program parameters and the linking of the shader program until after the display list is complete, or, more likely, create the program and then put just the glUseProgram( ) and drawing commands in the display list. There is rarely a good reason to have calls to glProgramParameteri( ) in a display list.

If you are using the glProgramParameteri( ) functions instead of the layout identifiers, those functions must be called, and all these parameters set, before the shaders are linked in the application.

There are some additional new GLSL functions for geometry shaders. These are

- EmitVertex( ): send the vertex you have been developing on to the second primitive assembly step.

- EndPrimitive( ): take all the vertices that have been sent to primitive assembly and create a geometric primitive to send on for further processing.

These are illustrated in the examples below, but they are pretty self-explan-atory. You should expect to have several instances of EmitVertex( ) as you go through the shader program, but you may or may not call EndPrimitive( ), depending on whether you are emitting only one primitive from the shader, or several. There is no need to call EndPrimitive( ) at the end of the geometry shader; this is implied.

New GLSL Variables and Variable Types

There are new kinds of variables that can be used in the geometry shader. If there is a geometry shader, output variables from the vertex shader are col-lected by the primitive assembly step and passed to the geometry shader once enough vertices have been collected for the current primitive's topology type. The user-defined variables that are input to the geometry shader from the ver-tex shader are declared in the vertex shader as out and in the geometry shader as in. The geometry shader's output variables, emitted to be interpolated in the rasterizer, are declared as out.

Geometry shaders use GLSL variables just like the vertex, tessellation, and fragment shaders. Geometry shaders can access uniform variables, just like the other shaders, and geometry shaders can access all the uniform variables from the application (as well as the standard OpenGL-defined variables, such as the transformation matrices, if you are working in compatibility mode). Thus, you can transform the original vertices in the vertex shader, or transform them as they are being emitted from the geometry shader, whichever is more conve-nient. However, there are several new GLSL variables to describe the data that comes to the geometry shader from the vertex or tessellation shader. These are described in detail in the next section.

Communication between a Vertex or Tessellation Shader and a Geometry Shader

If there is a geometry shader, variables from the vertex or tessellation shader are collected by a primitive assembly step and passed to the geometry shader once enough vertices have been collected for the current topology type.

The geometry shader will take all the products of the vertex or tessel-lation shader, from the geometric parts (gl_Position, ...) to the appearance parts (vColor, vST, ...) and use them as parts of the primitives it assembles. Notice that a vertex shader does not change the geometric primitive that is defined in your application, but is free to write out values as needed for the primitives it assembles.

If a vertex or tessellation shader writes variables as	Then the geometry shader will read them as	And will write the new variables as
gl_Position	gl_PositionIn[•]	gl_Position
gl_PointSize	gl_PointSizeIn[•]	gl_PointSize
gl_Layer	gl_LayerIn[•]	gl_Layer
gl_PrimitiveID	gl_PrimitiveIDIn[•]	gl_PrimitiveID

In the geometry shader, the dimensions indicated by [•] are given by the variable gl_VerticesIn, although you will already know this by the type of geometry you are inputting. The dimensions are shown in the following table.

Input Topology Type	# Vertices in Arrays
GL_POINTS	1
GL_LINES	2
GL_LINES_ADJACENCY	4
GL_TRIANGLES	3
GL_TRIANGLES_ADJACENCY	6

The geometry shader can assign values to any of the GLSL variables in the right-hand column to define the properties of the vertices it emits. When the geometry shader calls EmitVertex( ), this set of variables is copied to a slot in the shader's primitive assembly step. So when the geometry shader calls EndPrimitive( ), or when the geometry shader ends (which implies that the primitive has ended), the vertices that have been saved in the primitive assembly step are assembled, rasterized, and further processed in the remainder of the standard graphics pipeline.

You may wonder why, if there is an EndPrimitive( ) function, we have not mentioned a BeginPrimitive( ) function. In fact, there is no such function; a primitive is deemed to begin at the start of the geometry shader or at the return from any EndPrimitive( ) call. There is also no need to call EndPrimitive( ) at the end of the geometry shader; this is implicit in the shader's end, and ending any active primitive is part of the shader finishing process. If it feels wrong to you to have no BeginPrimitive( ) function, it's simple enough to create an empty function by

```
#define BeginPrimitive( ) ;
```

Normals in Geometry Shaders

When we discussed vertex shaders, we recognized that handling only one vertex at a time made it difficult to compute normals based on cross products of edges. If we did not have enough information to compute analytic normals from the changed vertex geometry, we could not get the normals we needed for the ambient-diffuse-specular lighting model.

Working with geometry shaders, we still want to use normals computed from the original geometry whenever we can, because that is better information than normals computed from cross products of edges. However, geometry shaders do give us access to all the information in all the vertices of an input triangle or triangle with adjacency, and this can let us compute cross-product normals. In fact, it may well be worth adding a geometry shader to an application that uses a vertex or tessellation shader but that does not support analytic normals, simply to be able to compute the cross-product normals for lighting.

Examples

Perhaps the best way to become familiar with geometry shaders is to consider several examples that operate in different ways. Below we have four examples, with the first two examples showing the use of geometry shaders to create limited LOD effects, and the next two examples showing instances where geometry shaders create new geometry to add extra meaning to a figure. The first example takes four vertices (two vertices with adjacent vertices) and produces a Bézier spline curve. The second example takes a triangle and outputs the same triangle, but shrunk about its centroid. The third example takes a single triangle and expands it into an octant of a sphere. The fourth example takes a 3D object and develops the silhouette of the object.

Bézier Curves

In our first geometry shader example, we will show how you can expand four points into a Bézier curve with a variable number of line segments. The GLIB file shown sets up the example in the same way we saw in Chapter 3, with some additions for geometry shaders. These are

- Specifying the types of input and output geometry.
- Specifying the geometry shader to be used.
- Setting the input values for the `LinesAdjacency` primitive.

Note the use of the LinesAdjacency primitive. Figure 12.3 shows the fixed-function handling of this primitive—a line from point #1 to point #2. But with a geometry shader turned on, this primitive is really just a way of getting four grouped points into the shader. What you do with them after that is up to you. So, in this case, the geometry shader will turn those four points into a line strip. The vertex and fragment shaders are not given, because they are very simple and very standard; the vertex shader simply sets gl_Position from the ModelViewProjection matrix and the vertex position, and the fragment shader simply sets the vec4 fFragColor.

Bezier.glib

```
Vertex bezier.vert
Geometry bezier.geom
Fragment bezier.frag
Program Bezier uNum <2 10 50>

LineWidth 3.
LinesAdjacency [0. 0. 0.] [1. 1. 1.] [2. 1. 2.] [3. -1. 0.]
```

The geometry shader is the key point of this example. It calculates the standard Bézier curve by using the standard basis on the four points in the input line with adjacency and then calculates the vertices on that curve by taking evenly spaced points in the parameter space:

$$P(t) = (1-t)^3 P_0 + 3t(1-t)^2 P_1 + 3t^2(1-t)P_2 + t^3 P_3.$$

Each point that is generated is emitted into a line strip. When the geometry shader ends, there is an implicit EndPrimitive( ) that sends the line strip on to the rest of the graphics pipeline.

Bezier.geom

```
#version 330
#extension GL_EXT_geometry_shader4: enable
uniform int uNum;

layout( lines_adjacency )  in;
layout( line_strip, max_vertices=1024 )  out;

void main( )
{
   float dt = 1. / float(uNum);
   float t = 0.;
   for( int i = 0; i <= uNum; i++, t += dt )
   {
```

```
        float omt = 1. - t;
        float omt2 = omt * omt;
        float omt3 = omt * omt2;
        float t2 = t * t;
        float t3 = t * t2;
        vec4 xyzw = omt3 * gl_PositionIn[0] +
        3. * t * omt2 * gl_PositionIn[1] +
        3. * t2 * omt * gl_PositionIn[2] +
         t3 *   gl_PositionIn[3];
        gl_Position = xyzw;
        EmitVertex( );
    }
}
```

The result of this shader's operation is shown in Figure 12.4 for two different values of the *glman* slider variable uNum. You can see the granularity of the curve for a small number of segments and the smoothness for a large number, as you would expect.

Note that it would have made no difference if the matrix transformation had been made in the geometry shader with

Figure 12.4. The Bézier curve (top), with uNum = 5, and the Bézier curve (bottom), with uNum = 25.

gl_Position = uModelViewProjectionMatrix*xyzw;

as the last statement before EmitVertex( ) instead of multiplying by uModelViewProjectionMatrix in the vertex shader. The interpolations that are done for the Bézier curve are the same in clipping space as they are in the original world space. In either case, the vertices are multiplied by the ModelViewProjection matrix and are then ready for processing further down the graphics pipeline.

Shrinking Triangles

An interesting question about any 3D object is how many triangles were used to create it. In the shrinking triangles example, shown in Figure 12.5, each triangle in the model is shrunken slightly about its centroid before it is displayed. This opens up a gap between the triangles, so each one is visible. Notice that the light on each triangle is exactly in agreement with its usual diffuse lighting, and you can see through the gaps between the triangles to the triangles on the back side of the model.

This geometry shader is shown below. It calculates the centroid of each triangle, calls the ProduceVertex( ) function to compute the light intensity, and moves each vertex toward the centroid, based on a uniform slider variable *uShrink*:

$$V' = \text{Centroid} + uShrink * (V - \text{Centroid}).$$

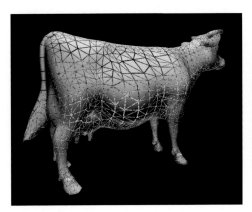

Figure 12.5. Two geometric figures with their component triangles shrunken.

When uShrink is 1., the vertices are unaltered. When uShrink is 0., all vertices are moved to the centroid. Clearly, neither of these is very valuable, so a value somewhere in between is called for. Notice that computing the centroid requires knowledge of the entire triangle, and so using a vertex shader by itself would not work.

```
#version 330
#extension GL_EXT_geometry_shader4: enable

layout( triangles )  in;
layout( triangle_strip, max_vertices=32 )  out;

uniform float uShrink;

in vec3 vNormal[3];

out float gLightIntensity;

const vec3 LIGHTPOS = vec3( 0., 10., 0. );

vec3 V[3];
vec3 CG;

void
ProduceVertex( int v )
{
  gLightIntensity = dot( normalize(LIGHTPOS-V[v]), vNormal[v]);
  gLightIntensity = abs( gLightIntensity );
```

```
    gl_Position = uModelViewProjectionMatrix *
        vec4( CG + uShrink * ( V[v] - CG ), 1. );
    EmitVertex( );
}
void
main( )
{
    V[0] = gl_PositionIn[0].xyz;
    V[1] = gl_PositionIn[1].xyz;
    V[2] = gl_PositionIn[2].xyz;
    CG = ( V[0] + V[1] + V[2] ) / 3.;
    ProduceVertex( 0 );
    ProduceVertex( 1 );
    ProduceVertex( 2 );
}
```

Sphere Subdivision

In this sphere subdivision example, we will start with a single triangle in the first octant of the sphere whose vertices lie on the positive coordinate axes. This triangle will be viewed as parameterized by two variables, which are multiplied by two adjacent edges of the triangle to determine all the interior points of the triangle. The triangle with this parameterization is shown in Figure 12.6, where the coordinates shown represent the values of the parameter pair.

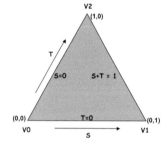

Figure 12.6. A triangle parameterized by two edges.

This triangle is subdivided by choosing values of s and t for appropriate points and using them to define new triangles. A parametric form of this is given by

$$V(s,t) = V_0 + s * (V_1 - V_0) + t * (V_2 - V_0),$$

with

$$s, t \geq 0$$

and

$$s + t \leq 1.$$

For example, in the triangles shown in Figure 12.7, the transition from level 0 to level 1 is obtained by taking the three parameter pairs (0.5, 0), (0, 0.5), and (0.5, 0.5) to define the three added points needed for the subdivision.

The vertex shader is straightforward and simply passes the aVertex value through to gl_Position. The fragment shader takes the input color and calculates fFragColor by multiplying the light intensity by the color, as we saw in earlier chapters. Neither of these needs to be presented further.

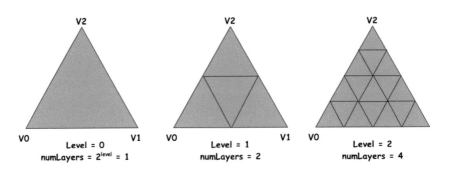

Figure 12.7. The original triangle (left) is subdivided into four triangles (middle), and then each of these four is subdivided again into four (right).

spheresubd.geom

The geometry shader has three parts: some header information, a function that produces a vertex from a pair (s,t) of parameters, and the main shader function. The header information for the shader is below; this supplies the level that is set in the GLIB file, the light intensity that the geometry shader will develop to pass on to rasterization, and the values of the three vertices of the triangle that we will subdivide.

```
#version 330
#extension GL_EXT_geometry_shader4: enable

layout( triangles )  in;
layout( triangle_strip, max_vertices=1024 )  out;

uniform int uLevel;
out float gLightIntensity;

vec3 V0, V01, V02;
```

The function `ProduceVertex( )` below produces a vertex from the parameters s and t in the parameterized definition of a triangle as shown above. The position computation uses the point v, derived from the parameters and normalized as a unit vector to give it a unit distance from the center of the sphere, as the suface normal. That position is then multiplied by the radius of the sphere to place it on the surface of the sphere. Thus, when the triangle is subdivided, the results are triangles whose vertices are on the surface of the sphere. The variables V0, V01, and V02 are, respectively, vertex 0, the vector from vertex 0 to vertex 1, and the vector from vertex 0 to vertex 2, as shown in Figure 12.7. The rest of the computations of light intensity and actual projected position are familiar because they are the same as would be made in a vertex shader. We saw the EmitVertex( ) function above; it passes the vertex on to be collected into a geometric primitive and then to go the rest of the graphics pipeline.

```
void ProduceVertex( float s, float t )
{
   const vec3 LIGHTPOS = vec3( 0., 10., 0. );
   vec3 v = V0 + s*V01 + t*V02;
   v = normalize(v);
   vec3 n = v;
   vec3 TransNorm = normalize(uNormalMatrix*n);
   vec4 ECposition = uModelViewMatrix*vec4((Radius*v), 1.);
   gLightIntensity = dot( normalize(LIGHTPOS-ECposition.xyz),
                  TransNorm );
   gLightIntensity = abs( gLightIntensity);
   gl_Position = uProjectionMatrix * ECposition;
   EmitVertex( );
}
```

The main( ) function in the geometry shader is given below. It increments through the *t* and *s* parameters, in that order, and emits a triangle from each set of three vertices it computes with the function above. Notice that the *t* parameter is used to control the primary direction of subdivision through the triangle, and the *s* parameter to control the secondary direction. The level of subdivision that is shown in Figure 12.8 is used to set the increments in *t* and the number of the *t* increment is used to set the increment in *s*. This nested incrementing is a bit obscure when you first look at it, but it's soon understood if you look carefully.

```
void
main( )
{
   V0  =    gl_PositionIn[0].xyz;
   V01 = ( gl_PositionIn[1] - gl_PositionIn[0] ).xyz;
   V02 = ( gl_PositionIn[2] - gl_PositionIn[0] ).xyz;

   int numLayers = 1 << uLevel;
   float dt = 1. / float( numLayers );
```

```
float t_top = 1.;
float t_bot = 1. - dt;
for( int it = 0; it < numLayers; it++, t_top = t_bot,
    t_bot -= dt )
{
    float smax_top = 1. - t_top;
    float smax_bot = 1. - t_bot;

    int nums = it + 1;
    float ds_top = smax_top / float( nums - 1 );
    float ds_bot = smax_bot / float( nums );

    float s_top = 0.;
    float s_bot = 0.;

    for( int is = 0; is < nums; is++,
        s_top += ds_top, s_bot += ds_bot )
    {
        ProduceVertex( s_bot, t_bot );
        ProduceVertex( s_top, t_top );
    }

    ProduceVertex( s_bot, t_bot );
    EndPrimitive( );

}
}
```

The results of this shader, when you start with two four-sided pyramids, are shown in Figure 12.8. The figure shows the resulting approximations for several different subdivision levels. Level 3 is a reasonable approximation of a sphere, and it would not take many more levels to make this sphere look very good indeed. The fact that this expansion can include a varying number of subdivisions makes it a good candidate for LOD operations and the like.

However, there is one subtle problem with using geometry shaders for general LOD work. For speed, emitted vertices are meant to be carried in memory on the graphics chip. Thus, there is a limited amount of space to hold them. As of this writing, most graphics cards limit geometry shaders to 1024 emitted vertices. This is good for line LOD, such as the Bézier curve, but surface LOD, such as the sphere, consumes those 1024 very quickly. The tessellation shader is probably a better way to do actual surface LOD.

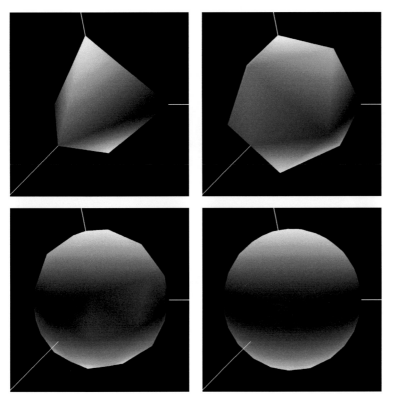

Figure 12.8. A single triangle in the first octant (level = 0) expanded to approximate section of a sphere in that octant, with level = 1 at the top right, level = 2 at the bottom left, and level = 3 at the bottom right.

3D Object Silhouettes

A clever way to detect an edge in a 3D silhouette is that a silhouette edge is shared by adjacent triangles, with one facing toward the eye and the other facing away from the eye. You can determine the way each triangle faces by calculating the dot product of the triangle surface normal and the eye vector and testing if its sign is positive or negative. In the triangle with adjacency shown in Figure 12.9, this test is applied to the central triangle and each of the triangles adjacent to it. One such pair of triangles is highlighted in the figure.

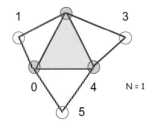

Figure 12.9. The structure of triangles that gives a line segment of the silhouette.

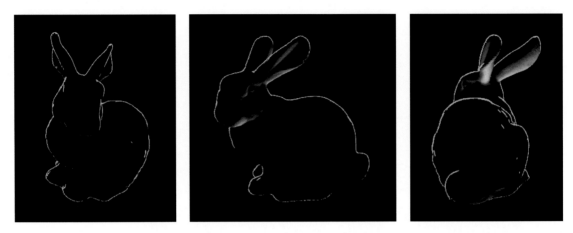

Figure 12.10. Three views of the bunny, with minimal lighting from below, showing the silhouette edges.

The input and output geometry types for this geometry shader are triangles with adjancey and line strip, respectively. The *glman* objAdj command is similar to the obj command, but it parses the original obj file to determine adjacency information, so that triangle-with-adjacency primitives are available to the geometry shader.

As before, the vertex and fragment shader files are omitted. The vertex shader only performs the ModelViewProjection transformation, and the fragment shader only sets the pixel color; these are completely routine.

The geometry shader works by taking a triangle with adjacency and calculating the face normal to each of the four triangles, making sure that each normal faces correctly with the standard triangle conventions. The vertex shader has already placed the vertices into 3D eye space, so the normals can be compared by simply comparing their z components. If there is a sign difference between the z component of the normal of the center triangle and the z component of the normal of an adjacent triangle, then their common edge is drawn by emitting two vertices and ending the primitive. Notice that each edge of the middle triangle is checked because, in principle, the silhouette could include any of them. The result of this shader is shown in Figure 12.10.

Geometry Shader silh.geom

```
#version 330
#extension GL_EXT_geometry_shader4: enable
```

```
layout( triangles_adjacency )  in;
layout( line_strip, max_vertices=32 )  out;

void main( )
{
  vec3 V0 = gl_PositionIn[0].xyz;
  vec3 V1 = gl_PositionIn[1].xyz;
  vec3 V2 = gl_PositionIn[2].xyz;
  vec3 V3 = gl_PositionIn[3].xyz;
  vec3 V4 = gl_PositionIn[4].xyz;
  vec3 V5 = gl_PositionIn[5].xyz;

  vec3 N042 = cross( V4-V0, V2-V0 );
  vec3 N021 = cross( V2-V0, V1-V0 );
  vec3 N243 = cross( V4-V2, V3-V2 );
  vec3 N405 = cross( V0-V4, V5-V4 );

// rashly assume all 4 normals are really meant to be
// within 90 degrees of each other:

  if( dot( N042, N021 ) < 0. )
    N021 = -N021;

  if( dot( N042, N243 ) < 0. )
    N243 = -N243;

  if( dot( N042, N405 ) < 0. )
    N405 = -N405;

  // look for a silhouette edge between triangles 042 and
  // 021:

  if( N042.z * N021.z < 0. )
  {
    gl_Position = uProjectionMatrix* vec4( V0, 1. );
    EmitVertex( );
    gl_Position = uProjectionMatrix* vec4( V2, 1. );
    EmitVertex( );
    EndPrimitive( );
  }

  // look for a silhouette edge between triangles 042 and
  // 243:

  if( N042.z * N243.z < 0. )
  {
    gl_Position= uProjectionMatrix* vec4( V2, 1. );
    EmitVertex( );
```

```
    gl_Position= uProjectionMatrix* vec4( V4, 1. );
    EmitVertex( );
    EndPrimitive( );
}

// look for a silhouette edge between triangles 042 and
// 405:

if( N042.z * N405.z < 0. )
{
    gl_Position= uProjectionMatrix* vec4( V4, 1. );
    EmitVertex( );
    gl_Position= uProjectionMatrix* vec4( V0, 1. );
    EmitVertex( );
    EndPrimitive( );
}
}
```

Exercises

1. Implement the silhouette for new geometry as specified by your instructor, and implement variations for both, such as

   a. Vary the color of the silhouette edge to reflect the direction of the edge.

   b. Vary the color of the silhouette lines to reflect the primitive ID of each segment.

2. Create a surface of various degrees of smoothness from four 3D vertices using bilinear interpolations. Use GL_LINES_ADJACENCY to input the vertices together. For the collection of vertices, break them up into an arbitrary number of triangles like this:

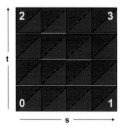

using the bilinear equation

$$Q(s,t) = (1-s)(1-t)Q_0 + s(1-t)Q_1 + (1-s)tQ_2 + stQ_3, \quad 0 \le s,t \le 1.$$

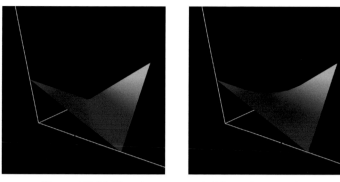

Figure 12.11. Two images created from four vertices.

So instead of drawing a non-planar quad as two creased triangles (Figure 12.11 (left)), it would be drawn as a smooth bilinear surface (Figure 12.11 (right)).

Notice that you can also interpolate vertex colors this way. This is useful in data visualization, where we affectionately call this object a "superquad."

3. In Figure 12.10 we showed the silhouette edges of the Stanford bunny. Take another .obj file that describes an object with adjacency and implement the silhouette edges of that object. What happens to the silhouette edges as you move the object around?

4. In the Chapter 15 we describe the hedgehog plot application of geometry shaders. Work through this example and apply it to an object of your choice. See if you can create a more realistic version of hair (color, lighting, shading) than the very simple one given there.

13

Tessellation Shaders

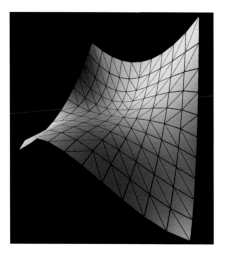

Tessellation in computer graphics is a process that divides a surface into a smoother mesh of triangles. An example of this kind of tessellation is shown in Figure 13.1.

What Are Tessellation Shaders?

Tessellation shaders are one of the stages available in OpenGL to create the geometry for a scene. New with OpenGL 4.0, they interpolate geometry to create additional geometry that can

- Let you perform adaptive subdivision based on a variety of criteria such as size or curvature,

- Let you provide coarser models that can be refined in the GPU, giving you a kind of geometric compression,

- Let you apply detailed displacement maps without supplying equally detailed geometry,

- Let you adapt visual quality to the required level of detail,

- Let you create smoother silhouettes, or

- Let you perform skinning more easily.

Overall this lets you increase the quality of your final images. So why not just add more geometric detail right in your application program? The best answer is that tessellation shaders have access to all the information in the graphics pipeline, and thus can adapt to the display situation. Tessellation shaders are at their very best when they choose tessellation parameters, not statically but dynamically, based on the current transformations, curvatures, screen coverage, etc.

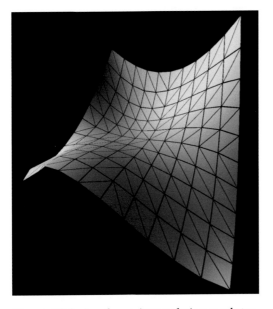

Figure 13.1. A polygon-interpolating mesh tessellation from a GLSL shader.

How does the tessellation shader fit into our overall shader world? The tessellation stage is applied between the vertex shader (Chapter 7) and the next shader stage in the pipeline, which could be either the geometry shader (Chapter 12) or the fragment shader (Chapter 8). This makes intuitive sense, because the vertex shader modifies vertices individually with no reference to the primitives they lie in. The tessellation shader amplifies a single primitive, and the geometry shader can provide additional primitives based on the original primitive. The GLSL view of the graphics pipeline is shown here in Figure 13.2 with the tessellation stage highlighted.

When we say "tessellation shader," we generally mean both the tessellation control shader (TCS) and the tessellation evaluation shader (TES), unless we say otherwise.

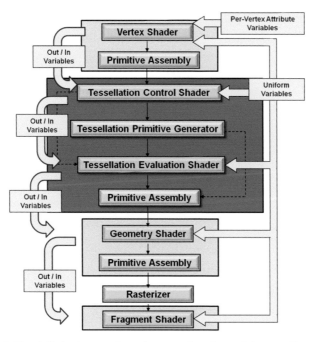

Figure 13.2. The full shader pipeline showing the place of the tessellation shaders.

Tessellation Shaders or Geometry Shaders?

Both geometry shaders and tessellation shaders are capable of creating new geometry from existing geometry, and both have uses in giving you level-of-detail support, so you might be confused about when to use each type. While their capabilities are in some ways similar, there are distinct differences. A tessellation shader gives you more geometry, but all the new geometry is of the same sort as you started with—you can get more segments for a line, more triangles for a triangular patch, or more isolines or quads for a quad patch, but you always get the same geometry. You should use a tessellation shader when you need to generate many new vertices and one of the tessellation topologies will suit your needs, or if your required patch input involves many (more than six[1]) vertices.

On the other hand, a geometry shader gives some different capabilities. You must use a geometry shader when you need to convert to different geometry topologies, such as presented in the silhouette and hedgehog shaders (tri-

---

1. Why six? The input to a geometry shader can have as many as six vertices when you use the triangles-with-adjacency topology.

angles → lines) or the explosion shader (triangles → points), or if you need some sort of geometry processing to come after the tessellation shader (such as the shrink shader you saw earlier, which we will use here to show what the tessellation stages are actually doing).

Finally, the fact that geometry shaders follow tessellation shaders in the vertex pipeline creates a limitation on using tessellation shaders. A tessellation shader can only emit line segments and triangles; it cannot emit any geometry with adjacency. If you need to create new geometry in a geometry shader and this geometry requires adjacency, the geometry shader cannot follow a tessellation shader and so you cannot use tessellation shaders.

Tessellation Shader Concepts

Tessellation shaders are conceptually simple but, like textures, require quite a bit of detail to set up.

Input to the tessellation shaders uses a new graphics primitive: the *patch*. This is specified in your OpenGL program with

```
glBegin( GL_PATCHES );
    glVertex3f( . . . );
    glVertex3f( . . . );
glEnd( );
```

Even if you are using vertex arrays or buffers instead of glBegin–glEnd, the topology type is still GL_PATCHES. There is no implied order in the list of vertices. The meaning of the order is up to you. You just need to pick a consistent convention for the type of geometry you are tessellating. As we will see in some later examples, the vertex values need not even be actual coordinates; we can even use them as geometric parameters. You also need to set up some data that describes the patch. The function

```
glPatchParameteri( GL_PATCH_VERTICES, num );
```

defines the number of vertices in the patch. Like other OpenGL topologies, you don't need a glEnd–glBegin to start a new primitive. Just keep listing vertices. In this case, one patch is complete after *num* vertices, and a new one gets started.

As you see in Figure 13.2, there are two tessellation shader types that work together. The first is the tessellation control shader (TCS). Its function is to prepare the final control points and to determine how much to tessellate. It is invoked once for each output control point and takes as input *num* transformed patch vertices from the vertex shaders. It gets to see the entire set of patch data. It transforms the input coordinates to a regular surface representation, and computes the required tessellation level based on distance to the eye, screen space spanning, hull curvature, displacement roughness, or whatever criteria make most sense for your application.

The TCS takes as input an array `gl_in[ ]` of structures, one structure per control vertex, that contain

```
vec4 gl_Position;
float  gl_PointSize;
float  gl_ClipDistance[ ];
```

as well as these single variables:

- `int gl_InvocationID`, which tells you which output vertex you are working on. This *must* be the value used to index a write into the `gl_out[ ]` array. You can read all other `gl_out` array values, but you can only write your own.

- `int gl_PatchVerticesIn` is the number of vertices in each patch and the dimension of `gl_in[ ]`

- `int gl_PrimitiveID` is the number of primitives since the last `glBegin( )` (the first one is #0)

The TCS must let the pipeline know how many final control points will be output.[2] This is done with the `layout` qualifier as follows:

```
layout( vertices = N ) out;
```

The output from the TCS includes `gl_out[ ]`, an array of structures that is the same size as the *N* that is specified by the `layout` qualifier. Each structure contains

```
vec4 gl_Position;
float  gl_PointSize;
float  gl_ClipDistance[ ];
```

as well as the additional output variables

- `patch out float gl_TessLevelOuter[4]`, an array containing up to four levels of tessellation at the outer edges, and

---

2. The number of output control points has to do with the geometric equations you are using for this patch. It has nothing to do with how many output primitives will eventually be produced. That specification is called setting the "tessellation levels," and is coming up in a moment.

- `patch out float gl_TessLevelInner[2]`, an array containing up to two levels of tessellation at the inner edges.

The outer and inner tessellation levels define the number of subdivisions for the perimeter and the interior of the input primitive, respectively, and also control the output of the TES. A TCS can also access the output data for its processing. You can also have other output variables from a TCS. User-defined variables defined per-vertex are qualified as "out," while user-defined variables defined per-patch are qualified as "patch out."

TCS instances run mostly independently, with undefined relative execution order. The built-in `barrier( )` function provides some control over TCS relative execution order by causing all instances of TCSs to wait. This allows synchronization points where no TCS shader invocation will continue until all TCS shader invocations have reached the barrier. This is important because an instance of a TCS can read variables from other TCS instances that might not yet have been written. The `barrier( )` function may only be called inside the main entry point of the TCS and may not be called in potentially divergent flow control. In particular, `barrier( )` may not be called inside a switch statement, in either sub-statement of an if statement, inside a do, for, or while loop, or at any point after a return statement in the function `main( )`.

The tessellation patch generator (TPG) is not a user-programmable shader stage, but a new fixed-function pipeline stage; you can't change its operation except by setting parameters. It is invoked one time per patch. It looks at the tessellation levels set by the TCS and creates the right number of tessellated triangles, quads, or lines, and outputs their positions as parametric coordinates in semi-regular barycentric (u,v,w) coordinates.

The second tessellation shader type is the tessellation evaluation shader (TES). It reads the (u,v,w) coordinates from the TPG and the output vertex coordinates from the TCS, and then determines output (x,y,z) coordinates, interpolates any attributes, and applies any displacements. There is one instance of a TES invoked per output vertex being generated. If you are using the TES but no TCS, your main program needs to set up some of the data that the TCS would normally provide. This is done with the functions

```
glPatchParameterfv( GL_DEFAULT_OUTER_LEVEL, float [4] );
glPatchParameterfv( GL_DEFAULT_INNER_LEVEL, float [2] );
```

that define the outer and inner levels of divisions for the interpolations, as we saw in the discussion of the TCS. The outer and inner levels define the number of subdivisions for the perimeter and the interior of the input polygon, respectively.

The interpolation pattern generated by the TPG is defined by a layout qualifier in the TES.[3] When used for defining the TES production, it has the form

$$\text{layout}(\left\{\begin{matrix} \text{triangles} \\ \text{quads} \\ \text{isolines} \end{matrix}\right\}, \left\{\begin{matrix} \text{equal\_spacing} \\ \text{fractional\_even\_spacing} \\ \text{fractional\_odd\_spacing} \end{matrix}\right\}, \left\{\begin{matrix} \text{ccw} \\ \text{cw} \end{matrix}\right\}, \text{point\_mode) in;}$$

The first parameter specifies the tessellation pattern: should the tessellation primitive generator subdivide a triangle into smaller triangles, a quad into triangles, or a quad into a collection of line segments, respectively? The second parameter specifies the spacing of the segments, the third the orientation of the triangles (if any) that are produced; specifying point_mode tells the TES is to produce a point at each output vertex rather than triangles or lines. Equal spacing and counterclockwise orientation are the defaults.

A typical invocation of this layout line might be

```
layout( triangles, equal_spacing, ccw ) in;
```

The TES has access to an input variable gl_in[ ], which is identical to the gl_out[ ] from the TCS, as well as the single variables

```
in int gl_PatchVerticesIn;
in int gl_PrimitiveID;
in vec3 gl_TessCoord;
```

It writes the information for the one vertex it is computing to the three output variables

```
vec4 gl_Position;
float gl_PointSize;
float gl_ClipDistance[ ];
```

The write to gl_Position is required. The write to the other two is optional.

In addition to the built-in variables mentioned, both the TCS and the TES can take user-defined variables. User-defined variables that are defined per-vertex are qualified as out or in, while user-defined variables defined per-patch are qualified as patch out or patch in.

---

3. This seems confusing, having the TES essentially "pass information upstream" to the TPG. Don't let it worry you. The shader compile and linking process takes care of this.

Outer and Inner Division Levels

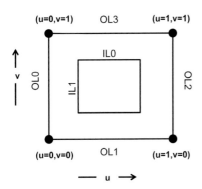

Figure 13.3. The division levels for the quad output interpolation.

While we have seen that the outer and inner division levels represent the number of divisions of the boundary and interior of a primitive, respectively, we should look at this in a little more detail. The outer level is set by a four-element floating point array, while the inner level is set by a two-element floating point array. These are handled differently by the output interpolation patterns as follows.[4]

For the quad output interpolation pattern, the division levels are shown in Figure 13.3. The key point in the figure is the sequence in which the outer level (OL0, OL1, OL2, OL3) and the inner level (IL0, IL1) elements are applied.

The triangle output interpolation is specified in terms of barycentric coordinates. This coordinate system gives a unique representation for any point in terms of three coordinates (u,v,w), as described in Figure 13.4.

For the triangles interpolation pattern, the division levels are shown in Figure 13.5. The key point in the figure is the sequence in which the outer level (OL0, OL1, OL2) and the inner level (IL0) elements are applied. (The components that are not used are not shown in the vectors and need not be set.)

For the isolines pattern, the division levels are shown in Figure 13.6. The outer level has only two values (OL0, OL1), and the inner level is not used at all. Again, the components that are not used need not be set. If OL0 is set to 1, only a single curve will be drawn. Essentially, OL0 determines how many isolines are to be drawn, while OL1 determines how many components are to be in each isoline.

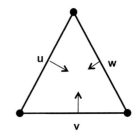

Figure 13.4. Barycentric coordinates in a triangle.

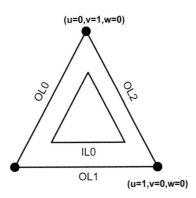

Figure 13.5. The division levels for the triangles output interpolation.

---

4. In the interest of not making you run away screaming from excruciating detail, we discuss what the tessellation levels mean only in very general terms. It is easiest to get a feel for what this actually means by experimenting with the example code. The full (excruciating) detail can be found in the OpenGL specification at http://opengl.org → Documentation → Specifications → OpenGL 4.2 core specification, in the tessellation section. Don't say we didn't warn you.

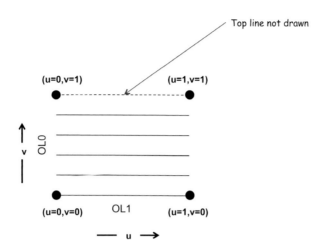

Figure 13.6. The division levels for the isolines output interpolation.

Issues in Setting Tessellation Levels

GLSL will let you set any tessellation levels you like for the inner and outer levels of your patches, but you need to pay attention to your overall scene as you set these levels. One reason is aesthetic—you want to set your levels high enough to achieve a satisfactory image, but no higher. There is a more important reason, however. If you have two pieces of geometry with patches that share an edge, using different outer tessellation levels for the edge in the different patches will clearly lead to cracks where the edges of the patches meet. Keeping the tessellation levels the same is only a necessary condition, of course; you must also ensure that the computations on the patches in the TES are the same so that the edges align.

Examples

In this section we'll look at four examples: one with output using an isolines pattern, one with output using a quads pattern, one with output using a triangles pattern, and one that implements point-normal (PN) triangles. These will show you how many of the tessellation shader operations fit together and should help you get started on your own work. Each example is set up to work with *glman*, so a .glib file is presented along with the shader files; it should be straightforward to see how to pass the same information to the shaders from an application.

Isolines

The first example uses tessellation shaders with isolines to create a familiar Bézier cubic curve with four control points, as shown in Figure 13.7. This curve is given by the equation

$$P(u) = (1-u)^3 P_0 + 3u(1-u)^2 P_1 + 3u^2(1-u)P_2 + u^3 P_3, \qquad (1)$$

where u is the single curve parameter and the polynomials $(1-u)^3$, $3u(1-u)^2$, $3u^2(1-u)$, and u^3 are the standard Bernstein basis functions for Bézier curves.

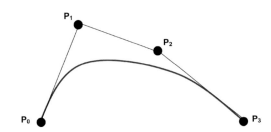

Figure 13.7. A Bezier curve with four control points.

The tessellation control shader (TCS) figures out how much to tessellate the curve based on screen area, curvature, or other factors. The tessellation primitive generator (TPG) generates u (or $[u,v,w]$) values for as many subdivisions as the TCS asked for, and the tessellation evaluation shader computes the (x,y,z) coordinates based on the TPG's u values, using the equation derived by expanding (1):

$$P(u) = u^3(-P_0 + 3P_1 - 3P_2 + P_3) + u^2(3P_0 - 6P_1 + 3P_2) + u(-3P_0 + 3P_1) + P_0. \qquad (2)$$

The final result is to be the familiar curve shown in Figure 13.8.

Figure 13.8. The Bézier curve with its positions at uniform values of u.

To show how to generate the tessellated figure from the given control points, we will show several pieces of code: the first is some code you would place in your main program, the second is the .glib file you would use to set up this example through *glman*, the third is the TCS shader file, and the fourth is the TES shader file.

Some code you might place in your main program is

```
glPatchParameteri( GL_PATCH_VERTICES, 4 );

glBegin( GL_PATCHES );
    glVertex3f( x0, y0, z0 );
    glVertex3f( x1, y1, z1 );
    glVertex3f( x2, y2, z2 );
    glVertex3f( x3, y3, z3 );
glEnd( );⁵
```

---

5. You can also use **GL_PATCHES** with vertex arrays and vertex buffer objects.

Alternately, if you are developing your shaders through *glman*, you could use the .glib file below, which uses specific values for the four patch vertices.

```
##OpenGL GLIB
Perspective 70
LookAt 0 0 3 0 0 0 0 1 0

Vertex          beziercurve.vert
TessControl     beziercurve.tcs
TessEvaluation  beziercurve.tes
Fragment        beziercurve.frag
Program BezierCurve uOuter1 <3. 5. 50.>

Color 1. 1. 0.

NumPatchVertices 4
glBegin gl_patches
   glVertex 0. 0. 0.
   glVertex 1. 1. 1.
   glVertex 2. 1. 0.
   glVertex 3. 0. 1.
glend
```

The vertex and fragment shaders would be the minimal shaders you have seen in the chapters on these shaders, and the TCS shader `beziercurve.tcs` could be

```
#version 400
#extension GL_ARB_tessellation_shader: enable

uniform float uOuter1;

layout( vertices = 4 ) out;  // same size as input,
                             // (but doesn't have to be)

void main( )
{
   gl_out[ gl_InvocationID ].gl_Position =
                  gl_in[ gl_InvocationID ].gl_Position;

   gl_TessLevelOuter[0] = 1.;
   gl_TessLevelOuter[1] = uOuter1;
}
```

A new detail in this code is the `gl_InvocationId` value. This value is the output vertex number that corresponds to this instance of the TCS shader. In this case, the components of the gl_in array are simply copied to the gl_out array, where they will serve as inputs to the TES shader. The other new detail is the gl_TessLevelOuter[ ] array that is to set the tessellation levels for the outer level in the TES.

Finally, we see the TES shader beziercurve.tes that uses the isolines pattern for its layout. Notice that the gl_Position value is computed with vector arithmetic since the p[0-3] parameters from the TCS are all vec4 values. And, because vec4 arithmetic is being used, this code will also work for *rational* Bézier cubic curves.

In this example, the variable gl_TessCoord is the (u,v,w) value of the vertex being processed by the TES, and the value of the curve parameter u is derived from the x-coordinate of this variable. Other ways of developing the single parameter u are also possible.

```
#version 400
#extension GL_ARB_tessellation_shader: enable

layout( isolines, equal_spacing) in;

void main( )
{
   vec4 p0 = gl_in[0].gl_Position;
   vec4 p1 = gl_in[1].gl_Position;
   vec4 p2 = gl_in[2].gl_Position;
   vec4 p3 = gl_in[3].gl_Position;

   float u = gl_TessCoord.x;

   // the basis functions:
   float b0 = (1.-u) * (1.-u) * (1.-u);
   float b1 = 3. * u * (1.-u) * (1.-u);
   float b2 = 3. * u * u * (1.-u);
   float b3 = u * u * u;

   gl_Position = b0*p0 + b1*p1 + b2*p2 + b3*p3;
}
```

We assign the intermediate p[0-3] variables here to make the code more readable. In general, the GLSL compiler will optimize this away rather than creating temporary variables it doesn't really need. Similarly, we can safely write out the b[0-3] variables in full detail for readability, and the GLSL compiler will assemble like terms rather than re-compute them.

Figure 13.9 shows the coordinate axes as well as two examples of the curve generated by these shaders. In the left image, you can easily see the five

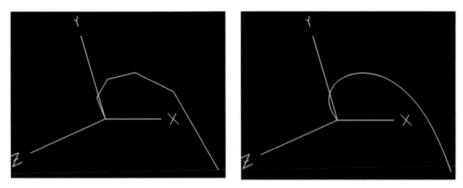

Figure 13.9. Two Bézier curves with outer1 = 5 (left) and outer1 = 50 (right).

segments that correspond to that value for outer1; in the right image you cannot see the individual segments because of the much larger outer1 value.

We will see a little more about the isolines layout when we work through the Bézier surface example in the next section.

Bézier Surface

A bicubic Bézier surface patch is defined by 16 control points $\{P_{ij} | 0 \le i, j \le 3\}$. The patch is a function of two parameters, u and v, with basis functions given by the products of the basis functions for Bézier curves, and is given by

$$P(u,v) = \begin{bmatrix} (1-u)^3 & 3u(1-u)^2 & 3u^2(1-u) & u^3 \end{bmatrix} \begin{bmatrix} P_{00} & P_{01} & P_{02} & P_{03} \\ P_{10} & P_{11} & P_{12} & P_{13} \\ P_{20} & P_{21} & P_{22} & P_{23} \\ P_{30} & P_{31} & P_{32} & P_{33} \end{bmatrix} \begin{bmatrix} (1-v)^3 \\ 3v(1-v)^2 \\ 3v^2(1-v) \\ v^3 \end{bmatrix}.$$

An example of a Bézier patch is shown in Figure 13.10. This shows the familiar way that the surface responds to the position of the control points and how the surface can be said to interpolate these points. Thus we can consider that a tessellation shader could interpolate the quad defined by P_{00}, P_{03}, P_{33}, and P_{30} with the interpolation defined by the other control points.

The code components for this example are similar to those for the Bézier curve, but involve more control points and a more complex set of outer and inner subdivision parameters. If you begin this from an OpenGL application, you might have code like this in the application. The order of the control points is unimportant, but must be consistent with your uses in the TCS and TES; pick a convention yourself and stick to it!

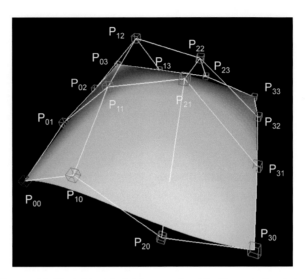

Figure 13.10. A bicubic Bézier patch with 16 control points.

```
glPatchParameteri( GL_PATCH_VERTICES, 16 );

    glBegin( GL_PATCHES );
        glVertex3f( x00, y00, z00 );
        glVertex3f( x10, y10, z10 );
        glVertex3f( x20, y20, z20 );
        glVertex3f( x30, y30, z30 );
        glVertex3f( x01, y01, z01 );
        glVertex3f( x11, y11, z11 );
        glVertex3f( x21, y21, z21 );
        glVertex3f( x31, y31, z31 );
        glVertex3f( x02, y02, z02 );
        glVertex3f( x12, y12, z12 );
        glVertex3f( x22, y22, z22 );
        glVertex3f( x32, y32, z32 );
        glVertex3f( x03, y03, z03 );
        glVertex3f( x13, y13, z13 );
        glVertex3f( x23, y23, z23 );
        glVertex3f( x33, y33, z33 );
    glEnd( );
```

Alternately, if we are developing the tessellation shaders using *glman,* we could use a .glib file like the one below to set this up. Note that this sets up a uniform slider variable uShrink that would be used by a geometry shader to produce shrunken triangles to show the tessellation structure. Again, we use specific values for the 16 control points.

```
##OpenGL GLIB
Perspective 70

Vertex          beziersurface.vert
TessControl     beziersurface.tcs
TessEvaluation  beziersurface.tes
Geometry        beziersurface.geom
Fragment        beziersurface.frag
Program BezierSurface                        \
        uOuter02 <1. 10. 50.>                \
        uOuter13 <1. 10. 50.>                \
        uInner0  <1. 10. 50.>                \
        uInner1  <1. 10. 50.>                \
        uShrink  <0. 1. 1.>                  \
        uLightX  <-10. 0. 10.>               \
        uLightY  <-10. 10. 10.>              \
        uLightZ  <-10. 10. 10.>

Color 1. 1. 0.

NumPatchVertices 16
glBegin gl_patches
 glVertex 0. 2. 0.
 glVertex 1. 1. 0.
 glVertex 2. 1. 0.
 glVertex 3. 2. 0.

 glVertex 0. 1. 1.
 glVertex 1. -2. 1.
 glVertex 2. 1. 1.
 glVertex 3. 0. 1.

 glVertex 0. 0. 2.
 glVertex 1. 1. 2.
 glVertex 2. 0. 2.
 glVertex 3. -1. 2.

 glVertex 0. 0. 3.
 glVertex 1. 1. 3.
 glVertex 2. -1. 3.
 glVertex 3. -1. 3.
glEnd
```

The TCS shader beziersurface.tcs is similar to the TCS shader in the Bézier curve example. In the TCS shader for the patch we pick up the values of the uniform slider variables uOuter* and uInner* and use them to set up the standard variables gl_TessLevelOuter[ ] and gl_TessLevelInner[ ].

```
#version 400
#extension GL_ARB_tessellation_shader : enable

uniform float uOuter02, uOuter13, uInner0, uInner1;

layout( vertices = 16 ) out;

void main( )
{
   gl_out[ gl_InvocationID ].gl_Position =
      gl_in[ gl_InvocationID ].gl_Position;

   gl_TessLevelOuter[0] = gl_TessLevelOuter[2] = uOuter02;
   gl_TessLevelOuter[1] = gl_TessLevelOuter[3] = uOuter13;
   gl_TessLevelInner[0] = uInner0;
   gl_TessLevelInner[1] = uInner1;
}
```

Figure 13.11 reminds us of the meaning of the outer and inner tessellation levels for a quad interpolation pattern. In this TCS, the variables uOuter* and uInner* are copied to the elements of gl_TessLevelOuter[ ] and gl_TessLevelInner[ ] so that opposite sides of the exterior and the interior of the patch have the same value. This need not be the case, and an exercise suggests that you experiment with the tessellation levels.

The TES beziersurface.tes is similar to that for the Bézier curve, but only because it involves more control points and more basis functions. The most important thing to note in this shader is the parameters to the layout qualifier. While we used an isolines pattern in the curve example, here we use a quads pattern and must also specify the orientation of each quad. When you see the output in Figure 13.12, you will see that the tessellation is a collection of quads, each of which is actually being drawn as two triangles. So specifying the quads pattern does not give you quads; it gives you *triangles* based on a *quad* interpolation pattern.

Finally, this TES not only outputs the required gl_Position but also computes the partial derivatives of the surface in both the *u* and *v* directions and, by a cross product, the out variable normal—the normal to the sur-

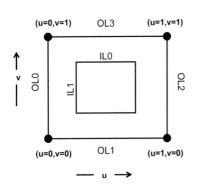

Figure 13.11. The outer and inner levels for a quad interpolation pattern.

face at that position. This normal is then used to produce the light intensity for
the shaded patch shown in the figures.

```
#version 400
#extension GL_ARB_tessellation_shader : enable

layout( quads, equal_spacing, ccw ) in;

out vec3 teNormal;

void main( )
{
  vec3 p00 = gl_in[  0 ].gl_Position;
  vec3 p10 = gl_in[  1 ].gl_Position;
  vec3 p20 = gl_in[  2 ].gl_Position;
  vec3 p30 = gl_in[  3 ].gl_Position;
  vec3 p01 = gl_in[  4 ].gl_Position;
  vec3 p11 = gl_in[  5 ].gl_Position;
  vec3 p21 = gl_in[  6 ].gl_Position;
  vec3 p31 = gl_in[  7 ].gl_Position;
  vec3 p02 = gl_in[  8 ].gl_Position;
  vec3 p12 = gl_in[  9 ].gl_Position;
  vec3 p22 = gl_in[ 10 ].gl_Position;
  vec3 p32 = gl_in[ 11 ].gl_Position;
  vec3 p03 = gl_in[ 12 ].gl_Position;
  vec3 p13 = gl_in[ 13 ].gl_Position;
  vec3 p23 = gl_in[ 14 ].gl_Position;
  vec3 p33 = gl_in[ 15 ].gl_Position;

  float u = gl_TessCoord.x;
  float v = gl_TessCoord.y;

  // the basis functions and their derivatives:

  float bu0 = (1.-u)  * (1.-u) * (1.-u);
  float bu1 = 3.  * u * (1.-u) * (1.-u);
  float bu2 = 3.  * u * u * (1.-u);
  float bu3 = u   * u * u;

  float dbu0 = -3.  * (1.-u) * (1.-u);
  float dbu1 =  3.  * (1.-u) * (1.-3.*u);
  float dbu2 =  3.  * u *       (2.-3.*u);
  float dbu3 =  3.  * u *       u;

  float bv0 = (1.-v) * (1.-v) * (1.-v);
  float bv1 = 3. * v * (1.-v) * (1.-v);
  float bv2 = 3. * v * v * (1.-v);
  float bv3 = v * v * v;
```

```
float dbv0 = -3.  * (1.-v) * (1.-v);
float dbv1 =  3.  * (1.-v) * (1.-3.*v);
float dbv2 = 3.   * v * (2.-3.*v);
float dbv3 =  3.  * v * v;

// finally we get to compute something

gl_Position =
       bu0 * ( bv0*p00 + bv1*p01 + bv2*p02 + bv3*p03 )
     + bu1 * ( bv0*p10 + bv1*p11 + bv2*p12 + bv3*p13 )
     + bu2 * ( bv0*p20 + bv1*p21 + bv2*p22 + bv3*p23 )
     + bu3 * ( bv0*p30 + bv1*p31 + bv2*p32 + bv3*p33 );

vec4 dpdu =
       dbu0 * ( bv0*p00 + bv1*p01 + bv2*p02 + bv3*p03 )
     + dbu1 * ( bv0*p10 + bv1*p11 + bv2*p12 + bv3*p13 )
     + dbu2 * ( bv0*p20 + bv1*p21 + bv2*p22 + bv3*p23 )
     + dbu3 * ( bv0*p30 + bv1*p31 + bv2*p32 + bv3*p33 );

vec4 dpdv =
       bu0 * ( dbv0*p00 + dbv1*p01 + dbv2*p02 + dbv3*p03 )
     + bu1 * ( dbv0*p10 + dbv1*p11 + dbv2*p12 + dbv3*p13 )
     + bu2 * ( dbv0*p20 + dbv1*p21 + dbv2*p22 + dbv3*p23 )
     + bu3 * ( dbv0*p30 + dbv1*p31 + dbv2*p32 + dbv3*p33 );

teNormal = normalize( cross( dpdu.xyz, dpdv.xyz ) );
}
```

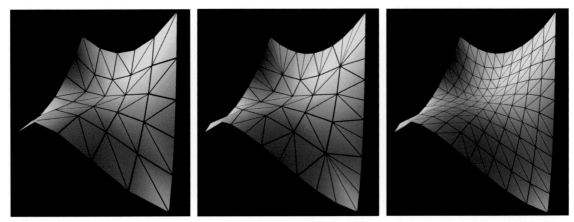

Figure 13.12. The shader output for different outer and inner tessellation levels: outer = inner = 5 (left); outer = 10, inner = 5 (middle); outer = inner = 10 (right).

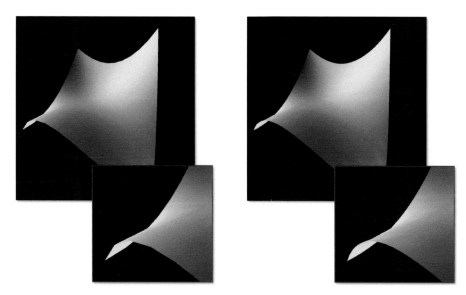

Figure 13.13. A tessellated surface (left) with outer tessellation level 10, showing facets along the edges, and (right) with outer tessellation level 30, showing a smooth edge.

The output of these shaders using *glman* is shown in Figure 13.12.

An important question about tessellation levels is how to use them for making effective images. When a patch edge is visible, you may find that a tessellation level that is perfectly adequate for a patch interior may look clumsy on the edge. We illustrate this in Figure 13.13, where the same patch shown in Figure 13.12 is examined in more detail at an edge where there is rapid change. Here the value of a larger outer tessellation level is clear from the appearance of the edge.

In the image on the left, the lower-left corner has outer tessellation level ten, which is not enough and so the lower boundary looks coarse. In the image on the right, the outer tessellation level has been changed to 30, resulting in a smooth-looking boundary. In both images, the inner tessellation levels were set to 10 which, in this case, were enough for standard smooth shading.

Finally, we return to the isolines pattern and use the Bézier patch example to extend the Bézier curves example and produce multiple isolines. First, in the .glib file you replace the layout qualifier by one that specifies the isolines pattern instead of the quad pattern, as in the code

```
layout( isolines, equal_spacing) in;
```

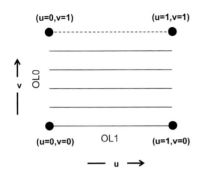

Figure 13.14. The effect of the two outer tessellation parameters.

Second, note that the two outer tessellation parameters are the number of isolines and the number of points in each isoline, respectively, while the inner tessellation parameter is ignored, as in Figure 13.14.

Some different values of inner and outer spacing for isolines is shown in Figure 13.15. Of course to produce these you must eliminate the shrink geometry shader in the .glib file, since you will not be producing any triangles for it to shrink. You will also need to move the lighting and the multiplication by the projection matrix from the geometry shader to the tessellation evaluation shader.

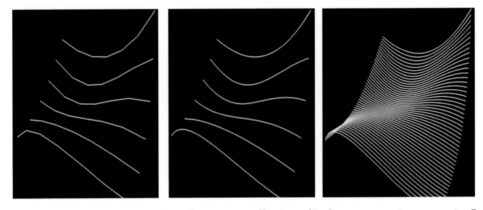

Figure 13.15. The Bézier surface shown as a collection of isolines. uOuter0 = uOuter1 = 5 (left); uOuter0 = 5., uOuter1 = 50 (middle); uOuter0 = uOuter1 = 50 (right).

Sphere Subdivision

Spheres offer some interesting display challenges. The simplest kind of sphere display is the GLUT sphere; this subdivides the sphere along latitude and longitude. There are times when you want to display a sphere while controlling the number and layout of the triangles to achieve an appropriately smooth surface. In this example we use the triangles pattern for the tessellation layout.

Sphere Octants

As a first example, let's consider a single octant of a sphere. This has a triangle at its base with vertices on each coordinate axis. If we take this as our
base geometry and interpolate it with a triangle pattern, we can see some of
the essential features of a triangle tessellation. The .glib file for this example,
octantsubd.glib, is straightforward, with uniform slider variables for the tessellation levels for you to experiment with. The geometry here is simply the
three-vertex patch in the first octant.

```
##OpenGL GLIB

Vertex          octantsubd.vert
TessControl     octantsubd.tcs
TessEvaluation  octantsubd.tes
Geometry        octantsubd.geom
Fragment        octantsubd.frag
Program OctantSubd                \
        uRadius <0. 1. 3.>        \
        uOuter0 <1. 25. 50.>      \
        uOuter1 <1. 25. 50.>      \
        uOuter2 <1. 25. 50.>      \
        uInner <1. 10. 50.>       \
        uShrink <0. 1. 1.>

Color 1. 1. 0.

NumPatchVertices 3
glBegin gl_patches
    glVertex 1. 0. 0.
    glVertex 0. 1. 0.
    glVertex 0. 0. 1.
glEnd
```

The vertex shader applies the modelview matrix to the vertex geometry.
The corresponding TCS file, octantsubd.tcs, copies the gl_Position values
from the gl_in[ ] array to the gl_out[ ] array for each vertex of the primitive
and calculates the tessellation levels from the .glib values.

```
#version 400 compatibility
#extension GL_ARB_tessellation_shader : enable

uniform float uOuter0, uOuter1, uOuter2, uInner;
uniform float uRadius;
```

```
layout( vertices = 3 ) out;

void main( )
{
  gl_out[ gl_InvocationID ].gl_Position =
                gl_in[ gl_InvocationID ].gl_Position;

  gl_TessLevelOuter[0] = uRadius * uOuter0;
  gl_TessLevelOuter[1] = uRadius * uOuter1;
  gl_TessLevelOuter[2] = uRadius * uOuter2;
  gl_TessLevelInner[0] = uRadius * uInner;
}
```

The TES shader created by the file octantsubd.tes below interpolates the input vertices with the tessellation coordinates gl_TessCoord[ ] using the triangles pattern. It applies the modelview matrix to get the position of each vertex in the tessellated output.

```
#version 400 compatibility
#extension GL_ARB_tessellation_shader : enable

uniform float uRadius;

layout( triangles, equal_spacing, ccw) in;

void main( )
{
  vec3 p0 = gl_in[0].gl_Position.xyz;
  vec3 p1 = gl_in[1].gl_Position.xyz;
  vec3 p2 = gl_in[2].gl_Position.xyz;

  float u = gl_TessCoord.x;
  float v = gl_TessCoord.y;
  float w = gl_TessCoord.z;

  gl_Position = uModelViewMatrix *
    vec4(uRadius*normalize(u*p0+v*p1+w*p2),1.);
}
```

The expression uRadius*normalize(...) is in the gl_Position computation to "puff" out the points to be a constant-radius spherical surface instead of a planar triangle.

Because this is the first triangle-pattern tessellation we have seen, we should remind ourselves about the outer and inner tessellation levels in this example. Figure 13.16 recalls the meaning of outer and inner tessellation levels for triangles; the first inner tessellation level controls the number of subdivisions along each triangle except the outermost, and the first three outer tessellation levels control the number of subdivisions along the three outer edges. The examples shown here use the tessellation levels rather conservatively, but in an exercise you are encouraged to try out different variations on these levels.

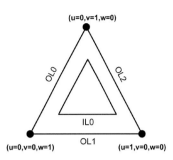

Figure 13.16. The meaning of tessellation levels for triangles.

In the images created by this example, we can see the effect of different tessellation levels. Figure 13.17 shows the sphere quadrant with two different tessellation levels; on the left we have outer = 10 and inner = 5, while on the right we have outer = inner = 10. You can see that in both cases, each outer edge has ten subdivisions while the inner edge (each line parallel to an outer edge) of the left image has five subdivisions and the inner edge of the right image has ten. In an exercise you are invited to experiment with using different tessellation levels for the three outer edges of the octant.

When you include the radius in setting the tessellation levels as in the TCS, you see that the larger the sphere radius is, the larger the tessellation level. This gives you a level-of-detail capability that is illustrated in Figure 13.18. Note that the individual triangles in the tessellations are of similar size across all the images.

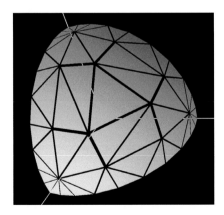 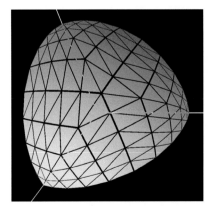

Figure 13.17. Two sphere octants with different tessellation levels: outer = 10, inner = 5. (left); outer = inner = 10 (right).

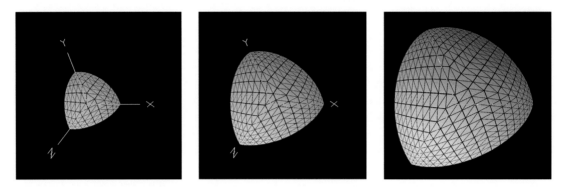

Figure 13.18. Three sphere octants with radius 1.0, 1.5, and 2.0 respectively. Regardless of tessellation level, each triangle is about the same size because the tessellation levels depend on the sphere radius.

Whole-Sphere Subdivision

A second sphere-subdivision example shows a different way to develop geometry from a tessellation shader. This example creates three spheres, each of which is defined by a single vertex in the patch vertex list. Each vertex is a vec4 value with center at (x,y,z) and with radius w, which is sufficient to define a sphere. We will see how this is handled in the TES. The .glib file for this example defines a set of uniform slider variables and is

```
##OpenGL GLIB

Vertex spheresubd.vert
TessControl spheresubd.tcs
TessEvaluation spheresubd.tes
Geometry spheresubd.geom
Fragment spheresubd.frag
Program SphereSubd              \
        uDetail <1. 30. 200.>   \
        uScale <0.1 1. 10.>     \
        uShrink <0. 1. 1.>      \
        uLightX <-10. 5. 10.>   \
        uLighY <-10. 10. 10.>   \
        uLightZ <-10. 10. 10.>

NumPatchVertices 1
```

```
glBegin gl_patches
  glVertex 0. 0. 0. .2    # x, y, z sphere center; w radius
  glVertex 0. 1. 0. .3
  glVertex 0. 0. 1. .4
glEnd
```

The vertex shader for this example, spheresubd.vert, gets the center and radius of the sphere from the input vertex value; it simply sets the output variables Center and Radius and sets the required gl_Position to the origin.

```
#version 400 compatibility

out vec3 vCenter;
out float vRadius;

void main( )
{
    vCenter = aVertex.xyz;
    vRadius = aVertex.w;

    gl_Position = vec4( 0., 0., 0., 1. );
}
```

The TCS, defined in spheresubd.tcs, takes the input from the vertex shader as two arrays, vRadius[ ] and vCenter[ ]. Each array has only one element in it, because the number of patch vertices was set to 1. The TCS sets up the tessellation levels for the primitive generator. It uses the uniform variable uDetail and the value of the radius to set the tessellation levels. Levels uOuter[0] and uOuter[2] are the number of divisions at the poles, uOuter[1] and uOuter[3] are the number of divisions at the vertical seams, and uInner[0] and uInner[1] give the real internal sphere detail.

```
#version 400 compatibility
#extension GL_ARB_tessellation_shader : enable

in vec3 vCenter[ ];
in float vRadius[ ];

patch out vec3 tcCenter;
patch out float tcRadius;

uniform float uDetail, uScale;

layout( vertices = 1 ) out;
```

```
void main( )
{
  gl_out[ gl_InvocationID ].gl_Position =
        gl_in[ 0 ].gl_Position;       // (0,0,0,1)

  tcRadius = vRadius[ 0 ];
  tcCenter = vCenter[ 0 ];

  gl_TessLevelOuter[0] = 2.;
```

//use scale and radius to help set the tessellation level

```
  gl_TessLevelOuter[1] = uScale*tcRadius*uDetail;
  gl_TessLevelOuter[2] = 2.;
  gl_TessLevelOuter[3] = uScale*tcRadius*uDetail;
  gl_TessLevelInner[0] = uScale*tcRadius*uDetail;
  gl_TessLevelInner[1] = uScale*tcRadius*uDetail;
}
```

The TES, given by spheresubd.tes, turns the tessellation coordinates u and v into angles, thus tessellating the sphere in spherical coordinates, and converts those into rectangular coordinates that are scaled and translated to get the actual triangle output coordinates. The normal is also computed as the radius vector.

```
#version 400 compatibility
#extension GL_ARB_tessellation_shader : enable

uniform float uScale;
layout( quads, equal_spacing, ccw) in;

patch in vec3 tcCenter;
patch in float tcRadius;

out vec3 teNormal;

const float PI = 3.14159265;

void main( )
{
  float u = gl_TessCoord.x;
  float v = gl_TessCoord.y;
  float w = gl_TessCoord.z;

  //-pi/2 <= phi <= pi/2
  // -pi <= theta <= pi
```

```
        float phi   =     PI * ( u - .5 ); // spherical coordinates
        float theta = 2. * PI * ( v - .5 );

        float cosphi = cos(phi);
        vec3 xyz = vec3( cosphi*cos(theta), sin(phi),
                            cosphi*sin(theta) );
        teNormal = xyz;

        xyz *= ( uScale * tcRadius );
        xyz += tcCenter;

        gl_Position = uModelViewMatrix * vec4( xyz,1. );
        // the shrink GS will multiply by the Projection matrix
    }
```

The output of these shaders is shown in Figure 13.19, where the same three
spheres have different levels of detail and different scale. As in the sphere
octant example, notice that the first image has larger triangles, while the second and third images have roughly the same level of detail since the radius is
used in defining the tessellation levels.

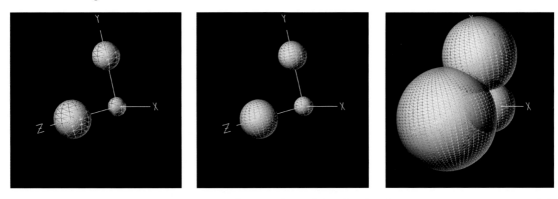

Figure 13.19. Three spheres as above with different values of detail and scale: uDetail = 30., uScale = 1. (left);
uDetail = 50., uScale = 1. (center); uDetail = 50., uScale = 2.5 (right).

Whole Sphere Subdivision while Adapting to Screen Coverage

This is good as far as it goes, but having to use uScale is restrictive. We would
much rather use our usual user interface (whatever that is) to arbitrarily scale,
rotate, and translate, and have the shader figure out what the right tessellation

levels should be. This would be especially useful in computer aided design and scientific data visualization, where smooth surfaces should stay smooth no matter how much you zoom in on them.

```glsl
#version 400 compatibility
#extension GL_ARB_tessellation_shader : enable
in vec3        vCenter[ ];
in float       vRadius[ ];
patch out vec3 tcCenter;
patch out float tcRadius;
uniform float  uDetail;
layout( vertices = 1 ) out;

void main( )
{
    tcCenter = vCenter[ 0 ];
    tcRadius = vRadius[ 0 ];

    // get the extreme points of the sphere:
    vec4 mx = vec4( vCenter[0] - vec3( vRadius[0], 0., 0. ), 1. );
    vec4 px = vec4( vCenter[0] + vec3( vRadius[0], 0., 0. ), 1. );
    vec4 my = vec4( vCenter[0] - vec3( 0., vRadius[0], 0. ), 1. );
    vec4 py = vec4( vCenter[0] + vec3( 0., vRadius[0], 0. ), 1. );
    vec4 mz = vec4( vCenter[0] - vec3( 0., 0., vRadius[0] ), 1. );
    vec4 pz = vec4( vCenter[0] + vec3( 0., 0., vRadius[0] ), 1. );

    // get the extreme points in clip space:
    mx = uModelViewProjectionMatrix * mx;
    px = uModelViewProjectionMatrix * px;
    my = uModelViewProjectionMatrix * my;
    py = uModelViewProjectionMatrix * py;
    mz = uModelViewProjectionMatrix * mz;
    pz = uModelViewProjectionMatrix * pz;

    // get the extreme points in NDC space:
    mx.xy /= mx.w;
    px.xy /= px.w;
    my.xy /= my.w;
    py.xy /= py.w;
    mz.xy /= mz.w;
    pz.xy /= pz.w;

    // how much NDC do the extreme points subtend?
    float dx = distance( mx.xy, px.xy );
    float dy = distance( my.xy, py.xy );
    float dz = distance( mz.xy, pz.xy );
    float dmax = sqrt( dx*dx + dy*dy + dz*dz );
```

```
    // set the tessellation levels from that information using
    // uDetail to make the conversion from NDC to screen space:
    gl_TessLevelOuter[0] = 2.;
    gl_TessLevelOuter[1] = dmax * uDetail;
    gl_TessLevelOuter[2] = 2.;
    gl_TessLevelOuter[3] = dmax * uDetail;
    gl_TessLevelInner[0] = dmax * uDetail;
    gl_TessLevelInner[1] = dmax * uDetail;
}
```

The big trick here is that the TCS is performing projection matrix multiply and homogeneous division itself. This is so that it can gain a sense of how large a region these points will subtend in normalized device coordinates (NDC), and thus how large the spheres will be when rendered on the screen. The outer and inner tessellations are then derived from that information. Here uDetail acts as a scale factor, and would normally be set by the application to reflect the size of the display window in pixels as well as some measure of your idea of what "pleasingly smooth" is.

The TES looks like this, which is the same as before except that there is no uScale:

```
#version 400 compatibility
#extension GL_ARB_tessellation_shader : enable

layout( quads, equal_spacing, ccw) in;

patch in float tcRadius;
patch in vec3  tcCenter;

out vec3 teNormal;

const float PI = 3.14159265;

void main( )
{
    float u = gl_TessCoord.x;
    float v = gl_TessCoord.y;
    float w = gl_TessCoord.z;

    float phi   = PI * ( u - .5 );
    float theta = 2. * PI * ( v - .5 );

    float cosphi = cos(phi);
    vec3 xyz = vec3( cosphi*cos(theta), sin(phi),
                        cosphi*sin(theta) );
```

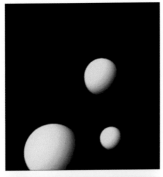

```
teNormal = xyz;

xyz *= tcRadius;
xyz += tcCenter;

gl_Position = uModelViewMatrix * vec4( xyz, 1. );
}
```

In Figures 13.20 and 13.21, notice that the number of triangles adapts to the screen coverage of each sphere, and that the size of the tessellated triangles stays about the same, regardless of radius or transformation.

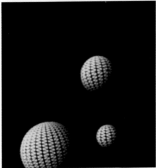

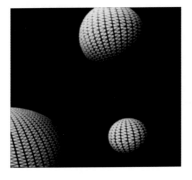 

Figure 13.21. The screen zoomed in (left) and rotated (right).

Figure 13.20. The original scene (left); with triangles shrunk to show tessellation (middle); zoomed out (right).

PN Triangles

This example shows how you can tessellate triangles with vertex normals, or point-normal (PN) triangles, to achieve significant levels of smoothness. This work is based on [45] and implements the techniques discussed there.

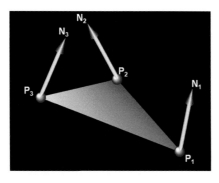 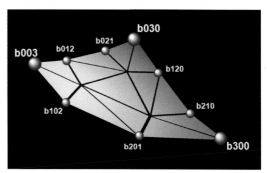

Figure 13.22. A PN triangle (left) and the Bézier control points of the curved PN triangle (right).

The left-hand image in Figure 13.22 shows the original triangle with three corner vertices and normals at those vertices. The general concept is to use this information to turn each PN triangle into a triangular Bézier patch, and create the Bézier control points. The Bézier patch equation can then be interpolated to any level of tessellation. The right-hand image in Figure 13.22 shows the Bézier control points of the curved PN triangle.

Now the geometry of a curved PN triangle that is defined by a triangular bicubic Bézier patch, which can be tessellated as shown in the images in Figure 13.23.

Below we give a complete set of shaders that handle PN triangles. They take input from a .glib file with uniform variables uScale, a scaling factor, uShrink, a shrinking factor for the geometry shader, and uInner and uOuter, inner and outer tessellation levels respectively. A white light is assumed, and its position is set in the geometry shader when the light intensity is computed. All these could easily be replaced to use these shaders from an application.

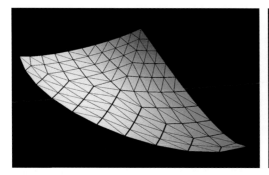 

Figure 13.23. A tessellated PN triangle showing the individual tessellations (left) and shown as one smooth surface (right).

The vertex shader, pntriangles.vert, is straightforward, taking its vertex location and normal from the standard variables and applying the scale value.

```
#version 400 compatibility
uniform float uScale;
out vec3 vNormal;

void main( )
{
   vec3 xyz = aVertex.xyz;
   xyz *= uScale;
   gl_Position = uModelViewMatrix * vec4( xyz, 1. );
   vNormal = normalize( uNormalMatrix * aNormal );
}
```

The TCS shader, pntriangles.tcs, is straightforward; it takes the position and normal values as arrays from the primitive assembly following the vertex shader, passes these on to the TES shader, and sets the required tessellation level values for the TES operation.

```
#version 400 compatibility
#extension GL_ARB_tessellation_shader : enable
uniform float uOuter, uInner;
uniform float uScale;

layout( vertices = 3 ) out;
in vec3 vNormal[ ];
out vec3 tcNormals[ ];

void main( )
{
   tcNormals[gl_InvocationID] =
        vNormal[gl_InvocationID];
   gl_out[ gl_InvocationID ].gl_Position =
        gl_in[ gl_InvocationID ].gl_Position;

   gl_TessLevelOuter[0] = uScale * Outer;
   gl_TessLevelOuter[1] = uScale * Outer;
   gl_TessLevelOuter[2] = uScale * Outer;
   gl_TessLevelInner[0] = uScale * Inner;
}
```

The TES shader, pntriangles.tes, is the most complex piece of the process because it sets up and executes the Bézier patch for the triangle, producing not only the position but also the normal for each vertex in the patch.

```glsl
#version 400 compatibility
#extension GL_ARB_tessellation_shader : enable
in vec3 tcNormals[ ];
out vec3 teNormal;

layout( triangles, equal_spacing, ccw) in;

void main( )
{
  vec3 p1 = gl_in[0].gl_Position.xyz;
  vec3 p2 = gl_in[1].gl_Position.xyz;
  vec3 p3 = gl_in[2].gl_Position.xyz;

  vec3 n1 = tcNormals[0];
  vec3 n2 = tcNormals[1];
  vec3 n3 = tcNormals[2];

  float u = gl_TessCoord.x;
  float v = gl_TessCoord.y;
  float w = gl_TessCoord.z;

  vec3 b300 = p1;
  vec3 b030 = p2;
  vec3 b003 = p3;

  float w12 = dot( p2 - p1, n1 );
  float w21 = dot( p1 - p2, n2 );
  float w13 = dot( p3 - p1, n1 );
  float w31 = dot( p1 - p3, n3 );
  float w23 = dot( p3 - p2, n2 );
  float w32 = dot( p2 - p3, n3 );

  vec3 b210 = ( 2.*p1 + p2 - w12*n1 ) / 3.;
  vec3 b120 = ( 2.*p2 + p1 - w21*n2 ) / 3.;
  vec3 b021 = ( 2.*p2 + p3 - w23*n2 ) / 3.;
  vec3 b012 = ( 2.*p3 + p2 - w32*n3 ) / 3.;
  vec3 b102 = ( 2.*p3 + p1 - w31*n3 ) / 3.;
  vec3 b201 = ( 2.*p1 + p3 - w13*n1 ) / 3.;

  vec3 ee = ( b210 + b120 + b021 + b012 + b102 + b201 ) / 6.;
  vec3 vv = ( p1 + p2 + p3 ) / 3.;
  vec3 b111 = ee + ( ee - vv ) / 2.;

  vec3 xyz = 1.*b300*w*w*w + 1.*b030*u*u*u + 1.*b003*v*v*v +
     3.*b210*u*w*w + 3.*b120*u*u*w + 3.*b201*v*w*w +
     3.*b021*u*u*v + 3.*b102*v*v*w + 3.*b012*u*v*v +
     6.*b111*u*v*w;
```

```
float v12 = 2. * dot( p2-p1, n1+n2 ) / dot( p2-p1, p2-p1 );
float v23 = 2. * dot( p3-p2, n2+n3 ) / dot( p3-p2, p3-p2 );
float v31 = 2. * dot( p1-p3, n3+n1 ) / dot( p1-p3, p1-p3 );

vec3 n200 = n1;
vec3 n020 = n2;
vec3 n002 = n3;
vec3 n110 = normalize( n1 + n2 - v12*(p2-p1) );
vec3 n011 = normalize( n2 + n3 - v23*(p3-p2) );
vec3 n101 = normalize( n3 + n1 - v31*(p1-p3) );

teNormal = n200*w*w + n020*u*u + n002*v*v +
           n110*w*u + n011*u*v + n101*w*v;

gl_Position = vec4( xyz, 1. );
}
```

Following the TES shader is the geometry shader, which takes a triangle as input and computes the light intensity and position for each vertex of the output triangle.

```
#version 400 compatibility
#extension GL_EXT_gpu_shader4: enable
#extension GL_EXT_geometry_shader4: enable

layout( triangles )  in;
layout( triangle_strip, max_vertices=32 )  out;

uniform float uShrink;
in vec3 teNormal[ ];
out float gLightIntensity;
const vec3 LIGHTPOS = vec3( 5., 10., 10. );
vec3 V[3];
vec3 CG;

void
ProduceVertex( int v )
{
  gLightIntensity =
    abs(dot(normalize(LIGHTPOS - V[v]),
normalize(teNormal[v])));
  gl_Position = uProjectionMatrix *
    vec4( CG + uShrink * ( V[v] - CG ), 1. );
  EmitVertex( );
}

void
main( )
```

```
{
    V[0] = gl_PositionIn[0].xyz;
    V[1] = gl_PositionIn[1].xyz;
    V[2] = gl_PositionIn[2].xyz;

    CG = ( V[0] + V[1] + V[2] ) / 3.;

    ProduceVertex( 0 );
    ProduceVertex( 1 );
    ProduceVertex( 2 );
}
```

And finally we have the fragment shader, pntriangles.frag, which takes the light intensity and applies it to the surface color.

```
#version 400 compatibility

in float gLightIntensity;
out vec4 fFragColor;

const vec3 COLOR = vec3( 1., 1., 0. );

void main( )
{
    fFragColor = vec4( gLightIntensity*COLOR, 1. );
}
```

The result of this treatment of PN triangles is shown in the treatment of a face defined as a triangle mesh, from [45]. Different treatments of the model's triangles yield different kinds of output quality. You should be careful when you use a technique such as this; you may end up creating an image that is too smooth to represent the reality your model has. Not all interpolations represent a reasonable approximation of reality!

A good example of the effect of using this tessellation on PN triangles is given by a detail of the cow model we saw in Chapter 12 on geometry shaders. In Figure 13.24 we see the detail at the base of the tail in the cow model. In the top row, the left-hand image is the simple Gouraud shading of the triangles in the tail, while the right-hand image improves the outer tessellation (outer = 2, inner = 1). Notice how much improvement there is just by increasing the outer tessellation. This is because smooth shading already helps the inner parts of triangles, but does nothing for the silhouettes. In the lower left image, the inner tessellation is also improved (outer = 2, inner = 2), while the lower right image shows the triangle structure by slightly shrinking all the triangles.

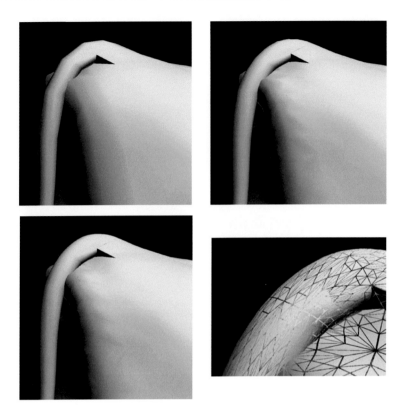

Figure 13.24. The cow's tail. Top row: smooth shading (left), improved outer tessellation (right). Bottom row: improved outer and inner tessellation (left), and detail (right).

Summary

Like many sophisticated features, tessellation shaders are very useful. There are many times when you would like to be able to specify a small amount of geometric detail and end up with a much larger amount. Those who have used RenderMan are already used to this because of RenderMan's automatic "microfaceting" feature. While OpenGL's tessellation shaders are not exactly the same as automated microfaceting, they are useful in many of the same ways. Thus, we can now perform some of the same surfacing and displacement mapping for which RenderMan has been so successfully used, but at interactive speeds.

Exercises

1. In the uniform variables in the `.glib` file for the Bézier curve, you will note that the variables `uOuter0` and `uOuter1` are slider uniform variables and can be set to a range of values. Experiment with these variables and note the result. Change the limits on the range of each and repeat the experiment.

2. Deliberately break the rules of good sense on tessellation levels to see the results. First, create two patches that share an edge and tessellate each with different outer tessellation levels to create holes between the two tessellated patches. Second, use wildly different inner and outer tessellation levels on a rectangular patch to see what the result looks like and to get a sense of how much difference between these might be reasonable.

3. Complete the Bézier surface example by supplying vertex, geometry, and fragment shaders for it. Experiment with the tessellation levels; start by giving different values to the two outer or two inner levels and note the result. Then add more uniform slider variables so that each of the four outer or inner levels is set separately, and note the result. It is quite possible to get really strange (and essentially unusable) results for some values of these levels; don't worry about that. It is useful to use the shrink geometry shader with this exercise so you can see the triangles more easily.

4. For a triangle tessellation, use a variety of values for the outer and inner tessellation levels. In particular, try out different values for the three outer levels and observe the results. It is useful to use the shrink geometry shader with this exercise so you can see the triangles more easily.

5. We have seen both sphere octant and whole-sphere examples in this chapter, but we have not compared their operation. Create a whole sphere from eight sphere octants and compare the quality of the resulting sphere with the whole-sphere quality. Can you say anything about the speed of drawing spheres these two ways?

6. Take one of your models based on triangles with vertex normals, or create a model of this sort, and apply the set of shaders given here for VN triangles. Examine the result carefully to see how it improves, or fails to improve, the concept you had in mind when you developed the model.

7. One of the historic uses of tessellation is to create a pattern of regular polygons or figures that fills a plane without any gaps or overlapping, like you see in the works of M.C. Escher. An example is shown in Figure 13.25.

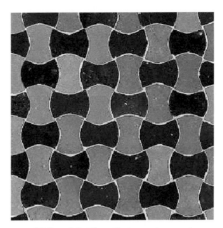

Figure 13.25. A pattern of Moorish tiles that creates a plane-covering tessellation.

Apply this pattern to a surface tessellation like some of the
ones shown in this chapter. Hint: you will need to create
a single repeatable rectangular tile with boundaries that
match up, as in the figure at the right, so that it can be repli-
cated across the surface like this:

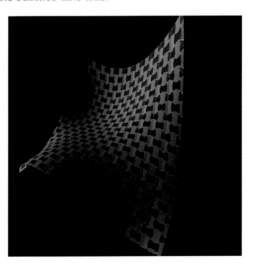

Another hint: it's not the GLSL tessellation that you need to worry about.
That doesn't change from the examples. Mostly you need to figure out where
in the whole 5-shader process you determine and assign the proper texture
coordinates.

14

The GLSL API

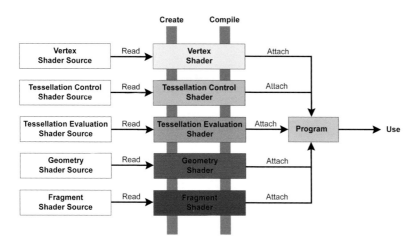

We have spent a lot of time talking about shaders outside the context of graphics applications that would use them. This is, of course, not the way the real world works, and in Chapter 15, we will see a number of exciting and important ways that shaders can contribute to creating meaningful images. To do that, however, you must integrate shader programming with your other graphics programming.

Shaders in the OpenGL Programming Process

So far, this book has focused on just writing the shader code itself, and not on the API boilerplate that goes around it. If you have been following along using

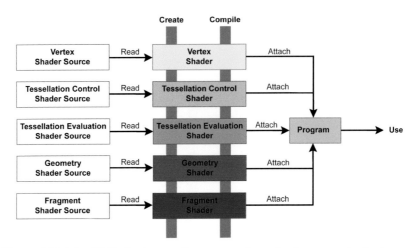

Figure 14.1. The GLSL shader-creation process from shader source to shader use.

glman, you probably realize that glman is handling a lot of infrastructure for you. Well, it's time to pull back the curtain and talk about how to hook GLSL shaders into an application.

As we have seen, shader programs replace fixed-function graphics operations that handle vertex, geometry, and fragment processing. When we use shaders, we must not only provide these files, but we must also carry out several steps, diagrammed in Figure 14.1, to integrate the shaders with our application. These steps are

1. Create the necessary shader source file(s).
2. Read each shader source file into a null-terminated text string to be compiled.
3. Create an empty shader object for each shader.
4. Give each shader object the text string of its shader source.
5. Compile each shader object.
6. Create an overall shader program.
7. Attach the shader objects to the program.
8. Link the shader program.
9. Specify that the shader program is to be used in place of the fixed-function pipeline.

When these are done, OpenGL will replace the fixed-function processing with your shaders until the application finishes or you deactivate or delete the shader program.

Handling OpenGL Extensions

At this time, shader programming with GLSL is new enough that many of the GLSL API calls are handled through OpenGL extensions. In order to manage extensions in a cross-platform way, we can use the *OpenGL Extension Wrangler Library* (*GLEW*). GLEW provides efficient run-time mechanisms for determining which OpenGL extensions are supported on the target platform. OpenGL core and extension functionality is exposed in a single header file. GLEW changes often to keep up with OpenGL developments. You can download GLEW from http://glew.sourceforge.net—you should check for new GLEW releases frequently.

In this chapter, we will refer to some GLSL functions that may be either EXT or ARB functions (that is, may not yet be fully integrated into the OpenGL standard), but GLEW will handle that and will replace a function name like glCreateProgram( ) with glCreateProgramEXT( ) or glCreateProgramARB( ) if either of those is the appropriate one for your system. In this chapter, we will only use the general function names and will leave EXT or ARB details up to GLEW.

You need to initialize GLEW in your application, probably in the function where you initialize your OpenGL system. The code below will do that for you.

```
#include "glew.h"

. . .

GLenum err = glewInit( );
if( err != GLEW_OK )
{
    fprintf( stderr, "glewInitError\n" );
    exit( 1 );
}

fprintf( stderr,"GLEW initialized OK\n" );
fprintf( stderr,"Status: Using GLEW %s\n",glewGetString(GLEW_
                VERSION) );
```

How Is a GLSL Shader Program Created?

The usual way of creating shader functionality is to create a collection of different types of shaders (e.g., vertex, tessellation, geometry, fragment) and collect them into a shader "program." This program will then be invoked ("used" in OpenGL terminology) during the rendering process to have this combination of shaders replace the fixed-function pipeline. An individual GLSL shader is exactly what you have been working with when you write vertex, geometry, or fragment shader files for *glman*. The only functional difference is in how you incorporate shaders in your application. A GLSL shader is written and stored as a plain text file to be incorporated into an OpenGL-based application, as we indicate above. You can use any kind of text-editing application to create the source file.

As you saw in Figure 14.1, there are a number of steps needed to incorporate shaders in an OpenGL application. The first step in this process is to read the shader source file into an ordinary null-terminated text string. This should be a familiar programming operation, but for completeness, the following example is a C++ source code fragment that reads a file into a null-terminated string whose address is str. From there, it can be compiled, attached to a shader program, and linked, so it can be used in your application.

```
#include <stdio.h>

FILE *fp = fopen( filename, "r" );
If ( fp == NULL ) {...} // report failure to open, and fail
                        // gracefully
fseek( fp, 0, SEEK_END );
int numBytes = ftell( fp ); // length of file

GLchar * str = new GLchar[numBytes+1];

rewind( fp );
fread( str, 1, numBytes, fp );
fclose( fp );
str[numBytes] = '\0'; // end byte string with NULL
```

The code fragment above uses the C++ new( ) operator, and in general we use C++ conventions in this chapter. If you are using C, you replace that line with the two lines

```
GLchar *str;
. . .
str = (GLchar *) malloc( numBytes + 1 );
```

and anywhere we use the C++ delete[ ] operator, you should use the C function free(...).

Creating and Compiling Shader Objects

Shader objects are unique objects: code groups that are downloaded from your application to the appropriate section of your graphics processor, where they can be used. There is a bit of processing involved in setting up a shader object. We cover that in this short section.

The process of creating a compiled shader object has three steps:

1. You must first create empty vertex, tessellation, geometry, or fragment shader objects. These will be identified with GLuint variables called handles that let you access them later. (The actual value of the handle has no meaning to your graphics application. Print it if you're curious. Just keep track of it and don't ever change it.)

2. You must next read the shader source string into the shader object. We described how you could create this string in the previous section.

3. Finally, you compile the shader object and check that the compilation was successful. This checking step is needed because shader compilation is not like standard language compilation; there is no automatic reporting of compilation problems.

The code fragment below shows how this is done for a vertex shader. The code to create and compile a geometry or fragment shader is made by simply replacing every reference to vertex shader by a reference to geometry or fragment shader, as you will see in the examples later in this chapter. This is a simpler version of the same operations in the full GLSLProgram class source listed in Appendix A; it shows the flow of activities needed to create and compile shaders.

```
int status;
int logLength;

// create an empty shader object
GLuint vertShader = glCreateShader( GL_VERTEX_SHADER );

// read the string into shader object
glShaderSource( vertShader, 1, (const GLchar **)&str, NULL );

// str is no longer needed and the memory can be freed
delete [ ] str;

// compile the shader object
glCompileShader( vertShader );
```

```
// check for OpenGL errors so far
CheckGlErrors( "Vertex Shader 1" );

// see if we had compilation errors
glGetShaderiv( vertShader, GL_COMPILE_STATUS, &status );
if( status == GL_FALSE )
{
    fprintf( stderr, "Vertex shader compilation failed.\n" );
    glGetShaderiv( vertShader, GL_INFO_LOG_LENGTH, &logLength
                    );
    GLchar *log = new GLchar [logLength];
    glGetShaderInfoLog( vertShader, logLength, NULL, log );
    fprintf( stderr, "\n%s\n", log );
    delete [ ] log;
    exit( 1 );
}
CheckGlErrors( "Vertex Shader 2" );
```

In the call to glCreateShader( ), the argument, GL_VERTEX_SHADER, has been highlighted. This is to emphasize that this is the only place that identifies what type of shader this is. Additional legal values are GL_TESSELLATION_CONTROL_SHADER, GL_TESSELLATION_EVALUATION_SHADER, GL_GEOMETRY_SHADER and GL_FRAGMENT_SHADER. This shader type is then stored in the shader object for later use. Other than this, each shader is compiled and attached the same way. It is important, of course, to set the shader type correctly so that the handling of the overall shader program knows what to do with each individual shader. Also, the compiler will sometimes produce different errors, depending on the type of shader; this is because certain things are legal in one type of shader but not others.

You will notice the construction (const GLchar **)&str for the shader source string. You can, of course, use a simpler construction for this and only read in a single string, but GLSL lets you construct a shader from a collection of source fragments that are stored in an array of strings and are only assembled at compile time. This gives you extra flexibility and lets you build a shader toolkit that is much finer grained than only having full shader source files.

As an example of taking this approach, you could use the same shader source, and insert the appropriate #define statements at the beginning by having each set of #defines in its own text file, letting you avoid time-consuming if tests. You can insert a common header file (a standard .h file) in the source if you like, or you can simulate the #include to re-use common pieces of code, such as frequently used functions.

As an idea of how this is done, consider the code fragment

```
GLchar *ArrayOfStrings[3];
ArrayOfStrings[0] = "#define SMOOTH_SHADING";
ArrayofStrings[1] = " . . . some commonly-used procedure
                . . . ";
ArrayofStrings[2] = " . . . the real vertex shader code
                . . . ";
glShaderSource( vertShader, 3, (GLchar **)ArrayofStrings,
                NULL );
```

This includes a #define statement, a common function, and the basic shader source.

If you want to prepare your shader source in a single file and still use this approach, you can either read the source into a string in a one-dimensional array, as

```
GLchar *buffer[1];
buffer[0] = " . . . the entire shader code . . . ";
glShaderSource( vertShader, 1, (GLchar **)buffer, NULL );
```

Or you can read the shader source into a single buffer, but cast its address as

```
GLchar *buffer = " . . . the entire shader code . . . ";
glShaderSource( vertShader, 1, (const GLchar **)&buffer,
                NULL );
```

The CheckGLErrors Function

The CheckGlErrors function is critical, because OpenGL does not report errors, so you need to ask. The CheckGlErrors function is shown below. It is an excellent idea to include this in all your OpenGL programs, not just shader programs, and to call it frequently. Simply knowing that errors occurred (as you would find when you checked GL_COMPILE_STATUS) is not enough; you need to get the list of errors from the compilation info log. Sometimes, errors occur well before their effects are felt, and with judicious use of this error checking function, you should be able to narrow down what the real error is and where it occurs.

```
void
CheckGlErrors( const char* caller )
{
   unsigned int gle = glGetError( );
```

```
if( gle != GL_NO_ERROR )
{
   fprintf(stderr,"GL Error discovered from caller %s:",
               caller);
   switch (gle)
   {
     case GL_INVALID_ENUM:
        fprintf( stderr, "Invalid enum.\n" );
        break;
     case GL_INVALID_VALUE:
        fprintf( stderr, "Invalid value.\n" );
        break;
     case GL_INVALID_OPERATION:
        fprintf(stderr,"Invalid Operation.\n");
        break;
     case GL_STACK_OVERFLOW:
        fprintf( stderr, "Stack overflow.\n" );
        break;
     case GL_STACK_UNDERFLOW:
        fprintf(stderr, "Stack underflow.\n" );
        break;
     case GL_OUT_OF_MEMORY:
        fprintf( stderr, "Out of memory.\n" );
        break;
     case GL_INVALID_FRAMEBUFFER_OPERATION;
        fprintf( stderr, "Framebuffer object is not
                    complete.\n" );
        break;
   }
   return;
}
return;
}
```

Creating, Attaching, Linking, and Activating Shader Programs

Once you have created the shader object(s) you want to use, you must create an overall shader program and attach the individual shaders to it. The shader program is the vehicle for making shader objects available to the OpenGL system, and activating a shader program tells the graphics card to use it to replace the appropriate parts of the fixed-function graphics operations.

Creating a Shader Program and Attaching Shader Objects

The glCreateProgram( ) function is used to create an empty shader program:

```
GLuint program = glCreateProgram( );
```

The variable program is just a handle and has no numerical significance to the application. To attach a shader to this program, use both the program and shader handles in glAttachShader( ) like this:

```
glAttachShader ( program, vertShader );
glAttachShader ( program, tesscontrolShader );
glAttachShader ( program, tessevaluationShader );
glAttachShader ( program, geomShader );
glAttachShader ( program, fragShader );
```

You don't need to have *all* these types of shaders in every program. The program will just consist of the shaders you have attached. This code should be placed in an initialization section of your application program. You can also create more than one shader program if you want to use different shaders in different parts of your application.

Linking Shader Programs

Before you can actually use the shader program you have just created, you must link the individual shader objects together, resolve their common variables, and link with any built-in support code. The linking uses the function

```
glLinkProgram( program )
```

If any shader objects are not included, the shader program will let the fixed-function processor continue to take on those functions.

Like compilation, linking a shader program can fail, and you should routinely check that linking is successful before assuming that the program is useable. The function

```
glGetProgramiv( program, GL_LINK_STATUS, &linkStatus )
```

returns a linkStatus of GL_TRUE if the program linked successfully; otherwise it returns GL_FALSE. Just as was the case when you compiled shader objects, you not only need to check for success, you also need to report any errors. The whole process looks like this:

```
int
LinkProgram( GLuint program )
{
  glLinkProgram( program );
  CheckGlErrors("LoadShader:Link 1");

  GLchar* infoLog;
  GLint infoLogLen;
  GLint linkStatus;
  glGetProgramiv( program, GL_LINK_STATUS, &linkStatus );
  CheckGlErrors("LoadShader:Link 2");

  if( linkStatus == GL_FALSE )
  {
    glGetProgramiv( program, GL_INFO_LOG_LENGTH,
    &infoLogLen );
    fprintf(stderr,"Failed to link program--Info Log
    Length = %d\n", infoLogLen );
    if( infoLogLen > 0 )
    {
      infoLog = new GLchar[infoLogLen+1];
      glGetProgramInfoLog( program, infoLogLen,
                             NULL, infoLog );
      infoLog[infoLogLen] = '\0';
      fprintf( stderr, "Info Log:\n%s\n", infoLog );
      delete [ ] infoLog;

    }
    glDeleteProgram( program );
    return 0;
  }

  return 1;
};
```

If the linking operation is successful, each of the program object's active uniform and attribute variables is assigned a location that can be queried with `glGetUniformLocation` and `glGetAttributeLocation`, as discussed later in this chapter.

Activating a Shader Program

Once a shader program is available, it must be activated. Activating the shader program switches the action of the graphics card so that your shader program takes over the necessary operations from the fixed-function processing. To make the program active, you use the statement

```
glUseProgram( program );
```

in your application. From this point until you next call glUseProgram( ), all graphics processing will use the shader code in this shader program.

To go back to using the fixed-function graphics pipeline, you simply tell the system to use a null shader program, like this:

Do not try to create or link shader programs within a display list, because these functions are executed *immediately* when they are processed, rather than being deferred until the list is called. You can, however, embed a call to glUseProgram( ) in a display list.

```
glUseProgram( 0 );
```

If you want to change shader programs, as you may well want to do if you want to use different shader programs for different parts of your display, you need not deactivate one shader before you activate another. Simply activate the new shader program at the point where you want to begin using it. The shader program being used is simply an attribute of the system; that is, another part of the OpenGL state.

You may create, compile, link, and activate shader programs at any point in your application, as long as the resulting active shader programs are complete before you actually use them. In practice, you may want to make this part of the initialization process for your application, the part that is usually executed only once when your application begins, and where you set up the application's graphics environment. You can then activate or deactivate your shaders whenever you like.

Finally, you can not only deactivate a shader program; you can actually delete it and all its components. This frees up the memory on the graphics board for other shader programs or other uses. All of the functions that build up a shader program have functional inverses, so you can

- Detach a shader object from a shader program with glDetachShader(shader).
- Delete a shader program with glDeleteProgram(program).
- Delete a shader object with glDeleteShader(shader).

You have some protection from incorrect ordering of these functions, because the actual effect of the function is delayed until it makes sense. If you ask for a program object to be deleted, but it is part of the current rendering state, it is not deleted until it is no longer part of the rendering context. If you ask for a shader to be deleted, but it is still attached to a program object, it is not deleted until after it has been detached. But it is probably much better to be systematic in removing program and shader objects, both to make your code easier to understand, and to avoid instances where the system might not adequately protect you.

Passing Data into Shaders

As you write any program with the OpenGL API, even if you don't intend that program to use GLSL shaders, you create data that the system will use in creating a scene. This is generally graphical data that describes the scene. For example, you can specify the color for each vertex, or you can create an array of vertices and a parallel array with data such as elevations, temperature, or any measured data. The data could be used in fixed-function operations by manipulating primitives based on your data, or with shader-based operations by putting the data into user-defined attribute or uniform data that you can access within the shader function(s). In these sections, we describe how you can create attribute, uniform, or sampler data for shaders, and we give some examples that show these in action.

Defining Uniform Variables in Your Application

GLSL uniform variables contain information that can change at most with each graphics primitive. You can think of these uniform variables as a sort of "global variables" that are available to all the shaders currently being used. If you want a shader to have data and that data isn't directly available from OpenGL, you can define your own uniform variables to give that data to a shader. Uniform variables are defined within a shader, and their values are set by the application. Uniform variables can hold any kind of data, including structs and arrays, as we saw with the built-in uniform variables.

The mechanism for defining and using your own uniform variables is indirect and somewhat unusual. When you define a uniform variable in your shader program, you simply declare the variable in the usual way:

```
uniform type name;
```

This associates a name and a type with the variable, but does not associate an address. An address is only assigned when the shader program is linked. Once linking has been done, an address is available for each variable. You query the address and then use it to set the variable from your application.

But how does the application get the address for a variable it does not know about? The application must know the name of the uniform variable in a linked shader program. It can then get the location (or address) with the function

```
GLint glGetUniformLocation(GLuint program, const GLchar *name);
```

Here `program` is the value returned from the `glCreateProgram( )` function, and `name` is the name (a text string) of the uniform variable. This function returns the address of the named variable within the named program object, so it can be used in the application. The uniform variable must be a simple variable, not an array or struct; these are handled differently. A uniform variable (either built-in or user-defined) is called *active* if the link operation finds that it can be accessed during program execution; a link operation must have been done (though it might not have succeeded) before the uniform variables in the shader program can be active.

You can think of this as creating a conduit from your application to the shader. The location you get from `glGetUniformLocation( )` is the place the conduit gets plugged into. You then use one of the `glProgramUniform*( )` functions to put data into the conduit to get it to the shader.

The application can set the value of a uniform variable whose location is known in three ways. The first way sets scalar or simple vector data with the function

```
glProgramUniform{i}{t}(GLuint program, GLint location, TYPE val)
```

where i can be 1, 2, 3, or 4, depending on the dimension of the variable, and t can be either f or i, depending on whether the type's base is floating-point or integer. The function causes the value of the parameter val to be loaded into the location indicated. This parameter can be a simple `vec1`, `vec2`, `vec3`, `vec4`, `ivec1`, `ivec2`, `ivec3`, or `ivec4`, but not an array of these types.

The second way sets array (vector) data with

```
glProgramUniform{i}{t}v(GLuint program, GLint location,
                    GLuint length, const TYPE *val)
```

where the meanings i and t are the same, but the data in `val` is a vector of the specified type (including `vec*` and `ivec*`) whose length is `length`.

Finally, the third way sets matrices, and is

```
glProgramUniformMatrix{i}fv( GLuint program, GLint location,
      GLuint count, GLboolean transpose, const GLfloat *val )
```

Notice that none of the glUniform* routines take a program handle as one of its arguments. Those routines set uniform variables in the *currently active* shader program. So, be sure that you call glUseProgram( ) on the correct program before setting that program's variables.

If i has the value 2, val must be a 2 × 2 matrix; if 3, a 3 × 3 matrix; and if 4, a 4 x 4 matrix. If transpose has value GL_FALSE, the matrix is taken to be in standard OpenGL column major order, while if transpose has value GL_TRUE, the matrix is taken to be in row-major order. The value of count is the number of matrices that are being passed, so if you are only passing a single matrix, that value is 1.

In Chapter 7 we talked about how it would sometimes be nice to be able to separate the Model and the Viewing matrices, instead of having them pre-combined into one ModelView matrix, as OpenGL does. If you are willing to manipulate the contents of those matrices yourself, then using matrix uniform variables is a good way to accomplish this.[1]

If you have defined a struct as a uniform variable, you cannot set the entire struct at once; you must use the functions above to set each field individually.

As an example, let's suppose that you wanted to pass a light location into your shaders. The following very short code fragment, to be used in your application, stores a Cfloat[3] variable named lightLoc in an application-defined uniform vec3 variable whose name is "uLightLocation". Note the use of the glGetUniformLocation function to find the location of the uniform variable and of the glProgramUniform3fv function to set that uniform variable, as well as the check to ensure that the variable was actually found.

```
//   in the shader:

uniform vec3 uLightLocation;

//   in the C / C++ application (after linking
//   the shader program):

float lightLoc[3] = { 0., 100., 0. };

GLint location = glGetUniformLocation( program,
                                       "uLightLocation" );
if( location < 0 )
   fprintf(stderr, "Uniform variable 'uLightLocation' not
            found\n");
else
   glProgramUniform3fv( program, location, 3, lightLoc );
```

---

1. Appendix B shows a C++ class that allows you to easily manipulate your own matrices.

Uniform Variables in Compatibility Mode

In compatibility mode, GLSL defines a number of built-in uniform variables that give you access to OpenGL state information, as we described in Chapter 5. There are a number of built-in uniform variables, including the ModelView, Projection, and Normal matrices, and all texture, light, and materials data. Your applications set these values through standard OpenGL functions and can use the associated uniform variables in your shaders.

In the discussion of the GLSL language, you saw a list of built-in uniform variables. Their names begin with gl_ and they give you access to all the OpenGL state values or values derived from these states. When a program object is made current, the built-in uniform variables that track the OpenGL state are initialized to the current value of those states, and any later OpenGL calls that modify state values update the built-in uniform variable that tracks those states. The most commonly used of these are shown in Table 14.1.

Standard OpenGL Function	Built-in Uniform Variable
transformations	mat4 gl_ModelViewMatrix
	mat4 gl_ModelViewProjectionMatrix
	mat4 gl_ProjectionMatrix
	mat3 gl_NormalMatrix

materials	struct gl_MaterialParameters {
	    vec4 emission;
	    vec4 ambient;
	    vec4 diffuse;
	    vec4 specular;
	    float shininess;
	} gl_Frontmaterial; gl_BackMaterial;

lights	struct gl_LightSourceParameters {
	    vec4 ambient;
	    vec4 diffuse;
	    vec4 specular;
	    vec4 position;
	    vec4 halfVector;
	    vec3 spotDirection;
	    float spotExponent;
	    float spotCutoff;
	    float spotCosCutoff;
	} gl_LightSource[gl_MaxLights];

textures	gl_TextureMatrix[i]

```
fog                              struct gl_FogParameters {
                                     vec4   color;
                                     float density;
                                     float start;
                                     float end;
                                     float scale;
                                 } gl_Fog
```

Table 14.1. Uniform variables defined by compatibility-mode OpenGL functions.

Defining Attribute Variables in Your Application

Attribute variables are a way to provide per-vertex data to a vertex shader. These are only available to a vertex shader. If any vertex-specific attribute data needs to be used by a shader, the vertex shader must first convert it to an out variable so the later shader can take it as an in variable. Here we describe the general approach to defining variables that describe properties of an individual vertex in your model.

Besides the usual attribute data such as the coordinates, normal, color, or texture coordinates of a vertex, you may also need to define other data to associate with a vertex. OpenGL lets applications define custom attributes to pass to a vertex shader. Each vertex attribute has an indexed location and can contain up to four values.

As with uniform variables, you need to determine the location of an attribute variable before you can set it:

```
GLint glGetAttribLocataion( program, GLchar * attribName );
```

where `attribName` is a character string of the name of the variable.

An application can specify a per-vertex attribute value using one of the functions

```
void glVertexAttrib{i}{t}{v}(GLuint location, TYPE val)
```

The value of i can be 1, 2, 3, or 4, depending on the dimension of the data to be given to that attribute. The value of t specifies the data type for the data to be given to the attribute; this can be b (byte), s (short), i (int), f (float), d (double), ub (unsigned byte), us (unsigned short), or ui (unsigned int). The suffix v means that the data is in vector form rather than as a list of scalars. These are consistent with the format of the glVertex* functions.

The parameter location is the particular symbol table location of the attribute variable you are setting, and the parameter or parameters val are the value(s) to be written to the attribute variable at that index. All the glVertexAttrib functions are expected to be used between glBegin and glEnd, just as the built-in attribute setting functions are.

The type of the data val is expected to match the type specified in the function name. However, since the vertex attributes are always stored in an array of type vec4, any byte, short, int, unsigned byte, unsigned short, or unsigned int will be converted into a standard GLfloat before it is actually stored.

Notice that the glVertexAttrib routine does not take a program handle as one of its arguments. This routine sets attribute variables in the *currently active* shader program. So, be sure that you call gluseProgram( ) on the correct program before setting that program's variables. (Presumably you would already have done this because to use glVertexAttrib( ) functions, you would be drawing something.)

In the short application code fragment below, we want to assign a vec2 attribute to each vertex of the triangle being drawn. The values to be assigned to that attribute for the three vertices are u0 and v0, u1 and v1, and u2 and v2. The role of the glVertexAttrib2f( ) function is to set these values for the attribute.

```
// in the vertex shader:
in vec2 aUV;    // a per-vertex attribute

// in the C / C++ global variables:

GLint UVloc;

// in the C / C++ graphics setup code (after linking the shader
// program):

UVloc = glGetAttribLocation( program, "aUV" );

if( UVloc < 0 )
    fprintf( stderr, "Cannot find Attribute variable 'aUV\n" );

// in the C / C++ display callback

if( UVloc > 0 )
{
    glBegin( GL_TRIANGLES );
        glVertexAttrib2f( UVloc, u0, v0 );
        glVertex3f( x0, y0, z0 );
        glVertexAttrib2f( UVloc, u1, v1 );
        glVertex3f( x1, y1, z1 );
```

```
        glVertexAttrib2f(  UVloc, u2, v2 );
        glVertex3f( x2, y2, z2 );
    glEnd( );
}
```

A visualization per-vertex attribute example could display pressure data on a surface. The usual way this would be presented with the fixed-function OpenGL would be to use the pressure to define the color at each vertex in the surface, and then—assuming a continuous pressure function on the surface—to send the surface's graphics primitives into the rendering stages, to be drawn with smooth shading. However, we could also define pressure to be an attribute variable with each vertex, and use that directly for drawing the surface, giving us more options on using color to present the pressure data.

The steps in doing this are as follows:

- Define the attribute variable in the application and set the variable to its appropriate value for each vertex as you define the vertex geometry.
- Pick up the value of the attribute variable in the vertex shader and write it to a varying variable so it can be interpolated smoothly across each graphics primitive.
- Use the varying variable's value to determine the color to be used in filling pixels.

This would let us add pressure contour lines, or would let us color different pressure regimes in distinct colors, or create other displays as needed. This idea will be explored more fully in Chapter 15.

Attribute Variables in Compatibility Mode

If you are working in compatibility mode, you may have a number of built-in attribute variables for a vertex shader to use directly or to pass along to other shaders. Each of the standard OpenGL functions that define a vertex (those you can call within a glBegin–glEnd pair) defines a built-in attribute variable that can be used by a vertex shader. These include

```
attribute vec4 gl_Color;
attribute vec3 gl_Normal;
attribute vec4 gl_Vertex;
attribute vec4 gl_MultiTexCoord0;
```

These variables correspond to the standard OpenGL vertex functions, as shown in Table 14.2.

Standard OpenGL Function	Built-in Attribute Variable
glVertex(...)	gl_Vertex
glColor(...)	gl_Color
glNormal(...)	gl_Normal
glSecondaryColor(...)	gl_SecondaryColor
glMultiTexCoord(i, ...)	gl_MultiTexCoordi, i=1..N
glFogCoordf(...)	gl_FogCoord

Table 14.2. Attribute variables defined by compatibility-mode OpenGL vertex functions.

A C++ Class to Handle Shader Program Creation

Appendix A shows a C++ class that is handy for shader creation and use. As a preview, here is how such an application would look:

```
#include "glslprogram.h"

float       Ad, Bd, NoiseAmp, NoiseFreq, Tol;
GLSLProgram *Ovals;
```

During setup:

```
Ovals = new GLSLProgram( );
Ovals->SetVerbose( true );
Ovals->SetGstap( true );
bool good = Ovals->Create( "ovalnoise.vert", "ovalnoise.frag" );
if( ! good  )
{
   fprintf( stderr, "GLSL Program Ovals wasn't created.\n" );
   <<handle the fact that the shaders did not compile or link>>
}
```

In the display callback:

```
Ovals->Use( );
// we assume the user has interactively changed the uniform
// vars:
Ovals->SetUniform( "uAd", Ad );
Ovals->SetUniform( "uBd", Bd );
Ovals->SetUniform( "uNoiseAmp",  NoiseAmp );
Ovals->SetUniform( "uNoiseFreq", NoiseFreq );
Ovals->SetUniform( "uTol", Tol );
```

```
// draw something:
glColor3f( 0., 1., 0. );
glutSolidTeapot( 1. );

// go back to the fixed-function pipeline:
Ovals->UseFixedFunction( );
. . .

// draw some items with the fixed-function pipeline:
. . .
```

Notes

- This example does not use a geometry shader but it could, just by listing the name of the .geom file. The Create( ) method accepts any number of shader file names, up to five.
- The handles for the individual shaders are hidden in the class. You really don't need to know them yourself.
- The handle for the overall shader program is hidden in the class. You really don't need to know it yourself.
- The uniform variable locations are also hidden in the class. They are determined once, and then looked up whenever they are needed.
- All compiler and linker error messages are sent to standard error. The application can determine if something failed, because the return from the GLSLProgram constructor is NULL.

The structure of this class can be found in the appendix, and the class code can be found in the online materials for the book.

Exercises

1. Take a project you wrote for fixed-function OpenGL and rewrite it with shader programs replacing the fixed-function vertex and fragment processing. Choose a straightforward program, not one that uses sophisticated graphics, because the goal of this exercise is simply to get shader programs working for you. Add something in the shaders that is not available in the original program, though.

2. We gave a general example of creating a user-defined attribute variable that holds the value of the pressure (a one-dimensional value) at each

point on a surface, so that a shader could color the surface in ways that communicate that pressure. Implement another visualization of the pressure besides the one(s) that we described in the text.

3. While OpenGL is a fully general graphics API that can be used by almost everyone who needs graphics, you can write shaders that only use the capabilities that you need. For example, the texture mapping functions in fixed-function OpenGL can work with a very large number of input formats for texture maps. Review the standard OpenGL texture map functions and list all the possible options for texture map inputs, and identify the set of operations that you would yourself expect to use.

15

Using Shaders for Scientific Visualization

So far, we have been cutting through the shader world in one direction—examining different capabilities of GLSL. In this chapter, we try cutting in another direction for a while—looking at an application focus. We will describe several ways in which shader programming can enhance the display of data. Clearly, there are many more ways to do this than just the few we illustrate, but the point is to show how different aspects of shader programming can be brought to bear on a single problem grouping.

There is much more to scientific visualization than we could begin to cover in this chapter, of course. Our approach will be to consider how some shader techniques from the previous chapters can be used for visualization. These will include image manipulation, geometry modification with vertex shaders, applications of textures, using fragment shaders to implement transfer functions and to carry out flow visualization, and using geometry shader techniques. This includes the whole range of shader techniques in the book, showing just how deeply shader programming has affected computer graphics applications.

Image-Based Visualization Techniques

The first few visualization techniques we describe are image based. They have already been covered in Chapter 10 on image manipulation, but it is useful to repeat them again here as we look at how they impact the understanding of data.

Image Negative

The first method displays the negative of an image. This is the most simple of the image shaders, but its use in visualization is surprisingly useful. Figure 15.1 shows a visualization image (a volume rendering, actually) of a mouse vertebra. The left-hand image in the figure is the original, and the right-hand one is the negative. Notice how the negative brings out subtle details that were not obvious in the original, especially the "pock marks" on the wall of the bone. Many visualization programs have a "display negative" button in their user interface for just this reason.

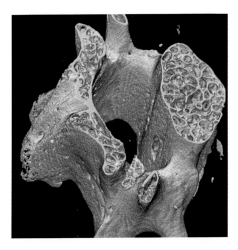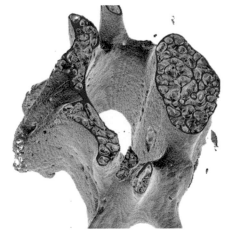

Figure 15.1. The original (left) and negative (right) of an image, showing how the negative often brings out new features.

Image Edge Detection

Another useful image shader in data visualization is the edge detection Sobel filter. As seen in Figure 15.2, the Sobel filter emphasizes the parts of the image where shading is changing quickly, usually the sharp edges. In this figure, the edges have been colored and superimposed on the original image, but it is sometimes also useful just to display the edges alone, as we did in Chapter 11.

Both the image negative and edge detection examples were implemented by looking at a static image, but in fact they can also become a post-process to any dynamic 3D rendering. To do this, use the OpenGL render-to-texture capability described in Chapter 9 to produce a texture image of the 3D scene, and then render a quadrilateral with this texture on it, using one of the image shaders.

Toon Rendering

Toon rendering, covered in Chapter 11, starts with edge detection and adds color quantization. It is sometimes an excellent way to perform architectural visualization, because it strongly brings out a building's key edges, while retaining the colors but de-emphasizing them. This is shown in Figure 15.3, which shows the Smithsonian Castle in Washington, DC both without (left) and with (right) toon shading.

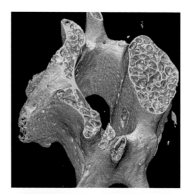

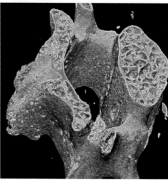

Figure 15.2. Edge detection emphasizes certain features.

Figure 15.3. Toon rendering for architectural visualization.

Hyperbolic Geometry

Often when you display highly detailed data, such as a large map, you want to be able to zoom into an area of interest. This usually forces much of the rest of the display off the screen, as it does in Figure 15.4.

What if you wanted to simply force the rest of the display to the *edges* of the screen, but not off it? One answer is to use *hyperbolic geometry*, which can be implemented very effectively in a vertex shader.

The reason for using hyperbolic geometry is to create a mathematical process that moves the parts of the scene farthest from the area of interest, asymptotically towards the edges of the display. One straightforward way of doing this uses polar coordinates. For a given (x,y) coordinate that has already been translated, you convert it into a polar (r,Θ) pair. You leave the angle Θ alone and manipulate the radius as follows:

$$r' = \frac{r}{r+k},$$

where k is a constant. As r increases, the theme of "something divided by something a little bigger" makes this fraction asymptotically approach 1. You then recombine this new radius with the original Θ to produce a new (x',y') that will always lie within a unit circle.

What does the constant k do? If k were 0, then all r' would be 1, that is, the entire scene would be forced to the edges. If k were ∞, then all r' would be 0, that is, the entire scene would be forced to a dot in the center. So adjusting

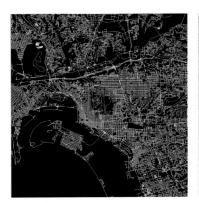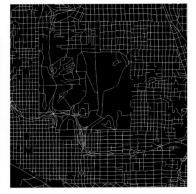

Figure 15.4. Linear zooming in Euclidean space.

 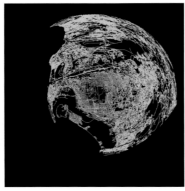 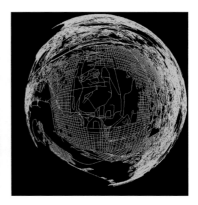

Figure 15.5. Zooming in polar hyperbolic space.

the value of k is a way to control how much of the scene is zoomed in upon and how much ends up at the edges. The images in Figure 15.5 show how this looks when applied to a street map of San Diego, while Figure 15.6 shows a hyperbolic rendering of a map of Corvallis, Oregon, that includes overlays for streets, buildings, and parks.

When doing shader programming, there is always a concern that needing to compute a handful of transcendental functions per vertex will kill performance. After all, turning an (x,y) into (r,Θ) involves using a square root and an arctan. Producing the final (x',y') involves using a sine and cosine. Fortunately, the equations simplify out all of these transcendantal functions except the square root:

$$r = \sqrt{x^2 + y^2},$$

$$x' = r' \cos \Theta = \left(\frac{r}{r+k} \right) \left(\frac{x}{r} \right) = \frac{x}{r+k}.$$

And, similarly,

$$y' = r' \sin \Theta = \left(\frac{r}{r+k} \right) \left(\frac{y}{r} \right) = \frac{y}{r+k}.$$

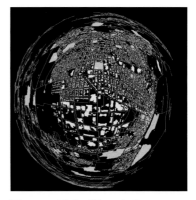

Figure 15.6. Hyperbolic geometry display of Corvallis, Oregon, showing streets (orange), buildings (yellow), and parks (green).

The vertex shader code to perform this is quite concise and looks like this:

```
uniform float   uK;
uniform float   uTransX;
uniform float   uTransY;

void main( )
{
   vec2 pos = ( uModelViewMatrix * aVertex ).xy;
   pos += vec2( uTransX, uTransY );
   float r = length( pos );
   vec4 pos2 = vec4( pos/(r + uK), 0., 1. );
   gl_Position = uProjectionMatrix * pos2;
}
```

In this case, a separate set of translations is explicitly being passed in, although the translations encapsulated in the ModelView matrix will work just fine. Also, it turns out that the scale factor encapsulated in the ModelView matrix can be used as another way to zoom in and out. If a uniform scale factor s is applied to the scene using glScalef( ), the resulting hyperbolic geometry equation would be

$$r' = \frac{sr}{sr + k} = \frac{r}{r + k/s}.$$

Thus, what we just thought of as k can actually also be thought of as $1/s$.

One other thing to notice is the use of the built-in GLSL length( ) function. Even though that same line could be written as

```
float r = sqrt( pos.x*pos.x + pos.y*pos.y );
```

it is always better to take advantage of built-in functions if they are available. At the worst, they will be the same speed as your own version. At best, though, they could take advantage of some features you don't have access to, and could be much faster.

If you are not comfortable with this fish-eye type of zoom, you could look at a Cartesian hyperbolic zoom, as shown in Figure 15.7. In this case, we do not go to polar coordinates, but use hyperbolic transformations for the rectangular coordinates, as

$$x' = \frac{x}{\sqrt{x^2 + k^2}},$$

$$y' = \frac{y}{\sqrt{y^2 + k^2}}.$$

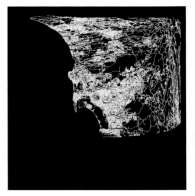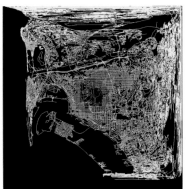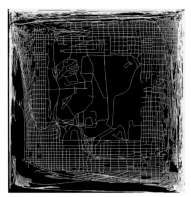

Figure 15.7. Zooming in Cartesian hyperbolic space.

Again, as k goes to zero, the transformations approach the identity, but as k increases, the hyperbolic effect increases. This approach makes the vertex shader code simpler, because you do not need to go through the polar coordinate conversion. The Cartesian hyperbolic vertex shader is left as an exercise.

3D Scalar Data Visualization

In this section, we are going to consider passing a 3D volume of data values into a shader in the form of a 3D texture, so that we can examine the volumetric data. There is a format setup in *glman* to make this easy for you to do, but you need to write your data in this file format yourself. To make this easier, below we give you an example of a short C++ program that writes a 32 × 32 × 32 texture file. This format is actually made to hold a floating-point 4D texture, as you can see in the actual file write statements, but here we are just using one of the four components, and leaving the other three empty. Instead of storing red, green, blue, and alpha (for example), we are just using the red component to hold a single value.

```
#include <stdio.h>
#include <math.h>
float ScalarValue( float, float, float );

const int NUMS = 32;
const int NUMT = 32;
const int NUMP = 32;
int
main( int argc, char *argv[ ] )
```

```
{
    FILE *fp = fopen( "vis3dtexture.tex", "wb" );
    if( fp == NULL )
    {
        fprintf( stderr,
          "Cannot create the output 3D texture file\n" );
        return 1;
    }

    fwrite( &NUMS, 4, 1, fp );
    fwrite( &NUMT, 4, 1, fp );
    fwrite( &NUMP, 4, 1, fp );

    float zero = 0.;
    for( int p = 0; p < NUMP; p++ )
    {
        float z = -1. + 2. * (float)p / (float)( NUMP-1 );
        for( int t = 0; t < NUMT; t++ )
        {
            float y = -1. + 2. * (float)t / (float)( NUMT-
                        1 );
            for( int s = 0; s < NUMS; s++ )
            {
                float x = -1. + 2. * (float)s / (float)
                    ( NUMS-1 );
                float value = HOWEVER YOU COMPUTE IT,
                 LOOK IT UP, ETC
                fwrite( &value, 4, 1, fp );
                fwrite( &zero, 4, 1, fp );
                fwrite( &zero, 4, 1, fp );
                fwrite( &zero, 4, 1, fp );
            }
        }
    }

    fclose( fp );
    return 0;
}
```

In the examples below, we will use the texture-file format to hold data that is a summation of decaying exponentials, approximating a temperature distribution in a room with individual heat sources, and whose walls are a heat sink. This data is available in the file vis3dtexture.tex with the resources for this book. In practice, up to four data components could be encapsulated at the same time, giving you more flexibility in what combinations you can visualize.

Point Clouds

A 3D texture is just data and needs a geometry to map itself to. A good start is to map it to a *3D point cloud*, a uniform mesh of 3D points. When you map the temperature distribution dataset above to a point cloud, you get the image in Figure 15.8.

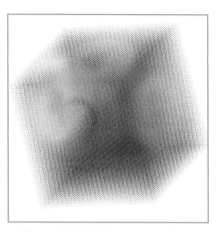

Figure 15.8. Uniform point cloud.

One of the interesting aspects of this approach is that the resolution of the point cloud does not have to exactly match the resolution of the dataset. Because this example uses texture mapping to access the data, the OpenGL display process will interpolate the data values to the cloud's point locations. Making the resolution of the point cloud *less* than that of the data is usually a bad idea, since some of the data values will be completely skipped over in the display. But you can easily give the point cloud a *higher* resolution and get a nicer-looking display.

Using a higher point cloud resolution assumes, of course, that interpolation makes sense for the particular data you have. It doesn't always. For example, suppose the data values represent integer-only data, such as the number of children per family. Even though a point cloud dot could exist between two data values, it makes no sense to combine half of one with half of the other to produce a data point that represents a fraction of a child. In this case, the resolution of the point cloud should be the *same* as the resolution of the data.

The GLIB file used to produce the point cloud above is

```
Texture  5 vis3dtexture.tex
Vertex   pointcloud.vert
Fragment pointcloud.frag
Program  PointCloud            \
         uTexUnit 5            \
         uMin <0. 0. 100>      \
         uMax <0. 100. 100.>
PointCloud 50 50 50
```

The vertex shader is also very short, since it just sets up the interpolation of the texture coordinates and performs the matrix transformation:

```
out vec3 vMCposition;
```

```
void main( )
{
   vMCposition  = aVertex.xyz;
   gl_Position  = uModelViewProjectionMatrix * aVertex;
}
```

The fragment shader shown below does all the work. Because the x coordinates go from −1 to 1, and the required s texture coordinates go from 0 to 1, the linear mapping is

$$s = \frac{x+1}{2}.$$

The same mapping applies to y and z to create the t and p texture coordinates. Once we have the s-t-p texture coordinates, we can look up the data value at this location, which is then used to set the color for this fragment.

```
const float SMIN =    0.;
const float SMAX = 100.;

uniform int    uTexUnit;
uniform float uMin, uMax;

in  vec3 vMCposition;

out vec4 fFragColor;

void
main( )
{
   vec3 stp = ( vMCposition + 1. ) / 2.; // maps [-1.,1.] to
                                         // [0.,1.]
   vec4 rgba = texture( uTexUnit, stp );
   float scalar = rgba.r;

   if( scalar < uMin )
      discard;

   if( scalar > uMax )
      discard;

   float t = ( scalar - SMIN ) / ( SMAX - SMIN );
   vec3 rgb = Rainbow( t );

   fFragColor = vec4( rgb, 1. );
}
```

Notice the use of the `Rainbow( )` function. This sets up the transfer function that defines the mapping between each scalar value and its assigned color. Routines like this are often written to accept a normalized input, in this case the variable called t. The value of t is 0 when the scalar value is a minimum and 1 when it is a maximum. In this way, the color mapping routine does not need to know anything about the nature of the scalar values. We cover transfer functions in more detail later in this chapter.

Figure 15.9. Culling dots based on scalar value.

Also notice the use of the uniform variables `uMin` and `uMax` in the fragment shader. They are assigned by sliders in the *glman* user interface, and are used to cull the display based on data values. In the image in Figure 15.9, the smallest values in the dataset have been culled.

This isn't a visualization book, but as we discuss visualization shaders, we need to talk about some fundamental visualization concepts. A disadvantage of the uniform point cloud is that it can create severe display artifacts. In orthographic projection mode, sometimes the dots line up, creating the "row of corn problem." In perspective projection mode, the alignment creates annoying (but often interesting) Moiré patterns. These two kinds of artifact are shown in Figure 15.10.

What can you do to avoid these artifacts? A common answer is to use a different type of point cloud, known as a *jitter cloud*. In a jitter cloud, the dots are randomly shifted by small amounts in x, y, and z, and the data values

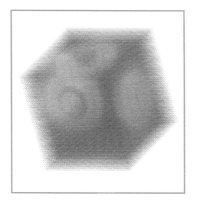
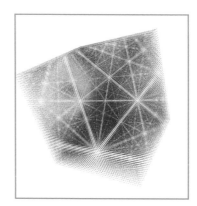

Figure 15.10. Artifacts in uniform point clouds; the "row of corn" problem, left, and Moiré patterns (right).

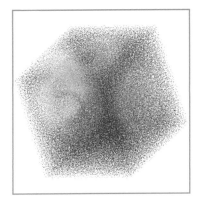 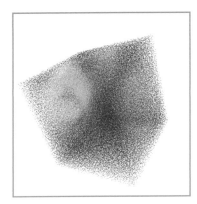

Figure 15.11. A JitterCloud display in orthographic (left) and perspective (right) projection.

are reinterpolated to those new points. To support this approach, *glman* has another GLIB file geometry option:

JitterCloud 50 50 50

In *glman*, a jitter cloud has its points (and thus its texture stp coordinates) perturbed. Results from using a JitterCloud in orthographic and perspective are shown in Figure 15.11. These are exactly the same as those in Figure 15.10, except for the jittercloud change. Note that the data values at the perturbed points are correct because they are looked up in the data texture based on their coordinates.

Another useful technique is to use the fragment shader's knowledge of the data values it is seeing to alter the appearance of the dots by changing

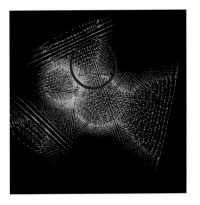 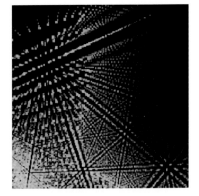

Figure 15.12. Changing a point's size to emphasize its scalar value.

their size. This is done by setting the gl_PointSize variable in the fragment shader. Setting this value has the same effect as calling the OpenGL function glPointSize( ). This allows you to emphasize data points with large data values by making them more visible. An example of doing this is shown in Figure 15.12.

Cutting Planes

Now that we have created this 3D texture of data values, is there anything else we can do with it? Yes! One of the most useful ways to visualize 3D data is with *cutting planes*. When you pass a cutting plane through a 3D dataset, you focus on specific planes of interest and leave out other areas that you don't care about right now. Also, a cutting plane display is a lot less cluttered than a point cloud.

There are two kinds of cutting planes. In one, you interpolate data values (and thus colors) at each pixel, and in the other, you create contour lines at a reduced set of pixels. As before, the color interpolation approach requires some sort of geometry to hang the data on. In this case, we will use the *glman* QuadXY primitive, which draws a quadrilateral in the X-Y plane from [−1,−1] to [1,1], by default at $z = 0$ (although we will change the z location with a slider). The vertex shader reads a z value from a slider uniform variable and sets up the model coordinates of the quadrilateral to be interpolated through the rasterizer:

```
uniform float uZ;

out vec3     vMCposition;

void main( )
{
   vMCposition     = aVertex.xyz;
   vMCposition.z = uZ;      // slide the cutting plane in Z
   gl_Position     = uModelViewProjectionMatrix*
                   vec4(vMCposition,1.);
}
```

The fragment shader uses those model coordinates to determine where each fragment is in texture coordinate space. This process reuses much of the fragment code from the *pointcloud* shader:

```
const float SMIN =   0.;
const float SMAX = 100.;
```

```glsl
uniform sampler2D   uTexUnit;
uniform float uMin, uMax;

in vec3   vMCposition;

out vec4 fFragColor;

void main( )
{
    vec3 stp = ( vMCposition + 1. ) / 2.;
    // maps [-1.,1.] to [0.,1.]

    if( any(    lessThan( stp, vec3(0.,0.,0.) ) ) )
        discard;

    if( any( greaterThan( stp, vec3(1.,1.,1.) ) ) )
        discard;

    float scalar = texture( uTexUnit, stp ).r;

    if( scalar < uMin )
        discard;

    if( scalar > uMax )
        discard;

    float t = ( scalar - SMIN ) / ( SMAX - SMIN );
    vec3 rgb = Rainbow( t );

    fFragColor = vec4( rgb, 1. );
}
```

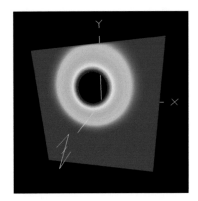

Figure 15.13. Interpolated color cutting plane.

Using the same 3D dataset as before, this process produces an image like that shown in Figure 15.13.

Notice the use of the `lessThan( )`, `greaterThan( )`, and `any ( )` functions. This also could have been expressed, equally correctly, as

```glsl
if( stp.s < 0. || stp.s > 1. )
    discard;

if( stp.t < 0. || stp.t > 1. )
    discard;

if( stp.p < 0. || stp.p > 1. )
    discard;
```

but that code would not have been able to exploit the inherent parallelism of the GPU.

Now, let's change the fragment shader to create contour lines. There are geometric ways to create contour lines with real OpenGL line segments, but for this example, we will use almost the same fragment shader code as we did above. Let's say we want contour regions at each 10 degrees of temperature. Then the main difference in the shader will be that we need to find how close each fragment's interpolated scalar data value is to an even multiple of 10. To do this, we say

```
float scalar10 = float( 10*int( (scalar+5.)/10. ) );
if( abs( scalar - scalar10 ) > uTol )
   discard;
```

Notice that this uses a uniform variable called uTol, which is read from a slider and has a range of 1 to 5. uTol is used to determine how close to an even multiple of 10 degrees we will accept, and thus how thick we want the contours to be. Various values for uTol produce the individual images in Figure 15.14.

Take a close look at what this fragment-based approach to contours gets you compared with a line-based approach. Notice that the contours have different thicknesses. This is an indication of how much area was within uTol of a 10-degree value. In addition to what the contour lines usually tell us, this type of display also lets us see how fast the data field is changing, i.e., the gradient. Thus, we can tell that the data is changing slower at the blue areas than at the red areas. This two-pieces-of-information-for-the-price-of-one-display feature is always appreciated in visualization.

 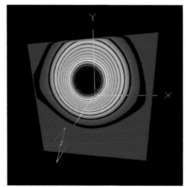 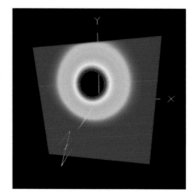

Figure 15.14. Contour lines using uTol values of 1, 4, and 5.

Also, notice that when uTol = 5., the uTol if-statement always fails, and we end up with the same display as we had with the interpolated colors. Thus, we don't actually need the separate *cutting plane* shader at all. Shaders that can do double duty are always appreciated!

It is also important to notice that the shaders maintain the mapping from the coordinates of the cutting planes to the texture coordinates that hold the data. This means that the cutting planes do not need to be oriented parallel to principal axes, but can be rotated into any orientation. It also means that the cutting geometry does not need to be a plane at all. It can be any shape for which you can produce the coordinates-to-texture mapping.

Volume Probe

Sometimes a cutting plane is too restrictive, that is, it is thin and flat. What if we want to map a colored representation of the scalar data to something that is not so thin and flat? What if we want to map it instead to something that is 3D? A variation on the cutting plane is to pass a 3D object through the scene and map data values to it. This called a *volume probe*. This technique uses a simple vertex shader and does most of its work in the fragment shader. The vertex shader, shown below, keeps track of the eye coordinates of each vertex.

```
out vec4 vECposition;

void main( )
{
    vECposition = uModelViewMatrix   * aVertex;
    gl_Position = uModelViewProjectionMatrix * aVertex;
}
```

The eye coordinates are then interpolated through the rasterizer, converted to *s-t-p* texture coordinates by the fragment shader, and finally looked up in the data texture. A fragment shader that does this is shown below.

```
const float SMIN =   0.;
const float SMAX = 120.;

uniform float     uMin, uMax;
uniform sampler3D uTexUnit;

in vec4   vECposition;

out vec4 fFragColor;
```

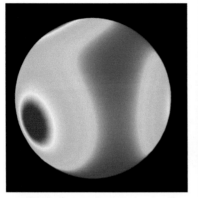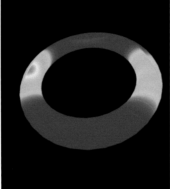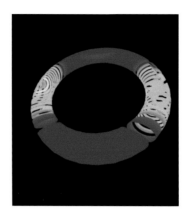

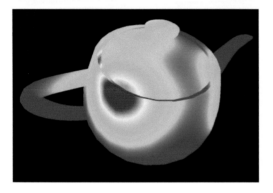

Figure 15.15. Volume probes through the 3D data-set: sphere, torus, torus with pixels discarded around even multiples of 10, and teapot, as was also shown in Figure 15.14.

```
void main( )
{
   vec3 stp = clamp( ( vECposition.xyz + 1. ) / 2.,  0., 1. );

   float scalar = texture( uTexUnit, stp ).r;

   if( scalar < uMin )
      discard;

   if( scalar > uMax )
      discard;

   float t = ( scalar - SMIN ) / ( SMAX - SMIN );
   vec3 rgb = Rainbow( t );

   fFragColor = vec4( rgb, 1. );
}
```

Of course, some choices of probe geometry make more sense than others. Two examples of volume probes are shown in Figure 15.15.

Direct Volume Rendering

So far, we have been visualizing 3D volumetric data with reduced geometry—
3D points or 2D planes. What if we want to peer into the *entire* volume at once?
This is known as *direct volume rendering*. There are a number of ways to do this.
One of the most common is to create many parallel interpolated color cutting
planes and composite (blend) them back-to-front. This works well as long as
you keep two things in mind:

1. As the eye moves, the planes need to be reoriented to always be perpendicular to the viewing direction, so that you never see the sides of a
   plane.
2. If you want OpenGL to do the compositing for you, you must draw the
   planes scene-back-to-scene-front, relative to the eye position, regardless
   of how the scene is oriented.

Instead of using that technique, we will describe a ray-casting approach,
because it's a more interesting use of shaders. Once again, we will use dummy
quadrilaterals, not because we want to display quadrilaterals, but because we
want to compute some display colors and need a place to put them. We position six quadrilaterals, looking like a cube, all one unit away from the origin, to
become the faces on which we will display the resulting fragments.

So envision the process this way. The volume data is in a 3D texture,
which you can think of as being bounded by the six quadrilaterals.[1] You are sitting on an arrow at one of the 3D fragments. Your task is to "fly" through the 3D
volume texture in a straight line, compositing colors as you go. You will paint
the final composited color onto the fragment at which you started your flight.

Starting at each fragment, we then need to choose a ray-casting direction.
We will start by choosing it in eye coordinates and will then convert it to texture coordinates, so that we can "fly" through the 3D texture. If we are using
an orthographic (parallel) projection, producing this direction is easy. Because
we are viewing the scene from the front, the direction will be (0, 0, −1) for all
fragments. If we are using a perspective projection, the tracing direction will
be a vector from the eye through the fragment being processed. We will use the
vertex shader to compute this vector for each vertex being processed, and then
let the rasterizer interpolate those vectors into each fragment.

---

[1] This is only a loose analogy. The quadrilaterals, and thus the fragments, are in the 3D world coordinate system. The volume data scalar values are in texture coordinates. We are going to force the
data volume inside the quadrilaterals with an equation that relates the quadrilaterals' [−1.,+1.] world
space to the texture coordinates' [0.,1.] space. Even though the quadrilaterals and the 3D volume
texture are in two different coordinate spaces, it is useful to think of them as being in the same space
with an equation that connects them.

After being multiplied by the ModelView matrix, each vertex lives in the Eye Coordinate space in which the viewer's eye position has been transformed to (0,0,0). We convert both the eye and the vertex coordinates into texture space like this:

```
vec4 vxyz = uModelViewMatrix*aVertex;    // vertex -> eye coords
vec3 vstp = ( vxyz.xyz + 1. ) / 2.;   // vertex -> tex coords
vec3 eye  = ( vec3(0.,0.,0.) + 1. ) / 2.; // eye -> tex coords
```

So, a vector from the eye through the vertex will be

```
stpvec = vstp - eye;
```

Depending on how the volume has been rotated and translated, `vstp` and `eye` could be well outside the range [0.,1.], even though they are supposed to be in texture coordinates. This is OK. We really aren't going to use their values, except to get the vector between them, which we will eventually scale to something smaller.

Now comes the tricky part. The vertex shader, shown below, takes its scene rotation from the ModelView matrix. It uses this in two ways. It rotates the cube quadrilaterals forward. This makes sense—we want the faces of the volume to appear to rotate.

But the tricky part is that the vertex shader also rotates the casting direction *backward*. Why is this? When we rotate the volume, we want it to appear that the 3D data texture is rotating along with the cube faces. But in OpenGL, textures themselves don't transform; only the texture coordinates do. Fortunately, transforming the texture is the inverse of transforming the texture coordinates. So, if you want to make it look like the data texture is rotating forward, you need to transform its texture coordinates backward. Since the casting direction is in texture coordinate space, its coordinates must be changed by the inverse of the desired texture transformation. In GLSL, to rotate the casting direction backward, we multiply it by the inverse of the ModelView matrix, encoded in the `mat4` variable, `uModelViewMatrixInverse`. This multiplication is operating on a vector, which has direction and magnitude, but no position. So, during that multiplication, we force the `w` component of the casting direction to be zero, so that we don't pick up any of the `uModelViewMatrixInverse` translations.

The longest possible flight path through the 3D data texture is from corner to opposite corner, which would be $\sqrt{3}$ long in texture coordinates, so the normalized casting distance is multiplied by $\sqrt{3}$. Then `vDirSTP` is divided by `uNumSteps`, the number of steps that we want to take samples at along the cast-

ing flight path. So, now vDirSTP is how much s, t, and p will change with each
casting step in the fragment shader's flight path.

```
const float SQRT3 = 1.73205; // longest path through a volume
                             // that is 1x1x1 in texture coords

uniform int  uNumSteps;    // # of steps to take through the
                           // volume

out vec3   vSTP0;       // starting location in texture coords
out vec3   vDirSTP;     // tracing step in texture coords

void main( )
{
    vSTP0 = (aVertex.xyz + 1.)/2.; // Convert [-1.,+1.]->[0.,1.]

    // leave the STP alone, rotate the position forward,
    // rotate the Dir backward

    vec3 stpvec;     // the vector to take through the volume
                     // in texture coords

    if( <<we're using orthographic projection >> )
        stpvec = vec3( 0., 0., -1. );   // all point in the
                                        // same direction

    if( <<we're using perspective projection >> )
    { vec4 vxyz = uModelViewMatrix * aVertex;
        // where this vertex is in eye space
      vec3 vstp = ( vxyz.xyz + 1. ) / 2.;
        // where the vertex is in texture coords
      vec3 eye = ( vec3(0.,0.,0.) + 1. ) / 2.;
        // where the eye is in texture coords
      stpvec = vstp - eye;
        // in perspective, the direction is a vector from
        // the eye to the vertex
    }

    vDirSTP = normalize( (uModelViewMatrixInverse *
                              vec4(stpvec, 0.) );
    vDirSTP *= SQRT3;
    vDirSTP /= float(uNumSteps);

    gl_Position = uModelViewProjectionMatrix * aVertex;
}
```

The fragment shader is where all the interesting graphics happens. Its arrow starts "flying" at the rotated model coordinate position of its fragment and steps through the

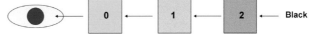

Figure 15.16. Determining the overall blending equation for multiple colored voxels.

data in the 3D volume, one vDirSTP at a time. If a step takes it outside the volume, it ignores that value. At each step, it samples the data from the 3D texture. Each of these samples is like a pixel with thickness, and so is called a *volume element*, or *voxel*. If that scalar value is outside the desired [Min,Max] range, the fragment shader doesn't discard the fragment as we did before, but sets the alpha value to 0. to indicate that this voxel makes no contribution to the final blended color along this flight path. Otherwise, it sets the alpha value to some value read from a *glman* slider variable.[2] If this voxel does make a contribution to the final blended color, the scalar value from the 3D volume texture is converted into an RGB color, in this case using a rainbow scale color transfer function.

The fragment shader composites data colors, as shown in Figure 15.16.

While the fragment shader will do the compositing front-to-back, it is more intuitive to derive the equations by looking at the situation from back-to-front. For the simple three-voxel example above, let's see what color will ultimately get displayed in this fragment, by breaking each step into its own equation. The arrow starts at the back of the volume, in this case voxel #2. It uses voxel #2's alpha value to blend the black background color with voxel #2's own color. It then moves forward and uses voxel #1's alpha value to blend the current color with voxel #1's own color. It then moves forward and continues the process:

$$color_{12} = \alpha_2 * color_2 + (1 - \alpha_2) * black,$$

$$color_{01} = \alpha_1 * color_1 + (1 - \alpha_1) * color_{12},$$

$$color^* = \alpha_0 * color_0 + (1 - \alpha_0) * color_{01},$$

We can algebraically combine these equations into one equation, like this:

$$
\begin{aligned}
color^* &= \alpha_0 * color_0 + (1 - \alpha_0) * \{color_{01}\} \\
&= \alpha_0 * color_0 + (1 - \alpha_0) * \{\alpha_1 * color_1 + (1 - \alpha_1) * [color_{12}]\} \\
&= \alpha_0 * color_0 + (1 - \alpha_0) * \{\alpha_1 * color_1 + (1 - \alpha_1) * [\alpha_2 * color_2 + (1 - \alpha_2) * black]\}.
\end{aligned}
$$

---

2. Using one alpha value for all voxels is a concession to keeping this code segment small and readable. Normally, you would get the proper alpha as a function of the scalar value to reflect what data ranges you are most interested in seeing.

Expanding everything gives

$$\text{color}^* = \alpha_0 * \text{color}_0 + (1 - \alpha_0)\, \alpha_1 * \text{color}_1 + (1 - \alpha_0)(1 - \alpha_1)\, \alpha_2$$
$$* \text{color}_2 + (1 - \alpha_0)(1 - \alpha_1)\,(1 - \alpha_2)\text{black}.$$

There's a pattern here, so let's look at how this appears when we move front-to-back. The fragment shader keeps a running alpha value called α^* (astar in the code below) and a running RGB color value called color^* (cstar). The variable α^* is the transparency factor that the next voxel's contribution will be multiplied by, and color^* is the combined color so far. These get updated with every step taken. The final value of color^* is then displayed at that fragment.

Why do it front-to-back when back-to-front seems more intuitive? The reason is that we can usually obtain significant time savings this way. If α^* ever becomes 0., this means that the arrow has encountered a completely opaque voxel and, thus, no data beyond that point will count toward the final color, so the code can safely break out of the loop. This may not sound like much, but over the course of thousands of fragments and hundreds of steps at each fragment, it can really add up!

```
const float SMIN =   0.;
const float SMAX = 120.;

uniform float      uMin;
uniform float      uMax;
uniform sampler3D uTexUnit;
uniform float      uTol;
uniform int        uNumSteps;
uniform float      uAmax;

in vec3        vSTP0;      // starting texture location
in vec3        vDirSTP;   // tracing step

out vec4       fFragColor;

void main( )
{
   float astar = 1.;
   vec3  cstar = vec3( 0., 0., 0. );
   vec3  STP   = vSTP0;

   for( int i = 0; i < uNumSteps; i++, STP += vDirSTP )
   {
      // keep looping if we're out of bounds:

      if( any(    lessThan( STP, vec3(0.,0.,0.) ) ) )
```

```
            continue;

        if( any( greaterThan( STP, vec3(1.,1.,1.) ) ) ) )
            continue;

        float scalar = texture( uTexUnit, STP ).r;

        float alpha = uAmax;

        if( scalar < uMin )
            alpha = 0.;

        if( scalar > uMax )
            alpha = 0.;

        float t = ( scalar - SMIN ) / ( SMAX - SMIN );
        vec3 rgb = Rainbow( t ); // transfer functions like this
                                 // will be covered in the next
                                 // section

        cstar += astar * alpha * rgb;
        astar *= ( 1. - alpha );

        // break out if the rest of the tracing won't matter:

        if( astar == 0. )
            break;
    }

    fFragColor = vec4( cstar, 1. );
}
```

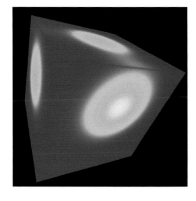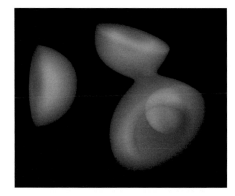

Figure 15.17. The data volume shown with all colors present (left) and with the lower values culled and a reduced alpha (right).

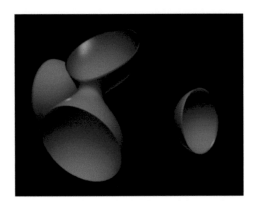

Figure 15.18. Isosurface.

Figure 15.17 shows the results of this shader. In the left-hand image, uMin and uMax are set to show all data values. Because you are looking at everything, some key parts of the volume might be obscured. It would then be very helpful if you cull away the values you really have no interest in. In the right-hand image, the low (blue) values have been culled, giving us a much better view of the shape of the middle-to-high values.

This same shader can be modified to produce isosurfaces as well. An isosurface is the locus of points corresponding to a specific scalar value in the volume, referred to as S*. All you have to do is change the volume rendering fragment shader to consider, in its march through the volume, only the first scalar value that is within a certain tolerance of S*. An example of this is shown in Figure 15.18. The actual code to do this is left as an exercise. (You knew that was coming, right?)

More on Transfer Functions

The mapping of a scalar value to its color was introduced in Chapter 8. This mapping was glossed over in the shaders that we discussed earlier in this chapter with the call to the Rainbow( ) routine. We should now look closer

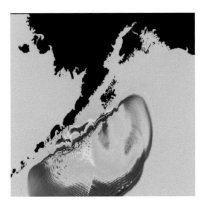

Figure 15.19. Two different transfer functions applied to tsunami data off the coast of the Aleutian Peninsula in Alaska. (Image courtesy of Chris Janik.)

at this. The mapping of data values to appearance (i.e., color and transparency) is known as a *color mapping*, and in the visualization world, the function that applies this mapping is more generally called a *transfer function*, *color map*, or *color ramp*. The appropriate use of transfer functions is a very important issue. By using different transfer functions, you can create very different mental models of patterns in the data.

Same data + different mapping = different insights.

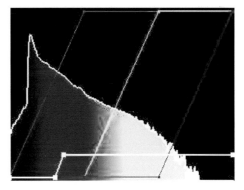

Figure 15.20. Red, green, blue, and alpha transfer function with the colors applied to a data histogram.

For example, in the tsunami wave simulation display in Figure 15.19, the patterns in the data come across quite differently, depending on the color mapping.

Often, visualization programs have a user interface for sculpting a transfer function. An example of such a sculpted function is shown in Figure 15.20. In this figure, the horizontal axis represents the range of scalar values. The red, green, and blue lines show how those color components change with respect to scalar value (in this case implementing a heated object scale). The white line is how alpha changes with respect to scalar value. The background shows a histogram of the data value frequency.[3]

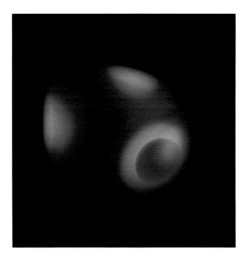

Figure 15.21. Previously seen volume with a different transfer function.

Figure 15.21 shows how the temperature distribution point cloud of Figure 15.8 looks with the heated object transfer function instead of the rainbow scale.

If you do not have a user interface for sculpting a transfer function, you can easily write your own transfer function. The sources for functions that implement the rainbow transfer function and the heated-object transfer function are shown here:

3. Actually, we usually use the *logarithm* of the frequency, because often some of the data values, especially the lowest values, occur much more often than all the others. Without the log function, the other values would scarcely be visible on the same set of axes. Many visualization programs have a similar looking user interface for sculpting a transfer function.

```
vec3
Rainbow( float t )
{
    t = clamp( t, 0., 1. );

// b -> c
    vec3 rgb = vec3( 0., 4. * ( t - (0./4.) ), 1. );

    // c -> g
    if( t >= (1./4.) )
        rgb = vec3( 0., 1., 1. - 4. * ( t - (1./4.) ) );

    // g -> y
    if( t >= (2./4.) )
        rgb = vec3( 4. * ( t - (2./4.) ), 1., 0. );

    // y -> r
    if( t >= (3./4.) )
        rgb = vec3( 1., 1. - 4. * ( t - (3./4.) ), 0. );

    return rgb;
}

vec3
HeatedObject( float t )
{
    t = clamp( t, 0., 1. );

    vec3 rgb = vec3( 3. * ( t - (0./6.) ), 0., 0. );

    if( t >= (1./3.) )
    {
        rgb.rg = vec2( 1., 3. * ( t - (1./3.) ) );
    }

    if( t >= (2./3.) )
    {
        rgb.gb = vec2( 1., 3. * ( t - (2./3.) ) );
    }

    return rgb;
}
```

Figure 15.22 shows a gallery of common themes for color transfer functions. Left to right and going down the gallery, these themes and some of their common uses are described in Table 15.1.

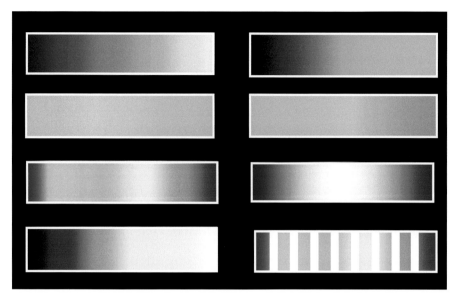

Figure 15.22. A gallery of color mappings.

Color Mapping	Comments
Grayscale	Black on one end and white on the other. It is simple and unambiguous. An example use is in x-rays.
Brightness	Black on one end and a solid color on the other.
Saturation	Gray on one end and a solid color on the other. Sometimes this is used to represent the validity or confidence of the data. The grayest areas are the areas of least confidence.
Two-color	Interpolation between multiple colors. This is often used on maps to show transitions from, say, desert to vegetation.
Rainbow	Mimics the visible portion of the electromagnetic spectrum. This is very common to anyone who learned the ROYGBIV color mnemonic in grade school.
Two-color with a neutral crossing	Common where crossing from one side to the other needs to convey a sense of neutrality, such as electrical charge in a molecule.
Heated object	The range of colors that you would see if you continuously heated a piece of metal. It goes from black to red to yellow to white. Star temperatures work this way too.
Contours	Involves artificially adding a set of lines into a color scale. This then shows up in your data as a set of contour lines.

Table 15.1. Some common color mappings and their common meanings.

For more examples, see [14], where transfer functions are called *color ramps* and are discussed in some detail.

In the example shown in Figure 15.20, the fragment shader has taken a data value from the 3D texture and applied the transfer function before displaying it. But wouldn't it just be easier to set the colors when the 3D texture was first created and then read them directly from the texture? After all, this would avoid a lot of per-fragment computation, wouldn't it?

While this would work, there are two reasons we don't like to do it this way:

1. It forces us to recreate the 3D color texture every time we want to change the transfer function.
2. The graphics color interpolation can turn out wrong.

The first reason is pretty obvious. By passing raw data through the graphics pipeline, the fragment shader can instantly start using a new color transfer function, depending on the value of an integer uniform variable. The input 3D data texture never changes.

But the second reason is more subtle, and has to do with how the graphics system interpolates through the rasterizer. Suppose we want to display a heated metal bar that has a temperature of 0° at the left end and a temperature of 100º at the right, as shown in Figure 15.23.

Figure 15.23. A bar with endpoints of different temperatures.

Figure 15.24. The bar above, but with a rainbow scale from left to right.

Figure 15.25. The bar above, but with colors interpolated from the end colors.

Now suppose we want to use a rainbow scale, so that the left end is blue, the right end is red, and the locations in between are colored as in Figure 15.24.

But suppose we take the naïve approach and draw the bar as a single quadrilateral with blue at the left end and red at the right end, drawing the bar using OpenGL smooth shading. Figure 15.25 shows what we would get. You see that you have no control over what lies between the two ends.

Because OpenGL interpolates each color component separately, it has no way to get the rainbow scale. In interpolating the left (r,g,b) to the right (r,g,b), the red component would go from 0 to 1, the green component would always be 0, and the blue component would go from 1 to 0. But if, instead, the temperatures at the corners were given as variables to be interpolated, then the interpolated *temperatures* throughout the quadrilateral could be mapped to colors using your transfer function in the fragment shader, exactly as you wanted.

Passing in Data Values with Your Geometry

So far we have dealt with data values that are just sort of "there" and have created artificial underlying geometry in order to view them. But there are a multitude of visualization problems in which data is attached to a very specific underlying geometry. How do we end up with the right colors being displayed on the geometry as easily and as efficiently as possible? How would we know if the colors chosen for Figure 15.26 are right?

The first approach is the non-shader way of doing things with fixed-function OpenGL. It amounts to doing the color mapping in the CPU part of the application and using the rasterizer to interpolate the colors. This is probably clearest if we use compatibility mode to describe the geometry:

```
glBegin( GL_QUADS );
   < convert s0 to r0,g0,b0,a0 >
   glColor4f( r0, g0, b0, a0 );
   glVertex3f( x0, y0, z0 );
   . . .
glEnd( );
```

Figure 15.26. Example of assigning a scalar value and its corresponding color, per vertex. being drawn. (Image courtesy of Chris Janik.)

This approach has worked for a long time with more or less success, but for the reasons just discussed, it is not as good as it could be. The next approach passes the original value with the vertex, rather than converting it to a vertex color. This takes advantage of the GLSL attribute variables, which can be attached to vertices and interpolated through the rasterizer:

```
glBegin( GL_QUADS );
  glVertexAttrib1f( location, s0 );
  glVertex3f( x0, y0, z0 );
  . . .
glEnd( );
```

This ends up giving the fragment program the actual data values, which can then be mapped into colors with the transfer function. Because there are actually several different attribute-setting glVertexAttrib* routines, several data values can be passed in for each vertex.

A variation on this approach is to be a little sneaky. You can also pass the scalar data value in with one call to glVertex4f( ):

```
glBegin( GL_QUADS );
  glVertex4f( x0, y0, z0, s0 );
  . . .
glEnd( );
```

Normally the fourth element of glVertex4f( ) is defined to be the homogeneous coordinate, w. In this case, though, we have used the fourth element to hold the scalar value at this vertex. However, the graphics pipeline still wants that element to be the homogeneous w when the coordinates are multiplied by the ModelView and Projection matrices, so the first thing we need to do in the vertex shader is to re-assign it to a varying variable and replace the w coordinate with something sensible:

```
out float vScalar;

void main( )
{
  ...
  vScalar     = aVertex.w;
  gl_Position =uModelViewProjectionMatrix*vec4(aVertex.xyz, 1.);
}
```

Terrain Bump-Mapping

Terrain mapping is a visualization use of the height-field bump-mapping we've seen before. Like the ripple bump-map shader we saw before, the idea is to create the illusion of lots more geometry detail than we really have. In fact, like the ripple example, the entire geometry is typically a single quad.

The geometry is a square quad, scaled to match the aspect ratio of the real terrain area. That part of the .glib file looks like this:

```
Scale  1.2569  1.  1.
QuadXY  .1  1.
```

This code shows the vertex shader. It sets up two variables for the fragment shader: the texture coordinates and the model coordinate position. The texture coordinates will be used to look up the terrain heights in a texture map. The model coordinates will be used for lighting. (We use model coordinates for lighting because we assume that, in the case of terrain, the light moves, but the geometry doesn't.)

```
out vec3    vMCposition;
out vec2    vST;

void main( )
{
    vST = aTexCoord0.st;
    vMCposition = aVertex.xyz;
    gl_Position = aModelViewProjectionMatrix * aVertex;
}
```

This code shows the fragment shader. The heights are sampled from a data texture. Like the ripple shader, it generates a normal by taking the cross product of two tangent vectors. It uses the normal in a lighting model that applies to a color that is selected based on elevation. The results of this shader, with two different height exaggerations, are shown in Figure 15.27.

```
uniform float    uLightX, uLightY, uLightZ; // light pos
uniform float    uExag;      // height exaggeration
uniform sampler2D uHgtUnit;  // where to find heights
uniform float    uLevel1;    // green-to-brown
uniform float    uLevel2;    // brown-to-white
uniform float    uTol;       // soften the transition

in vec3    vMCposition;
```

```glsl
in vec2       vST;

out vec4       fFragColor;

const float DELTA =    0.001;

const vec3 BLUE  =  vec3( 0.1, 0.1, 0.5 );
const vec3 GREEN =  vec3( 0.0, 0.8, 0.0 );
const vec3 BROWN =  vec3( 0.6, 0.3, 0.1 );
const vec3 WHITE =  vec3( 1.0, 1.0, 1.0 );

const float LNGMIN = -579240./2.;
const float LNGMAX =  579240./2.;
const float LATMIN = -419949./2.;
const float LATMAX =  419949./2.;

const float HGTMAX =  2891;

#define FP_TEXTURE  // if we are using a floating point texture
       // to contain the elevations, instead of a byte-texture

void main( )
{
  vec2 stp0 = vec2( DELTA,  0. );
  vec2 st0p = vec2( 0.   ,  DELTA );

  float west  =  texture( uHgtUnit, vST-stp0 ).r;
  float east  =  texture( uHgtUnit, vST+stp0 ).r;
  float south =  texture( uHgtUnit, vST-st0p ).r;
  float north =  texture( uHgtUnit, vST+st0p ).r;

#ifndef FP_TEXTURE
  west  *= HGTMAX;
  east  *= HGTMAX;
  south *= HGTMAX;
  north *= HGTMAX;
#endif

  vec3 stangent = vec3( 2.*DELTA*(LNGMAX-LNGMIN), 0.,
             uExag * ( east - west ) );
  vec3 ttangent = vec3( 0., 2.*DELTA*(LATMAX-LATMIN),
             uExag * ( north - south ) );
  vec3 normal = normalize(  cross( stangent, ttangent )  );
  float LightIntensity  =
   (dot(normalize(vec3(uLightX,uLightY,uLightZ)-
                      vMCposition),normal));
  if( LightIntensity < 0.1 )
    LightIntensity = 0.1;
```

```
    float here = texture( uHgtUnit, vST ).r;
#ifndef FP_TEXTURE
    here *= HGTMAX;
#endif
    vec3 color = BLUE;
    if( here > 0. )
    {
        float t = smoothstep( uLevel1-uTol, uLevel1+uTol, here );
        color = mix( GREEN, BROWN, t );
    }
    if( here > uLevel1+uTol )
    {
        float t = smoothstep( uLevel2-uTol, uLevel2+uTol, here );
        color = mix( BROWN, WHITE, t );
    }
    fFragColor = vec4( LightIntensity*color, 1. );
}
```

We need to talk a little more about the elevation data-texture. Every so often, you see a line that looks like this:

```
#ifndef FP_TEXTURE
```

In our case, we hid the elevations in an OpenGL floating-point texture. This is a handy way to do it, because you can store the elevations exactly as their actual decimal values. When you sample that texture, you get correct values back out. However, some graphics systems cannot handle float-point textures, or handle them slowly. In that case, you would store the eleva-

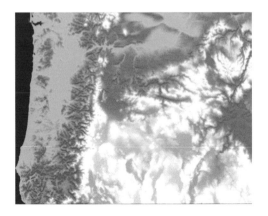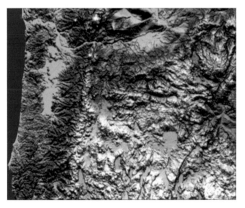

Figure 15.27. Terrain map of Oregon, USA. Height exaggeration = 1. (left) and 5. (right)

Figure 15.28. Zooming on the Willamette Valley, Oregon, USA.

tions in an unsigned-byte texture, but in doing so, you would first need to quantize the entire range of heights into the range 0–255. When GLSL samples this type of texture, it returns a range of 0. (corresponding to the unsigned byte 0) to 1. (corresponding to 255). To un-quantize these elevations, they must be multiplied by the maximum height. By using pre-processor directives, this shader code can handle it both ways.

As we discussed before, one of the great things about bump-mapping is that it is performed per-pixel. This means that as you zoom in, you just keep sampling the elevation texture finer and finer. In this example, we used a 2048 × 1152 texture, so we are able to zoom in quite a bit, as shown in Figure 15.28.[4]

Flow Visualization

Flow visualization is a common problem in scientific visualization that arises when simulating moving fluids or particles. In these cases, it is useful to show the paths that are being taken as the fluid or particles move through the volume.

2D Line Integral Convolution

Cabral and Leedom were the first to demonstrate the *line integral convolution* (LIC) technique [6] that smears the pixels of an image in the direction of a 2D flow field and thus shows the entire flow field at a glance. This algorithm can be implemented well in a fragment shader. Typically, this fragment shader takes two input image textures, one for the base image and one that has had the flow field function encoded in it. Let's look at this base image texture first.

The base image is going to be smeared in the direction of the flow at each pixel. We almost don't care what this base image is. It is usually white noise, but it can also be your favorite personal photo as well. The biggest concern is that there are no distinct patterns in it that might be mistaken for flow information. This is why white noise is such a good choice.

---

4. To create this texture, we wrote a software tool that takes a longitude-latitude range from the US Geological Survey National Elevation Dataset (USGS-NED) [44] and creates the .tex file.

Figure 15.29. Example color components for a 2D flow field.

The second texture is to encode the flow field. A 2D flow field has a (vx,vy) velocity component pair at every point in the field. A good way to capture this is with a 2D texture, letting the y component be represented by red and the y component by green. With floating point textures, the exact (vx,vy) can be stored in each texel's (r,g).

There is an unfortunate nuance here, though. Many graphics cards do not yet accelerate bilinear sampling of floating point textures. However, nearest-neighbor sampling of data such as a flow field often results in a very "chunky" looking display. If you are using such a graphics card, then a better solution is to represent the flow velocities in an unsigned byte texture. For example, a 2D circular flow field would be represented by a red scale that shows black for a negative x component and red for positive, and black for a negative y component and green for positive, as shown in Figure 15.29.

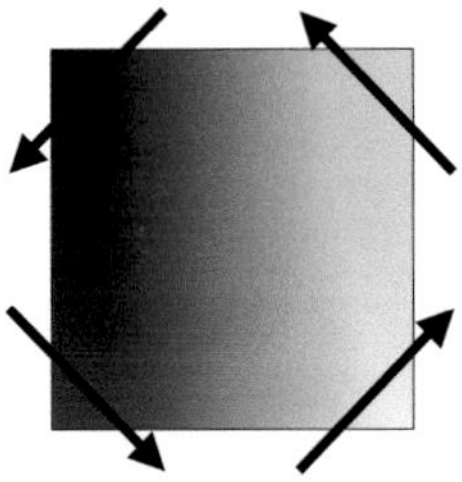

When these components are combined, the resulting 2D texture field looks like Figure 15.30. For example, the lower-right corner is yellow because it has both a positive x and y velocity component. The arrows in this figure show the direction that a circular LIC visualization would take.

In practice, we don't actually care what the texture looks like, and we rarely look at it except for fun. In fact, it is usually very difficult to tell from the image just what the flow field really is. We don't care. We just care about the data that is hiding in it.

Most of the work of LIC is in the fragment shader shown here:

Figure 15.30. Using color components to encode flow velocities.

```
uniform int uLength;
uniform sampler2D uImageUnit;
uniform sampler2D uFlowUnit;

in vec2  vST;

out vec4 fFragColor;

void main( )
{
```

```
// starting location:

vec2 v  = texture( uFlowUnit,vST ).xy;

vec3 color = vec3( texture( uImageUnit, vST ) );

vec2 st = vST;
for( int i = 0; i < uLength; i++ )
{
   st += v;
   st = clamp( st, 0., 1. );
   color += vec3( texture( uImageUnit, st ) );
}

st = vST;
for( int i = 0; i < uLength; i++ )
{
   st -= v;
   st = clamp( st, 0., 1. );
   color += vec3( texture( uImageUnit, st ) );
}

color /= float(uLength + uLength + 1);   // divide by # of
                                         // samples
fFragColor = vec4( color, 1. );
}
```

Figure 15.31 shows how this fragment shader works when applied to a noise image.

Figure 15.31. The circular LIC applied to a noise image. Left: length = 0 (the original image). Right: length = 50.

3D Line Integral Convolution

The same process can be used in 3D. Here, we have generated a 3D positional noise texture and a floating point 3D flow texture in which the x, y, and z flow directions have been encapsulated in the r, g, and b components of the texture, simply extending the 2D approach above. Again, most of the work is done in the fragment shader:

```
uniform int       uLength;
uniform float     uTol;
uniform float     uScale;
uniform sampler3D uImageUnit;
uniform sampler3D uFlowUnit;

in vec3  vSTP;

out vec4 fFragColor;

void main( )
{
   float Res = float(  textureSize( uFlowUnit, 0 ).s  );

   // flow field direction:

   vec3 v = texture( uFlowUnit, vSTP ).xyz;
   v *= uScale;
   v /= Res;

   // starting location:

   vec3 stp = vSTP;
   vec3 color = texture( uImageUnit, stp ).rgb;

   for( int i = 0; i < uLength; i++ )
   {
      stp += v;
      stp = clamp( stp, 0., 1. );
      vec3 new = texture( uImageUnit, stp ).rgb;
      color += new;
   }

   stp = vSTP;
   for( int i = 0; i < uLength; i++ )
   {
      stp -= v;
      stp = clamp( stp, 0., 1. );
      vec3 new = texture( uImageUnit, stp ).rgb;
      color += new;
   }
```

```
    color /= float(uLength + uLength + 1);
    fFragColor = vec4( color, 1. );
}
```

The geometry used here was a 3D box, containing only noise, to show the flow field on the outside of the volume. Volume rendering techniques could (and should) be used to see inside the volume. (This is left as an exercise.) Figure 15.32 shows the resulting image for four different convolution lengths.

The flow field equation used here is flow around a corner [24]:

$$v_x = -3 + 6x - 4x(y+1) - 4z,$$
$$v_y = 12x - 4x^2 - 12z + 4z^2.$$
$$v_z = 3 + 4x - 4x(y+1) - 6z + 4(y+1)z.$$

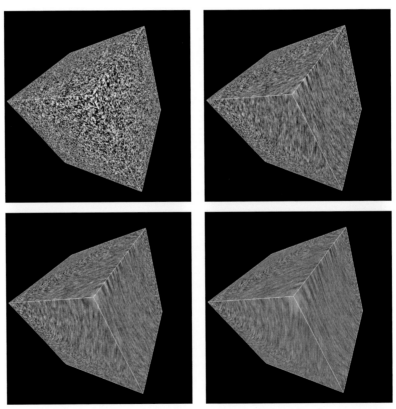

Figure 15.32. 3D line integral convolution (top left: length = 0, top right: length = 5, bottom left: length = 10, bottom right: length = 20).

Extruding Objects for Streamlines

If you place a weightless ping-pong ball in a 3D flow field and trace where it goes, the result will be a 3D streamline. Streamlines are useful in visualization because they give an animation "snapshot" of what is happening in the field and thus are good for helping viewers discern flowfield patterns. Now imagine that you are driving a small car along the streamline. The car has a direction in which it is traveling, and it feels like the centrifugal force is pushing you to the outside of the curve you are currently traveling through. There are mathematical terms for these directions. Let's name the curve you are driving on in the original flow field $P(t)$. The direction you are traveling is called the *tangent* and is denoted by $T(t)$. The direction that points to the center of the curve is the *normal*, denoted by $N(t)$, and a vector perpendicular to both of these is the *binormal*, denoted by $B(t)$. If you have the function $P(t)$ describing the curve and the function has first and second derivatives, you can get all three of these quantities with the Frenet equations:

$$T(t) = \text{normalize}(P'(t)),$$
$$B(t) = \text{normalize}(P'(t) \times P''(t)),$$
$$N(t) = B(t) \times T(t).$$

If you have a discrete series of points for the curve instead of a continuous curve, then you can still approximate $P(t)$ by treating the curve as piecewise linear or perform some other interpolation through the points. For each point on the curve, then, the parameter t is the fraction of the total distance that this point is along the combination of linear pieces.

Together, these three vectors constitute a moving coordinate system, or *frame*, along the curve. Knowing these characteristics of this curve, we can take a simple object and extrude it along the curve with the following transformation:

$$\begin{Bmatrix} x' \\ y' \\ z' \\ 1 \end{Bmatrix} = \begin{bmatrix} Tx & Nx & Bx & X \\ Ty & Ny & By & Y \\ Tz & Nz & Bz & Z \\ 0 & 0 & 0 & 1 \end{bmatrix} \begin{Bmatrix} x \\ y \\ z \\ 1 \end{Bmatrix}.$$

In this matrix, (x,y,z) are the points on the original (unwarped) object and Tx, Nx, Bx, etc., are the components of the tangent T, normal N, and binormal B that make up the coordinate frame at (X,Y,Z). The point (X,Y,Z) is the point in 3-space where we want the point (x,y,z) to be translated to after it has been reoriented.

When you apply this warp operation to a geometric object such as a cylinder, you get a representation of the path an object would take in the flow field. We call this general warped object a *streamtube*. We will show the behavior of this warp operation on the *glman* geometric arrow object defined with the command

```
Xarrow 200
```

This defines an arrow with 200 slices from left to right, aligned with the *x* axis, as shown in Figure 15.33. This large number of slices gives the arrow enough vertices for the vertex shader to produce a smooth warp.

In an application, you would normally pass in details about the flow field through a texture or other data structure. To simplify things here, we will just hard code the vertex shader to twist the arrow into a spiral. The properties of the spiral are defined by the *glman* uniform slider variables *uN* and *uK* that control the number of twists in the warped arrow and the total *x*-length of the warped arrow, respectively. Here is the vertex shader code to do this:

Figure 15.33. The original, unwarped arrow object.

```
const float R        = 2.;
const float PI       = 3.14159265;
const float TWOPI    = 2.*PI;
const float HALFWIDTH = 0.10;

uniform float uN;
uniform float uK;
uniform float uPeristaltic;
uniform float uSpeed;
uniform float Timer;

out float vColor;
out float vLightIntensity;

const vec3 LIGHTPOS = vec3( 5., 5., 10. );

void main( )
{
   vColor = aColor;

   vec3 vertex = aVertex.xyz;

   float t = ( vertex.x + 1. ) / 2.;   // change [-1.,1.]
                                       // to [0.,1.]

   float timer = fract( uSpeed*Timer );
   if( timer-HALFWIDTH <= t  &&  t <= timer+HALFWIDTH )
```

```
   {
      float mag = 1.+uPeristaltic*(1.+cos(PI*(t-timer)/
                                          HALFWIDTH) )/2.;
      vertex.yz *= vec2(mag,mag);
   }

   float x = R*cos( TWOPI*uN*t );
   float y = R*sin( TWOPI*uN*t );
   float z = uK * t;

   float xd = -R*TWOPI*uN*sin( TWOPI*uN*t );
   float yd =  R*TWOPI*uN*cos( TWOPI*uN*t );
   float zd =  uK;

   float xdd = -( TWOPI*TWOPI*uN*uN ) * x;
   float ydd = -( TWOPI*TWOPI*uN*uN ) * y;
   float zdd =  0.;

   vec3 T = normalize( vec3(xd,yd,zd) );
   vec3 B = normalize( cross( vec3(xd,yd,zd),
                              vec3(xdd,ydd,zdd) ) );
   vec3 N = normalize( cross(B,T) );

   vec3 xyz = vec3( 0., vertex.y, vertex.z );

   float xp = dot( vec3(T.x,N.x,B.x), xyz );
   float yp = dot( vec3(T.y,N.y,B.y), xyz );
   float zp = dot( vec3(T.z,N.z,B.z), xyz );

   vec3 newposition = vec3( x+xp, y+yp, z+zp );
   vec3 tpos = vec3( uModelViewMatrix *
                     vec4( newposition, 1. ) );

   float nxp = dot( T, aNormal );
   float nyp = dot( N, aNormal );
   float nzp = dot( B, aNormal );
   vec3 newnormal = vec3(nxp,nyp,nzp);
   vec3 tnorm = normalize( uNormalMatrix * newnormal );

   vLightIntensity  = dot( normalize(LIGHTPOS - tpos), tnorm );
   vLightIntensity  = abs( vLightIntensity );

   gl_Position = uModelViewProjectionMatrix *
                     vec4(newposition, 1.);
}
```

This vertex shader and a very standard fragment shader give you the warped arrow object shown in Figure 15.34.

Figure 15.34. The warped arrow.

Figure 15.35. The warped arrow with the peristaltic bulge.

You may have noticed the uniform variable called uPeristaltic. This *glman* uniform slider variable lets us create a dynamic visualization trick that's much easier to achieve with shaders. This shader uses the *glman* built-in *Timer* variable to cause part of the arrow to bulge, and the bulge travels with time. This is another example of two-pieces-of-information-for-the-price-of-one display. The full arrow shows the entire streamtube, and the moving bulge shows relative velocity, as shown in Figure 15.35. This is definitely one example worth running! It has a pig-in-the-python look to it, and is either one of the most interesting shader applications you will ever see, or one of the most disgusting.

Geometry Visualization

The GLSL geometry shader makes some additional techniques available for visualization applications. Here we discuss only two, but as the geometry shader capability becomes more widely available, we recognize that many more will be developed.

Silhouettes

Techniques for creating silhouettes were discussed earlier in Chapter 12. They are included again here because silhouettes are a valuable technique for visualizing 3D geometry. Figure 15.36 shows a carbon-50 molecule without and with silhouettes. Notice how the silhouettes make the outside edges of individual atoms a lot crisper and serve to help define the overall shape of the object.

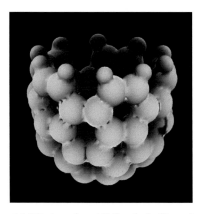 

Figure 15.36. A carbon-50 (buckyball) molecule without (left) and with (right) silhouettes.

Hedgehog Plots

The *hedgehog plot* is a visualization technique that uses a series of spikes perpendicular to a surface to give a sense of the shape of that surface. In computer graphics, we often use flat surfaces with different normals at the vertices, combined with smooth shading, to give the appearance of smooth surfaces. Using a geometry shader, we can also use the same input to create these spikes and produce a hedgehog plot of the surface.

The basic idea is shown in Figure 15.37. A triangle with separate normals at its vertices is passed to a geometry shader. The geometry shader then subdivides the triangle and interpolates the normals for each vertex in the new triangles, and also creates the line segments for the spikes. This is progressively shown from left to right as additional subdivisions are created.

   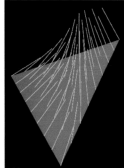

Figure 15.37. The original triangle with vertex normals (left) and with additional normals as the triangle is subdivided.

The hedgehog plot geometry shader is shown below. It takes triangles as inputs and outputs line strips. As these are single line spikes, it would be more efficient to output line segments, but these are not allowed as the output from a geometry shader. For fun, a uDroop variable has been added so that this shader can also do simple hair.

```glsl
#version 330
#extension GL_EXT_geometry_shader4: enable

layout( triangles )  in;
layout( line_strip, max_vertices=1024 )  out;

uniform int    uDetail;
uniform float uDroop;
uniform int    uLength;
uniform float uStep;

in vec3  vNormal[3];
in vec4  vColor[3];

out vec4 gColor;

vec3 Norm[3];
vec3 N0, N01, N02;
vec4 V0, V01, V02;

void
ProduceVertices( float s, float t )
{
    vec4 v = V0 + s*V01 + t*V02;
    vec3 n = normalize( N0 + s*N01 + t*N02 );

    for( int i = 0; i <= Length; i++ )
    {
        gl_Position = uProjectionMatrix * v;
        gColor = vColor[0];
        EmitVertex( );
        v.xyz += Step * n;
        v.y    -= uDroop * float(i*i);
    }
    EndPrimitive( );
}

void main( )
{
    V0  =    gl_PositionIn[0];
    V01 = ( gl_PositionIn[1] - gl_PositionIn[0] );
    V02 = ( gl_PositionIn[2] - gl_PositionIn[0] );
```

```
Norm[0] = vNormal[0];
Norm[1] = vNormal[1];
Norm[2] = vNormal[2];

if( dot( Norm[0], Norm[1] ) < 0. )
    Norm[1] = -Norm[1];

if( dot( Norm[0], Norm[2] ) < 0. )
    Norm[2] = -Norm[2];

N0  = normalize( Norm[0] );
N01 = normalize( Norm[1] - Norm[0] );
N02 = normalize( Norm[2] - Norm[0] );

int numLayers = 1 << uDetail;

float dt = 1. / float( numLayers );
float t = 1.;

for( int it = 0; it <= numLayers; it++ )
{
    float smax = 1. - t;

    int nums = it + 1;
    float ds = smax / float( nums - 1 );

    float s = 0.;
    for( int is = 0; is < nums; is++ )
    {
        ProduceVertices( s, t );
        s += ds;
    }

    t -= dt;
}
}
```

In Figure 15.38 we see the hedgehog shader applied to the cow dataset, which has normals at each vertex. You can see that indeed, when the spikes are short, they do give insight into the shape variations (for example, look at the cow's nose). Note also that each vertex has multiple spikes, corresponding to different triangles in the modeling. However, you can also see that when the normals are too long, the image turns from something insightful into a frightening Chia Pet.

 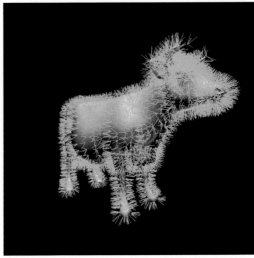

Figure 15.38. A cow's head showing detailed surface normals (left) compared with the "Chia Pet" cow (right).

Exercises

1. You have been given the Rainbow( ) and HeatedObject( ) color mapping routines. Now write: GrayScale( ), BlackGreen( ), GrayGreen( ), GreenBrown( ), BlueWhiteRed( ), and RainbowWithContours( ).

2. Sometimes it is useful to not show the scalar value as a continuous range but as a series of stepped values. This is called *quantizing*. Redo the volume tracing, but with quantized scalar values. The results should look something like the right-hand image in Figure 15.39.

3. Add a tolerance, uTol, to the *volumetrace* shader, as shown in Figure 13.40.

4. Add lighting to the volumetracing shader, as shown in Figure 15.41. Hint: to do this, you need to have surface normals, but a volume has no surface, so it shouldn't have normals. Fortunately, volume data has *pseudo-normals*, which can be used like real surface normals. You compute a pseudo-normal at a particular location by taking the gradient there,

$$\bar{n} = \left(\frac{\partial S}{\partial x}, \frac{\partial S}{\partial y}, \frac{\partial S}{\partial z} \right),$$

that is, by sampling scalar values around the point where you are now.

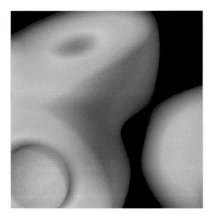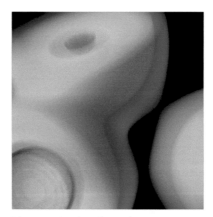

Figure 15.39. Volume rendering with quantized scalar values.

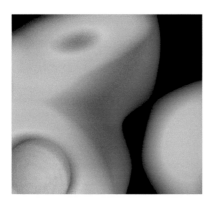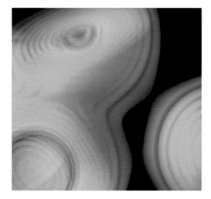

Figure 15.40. Volume rendering with tolerances on the scalar values.

Figure 15.41. Volume rendering with lighting.

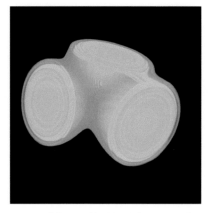 

Figure 15.42. Volume rendering with lighting and tolerances.

5. Set the tolerance in the lighted volume shader, as shown in Figure 15.42.
6. Redo the 3D line integral convolution example with a solenoid flow volume:

$$v_x = yz\left(x^2 + y^2\right),$$
$$v_y = xz\left(x^2 + z^2\right),$$
$$v_z = xy\left(x^2 + y^2\right).$$

This is shown in Figure 15.43.

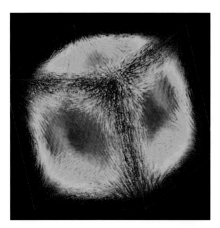 

Figure 15.43. 3D line integral convolution. (Image courtesy of Vasu Lakshmanan.)

Figure 15.44. A decimated line integral convolution. (Image courtesy of Vasu Lakshmanan.)

7. Redo the 3D line integral convolution example to perform volume rendering instead of just showing the outside of the volume.

8. Volume-rendered 3D line integral convolutions are very cluttered. Find ways to selectively decimate the volume so that the entire volume is not filled, as shown in Figures 15.43 and 15.44.

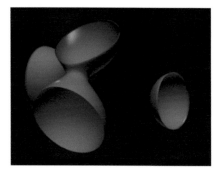

9. Adapt the direct volume rendering shader to render isosurfaces as shown in Figure 15.18, repeated above. Let the user give the S* value on a slider. Use lighting as discussed in Exercise 4 above.

16

Serious Fun

One of the great things about computer graphics is that it gives you the ability to create exciting images by simulating a number of special effects. It's a way to have fun and still convince people that you are doing serious work, which is why we have entitled this chapter "Serious Fun." We think you will find these effects to be both interesting and informative.

This chapter is something of a potpourri—or perhaps a bag of magic effects. The first area we will explore is light interference, through both a diffraction grating and an oil slick. The interaction of light with different parts of a surface creates some exciting surface effects that we explore with shaders. The next area is lenses that bend light as it passes through them, and we explore the way a lens affects our view of space by looking at lenses within a cube map. The third area is atmospheric effects and how they capture and distribute light within a scene, and we consider the familiar rainbow and the common, but perhaps less familiar, glory effect by simulating them with shaders and putting them in the context of scenes. We go on to note the various ways you can create an interesting path from zero to one and how we can manipulate motion with these techniques. Fog is next on the list, and we show how we can make fog more interesting by applying noise techniques to vary the fog's density. We then look at morphing (some might say "abusing") 3D geometry. A short excursion into a different kind of exploration gives us algorithmic art, where we operate on either pixels or texels to create some new kinds of 2D images. We then consider the concept of information in an image and explore a way we can provide information with pure motion. We close with a bang, with an explosion shader that the geometry shader makes possible. This gives you an indication of just how many things you can do with shaders, and we would love to hear from you, via the book's website, about your own creations.

Light Interference

The general concept of light interference is that two light waves can interfere with each other, reinforcing each other at times or canceling each other at

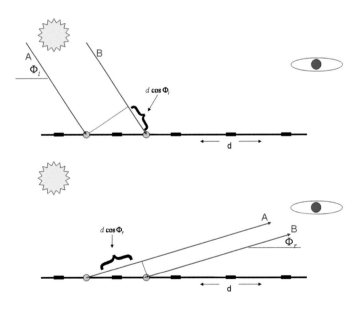

Figure 16.1. How a CD or DVD acts as a diffraction grating.

times. This effect can vary across a surface, changing the colors we see at different points. There are many ways this can happen, but we will look at two: diffraction gratings, such as the grooves on a CD or DVD, and oil slicks.

Diffraction Gratings

A diffraction grating is a surface containing a set of parallel lines that are very close together, as illustrated in Figure 16.1. One common example of this is the surface of a CD or DVD, in which case the "parallel lines" are concentric rings. On a CD, the distance d between adjacent tracks is 1600 nm, while on a DVD, d is 740 nm.

In this figure, we see that light arrives at a surface containing a diffraction grating with distance d between the grooves. The light arrives with an incident angle Φ_i with respect to the plane of the surface. It bounces in all directions, and some of it reflects toward the eye with a reflective angle Φ_r. Because the distance d between the grooves is very small with respect to the light and viewing distances, we will treat multiple rays as if they were parallel.

On the way to the surface, the light along path B travels $d * \cos(\Phi_i)$ farther than the light along path A, while on the way from the surface to the eye, the light along path A travels $d * \cos(\Phi_r)$ farther than along path B. The absolute difference between the lengths of the paths is

$$\Delta = \left| d * \left(\cos \Phi_i - \cos \Phi_r \right) \right|.$$

If the difference Δ is a multiple of the light's wavelength λ, $m\lambda$, then the waves of the two paths are in phase and that wavelength is reinforced. So the wavelengths λ^* that we see in this type of situation are all defined by

$$\lambda^* = \frac{\left| d * \left(\cos \Phi_i - \cos \Phi_r \right) \right|}{m}.$$

We know the values of Φ_i, Φ_r, and d. We just need to see what, if any, integer values of m would give us wavelengths in the visible spectrum. The following code shows the vertex shader. The eye coordinate position is retained, as well as the transformed tangent vector. Because the grooves are circular, the tangent vector to the grooves at a point (x, y) on the circle is $(-y, x)$. This is computed by the vertex shader to use in the fragment shader.

```
out vec3 vECposition;
out vec3 vTransfTangent;
```

```
void
main( )
{
  vECposition    = ( uModelViewMatrix * aVertex ).xyz;
  vTransfTangent = uNormalMatrix * vec3( -aVertex.y,
                                          aVertex.x, 0. );
  vTransfTangent = normalize( vTransfTangent ) ;
  gl_Position    = uModelViewProjectionMatrix * aVertex;
}
```

The fragment shader for the CD/DVD simulation is shown here:

```
uniform float uLightX, uLightY, uLightZ;   // from a slider
uniform float uD;                          // from a slider

in vec3 vECposition;
in vec3 vTransfTangent;

out vec4 fFragColor;

const float LAMBDAMIN = 400.;              // blue
const float LAMBDAMAX = 600.;              // red
const vec4  GRAY = vec4( .2, .2, .2, 1. );

int
AssignRGB( in float lambda, out vec3 color )
{
  if( lambda < LAMBDAMIN  ||  lambda > LAMBDAMAX )
    return 0;

  float t = ( lambda - LAMBDAMIN ) / ( LAMBDAMAX - LAMBDAMIN );
  color = Rainbow( t );
  return 1;
}

void main( )
{
  vec3 ToLight = normalize(vec3(uLightX,uLightY,uLightZ)
                    -vECposition);
  vec3 ToEye   = normalize(vec3(0.,0.,0.)
                    -vECposition);

  float sum   = dot(ToLight,vTransfTangent)
                    +dot(ToEye,vTransfTangent);
  float delta = uD * abs( sum );

  int mmin = int( floor( delta / LAMBDAMAX ) );
```

```
int mmax = int( ceil(  delta / LAMBDAMIN ) );

fFragColor = GRAY;
if( mmin > 0 )
{
  vec3 color = vec3( 0., 0., 0. );
  int count = 0;
  for( int m = mmin; m <= mmax; m++ )
  {
    float lambda = delta / float(m);
    vec3 col;
    int status = AssignRGB( lambda, col );
    if( status > 0 )
    {
      color += col;
      count++;
    }
  }

  if( count > 0 )
    fFragColor = vec4( color / float(count), 1. );
 }
}
```

Two vectors are created in this fragment shader. One vector goes from the fragment toward the light position (which is specified externally on sliders when this is used with *glman*), and one goes toward the eye position (which is at (0., 0., 0.)). Each of these is dotted with vTransfTangent, the tangent vector to the groove, which is parallel to the grooves at this fragment and acts like the "light channel" there.

These dot products tell us how much of each of these vectors lies in the direction of the transformed tangent.

Since the dot product distributes over vector addition, the first line of code could have been simplified as

```
float sum = dot(
ToLight+ToEye,
TransfTangent );
```

We didn't do that here, because this construct looks confusingly like the "halfway vector" often used in the specular lighting equation. It's not. Remember this distinction, so you are not tempted to add them together and normalize the result.

Because of the direction of these three vectors, one of the dot products will be positive and one will be negative. Because our equation calls for a subtraction and an absolute value,

$$\Delta = \left| d * \left(\cos \Phi_i - \cos \Phi_r \right) \right|,$$

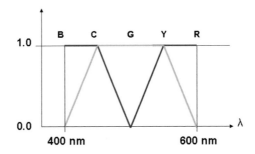

Figure 16.2. Hue spectral changes.

we can simply add the two dot products together.

```
float sum = dot(ToLight, TransfTangent) + dot(ToEye,
           TransfTangent);
float delta = D * abs( sum );
```

From this, Δ is computed and the wavelength equation is inverted to give us the required integer multipliers as a function of wavelength:

$$m = \frac{\left| d * \left(\cos \Phi_i - \cos \Phi_r \right) \right|}{\lambda}.$$

When the minimum and maximum wavelengths are substituted into this equation, we have the maximum and minimum integer multipliers, mmax and mmin respectively, for visible light. The fragment shader loops through these integer multipliers and computes a color for each one using the Rainbow( ) function that we used in the transfer function discussion in Chapter 15. That function is a reasonably good approximation of the visible portion of the electromagnetic spectrum, and it gives us a color distribution that looks like Figure 16.2.

It may be the case that for some points on the surface, mmin ≠ mmax. In those cases, we compute the colors for each wavelength and average the results. When we put all of this together, we get a final effect that looks like Figure 16.3.

This kind of diffraction effect is found in many places in nature, such as bird feathers and butterfly wings. Our ability to model the effect does not make it any less wonderful in nature!

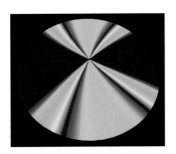

Figure 16.3. CD diffraction shader.

Oil Slicks

An oil slick is caused by a thin film of oil on top of water. It is very common to see these in streets and parking lots, especially right after a rain when it has not rained in a while. As shown in Figure 16.4, the light is partially reflected from the top surface of the oil and partially refracted down into the oil. At the oil-water interface, the light is reflected upward, and the reflected light then passes through the oil surface back into the air. The interference between the directly reflected and the refracted-then-reflected light causes the oil slick's visual effect.

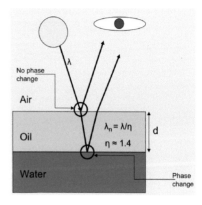

Figure 16.4. Light interacting with a thin oil film over water.

Here we see a similar computation of the wavelengths, but there is an interesting twist because the light undergoes a 180° phase change at the oil-water interface. The light that comes from the interface has a slightly longer path, which we will assume is simply $2d$ longer. The refractive index η of the oil means that the light in the oil has wavelength $\lambda_{out} = \lambda/\eta$, and the phase change means that the light coming out of the oil is a half wavelength out of phase with light that went in. The two light waves will then cancel if the added distance is a multiple of the wavelength of the light in the oil, $2d = m * \lambda_{out}$. The light waves will reinforce each other if the distance is a half wavelength off such a multiple, $2d = (m + 0.5) * \lambda_{out}$. So the wavelengths that we see in an oil slick are all defined by

$$\lambda^* = \frac{2d\lambda}{m + 0.5}.$$

We know d and η. We just need to see what, if any, integer values of m would give us wavelengths in the visible spectrum. We will assume that the oil on top of the water is in the shape of decaying exponential "hump," perturbed with a noise function. The vertex shader, then, records the current position in that hump and the location of the center center of the hump.

```
out vec3 vMCposition;
out vec3 vCenter;

void main( )
{
        vCenter     = vec3( 0., 0., 0. );
        vMCposition = aVertex.xyz;
        gl_Position = uModelViewProjectionMatrix * aVertex;
}
```

The fragment shader computes the height, applies the noise function to the radius of the current point, and uses it to compute the decaying-exponential hump height, d. It then inverts the equation

$$\lambda^* = \frac{2d\lambda}{m + 0.5}$$

to become

$$m = \frac{2d\eta}{\lambda} - 0.5$$

so that, like the DVD example, a minimum and maximum multiple can be computed. Those multiples are looped through, computing a wavelength at each, which is then turned into an RGB:

```
uniform sampler3D Noise3;
uniform float uMaxHeight;      // variables from sliders
uniform float uNoiseMag;
uniform float uA;

in vec3 vMCposition;
in vec3 vCenter;

out vec4 fFragColor;

const float ETA       = 1.4;   // oil index of refraction
const float LAMBDAMIN = 400.;  // blue
const float LAMBDAMAX = 600.;  // red
const vec4  BLACK     = vec4( 0., 0., 0., 0. );

int
AssignRGB( in float lambda, out vec3 color )
{
   if( lambda < LAMBDAMIN  ||  lambda > LAMBDAMAX )
      return 0;

   float t = ( lambda - LAMBDAMIN ) / ( LAMBDAMAX - LAMBDAMIN );
   color = Rainbow( t );
   return 1;
}

void
main( )
```

```
{
  vec4 nv    = texture( Noise3, vMCposition );
  float rad = distance( vMCposition.xy, vCenter.xy ) +
              uNoiseMag * ( nv.r - 0.5 );

  float d   = uMaxHeight * exp( -uA*rad*rad );
  int mmin = int( floor( 2.*d*ETA/LAMBDAMAX - .5 ) );
  int mmax = int( ceil(  2.*d*ETA/LAMBDAMIN - .5 ) );

  fFragColor = BLACK;
  if( mmin > 0 )
  {
    vec3 color = vec3( 0., 0., 0. );
    int count  = 0;
    for( int m = mmin; m <= mmax; m++ )
    {
      float lambda = 2.*d*ETA / ( float(m) + .5 );
      vec3 col;
      int status = AssignRGB( lambda, col );
      if( status > 0 )
      {
        color += col;
        count++;
      }
    }

    if( count > 0 )
      fFragColor = vec4( color / float(count), 1. );
  }
}
```

Figure 16.5 shows the effect of this function. As you would expect, the appearance of the oil slick can be changed dramatically by changing the values of uA and uNoiseMag, which, of course, is part of the fun!

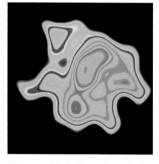

Figure 16.5. Results of the oil-slick shader.

Lens Effects

It can be very interesting to add lenses to a scene and to see how the scene looks through a lens. In this section, we will review the way light interacts with a single lens (more lenses takes us deeply into optics) and see how that can be used to create the effect of a lens in the scene.

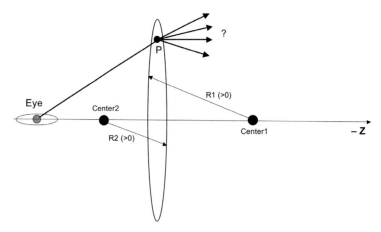

Figure 16.6. A diagram of a convex lens.

For any lens made of a material with a higher refractive index than air, as a ray of light from the eye to a point P enters the lens, it is bent toward the line of the normal to the lens at that point. As it then leaves the lens, it is bent away from the normal to the lens at the point where it leaves. Exactly what happens to the light depends on the directions of these normals and, of course, on the exact refractive index of the lens material relative to the air.

For a convex lens, normals point away from the centerline of the lens, $-z$ in Figure 16.6, and so a light ray from the eye is bent back toward the centerline. This has the effect of focusing light from the eye point on the centerline, which generally magnifies the appearance of any object on that. The image that is seen can either be seen upright or inverted, depending on its distance from the lens, as we will see later.

The focal length f of such a lens is given by the lensmaker's equation,

$$\frac{1}{f} = \left(\frac{\eta_{\text{lens}}}{\eta_{\text{env}}} - 1\right)\left(\frac{1}{R_1} - \frac{1}{R_2}\right),$$

where the values of η are the refractive indices of the lens and the environment. The way the light rays and the normals behave at the points where the rays enter and leave the lens is shown in more detail in Figure 16.7.

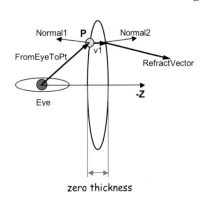

Figure 16.7. Light rays and intersections with a (convex) lens.

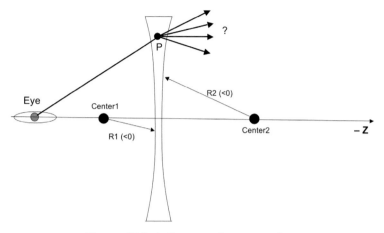

Figure 16.8. A diagram of a concave lens.

For a concave lens, shown in Figure 16.8, the normals point towards the centerline –z, and so rays of light from the eye are directed farther from the centerline rather than toward it. This has the effect of making things seen through the lens seem smaller.

In the next few figures, we will show how these lens behaviors are translated into actual images by GLSL shaders. In Figure 16.9, we see a scene in which the object we are looking at is in front of the lens's convergence point. The objects we see through the lens are upright and are magnified.

In contrast to Figure 16.9, we see in Figure 16.10 that if an object lies behind the convergence point, it is inverted when viewed through the lens. The magnification effect is not as strong here, and you begin to see some fisheye magnification lens effect within the area of the lens.

For a concave lens, as shown in Figure 16.11, we see an upright image, but the area within the image is seen as smaller than its actual size. We also see a fish-eye lens effect in this lens that reduces objects' size as rays toward the edge of the lens are bent more than rays toward its center.

The actual shader code for vertex and fragment shaders is shown below. First we include the vertex shader code, because it must compute the refraction vector for the lens as well as the familiar gl_Position value. In this example, you could let uR1 and uR2 be *glman* slider variables so you could experiment with the effect of lenses with different shapes.

Figure 16.9. Convex lens ($R_1 > 0$, $R_2 > 0$) with the object in front of the convergence point.

Figure 16.10. Convex lens ($R_1 > 0$, $R_2 > 0$) with the object behind the convergence point.

Figure 16.11. Concave lens ($R_1 < 0$, $R_2 < 0$).

```
uniform float uR1, uR2;

out vec3 vRefractVector;
const float ETA = 0.66;        // eta=in/out

void main( )
{
   vec3 P = ( uModelViewMatrix * aVertex ).xyz;
   vec3 Eye = vec3( 0., 0., 0. );     // just to make it clearer
   vec3 FromEyeToPt = normalize( P - Eye  ); // vector from eye
to pt

   vec3 Center1 = vec3( 0., 0., P.z - uR1 );
   vec3 Normal1 = normalize( sign(uR1) * ( P - Center1 ));

   vec3 v1 = refract(FromEyeToPt, Normal1, ETA);
   v1 = normalize( v1 );

   vec3 Center2 = vec3( 0., 0., P.z + uR2 );
   vec3 Normal2 = normalize( sign(uR2) * ( Center2 - P ));

   vec3 v2 = refract( v1, Normal2, 1./ETA );

   vRefractVector = v2;

   gl_Position = uModelViewProjectionMatrix * aVertex;
}
```

The fragment shader, by contrast, is much simpler. It simply computes the texture from the cube map based on the refraction vector returned by the vertex shader and blends that with white to get the effect of the lens not passing along all the light it receives. This also helps to make the lens visible in the scene.

```
uniform samplerCube uRefractUnit;

in vec3 vRefractVector;

out vec4 fFragColor;

const vec4 WHITE = vec4( 1.,1.,1.,1. );

void main( ) {
   vec4 refractcolor = textureCube( uRefractUnit,
                                    vRefractVector );
   fFragColor       = mix( refractcolor, WHITE, .3 );
}
```

Bathroom Glass

We can combine noise with bump-mapping and cube map refractions to simulate the effect of "bathroom glass"; that is, glass that has a wobbly enough surface that you can't exactly discern the detail of what is on the other side of it. To do this, we are going to use a single quad as our input geometry. Remember that one of the beauties of bump-mapping is that you can use fairly coarse geometry but make it look quite detailed because the computations take place per-pixel.

Here is the fragment shader. Because the input geometry is a single quad in the XY-plane, each fragment starts out with a normal vector of $(0,0,1)$. That normal vector is going to be perturbed twice, by rotating it around X and then around Y. That's the purpose of the RotateNormal( ) function. The angles to rotate about are generated by calling the noise function twice, using the fragment's model coordinates as an index.

```
uniform samplerCube uTexUnit;
uniform float       uNoiseAmp;
uniform float       uNoiseFreq;
uniform sampler3D   Noise3;

in vec3   vMCpos;
in vec3   vECpos;

out vec4 fFragColor;

const float ETA   = 1.4; // index of refraction
const vec4  WHITE = vec4( 1.,1.,1.,1. );

vec3
RotateNormal( float angx, float angy, vec3 n )
{
   float cx = cos( angx );
   float sx = sin( angx );
   float cy = cos( angy );
   float sy = sin( angy );

   // rotate about x:
   float yp =  n.y*cx - n.z*sx; // y'
   n.z      =  n.y*sx + n.z*cx; // z'
   n.y      =  yp;

   // rotate about y:
   float xp =  n.x*cy + n.z*sy; // x'
   n.z      = -n.x*sy + n.z*cy; // z'
```

```
   n.x       =  xp;

   return normalize( n );
}

void main( )
{
   vec3 eye      = vec3( 0., 0., 0. );
   vec3 eyeToPt = normalize( vECpos - eye );

   vec4 nvx = texture( Noise3, uNoiseFreq*vMCpos );
   vec4 nvy = texture( Noise3,
            uNoiseFreq*vec3(vMCpos.xy,vMCpos.z+0.5) );

   float angx = nvx.r + nvx.g + nvx.b + nvx.a; //  1. -> 3.
   angx = angx - 2.;           // -1. -> 1.
   angx *= uNoiseAmp;

   float angy = nvy.r + nvy.g + nvy.b + nvy.a; //  1. -> 3.
   angy =        angy - 2.;            // -1. -> 1.
   angy *=       uNoiseAmp;

   vec3 N = vec3( 0., 0., 1. ); // unperturbed normal
   N = RotateNormal( angx, angy, N );
   N = normalize( uNormalMatrix * N );
   // force the normal to point towards us:
   if( N.z < 0. )
      N = -N;

   vec3 reflectVector = reflect( eyeToPt, N );
   vec4 reflectColor  = textureCube( uTexUnit, reflectVector );

   vec3 refractVector = refract( eyeToPt, N, ETA );
   vec4 refractColor  = textureCube( uTexUnit, refractVector );
   refractColor       = mix( refractColor, WHITE, .3 );

   if( all(  equal( refractVector, vec3(0.,0.,0.) )  ))
      refractColor = reflectColor;

   fFragColor = mix( refractColor, reflectColor, uMix );
}
```

It is possible that the refract( ) function will fail and will tell us that it failed by returning the vector (0,0,0). Why could it fail? Like real refraction, it is possible that the angles will become such that, instead of refraction, you get internal reflection. You can detect this in Snell's law of refraction by being forced to take an arcsin of a value greater than 1. or less than −1. You can see

Figure 16.12. The unperturbed normal (left), a small value of `uNoiseAmp` (middle), and a larger value of `uNoiseAmp` (right).

this phenomenon in action if you lie at the bottom of a swimming pool and look up. Straight up, you will see the sky. As you look away from the straight-up vector you will still see the sky, but at some angle (about 50°) you will start to see the bottom of the pool reflected instead. To handle this properly, we check for that case and set the color to be what would have been reflected from the fragment rather than refracted. Figure 16.12 shows this in action.

Atmospheric Effects

There are many wonderful effects from sunlight (and even moonlight) in the atmosphere. In this section, we consider two effects, both caused by light interacting with water droplets in the atmosphere. The *rainbow* is probably the most familiar and has been important to people for all known history. The *glory*, caused by backscattering from much smaller water droplets such as clouds (near 10 μm in diameter), was once known primarily to mountain climbers because it depends on looking at a point immediately opposite the direction of light. Now it is most often seen when you are flying. Figure 16.13 shows the general concept of light being refracted at the surface of a water droplet and reflected internally within the droplet, including the fact that this varies slightly for different wavelengths of light. There are many other amazing atmospheric effects, such as halos, sunpillars, and sundogs; for a remark-

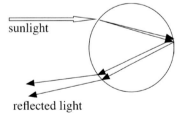

Figure 16.13. General light backscattering process, showing the different paths for different wavelengths of light.

ably complete and detailed discussion, see [12] or [26]. You should be able to adapt the techniques developed here to simulate them.

The approach we take to simulating these effects come from [4]. We take a Lee diagram, computed by the MiePlot application [25], showing the color of scattered light at different angles based on the radius of water droplets, and use that as a look-up map. The color of the effect at each point on a quad is then determined by the angle of that point from the eye, and that color is added to whatever color is already present. You can compute Lee diagrams that correspond to each of the effects we will discuss, so this approach works for each of our effects.

Rainbows

Everyone is familiar with rainbows. In Figure 16.14, we see a photograph of a rainbow at sunrise. Note the structure of the rainbow: from the outside, we see the common spectrum of light that we also see from a prism, with red going through orange, yellow, green, blue, indigo, and then violet. Then further inside, we see a general lightening in color as a white tint seems to be added to the scene. Although this figure does not show it, there can also be a secondary rainbow outside the primary one, with its colors reversed. In theory, though very rarely seen, there may even be further rainbows.

The structure of a rainbow comes from the reflection of light from the interior of water droplets in the air, as shown in Figure 16.13. This is examined in more detail in Figure 16.15, showing that the particular angles for a plain water droplet are approximately $41° \pm 1°$.

Figure 16.14. A rainbow photograph showing the way it affects light in the atmosphere.

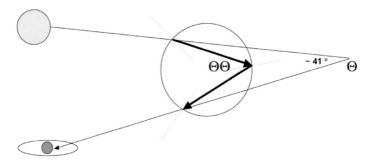

Figure 16.15. The path of light through a water droplet.

Table 16.1 shows these approximate angles for different wavelengths of light that correspond to the main colors we see in a rainbow. The angle Θ represents the main rainbow, and $\Theta\Theta$ represents the secondary rainbow.

Color	λ	η	Θ	$\cos\Theta$	$\Theta\Theta$	$\cos\Theta\Theta$
Red	≈ 650 nm	1.510	42°	0.743	50.0°	0.643
Green	≈ 500 nm	1.519	41°	0.755	51.5°	0.623
Blue	≈ 400 nm	1.528	40°	0.766	53.0°	0.602

Table 16.1. The approximate angles for a rainbow.

The actual computation of color for a rainbow in a scene could be done using angle computations in the fragment shader, as we did for the spotlight simulation in Chapter 8. This would involve creating a one-dimensional texture whose colors span the rainbow and using that texture with the angle values as texture coordinates. However, we have other resources, so it is probably simpler to use the approach of [4], with the Lee diagram for light scattering in the rainbow region, computed by MiePlot and shown in Figure 16.16.

We have created a texture map from this Lee diagram and have used it as a look-up table to return the color of the rainbow for various angles in a display. This is done by sampling a vertical line in the Lee diagram at a fixed value of the droplet radius. In Figure 16.17, we see the effect of this fragment shader computation for a plain gray quad (left), for a natural scene with the rainbow added (middle), and for the natural scene with an actual rainbow (right). In the first two cases, the color returned from the texture map is simply added to the color of the pixel to get the displayed color, though of course some of the image techniques discussed earlier could improve the blending. Additional effects like the secondary rainbow in the natural scene are not included in the simulation.

Note that we've manipulated the alpha component of the rainbow colors to smooth the outside edge of the rainbow and to show the lightened color inside the rainbow. These effects are not as strong as you might like, and an exercise invites you to work with the fragment shader to improve them. However, a significant problem in this simulation is that conditions are much more complex than simply creating a rainbow. In the real image, there was a rain squall about 100 yards from the camera but the camera location had no rain, so the tree in the foreground is much darker in the actual image because it was not in the rain. The background in the actual image is obscured by the heavy rain that causes the rainbow, but simulating that is not part of simulating the rainbow. We also have not included the secondary reflection in the raindrop that gives us the faint secondary rainbow in the photo. Without using this additional information, the simulated image in the middle of Figure 16.17 is about all we can do.

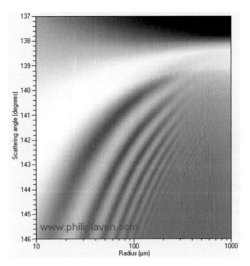

Figure 16.16. The Lee diagram of the color of a rainbow for different angles and water droplet radii.

Figure 16.17. A computed rainbow against a gray quad (left), against a natural scene (middle), and compared with an actual photo of the scene with a rainbow (right).

The fragment shader code for this simulation is given below, and it uses a number of uniform variables that come from *glib* sliders. These let you "tune" the rainbow to match real conditions, since the critical angles from the contrasolar point are not available in the plain photograph. These variables have been tuned to get the computed rainbow to align fairly well with the actual photograph, as shown, but the tuned values are not included here. See the exercises for more on tuning.

```
uniform float    uUpDown, uLeftRight, uInOut;
uniform float    uALF, uWhere;
uniform sampler2D uImageUnit, uRainbowUnit;

in vec2 vST;

out vec4 fFragColor;

const float PI      = 3.14159265;
const float outAngle = 41.
const float inAngle  = 39.
const vec4  LIGHTPOS = vec4( 0., 0., 40000., 1. );

void
main( )
{
//simulate directional light

//set up eye and texture coordinates
   vec3 irgb   = texture( uImageUnit, vST ).rgb;
   vec4 irgba  = vec4(irgb, 0.5);
   vec2 xy     = 100. * vST - 50.;
                   // set initial eyepoint to [-50, 50]
   vec3 EyePos = vec3(xy.x + uLeftRight, xy.y + uUpDown, uInOut);

//Compute angles
   float num     = length( EyePos.xy - LIGHTPOS.xy );
   float rAngle  = atan( num, uInOut );  // angle in radians
   float angle   = degrees( rAngle );    // angle in degrees
   float myAngle = angle;

//Convert myAngle to rainbow range
   if ( angle > outAngle )
   {
      myAngle = outAngle;
   }
   if ( angle < inAngle )
   {
      myAngle = inAngle;
```

```
    }
    float v = (outAngle - myAngle)/(outAngle - inAngle);

//Get colors by sampling RainbowUnit at the fixed value:
    vec2 Rainbowst = vec2(v, uWhere);
    vec3 rrgb = texture( uRainbowUnit, Rainbowst ).rgb;

//Set alpha components of color for blending
    vec4 rrgba = vec4( rrgb, uALF);

    //0.5 degree dropoff band at outside edge of rainbow
    if ( (angle > outAngle - 0.5) ) {
        rrgba.a = uALF*(1. - smoothstep(outAngle-0.5,
            outAngle, angle) );
    }

    //lighter color inside rainbow
    if (angle < inAngle)
    {
        rrgba.a = uALF*cos((inAngle - angle)/PI);
    }
    float alpha = rrgba.a;

//Approximation of the background
    if (alpha < 0.3 )
        alpha = 0.3;

    vec3 colorOut = (1. - alpha) * irgb + alpha * rrgb;
    fFragColor = vec4 (colorOut, 1);
}
```

The Glory

A glory is the effect of seeing a bright spot with a rainbow fringe at a point exactly opposite the sun. An example is shown in Figure 16.18. Note that you can actually see exactly where you are in the reflection (as the center of the halo) and that you can see several color fringes centered at that point.

Glories are caused by interference between frequencies of light backscattered toward the light source (the sun) from atmospheric water droplets, but the exact way this happens is obscure. Instead of trying to simulate this directly, we look for simulations that compute the color associated with the

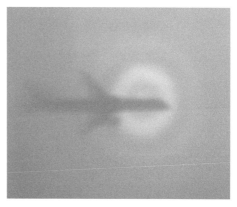

Figure 16.18. The glory as seen from an airplane. You can tell where the photographer was sitting by the center of the glory.

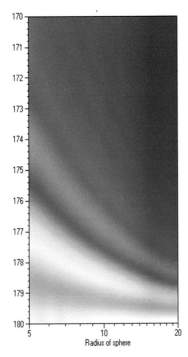

Figure 16.19. A Lee diagram of the color of the glory for different angles and water droplet radii. The radii are in μm.

effect. A Lie diagram for the glory is shown in Figure 16.19, computed from MiePlot for a range of water drop sizes. Notice that the sizes are much smaller—about an order of magnitude—than the sizes for the rainbow; the rainbow and the glory do not occur in the same atmospheric conditions. You will also note that there are, in fact, several bands of similar color. We will use this diagram as a look-up map as we did in the rainbow example, taking the radius as a constant set by the slider variable Radius and looking up the color based solely on the angle.

When we apply this approach to compute a glory, we see the effects shown in Figure 16.20 against a solid quad (left) and against a photograph of a cloud surface (right).

The code for the fragment shader that was used to create the right-hand image of Figure 16.20 is shown below; it is quite similar to the rainbow fragment shader. The background cloud image is loaded and associated with the uImageUnit in the GLIB file as was done in Chapter 9. The angle is set up relative to the direction to the sun, not the angle into the scene; these angles are complementary, so the computed angle must be subtracted from 180° for the texture look-up (recall the angles shown in Figure 16.15).

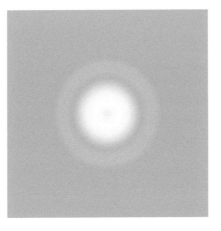 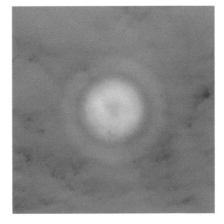

Figure 16.20. The glory effect, seen mixed against a solid white quad (left) and as added into a photograph of a cloud surface (right).

```
uniform float      uUpDown, uLeftRight, uInOut;
uniform float      uMix, uRadius;
uniform sampler2D uImageUnit, uGloryUnit;

in vec2  vST;

out vec4 fFragColor;

const float THEANGLE  = 160.;  // cutoff angle for our
                               // look-up texture
const vec4  LIGHTPOS = vec4( 0., 0., 40000., 1. );

void main( )
{
//Simulate directional light

//Get texture coordinates of fragment and convert to [-50, 50]
  vec3 irgb = texture( uImageUnit, vST ).rgb;
  vec2 xy   = 100. * vST - 50.;

//Compute angle from the light direction
  vec3 EyePos  = vec3(xy.x + uLeftRight, xy.y + uUpDown,
                                              uInOut);
  float dist   = length( LIGHTPOS.xy - EyePos.xy );
  float rAngle = atan( dist, uInOut );  // angle to point in
                                        // radians

  // the angle is measured from the direction to the sun; this
  // is 180 degrees at the contrasolar point and we avoid 180
  float angle  = 180. - degrees( rAngle );
  if( angle < THEANGLE )
     angle = THEANGLE;

  float v = ( 180. - angle )/( 180. - THEANGLE );
  if (v > .99)
    v = .99;  // avoiding 180

//get the glory texture color
  vec2 Gloryst  = vec2(v, uRadius);
  vec3 Gloryrgb = texture( uGloryUnit, Gloryst ).rgb;

//mix the glory and background colors
  vec3 colorOut = uMix * irgb + (1. - uMix) * Gloryrgb;
  fFragColor    = vec4( colorOut, 1 );
}
```

Fun with One

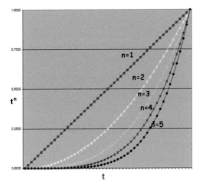

Figure 16.21. Comparison of shapes of t^n functions.

Many GLSL variables range linearly from 0. to 1., such as texture components, the noise function, color components, etc. But just because a variable ranges *linearly* from 0. to 1. doesn't mean that you have to actually use it that way. There are a number of ways you can manipulate the range [0.,1.] to get different effects. This is especially fun with the *glman* Timer function, introduced in Chapter 4 and discussed in the next section. Some of the possibilities are shown in Table 16.2, and the shapes of some of these functions are shown in Figures 16.21 to 16.23.

Effect	Code

Collection of curves from 0. to 1.	`float tm = Timer;`
	`float tm = Timer*Timer;`
	`float tm = Timer*Timer*Timer;`
	`float tm = 3.*Timer`^{2}` - 2.*Timer`^{3}`;`
	`float tm = 10.*Timer`^{3}` - 15.*Timer`^{4}` + 6.*Timer`^{5}

Ramp from 0. to 1. and back to 0.	`float tm;`
	`if( Timer <= .5 )`
	`  tm = 2.*Timer;`
	`else`
	`  tm = 2. - 2.*Timer;`

Smooth oscillation from –1. to 1. and back to –1.	`float tm = sin( 2.*π*Timer );`
Faster oscillation with parameter S.	`float tm = sin( 2.*π*S*Timer );`
Bigger oscillation with parameter M.	`float tm = M * sin( 2.*π*S*Timer );`
Smooth oscillation from 0. to 1. and back to 0.	`float tm = .5 + .5*sin(2.*π*Timer );`

Table 16.2. Some effects of different functions with range between 0 and 1.

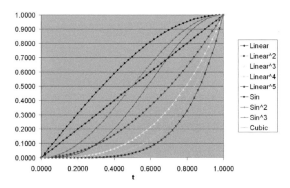

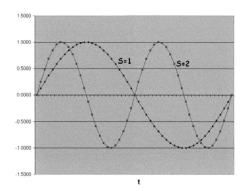

Figure 16.22. Comparison of shapes of t^n, sin, and cubic functions.

Figure 16.23. Comparison of shapes of $\sin(2\pi st)$ functions.

Using the glman Timer Function

The *glman* tool has a built-in Timer function that ranges from 0. to 1. in 10 seconds, by default, though you can make that interval any length you choose. All you have to do is declare a uniform floating-point variable named Timer:

```
uniform float Timer;
```

in your shader, and it will magically be assigned a number that repeatedly ramps from 0. to 1. over time. We can use the Timer function within a shader to create moving effects, using the "Fun with One" ideas in the previous section to get many different kinds of motion. You can get similar effects in your applications using the GLUT timer events.

Disco Ball

You can also take advantage of the Timer in many kinds of animation processes. As an example of this, consider the disco ball example shown in Figure 16.24, where several geometric objects are lit by a set of moving lights.

The scene uses a variable number of lights, controlled by a uniform slider variable in the fragment shader. The vertex shader for the disco example simply sets up the usual normal, eye coordinate position, light intensity, and gl_Position. This is familiar and so is not included here, but we do show the fragment shader for the disco example. It uses the uniform Timer variable, in the highlighted statement in the code below. This controls the offset angle of

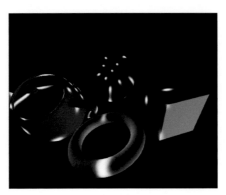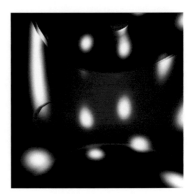

Figure 16.24. The disco light effect.

the lights—the only animated part of the scene—so that they swirl around the
space.

It might look like there are multiple light sources, but there really is just
one. A real disco ball appears to be multiple light sources because of the flat
mirrored facets on the ball itself. The fragment shader below looks at the angle
between the fragment, the disco ball, and the single light source. It then quan-
tizes that angle to see how close one of the simulated mirrored facets comes
to reflecting the light source to that fragment. It then uses that light intensity,
combined with a raise-to-a-power dropoff, to illuminate the fragment.

```glsl
uniform int    uNum;   // # of mirrors in each spherical direction
uniform float Timer; // built-in glman timer function

in vec3  vECpos;
in vec4  vColor;
in float vLightIntensity;

out vec4 fFragColor;

const float DMIN       = 0.980;   // minimum cosine for no light
const vec3  BALLPOS    = vec3( 0., 2., 0. );
const vec3  LIGHTPOS   = vec3( 2., 0., 0. );
const vec3  LIGHTCOLOR = vec3( 1., 1., 1. );
const float PI         = 3.14159265;

void main( )
{
   int numTheta = uNum;
   int numPhi   = uNum;
   float dtheta = 2. * PI / float(numTheta);
   float dphi   =      PI / float(numPhi);
```

```
    vec3 BP = vECpos - BALLPOS;
    float angle = radians(Timer*360.);
    float c = cos( angle );
    float s = sin( angle );
    vec3 bp;
    bp.x =  c*BP.x + s*BP.z;
    bp.y =  BP.y;
    bp.z = -s*BP.x + c*BP.z;

    vec3 BL = LIGHTPOS - BALLPOS;
    vec3 H = normalize( normalize(BL) + normalize(bp)  );
    float x = H.x;
    float y = H.y;
    float z = H.z;
    float xz = length( H.xz ); // = sqrt( x^2 + z^2 );
    float phi = atan( y, xz );
    float theta = atan( z, x );

    int itheta = int( floor( ( theta + dtheta/2. ) / dtheta ) );
    int iphi   = int( floor( ( phi   + dphi/2.   ) / dphi   ) );

    float theta0 = dtheta * float(itheta);
    float phi0   = dphi   * float(iphi);

    vec3 N0;
    N0.y = sin(phi0);
    xz   = cos(phi0);
    N0.x = xz*cos(theta0);
    N0.z = xz*sin(theta0);

    float d = max( dot( N0, H ), 0. );
    if( d < DMIN )
       d = 0.;
    d = pow( d, 5000. );      // much quicker drop-off

    fFragColor = vec4( vColor.rgb * vLightIntensity +
                 d * LIGHTCOLOR, vColor.a ) ;
}
```

Figure 16.24 (left) shows how this would look if a group of GLUT solids were on the dance floor together. Of course, lighting equations can apply to the inside of objects just as well as the outside, if you want them to (as you usually do). Figure 16.24 (right) shows the inside of the teapot. If the SIGGRAPH conference ever creates a nightclub venue, we have no doubt it will look like this!

Fog, with and without Noise

OpenGL allows you to create the appearance of fog and haze in the background of your scene. This is used to good effect, especially in games and simulators, to hide the far clipping plane. Objects can be clipped from the scene as they recede into the background without them appearing to "pop" out of view. However, the standard OpenGL fog looks too uniform. That is, everything at the same depth gets the same amount of fog blended into it. Real fog doesn't behave that way. This example fragment shader shows how using a 3D noise function to modulate a fragment's Z depth can be used to create a less uniform fog effect. This is shown in Figure 16.25 that we call "Dinos in the Mist."

```glsl
uniform float uNoiseScale;
uniform float uNoiseFreq;
uniform float uDepthFront, uDepthBack;
uniform sampler3D Noise3;

in float vZ;          // equal to -EC.z (dist in front of the eye)
in vec4  vColor;
in vec3  vMCposition;
in float vLightIntensity;

out vec4 fFragColor;

const vec4 FOG = vec4( 0.5, 0.5, 0.5, 1. );

void
main( )
{
   vec4  nv  = texture( Noise3, uNoiseFreq * vMCposition );
   float size = nv.r + nv.g + nv.b + nv.a;          // [1.,3.]
   size -= 2.;                                      // [-1.,+1.]
   float deltaz = uNoiseScale * size;

   float fogFactor =
         ((vZ+deltaz) - uDepthFront)/(uDepthBack - uDepthFront);
   fogFactor = clamp( fogFactor, 0., 1. );
   fogFactor = smoothstep( 0., 1., fogFactor );

   vec3 rgb = mix( vColor.rgb * vLightIntensity, FOG.rgb,
                   fogFactor );
   fFragColor = vec4( rgb, 1. );

}
```

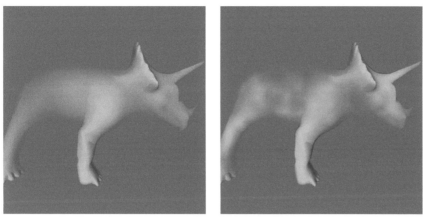

Figure 16.25. Fog, without (left) and with (right) noise.

Morphing 3D Geometry

Ever since the movie *Willow* (1988), morphing 3D geometry has been a mainstream topic in computer graphics. It would be fun to use shaders to do this in a general way. Unfortunately, morphing one general 3D object to another general 3D object is quite difficult because you need to create a careful correspondence between both sets of vertices, which is hard to do in an automated way. However, we can morph between two known shapes, such as a sphere to a disk, as shown in Figure 16.26. As we are altering vertex coordinates, most of the work is done by the vertex shader, shown here. The object is originally defined as a sphere, but its texture coordinates (aTexCoord0.st) are used to

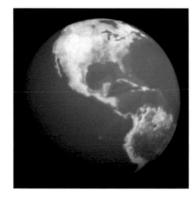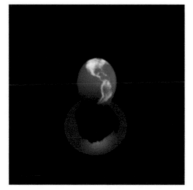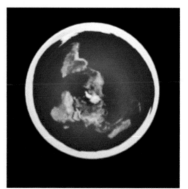

Figure 16.26. Morphing between a sphere and a disk. From left to right, uBlend is 0.0, 0.5, and 1.0.

produce the polar coordinates (r, Θ) of the disk. Thus we have two sets of coordinates and use the uBlend variable to mix between them.

```
uniform float uBlend;

out vec4  vColor;
out float vLightIntensity;
out vec2  vST;

const float TWOPI   = 2.*3.14159265;
const vec3  LIGHTPOS = vec3( 5., 10., 10. );

void main( )
{
    // original model coords (sphere):

    vec4 vertex0 = aVertex;
    vec3 norm0   = aNormal;

    // circle coords:

    vST = aTexCoord0.st;
    float s = aTexCoord0.s;
    float t = aTexCoord0.t;
    float radius = 1.-t;
    float theta = TWOPI*s;
    vec4  circle = vec4( radius*cos(theta), radius*sin(theta),
                         0., 1. );
    vec3 circlenorm = vec3( 0., 0., 1. );

    // blend:

    vec4 theVertex = mix( vertex0, circle, uBlend );
    vec3 theNormal = normalize( mix( norm0, circlenorm, uBlend ));

    // do the lighting:

    vec3 tnorm       = normalize( vec3( uNormalMatrix *
                                        theNormal ) );
    vec3 ECposition = vec3( uModelViewMatrix * theVertex );
    vLightIntensity = abs( dot(normalize(LIGHTPOS -
                                         ECposition),tnorm));
    if( vLightIntensity < 0.2 )
       vLightIntensity = 0.2;

    vColor = aColor;
    gl_Position = uModelViewProjectionMatrix * theVertex;
}
```

Figure 16.27. Morphing between a dino and a cube. From left to right, uBlend is 0.0, 0.5, and 1.0.

The rightmost image in Figure 16.26 is an interesting way to visualize the planet: as a polar disk with the angle corresponding to longitude and the radius corresponding to latitude.

We can also go one step more towards general morphing—a general shape to a known shape (in this case a cube), shown in Figure 16.27. Again, most of the work is done in the vertex shader. The original vertices are blown up like a balloon and are then clamped to fixed sides. Again, two sets of 3D coordinates are created and then mixed between.

```
uniform float uBlend;

out vec4   vColor;
out float vLightIntensity;

const float SIDE    = 2.;
const vec3 LIGHTPOS = vec3( 5., 10., 10. );

void main( )
{
  vec4 vertex0 = aVertex;
  vertex0.xyz *= 4./length(vertex0.xyz);

  vertex0.xyz = clamp( vertex0.xyz, -SIDE, SIDE );

  vec3 tnorm        = normalize( uNormalMatrix * aNormal );
  vec3 ECposition   = vec3( uModelViewMatrix * aVertex );
  vLightIntensity   = abs( dot(normalize(LIGHTPOS - ECposition),
                          tnorm));
  if( vLightIntensity < 0.2 )
    vLightIntensity = 0.2;
```

  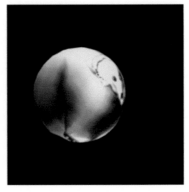

Figure 16.28. Morphing between a dino and a sphere. From left to right, uBlend is 0.0, 0.5, and 1.0.

```
        vColor = aColor;
        gl_Position = uModelViewProjectionMatrix *
                    mix( aVertex, vertex0, uBlend );
    }
```

In a very similar way, you can also morph between a general object and a sphere, as shown in Figure 16.28. All you need to do is leave out the part about clamping to the fixed sides.

Algorithmic Art

Algorithmic art is a field in which interesting images are generated through the use of computer algorithms. An introduction to the concept may be found at [1]. The field is very broad, and many aspects of it are perfect for implementing with shaders, especially those that create images based on the positions of pixels on the screen. We have already seen how Mandelbrot and Julia sets are generated in this way.

Connett Circles

One particular (and very simple) example of an algorithm that generates what are called Connett Circles is the Circle^2 algorithm [15], discovered by J. E. Connett. In this algorithm, each fragment's x- and y-coordinates are examined to see what circle radius they lie on. That radius is squared and cast to an integer. If that integer is odd, the fragment is discarded. If it is even, then a color is assigned to it and it is plotted in that color.

There are two ways to handle the coordinates for a fragment. One is to use the actual screen coordinates, and the other is to handle the coordinates on the surface. Both are available to you through GLSL. If you are working with *glman*, you can start with a simple quad with texture coordinates. The *glman* built-in quad has texture coordinates st that each range between 0 and 1, so if you multiply them by the size of the window and arrange for the quad to exactly fill the window, unit steps in the *st* space will match unit pixels in the display. Alternately, you can use the values of vFragCoord.xy to get the exact pixel coordinates for each fragment.

The fragment shader code for this is listed below, with the getColor (float t) function only stubbed; you can fill that in or use any other color function of one variable that you like. The #ifdef SCREEN logic lets you select either screen coordinates or screen-equivalent texture coordinates on your geometry. The GLIB file and vertex shader files are very much like those we saw in Chapter 10, except that no actual texture file is loaded. This code works with *glman* and assumes that the geometry is a simple quad with texture coordinates. Note that the dot function is a fast way to get the square of the radius.

```
#define SCREENSIZE 1200.
#define SCREEN

uniform float     uSide;
uniform sampler2D uVoidUnit;

in vec2 vST;

out vec4 fFragColor;

vec3
GetColor( float t )
{
    ...
}

void main( )
{
#ifdef SCREEN
    vec2 xy = uSide * gl_FragCoord.xy;
#else
    vec2 xy = uSide * vST;
#endif
```

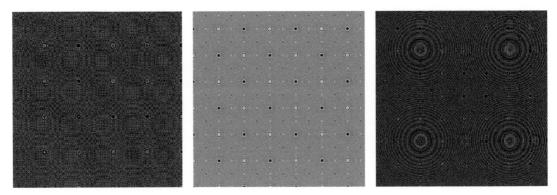

Figure 16.29. Three examples of images generated by the Circle² algorithm, with uSIDE = .875 (left), uSIDE = 1.00 (middle), and uSIDE = 1.08 (right).

```
float t = dot( xy, xy );
int c = int( t );
if ( (c % 2) != 0 ) discard;
t = float( c%360 )/359.;

vec3 myColor = GetColor( t );
fFragColor = vec4( myColor, 1.);
}
```

Some sample images from this shader are shown in Figures 16.29 and 16.30. Figure 16.29 shows three views with the algorithm above and three different values of uSIDE, showing how much this small change affects the images. (When you try this for yourself, you may find different results for these values

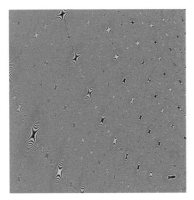

Figure 16.30. The Circle² algorithm used on the object side, viewed obliquely, with uSIDE = 1.00.

of uSIDE; the algorithm is sensitive to the resolution of your image. These were done for a 1200 × 1200 image.) Note the very subtle rainbow circles with center at the lower left of the image with uSIDE = .875 and the very strong Moiré circles in the image with uSIDE = 1.08. These secondary effects are common in the images and make them more interesting.

In Figure 16.30, we look at an image that uses the object-side coordinates, and in order to increase the brightness and the effect of this image, we did not use the pixel-discard logic. Since we are working on the object side rather than the screen side, we can manipulate the object; in this case, we rotated the quad a bit so that we are getting an oblique view of the quad instead of a straight-on view. This makes a striking difference in the image, as you can see.

Making Information Visible Through Motion

We have seen many examples of shader programming being used to create effective graphics that communicate information to the user using various geometric methods. However, it may be interesting to think about using graphics to make information visible through motion rather than geometry. Dan Sandin explored this concept as long ago as the late 1980s [40] and computer graphics shaders give us better tools to illustrate this. Sample shader functions to do this are given below.

The vertex shader is simple, merely copying the attribute values of vertex location (in model space) and texture coordinates to output variables that are then available to the fragment shader, and setting the global gl_Position variable. This is standard but is included for completeness.

```
out vec3 vMCposition;
out vec2 vST;

void main( )
{
   vMCposition = aVertex.xyz;
   vST         = aTexCoord0.st;
   gl_Position = uModelViewProjectionMatrix * aVertex;
}
```

The fragment shader reads in two textures, a white noise texture and a mask texture, and moves pixels from the white noise texture either left or right depending on the value in the mask texture. This motion difference lets you distinguish areas in the mask texture so you can get information from the mask through motion in the white noise. Just what kind of information can be distinguished remains an open research question, and we suggest some explorations in this area in one of this chapter's exercises.

```
uniform   sampler2D uRandomUnit, uMaskUnit;
uniform   float Timer;    // from glman

in vec3 vMCposition;
in vec2   vST;

out vec4 fFragColor;

void main( )
{
   vec2 st   = vST;
```

```
vec3 Rrgb = texture( uRandomUnit, st ).rgb;
vec3 Mrgb = texture( uMaskUnit,   st ).rgb;
vec3 color;

float T = 1024.*Timer;

if ( Mrgb.r > 0.5 ) // white part of mask
{
   st = vec2( st.s + T/1024., st.t );
   color = texture( uRandomUnit, st ).rgb;
}
else // black part of mask
{
   st = vec2( st.s - T/1024., st.t );
   color = texture( uRandomUnit, st ).rgb;
}
fFragColor = vec4( color, 1.);
}
```

We wish we could show you this technique in action, but the key word is *action*: it is the action of motion that shows the content of the mask texture. Since you are reading this in print, which does a poor job of supporting animation, we cannot do this; any freeze-frame capture of the output simply shows the white noise texture. Instead we urge you to download the textures (random.bmp and mask.bmp) shown in Figure 16.31, see the effect, and then see what more you can do, as suggested in an exercise.

Figure 16.31. The white noise texture (left) and a possible mask texture (right).

An Explosion Shader

We hope you have found the potpourri of examples in this chapter as interesting to read as we found it to create, but we thought we would like the book to end with a bang—so we close with an explosion shader, whose effect is shown in Figure 16.32. This example uses a geometry shader to take a collection of triangles, subdivides each of them into a number of discrete points, and then has the points undergo projectile physics motion as if an explosion had driven them all apart. The geometry shader uses the same parametric triangle subdivision scheme as was used in Chapter 12, but instead of subdividing triangles into smaller triangles, it subdivides them into points. The geometry shader is shown here.

```
#version 330
#extension GL_EXT_geometry_shader4: enable
#extension GL_EXT_gpu_shader4: enable

layout( triangles )  in;
layout( points, max_vertices=1024 )  out;

uniform int   uLevel;
uniform float uGravity;    // < 0.is down
uniform float uT;
uniform float uVelScale;

out float gLightIntensity;

const vec3 LIGHTPOS = vec3( 0., 0., 10. );

vec3 V0, vV01, vV02;
vec3 CG;
vec3 Normal;

void
ProduceVertex( float s, float t )
{
   vec3 v = V0 + s*V01 + t*V02;
   gLightIntensity  = dot( normalize(LIGHTPOS - v),
                           Normal );
   gLightIntensity = abs( gLightIntensity );

   vec3 vel = uVelScale * ( v - vCG );
```

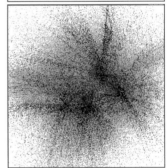
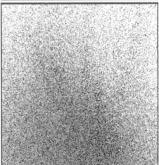

Figure 16.32. Exploding dinosaur at times 0.0, 0.3, 0.5, and 11.

```
        v += vel*uT + 0.5*vec3(0., uGravity, 0.)*uT*uT;
        gl_Position = uProjectionMatrix * vec4( v, 1. );
        EmitVertex( );
}

void
main( )
{
    V01 = ( gl_PositionIn[1] - gl_PositionIn[0] ).xyz;
    V02 = ( gl_PositionIn[2] - gl_PositionIn[0] ).xyz;

    Normal = normalize( cross( V01, V02 ) );

    V0  = gl_PositionIn[0].xyz;
    CG  = ( gl_PositionIn[0].xyz + gl_PositionIn[1].xyz
          + gl_PositionIn[2].xyz ) / 3.;

    int numLayers = 1 << uLevel;

    float dt = 1. / float( numLayers );
    float  t = 1.;

    for( int it = 0; it <= numLayers; it++ )
    {
        float smax = 1. - t;
        int   nums = it + 1;
        float   ds = smax / float( nums - 1 );
        float    s = 0.;

        for( int is = 0; is < nums; is++ )
        {
            ProduceVertex( s, t );
            s += ds;
        }

        t -= dt;
    }
}
```

Exercises

1. Adapt the CD/DVD shader example to look more realistic by applying cube-mapping as well as diffraction to add a reflection of a scene in the colored disk. Do the same to add the reflection of sky clouds in the oil slick.

2. Change the uSIDE slider uniform variable in the Circle² algorithm to be a uniform Timer variable and note the effect of this animation on the nature of the images.

3. Generalize the previous exercise by taking any shader that includes a *glman* slider variable (for example, the ablation shader from Chapter 9) and replacing the slider variable by a variable based on the Timer function that is modified by a "Fun with One" function. Use several versions of the function and notice the different effects.

4. Revisit the rainbow example using the GLIB file with the corresponding vertex and fragment shaders. Do your own computation of the parameters to match any rainbow photograph of your choice and modify the shaders as needed to create a better blending of the raw rainbow with the background scene.

5. We saw that the effects of rainbows or glories are modified by the environment in which they occur. For example, Figure 16.19 is not really right because the glory won't really be reflected from those areas where there aren't any clouds. Modify the fragment shader for the glory so that the color of the background affects the alpha of the glory, thus making the composited image more accurate.

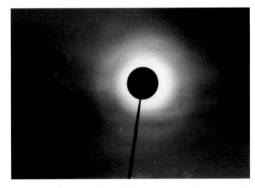

Figure 16.33. A solar corona, from [17]. Courtesy of Richard Fleet, used by permission.

6. While rainbows and glories are created by reflections from near the contrasolar point, coronas are created by reflections from small water drops at small angles near the sun. See Figure 16.33, [12] or [17] for examples and note that you can create simulations of coronas with HaloSim (see [13]). Write a shader that creates a corona around a point as if that point were the sun.

7. Other solar phenomena are caused by ice in the upper atmosphere. These can be quite amazing, but here we only consider the so-called 22° corona caused by ice crystals in very high thin cirrus clouds. See Figure 16.34, [12] or [17] for examples. Write a shader that simulates the solar corona.

8. Explain the patterns you see in the Circle² algorithm.

Figure 16.34. A 22° solar corona.

9. In the morphing examples, the "correct" range of values for uBlend is [0.,1.]. What happens if uBlend < 0.? What happens if uBlend > 1.? Can you explain why you end up with these shapes?

10. Experiment with the Circle^2 algorithm by using a power other than 2 for the distance computation. How does that affect the images?

11. Use texture coordinates on an object to computer a Circle^2 texture directly on the surface of the teapot.

12. Change the color transfer function in the Circle^2 algorithm and notice the difference in the images you produce. Compare a relatively monochromatic transfer function (a simple grayscale, for example, or a black → red → yellow → white range) to a very chromatic function (a full rainbow scale, for example) and note the changes in the patterns.

13. Modify the cube morphing to produce spherical morphing as we showed in Figure 16.27. How many other variations can you come up with?

14. Investigate another kind of algorithmic art (probably 2D) that you can find. This can come from the 2D fractal world (look at the literature based on the Mandelbrot or Julia sets), from simulating surfaces as described in Chapter 7, or from general searches on "algorithmic art." If it's *really* cool, let us know via the book's website.

15. Implement the "moving pixels" shader to see how it works. Create different kinds of mask textures, with different text, different fonts, or with different shapes. Try this with a color white noise (available with the book's materials as randomColor.bmp) to test whether color noise carries the motion information as well as the monochrome noise.

16. Figure 16.32 doesn't just show points; it shows light-shaded points. Modify the given explosion geometry shader to compute a light intensity for each point, which will then be picked up and used by the fragment shader.

A GLSLProgram C++ Class

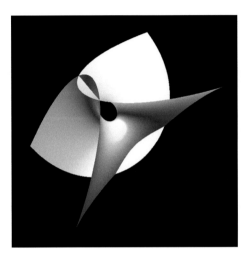

The act of creating, compiling, linking, using, and passing parameters to shaders is very repetitive. For some of our own work, we have found it helpful to create a C++ class called GLSLProgram that implements this process. This class has the tools to manage all the steps of shader program development and use, including source file opening, loading, and compilation. Some of the individual methods were presented in Chapter 14. It also has methods that implement setting attribute and uniform variables. This source is available on the book's website.

The following methods are supported by the class

```
bool  Create(  char *, char * = NULL, char * = NULL,
               char * = NULL, char * = NULL );
bool  IsValid( );
```

```
void  SetAttribute( char *, int );
void  SetAttribute( char *, float );
void  SetAttribute( char *, float, float, float );
void  SetAttribute( char *, float * );
void  SetAttribute( char *, Vec3& );
void  SetGstap( bool );
void  SetInputTopology( GLenum );
void  SetOutputTopology( GLenum );
void  SetUniform( char *, int );
void  SetUniform( char *, float );
void  SetUniform( char *, float, float, float );
void  SetUniform( char *, float[3] );
void  SetUniform( char *, Vec3& );
void  SetUniform( char *, Matrix4& );
void  SetVerbose( bool );
void  Use( );
void  UseFixedFunction( );
```

The Create( ) method takes up to five shader file names as arguments. From the filename extension, it figures out what type of shader it is, loads it, compiles it, and links them all together. All errors are written to *stderr*. The IsValid( ) method can be called if your application wants to know if everything succeeded or not.

The SetAttribute( ) methods set attribute variables, destined for the vertex shader. The SetUniform( ) methods set uniform variables, destined for any of the shaders.

The Use( ) method makes this shader program active, so that it affects any subsequent drawing that you do. UseFixedFunction( ) returns the state of the pipeline to use the fixed-functionality (if it's available).

The SetGstap( ) method is there to give you the option to have the *gstap.h* code included automatically. Just pass true as the argument. Call this before you call the Create( ) method.

Here is an example of using the GLSLProgram class.

```
#include "glslprogram.h"

float      Ad, Bd, NoiseAmp, NoiseFreq, Tol;
GLSLProgram *Ovals;

. . .

// set everything up once:

Ovals = new GLSLProgram( );
Ovals->SetVerbose( true );
```

```
Ovals->SetGstap( true );
bool good = Ovals->Create( "ovalnoise.vert", "ovalnoise.frag" );
if( ! good )
{
  fprintf( stderr, "GLSL Program Ovals wasn't created.\n" );
  . . .
}

. . .


// do this in the display callback:

Ovals->Use( );
Ovals->SetUniform( "uAd", Ad );
Ovals->SetUniform( "uBd", Bd );
Ovals->SetUniform( "uNoiseAmp", NoiseAmp );
Ovals->SetUniform( "uNoiseFreq", NoiseFreq );
Ovals->SetUniform( "uTol", Tol );
glColor3f( 0., 1., 0. );
glutSolidTeapot( 1. );

Ovals->UseFixedFunction( );

. . .
```

B

Matrix4 C++ Class

One of the trends in OpenGL is to have the application developer bear the responsibility to manipulate and provide the needed transformation matrices. We have created a 4 × 4 matrix class called `Matrix4` to handle a lot of this work. The following methods are supported by the class

```
Matrix4( );
Matrix4( const Matrix4& );
Matrix4( float, float, float, float, float, float, float, float,
         float, float, float, float, float, float, float, float );
Matrix4( float [4][4] );

Matrix4& Frustum( float, float, float, float, float, float );
Matrix4& FrustumZ( float, float, float, float, float, float,
                   float );
```

```
float  GetDeterminant( );
float  GetElement( int, int );
Matrix4  GetInverse( );
Matrix4  GetInverse3( );
void GetMatrix4( float [4][4] );
void GetMatrix43( float [3][3] );
Matrix4  GetTranspose( );
Matrix4  GetTranspose3( );
Matrix4& Invert( );
Matrix4& Invert3( );
Matrix4& LoadIdentity( );
Matrix4& LookAt( float, float, float,  float, float, float,
                 float, float, float );
Vec3 MultBy( Vec3 );
Matrix4& operator=( const Matrix4& );
Matrix4  operator*( float );
Matrix4  operator*( Matrix4& );
Point3 operator*( Point3& );
Vec3 operator*( Vec3& );
Matrix4& operator*=( Matrix4& );
Matrix4& operator*=( float );
Matrix4  operator+( Matrix4& );
Matrix4& operator+=( Matrix4& );
Matrix4  operator-( Matrix4& ); // binary
Matrix4& operator-( );   // unary
Matrix4& operator-=( Matrix4& );
Matrix4& operator-=( float );
Matrix4& Ortho( float, float, float, float, float, float );
Matrix4& Ortho2D( float, float, float, float );
Matrix4& Perspective( float, float, float, float );
Matrix4& PopMatrix4( );
Matrix4& Print( char * = "", FILE * = stderr );
Matrix4& PushMatrix4( );
Matrix4& Rotatef( float, float, float, float );
Matrix4& Scalef( float, float, float );
Matrix4& SetElement( int, int, float );
Matrix4& SetMatrix4( float [4][4] );
Matrix4& SetMatrix43( float [3][3] );
Matrix4& StereoPerspective( float, float, float, float, float,
                            float );
Matrix4& Translatef( float, float, float );
Matrix4& Transpose( );
```

The method names have been selected to mimic OpenGL procedure names wherever possible, such as

```
Matrix4& Rotatef( float, float, float, float );
```

```
Matrix4& Scalef( float, float, float );
Matrix4& Translatef( float, float, float );
```

The default constructor sets the matrix to identity, but you can also explicitly do that with the LoadIdentity( ) method.

There are many operator overloads, so that you can use matrices in expressions, such as

```
Matrix4 R;
R.Rotatef( 30., 1., 0., 0. );
Matrix4 T;
T.Translatef( 2., 3., 4. );
Matrix4 P = R * T;
```

Many of these methods return a reference to the result so that they can be chained together, like this:

```
Matrix4 Comp;
Comp.LoadIdentity( ).Translatef(-A,-B,-C).Scalef(3.,4.,1.).
Translatef(A,B,C).Print("Composite = ");
```

These operations are evaluated left-to-right.

Here are some examples of using the Matrix4 class:

```
#include "matrix4.h"

Matrix4 I;
I.Print( "I = " );

Matrix4 R;
R.Rotatef( 30., 1., 0., 0. );
R.Print( "R = " );

Ovals->SetUniform( "uModelMatrix", R );

Matrix4 T;
T.Translatef( 2., 3., 4. );
T.Print ( "T = " );

Matrix4 P = R * T;
P.Print( "P1 = " );

P = T * R;
P.Print( "P2 = " );

Matrix4 RI = R;
```

```
RI.Invert( );
RI.Print( "Rinverse = " );
RI *= R;
RI.Print( "Rinverse * R = " );

Matrix4 Comp;
Comp.LoadIdentity( ).Translatef(-A,-B,-C).Scalef(3.,4.,1.).
Translatef(A,B,C).Print("Composite = ");
Comp.Invert( ).Print( "Composite Inverse = " );

fprintf( stderr, "Determinant of Composite Inverse = %8.3f\n",
Comp.GetDeterminant( ) );
```

Vec3 C++ Class

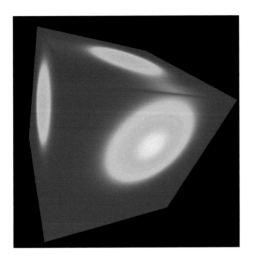

It is also helpful to have a 3-element vector class. Here is one called vec3. These are its methods:

```
vec3( float = 0., float = 0., float = 0. );
vec3( const vec3& );
vec3&  operator=( const vec3& );
vec3&  operator*=( float );
vec3   operator+( const vec3& );
vec3&  operator+=( const vec3& );
vec3   operator-( const vec3& );     // binary -
vec3   operator-( );  // unary -
vec3&  operator-=( const vec3& );
vec3   Cross( vec3 );
float  Dot( vec3 );
void   GetVec3( float * );
```

```
float   Length( );
void    Print( char * = "", FILE * = stderr );
Vec3    Unit( );
Vec3&   Unitize( );
```

Several operators are overloaded so you can use these vectors in expressions, such as

```
Vec3 a( 1., 2., 3. );
Vec3 b( 4., 5., 6. );
Vec3 e = a + b;
```

Another class, Point3, is sub-classed from Vec3. A Point3 variable can use all the same methods a Vec3 class variable can, but by using the Point3 name you are making it clear that the three-element array is meant to be a point (with positions) instead of a vector (with directions):

```
Point3 Q( 1., 2., 0. );
Point3 R( 5., 3., 0. );
Vec3 S = R - Q;
```

Some of these methods return a reference to the result so that they can be chained together, like this:

```
float i = c.Dot( a.Cross(b) );

Vec3 normal = ( R - Q ).Cross( S - Q );

Here are some examples of using the Vec3 class.

#include "vec3.h"

Vec3 b( 1., 2., 3. );
Vec3 c( 5., 6., 7. );
Vec3 d( c );

Vec3 a = c;
a.Unitize( );
a.Print( "a =" );
b.Print( "b =" );
c.Print( "c =" );
d.Print( "d =" );

a = Vec3( 2., -5., 8. );
a.Print( "a =" );
```

```
Vec3 ma = -a;
ma.Print( "-a = " );

Vec3 e = a + b;
e.Print( "e =" );

e *= 3.;
e.Print( "e =" );

float f = ( a + b ).Length( );
fprintf( stderr, "f = %8.3f\n", f );

float g = a.Dot( (b+c).Unit( ) );
fprintf( stderr, "g = %8.3f\n", g );

Vec3 h = a.Cross(b);
h.Print( "axb =" );

float i = c.Dot( a.Cross(b) );
fprintf( stderr, "c.(axb) = %8.3f\n", i );

Point3 Q( 1., 2., 0. );
Point3 R( 5., 3., 0. );
Point3 S( 3., 6., 0. );
Vec3 normal = ( R-Q ).Cross( S-Q );
normal.Print( "normal = " );
float area = normal.Length( ) / 2.;
fprintf( stderr, "triangle area = %8.3f\n", area );
```

D

Vertex Array Class

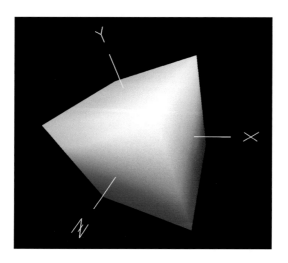

OpenGL encourages you to use vertex arrays (VAs) and vertex buffer objects (VBOs) instead of glBegin-glEnd for three reasons:

1. VAs and VBOs are much more efficient than using glBegin-glEnd.

2. glBegin-glEnd has been deprecated in OpenGL-desktop from version 3.0 onward, and might actually go away at some time in the future.

3. glBegin-glEnd has been completely eliminated from OpenGL-ES 2.0 and so cannot be used if you want your application to run on both desktop and mobile platforms.

There is no question that using glBegin-glEnd is convenient, especially when beginning to learn OpenGL. With this in mind, here is a C++ class1 that looks like the application is using glBegin-glEnd, but inside its data structures are preparing to use VAs and VBOs when the class's Draw( ) method is called:

```
void CollapseCommonVertices( bool );
void Draw( );
void glBegin( GLenum );
void glColor3f( GLfloat, GLfloat, GLfloat );
void glColor3fv( GLfloat * );
void glEnd( );
void glNormal3f( GLfloat, GLfloat, GLfloat );
void glNormal3fv( GLfloat * );
void glTexCoord2f( GLfloat, GLfloat );
void glTexCoord2fv( GLfloat * );
void glVertex2f( GLfloat, GLfloat );
void glVertex2fv( GLfloat * );
void glVertex3f( GLfloat, GLfloat, GLfloat );
void glVertex3fv( GLfloat * );
void Print( FILE * = stderr );
void RestartPrimitive( );
void SetTol( float );
void SetVerbose( bool );
void UseBufferObjects( bool );
```

The UseBufferObjects( ) method declares whether a VBO should be used instead of a VA. As VBOs are stored in the graphics card memory and thus only ever need to be transmitted from host memory once, VBOs are almost always preferable.

Passing a true to the CollapseCommonVertices( ) method says that you want any vertices closer to each other than the distance specified in SetTol( ) collapsed to be treated as a single vertex. The advantage to this is that the single vertex only gets transformed once. The disadvantage is that the collapsing process takes time, especially for large lists of vertices.

The RestartPrimitive( ) method invokes an OpenGL-ism that restarts the current primitive topology without starting a new VA or VBO. This saves overhead. It is especially handy for "never-ending" topologies such as triangle strips and line strips.

Here is an example of using the *VertexArray* class and the image it produces (see Figure D.1):

---

1. The source for this class is available on the book's web site: http://www.cgeducation.org

```
#include "vertexarray.h"

GLfloat CubeVertices[ ][3] =
{
    { -1., -1., -1. },
    {  1., -1., -1. },
    { -1.,  1., -1. },
    {  1.,  1., -1. },
    { -1., -1.,  1. },
    {  1., -1.,  1. },
    { -1.,  1.,  1. },
    {  1.,  1.,  1. }
};

GLfloat CubeColors[ ][3] =
{
    { 0., 0., 0. },
    { 1., 0., 0. },
    { 0., 1., 0. },
    { 1., 1., 0. },
    { 0., 0., 1. },
    { 1., 0., 1. },
    { 0., 1., 1. },
    { 1., 1., 1. }
};

GLuint CubeIndices[ ][4] =
{
    { 0, 2, 3, 1 },
    { 4, 5, 7, 6 },
    { 1, 3, 7, 5 },
    { 0, 4, 6, 2 },
    { 2, 6, 7, 3 },
    { 0, 1, 5, 4 }
};


VertexArray *VA;


. . .


// this goes in the part of the program where graphics things
// get initialized once:

VA = new VertexArray( );   // create an instance of the class
            // the real "constructor" is in the glBegin method
```

```
VA->CollapseCommonVertices( true );
VA->UseBufferObjects( true );
VA->SetTol( .001f );

VA->glBegin( GL_QUADS );

for( int i = 0; i < 6; i++ )
{
  for( int j = 0; j < 4; j++ )
  {
    GLuint k = CubeIndices[i][j];
    VA->glColor3fv( CubeColors[k] );
    VA->glVertex3fv( CubeVertices[k] );
  }
}

VA->glEnd( );


VA->Print( );// verify that vertices were really collapsed

. . .

// this goes in the display-callback part of the program:

VA->Draw( );
```

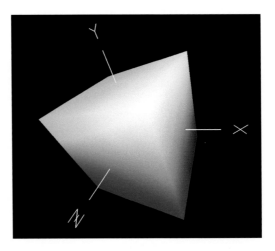

Figure D.1. The cube drawn by this code example, with axes added to show how the colors correspond to the vertex coordinates.

This next example shows drawing gridlines on a terrain map. The already-defined Heights[] array holds the terrain heights. This is a good example of using the RestartPrimitive( ) method so that the next grid line doesn't have to be in a new line strip. In this way, the entire grid is saved as a *single* line strip and is drawn by blasting a *single* VA / VBO into the graphics pipeline.

```
VertexArray *VA;

    . . .


// this goes in the part of the program where graphics things
// get initialized once:

VA = new VertexArray( );   // create an instance of the class
            // the real "constructor" is in the glBegin method

VA->CollapseCommonVertices( true );
VA->UseBufferObjects( true );
VA->SetTol( .001f );

int x, y;     // loop indices
float ux, uy;// utm coords

VA->glBegin( GL_LINE_STRIP );

for( y = 0, uy = meteryMin; y < NumLats; y++, uy += meteryStep )
{
  VA->RestartPrimitive( );
  for( x = 0, ux = meterxMin; x < NumLngs x++, ux += meterxStep
)
  {
      float uz = Heights[ y*NumLngs + x ];
      VA->glColor3f( 1., 1., 0. ); // single color = yellow
      VA->glVertex3f( ux, uy, uz );
  }
}

for( x = 0, ux = meterxMin; x < NumLngs; x++, ux += meterxStep )
{
  VA->RestartPrimitive( );
  for( y = 0, uy = meteryMin; y < NumLats; y++, uy +=
                                            meteryStep )
  {
     float uz = Heights[ y*NumLngs + x ];
     VA->glColor3f( 1., 1., 0. );
```

```
        VA->glVertex3f( ux, uy, uz );
    }
}

VA->glEnd( );


  .  .  .


// this goes in the display-callback part of the program:

VA->Draw( );
```

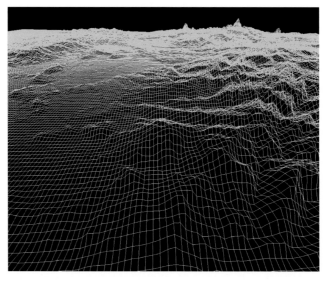

Figure D.2. A wireframe terrain map drawn as a single line strip in a vertex buffer object.[2]

---

[2] If you're interested in timing, this dataset had 1024 × 569 grid points, and displayed at 1,000 FPS on an NVIDIA GTX 480.

References

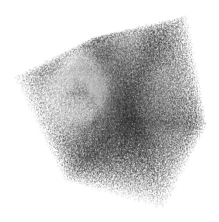

[1]   "Algorithmic Art." *Wikipedia*. Available at http://en.wikipedia.org/wiki/Algorithmic_art, 2011.

[2]   M. J. Bailey and D. Clark. "Using OpenGL and ChromaDepth to Obtain Inexpensive Single-Image Stereovision for Scientific Visualization." *Journal of Graphics Tools*. 3:3 (1999), 1–9.

[3]   Mike Bailey, Matt Clothier, and Nick Gebbie. "Realtime Dome Imaging and Interaction: Towards Immersive Design Environments." *Proceedings of ASME 2006 International Design Engineering Technical Conference*, DETC2006-99155. New York: ASME, September 2006.

[4]   Clint Brewer. "Rainbows and Fogbows: Adding Natural Phenomena." NVIDIA SDK White Paper, 2004.

[5]   Wilhelm Burger and Mark J. Burge. *Digital Image Processing: An Algorithmic Introduction using Java*. New York: Springer, 2007.

[6]   Brian Cabral and Leith (Casey) Leedom. "Imaging Vector Fields Using Line Integral Convolution." In *Proceedings of SIGGRAPH '93, Computer Graphics Proceedings, Annual Conference Series,* edited by James T. Kajiya, pp. 263–270. New York: ACM Press, 1993.

[7]   California Institute of Technology. "Mars Exploration Rovers." *Jet Propulsion Laboratory.* Available at http://marsrovers.jpl.nasa.gov/gallery, 2011.

[8]   Edwin Catmull and Raphael Rom. "A Class of Local Interpolating Splines." In *Computer Aided Geometric Design,* edited by R. E. Barnhill and R. F. Riesenfeld, pp. 317–326. New York: Academic Press, 1974.

[9]   *Codemonsters.* http://www.codemonsters.de/home/content.php?show=cubemaps

[10] Robert L. Cook. "Shade Trees," *Proc. SIGGRAPH '84, Computer Graphics* 18:3 (1984), 223–231.

[11] Robert L. Cook and Tony DeRose. "Wavelet Noise." *Proc. SIGGRAPH '05, Transactions on Graphics* 24:3 (2005), 803–811.

[12] Les Cowley. "Atmospheric Optics." Available at http://www.atoptics.co.uk/, 2008.

[13] Les Cowley. "HaloSim3 Software." *Atmospheric Optics.* Available at http://www.atoptics.co.uk/halo/halfeat.htm.

[14] Steve Cunningham. *Computer Graphics: Programming in OpenGL for Visual Communication.* Upper Saddle River, NJ: Pearson Prentice Hall, 2007.

[15] A. K. Dewdney. *The Armchair Universe.* New York: W. H. Freeman, 1988.

[16] Randima Fernando and Mark Kilgard. *The Cg Tutorial: The Definitive Guide to Programmable Real-Time Graphics.* Boston: Addison-Wesley Professional, 2003.

[17] Richard Fleet. *Glows, Bows, and Haloes.* Available at http://www.dewbow.co.uk/, 2008.

[18] James D. Foley, Andries van Dam, Steven K. Feiner, and John F. Hughes. *Computer Graphics: Principles and Practice,* Second edition. Boston: Addison-Wesley Professional, 1996.

[19] Andrew S. Glassner. *Principles of Digital Image Synthesis.* San Francisco: Morgan-Kaufman, 1995.

[20] Jens Gruschel. "Blend Modes." *Pegtop Software.* Available at http://www.pegtop.net/delphi/articles/blendmodes/, 2006.

[21] David Hutchison. "Introducing DLP 3-D TV." Texas Instruments White Paper, 2007.

[22] James Kajiya and Timothy Kay. "Rendering Fur with Three Dimensional Textures," *Proc. SIGGRAPH '89, Computer Graphics* 23:3 (1989), 271–280.

[23] John Kessenich, Dave Baldwin, and Randi Rost. "The OpenGL Shading Language." *OpenGL.* Available at http://www.opengl.org/registry/doc/GLSLandSpec.Full.1.20.u.pdf, 2006.

[24] David Knight and Gordon Mallinson. "Visualizing Unstructured Flow Data Using Dual Stream Functions." *IEEE Transactions on Visualization and Computer Graphics* 2:4 (1996), 355–363.

[25] Philip Laven. *MiePlot.* Available at http://www.philiplaven.com/mieplot.htm, 2011.

[26] Philip Laven. "The Optics of a Water Drop: Mie Scattering and the Debye Series." *Applied Optics* 44:27 (2005), 5675–5683.

[27] Lenny Lipton. *The CrystalEyes Handbook*. StereoGraphics Corporation, 1991.

[28] Benoit Mandelbrot. *The Fractal Geometry of Nature*. New York: W H Freeman, 1977.

[29] William R. Mark, R. Steven Glanville, Kurt Akeley, and Mark J. Kilgard. "Cg: A System for Programming Graphics Hardware in a C-like Language." *Proc. SIGGRAPH '03, Transactions on Graphics* 22:3 (2003), 896–907.

[30] James D. Murray and William Van Ryper. *Encyclopedia of Graphics File Formats*, 2nd edition. Sebastopol, CA: O'Reilly & Associates, 1996.

[31] Marc Olano and Anselmo Lastra. "A Shading Language on Graphics Hardware: The PixelFlow Shading Language." In *Proceedings of SIGGRAPH '98, Computer Graphics Proceedings*, Annual Conference Series, edited by Michael Cohen, pp. 159–168. Reading, MA: Addison-Wesley, 1998.

[32] "OpenGL Registry." OpenGL. *OpenGL Language and Reference Pages*, http://www.opengl.org/registry/, 2011.

[33] Craig Peeper and Jason Mitchell. "Introduction to the DirectX 9 High-Level Shader Language." In *ShaderX2: Shader Programming Tips and Tricks with DirectX 9.0*, edited by Wolfgang Engel, pp. 1–61. Plano, TX: Wordware Publishing, 2003.

[34] Ken Perlin. "An Image Synthesizer." *Proc. SIGGRAPH '85, Computer Graphics* 19:3 (1985), 287–296.

[35] Ken Perlin. "Improving Noise." *Proc. SIGGRAPH '02, Transactions on Graphics* 21:3 (2002), 681–682.

[36] Heinz-Otto Pietgen and Dietmar Saupe, editors. *The Science of Fractal Images*. New York: Springer-Verlag, 1988.

[37] Pixar. "Properties of RenderMan Noise Functions." *PhotoRealistic RenderMan*, SIGGRAPH '96 Course Notes.

[38] Pixar. "The RenderMan Interface Specifications, version 3.2." *Renderman*. Available at https://renderman.pixar.com/products/rispec/index.htm, 2000.

[39] Kekoa Proudfoot, William Mark, Svetoslav Tzvetkov, and Pat Hanrahan. "A Real-Time Procedural Shading System for Programmable Graphics Hardware." In *Proceedings of SIGGRAPH 2001, Computer Graphics Proceedings*, Annual Conference Series, edited by E. Fiume, pp. 159–170. Reading, MA: Addison-Wesley, 2001.

[40] Dan Sandin. "Random Dot Motion," *SIGGRAPH Video Review* 42, 1989.

[41] Dave Shreiner, et al., *OpenGL Programming Guide*, eighth edition. Reading, MA: Addison-Wesley, 2011.

[42] Maureen Stone. *A Field Guide to Digital Color*. Natick, MA: A K Peters, 2003.

[43] Steve Upstill. *The RenderMan Companion*. Reading, MA: Addison-Wesley, 1990.

[44] U.S. Geological Survey. "National Elevation Dataset." *U.S. Geological Survey*. Available at http://ned.usgs.gov, 2006.

[45] Alex Vlachos, Jörg Peters, Chas Boyd, and Jason Mitchell, "Curved PN Triangles," *Proceedings of the 2001 Symposium on Interactive 3D Graphics*, pp.159–166. New York: ACM, 2001.

[46] George Wolberg. *Digital Image Warping*. Los Alamitos, CA: IEEE Computer Society Press, 1990.

Index